Donated in Memory of

Naomi Hickey Bideau

Mother of
Bill Hickey
UTSA Staff

September 2008

From
Contributors to the
UTSA Memorial Book Fund

University of Texas at San Antonio

Self-Efficacy in SPORT

DEBORAH L. FELTZ, PHD

Professor and Chairperson
Department of Kinesiology
Michigan State University
East Lansing, Michigan

SANDRA E. SHORT, PHD

Chairperson and Professor
Department of Physical Education, Exercise Science, and Wellness
University of North Dakota
Grand Forks, North Dakota

PHILIP J. SULLIVAN, PHD

Associate Professor
Department of Physical Education and Kinesiology
Brock University
St. Catherines, Ontario, Canada

Human Kinetics

Library of Congress Cataloging-in-Publication Data

Feltz, Deborah L.
 Self-efficacy in sport / Deborah L. Feltz, Sandra E. Short, and Philip J. Sullivan.
  p. cm.
 Includes bibliographical references and index.
 ISBN-13: 978-0-7360-5999-2 (hard cover)
 ISBN-10: 0-7360-5999-7 (hard cover)
 1. Sports--Psychological aspects. 2. Athletes--Psychological aspects. 3. Sports
teams--Psychological aspects. 4. Coaching (Athletics)--Psychological aspects. 5.
Succcess. I. Short, Sandra E. II. Sullivan, Philip Joseph, 1969- III. Title.
 GV706.4.F45 2008
 796.01--dc22

                                                                    2007009991

ISBN-10: 0-7360-5999-7
ISBN-13: 978-0-7360-5999-2

The Web addresses cited in this text were current as of March 5, 2007, unless otherwise noted.

Acquisitions Editor: Myles Schrag; **Developmental Editor:** Judy Park; **Assistant Editors:** Heather M. Tanner and Melissa McCasky; **Copyeditor:** Joyce Sexton; **Proofreader:** Joanna Hatzopoulos Portman; **Indexer:** Susan Danzi Hernandez; **Permission Manager:** Dalene Reeder; **Graphic Designer:** Robert Reuther; **Graphic Artist:** Denise Lowry; **Photo Manager:** Laura Fitch; **Cover Designer:** Nancy Rasmus; **Photographer (interior):** © Human Kinetics; **Art Manager:** Kelly Hendren; **Illustrator:** Al Wilborn; **Printer:** Edwards Brothers

Printed in the United States of America   10 9 8 7 6 5 4 3 2 1

Human Kinetics
Web site: www.HumanKinetics.com

United States: Human Kinetics, P.O. Box 5076, Champaign, IL 61825-5076
800-747-4457
e-mail: humank@hkusa.com

Canada: Human Kinetics, 475 Devonshire Road Unit 100, Windsor, ON N8Y 2L5
800-465-7301 (in Canada only)
e-mail: orders@hkcanada.com

Europe: Human Kinetics, 107 Bradford Road, Stanningley, Leeds LS28 6AT, United Kingdom
+44 (0) 113 255 5665
e-mail: hk@hkeurope.com

Australia: Human Kinetics, 57A Price Avenue, Lower Mitcham, South Australia 5062
08 8372 0999
e-mail: info@hkaustralia.com

New Zealand: Human Kinetics, Division of Sports Distributors NZ Ltd.
P.O. Box 300 226 Albany, North Shore City, Auckland
0064 9 448 1207
e-mail: info@humankinetics.co.nz

For my parents, Vivian and Allen,
who believed that I was capable of anything
toward which I put my effort
and for modeling a thirst for life-long learning.

Deborah L. Feltz

For my parents, Eileen and Laurie,
husband, Martin, and children, Stoker and Brecken,
for their roles in building and maintaining my confidence.

Sandra E. Short

For my wife, Sue, and my children, Tim and Abby.
Thanks for all your support.

Philip J. Sullivan

Contents

Preface

S elf-efficacy is a recognizable and valuable attribute within sport. Play-ers, coaches, and sport psychologists all know the powerful effects that this psychological construct can have on thoughts, feelings, and behavior, especially performance:

- Athletes refer to self-efficacy as confidence and often attribute success-ful accomplishments to "being confident" and unsuccessful performances to "not having enough confidence" or to losing confidence. In team sports, ath-letes recognize that it is important to have confidence not only in themselves but also in the entire team—especially in those who play critical positions, such as a goaltender in ice hockey or a pitcher in baseball.

- Coaches are extremely interested in knowing about methods that can be used to help athletes build, maintain, and regain confidence. They also understand that their own confidence in their ability to coach is important and can have a powerful effect on their athletes.

- Sport psychology consultants are often called upon to design psycho-logical skills training programs that include efficacy-enhancing strategies. When designing their interventions, consultants use materials to assist them and may consult with researchers who have devoted their time to studying efficacy beliefs in sport.

Clearly there is a dynamic interplay among athletes, coaches, sport psy-chology consultants, and efficacy researchers. What seems to be missing, however, is a comprehensive, up-to-date summary and analysis of what we currently know about efficacy beliefs in sport. No one, until now, has ever written an entire book dedicated to this important topic in sport.

This book is a "go to" reference on efficacy research. It will be of consid-erable value to those involved in or considering doing research in this area. It is also a "must have" for scholar-practitioners interested in theoretically based and research-tested guidelines and recommendations for interventions. The approach we use in this book is a balance of conceptual background, research summaries and reviews, application, and critical thoughts regarding current and important issues. Kurt Lewin once said that there is nothing as practical as a good theory. Perhaps nowhere in psychology is this concept as fundamental as it is in sport psychology. And, within sport psychology, the efficacy construct has probably achieved the most remarkable balance between theory, research, and application. Indeed, our firm belief that efficacy is the prototypical construct for such balance is central to our book and is reflected in its content.

The book has three main parts and contains nine chapters. Part I deals with the conceptual nature of efficacy beliefs and its place in sport psychology. In the second part, we divide efficacy beliefs into the three main components recognized in sport—self-efficacy, team efficacy, and coaching efficacy. One chapter is devoted to each of these areas. The third part of the book is devoted to efficacy techniques, with separate chapters for athletes, teams, and coaches, and a final discussion of future directions and a summary of current and critical issues.

The first chapter presents the fundamental components of Bandura's efficacy theory as based within social cognitive theory. Self-efficacy theory has withstood the test of time and has been relatively unchanged since its inception in 1977. Since then, however, hundreds of studies, just within sport, have included efficacy beliefs in some form (i.e., task efficacy, self-regulation, etc.). Advances regarding efficacy measurement are also included here. Keeping up with the research on self-efficacy can be challenging for anyone, and incorporating it into scholarly inquiry and professional practice can be even harder. For this reason, we have included an annotated bibliography at the end of the book containing all of the research studies on efficacy beliefs in sport that we discovered during our writing of this book. This unique aspect prevents the book from being just a long literature review.

The second chapter provides extensive coverage of measurement guidelines and issues in the area of self-efficacy in sport. Bandura's guidelines for constructing efficacy scales are reviewed; sample scales are provided; and special issues in measuring efficacy beliefs in the sport context are covered. In addition, we review considerations for measuring collective efficacy at the team level, and we present our coaching efficacy measure.

The next three chapters are all similarly organized. First, we review the specific dimension of efficacy that we are discussing (chapter 3, self-efficacy; chapter 4, team efficacy; and chapter 5, coaching efficacy) in terms of its definition and conceptualization within social cognitive theory. We present a summary of what is known about the sources of these efficacy beliefs, and also what is known about the outcomes. Although performance is the most widely researched outcome of one's efficacy beliefs, it is not the only one. Influential behaviors such as commitment and burnout, as well as attitudes such as satisfaction, are also related to one's efficacy. Together, these chapters explain why efficacy is important and how we know this.

Part III offers suggestions for efficacy interventions. These chapters are a must-read for theoretical and research-based ideas for building and maintaining efficacy in athletes (chapter 6), teams (chapter 7), and coaches (chapter 8). We know that there is often a time lag between research and practice, and the contents of this section bridge the gap, in a format that is easy to understand, for those who are looking for practical advice. These chapters can be considered "stand-alone" in that understanding the information provided is not dependent on the previous sections. Thus, the chapters are intentionally redundant in terms of information that has application for more than one chapter.

The final chapter of the book is titled "Future Directions for Research on Efficacy Beliefs." The simplicity of the title may be misleading because its contents contain an analysis of current and critical issues.

We believe that this book is the most comprehensive and up-to-date analysis of what is currently known from the last 25 years of efficacy research in sport, as well as a map for the future for research on efficacy in sport.

Acknowledgments

We wish to acknowledge our colleagues Eva Monsma, Sheldon Hanton, Sian Beilock, and Daniel Gould for their input, encouragement, and friendship throughout this book-writing process. We are also thankful to Robert Weinberg for his review and helpful suggestions for improving the readability of the book. We also wish to acknowledge several graduate students who helped us with various tasks, including parts of the annotated bibliography, graphics, and permissions: Graig Chow, Lori Dithurbide, Teri Hepler, Nicholas Myers, and Lindsay Ross-Stewart. Each of us also has special people we wish to acknowledge.

Deborah Feltz: I wish to acknowledge my coauthors and former students, Sandra and Philip, for spurring me on to undertake this book. It came to fruition because of our sense of collective efficacy. Also, for the past 26 years, I have had more than 30 talented graduate students who have collaborated with me to help build a program of research in self-efficacy and sport. I acknowledge my gratitude to them. Lastly, I especially acknowledge Linda and Luke for helping me balance work and family.

Sandra Short: I would like to acknowledge my coauthors, Deb and Phil. Your positive influences on my life have generalized well beyond the academic domain. I would also like to thank my Mom, my best friend, for being there for my family, especially during those times when I was busy writing this book. And to my family, Martin, Stoker, and Brecken, for always making me feel like "mother of the year."

Philip Sullivan: I have to thank my coauthors Deb and Sandra, not just for the opportunity to collaborate on this book, but for 10 years of support and teamwork.

PART

I

Understanding Self-Efficacy Theory

Part I of this book examines the conceptual and structural nature of self-efficacy theory as it applies to sport. We present the fundamental components of Bandura's (1977) self-efficacy theory as they relate to sport behavior in athletes, teams, and coaches. We also discuss the measurement of efficacy beliefs as prescribed by self-efficacy theory and as they pertain to the context of sport.

1

Self-Efficacy Theory in Sport

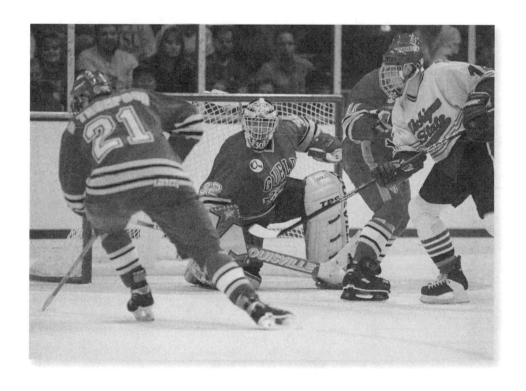

> Self-confidence is the first requisite to great undertakings.
>
> *Samuel Johnson, 18th century English writer*

Successful performance in sport is based, in part, on psychological factors. Athletes, of course, must have the relevant physical skills and capabilities to perform, but some athletes are less confident than others that they can perform as skillfully, cope with performance pressure, or sustain the hard work necessary to perfect their skills. Athletes also recognize that it is essential to have not only confidence in teammates who play the critical positions, such as a goaltender in ice hockey or a pitcher in softball, but also a more generalized belief that their team has the ability to be successful. Coaches, as well, can influence team and individual confidence through their expectations, behavior, and interactions with their athletes. Their own confidence in their coaching skills also can have a powerful effect on their athletes. Bandura's (1977, 1997) theory of self-efficacy (and its collective efficacy extension) has been proposed as a cognitive explanation for differences in the abilities of people, teams, and organizational leaders to carry out challenging tasks, including tasks in the athletic arena. In fact, self-efficacy is considered to be one of the most influential psychological constructs mediating achievement striving in sport (Feltz, 1988b, 1994).

In this chapter, we begin by providing an overview of self-efficacy theory, including how efficacy judgments are formed and their relationship to motivation and performance. We outline the different types of efficacy beliefs that are examined in sport and examine concepts that are not self-efficacy, but are related to self-efficacy. The chapter ends with a section on criticisms of self-efficacy theory. We consider some research examples to help give context to some of the theoretical relationships, but most of the research is described in greater detail in the following chapters.

Self-Efficacy Theory

Bandura's (1977, 1997, 2001) theory of self-efficacy was developed within the framework of social cognitive theory. In social cognitive theory, individuals are viewed as proactive agents in the regulation of their cognition, motivation, actions, and emotions rather than as passive reactors to their environment. Bandura refers to this view as an agentic perspective of social cognitive functioning (Bandura, 2001). As agents, people use forethought, self-reflection, and self-regulation to influence their own functioning. Social cognitive theory also posits a network of causal structures that depend on people's own agentic behaviors (e.g., persistence), personal factors (e.g., knowledge and beliefs), and environmental conditions (e.g., interactions with others). This network represents a reciprocal process in which the triadic factors all operate as interacting determinants of one another to explain motivation and behavior (Bandura, 1986b, 1997). For instance, a coach's positive feedback behavior can influence what an athlete believes that she or he can achieve and goals the athlete sets, which can influence the effort to reach those goals. The effort, in turn, can influence a coach's reaction to the athlete (see figure 1.1).

Within this social cognitive framework of human functioning, self-efficacy theory addresses the role of self-referent beliefs as the core agentic factor that determines people's goal-directed behavior. Bandura (1986b, 1997) refers to self-efficacy as a common cognitive mechanism that mediates between selected self-appraisal information and people's subsequent thought patterns, emotional reactions, motivation, and behavior. Such motivated behaviors and thought patterns are important contributors to performance in sport. High-efficacious athletes are not afraid to pursue challenging goals; they cope with pain; and they persevere through setbacks. Athletes with low self-efficacy avoid difficult goals, worry about possible injury, expend less effort, and give up in the face of failure.

Although self-efficacy theory was originally proposed to account for the different results achieved by diverse methods used in clinical psychology for

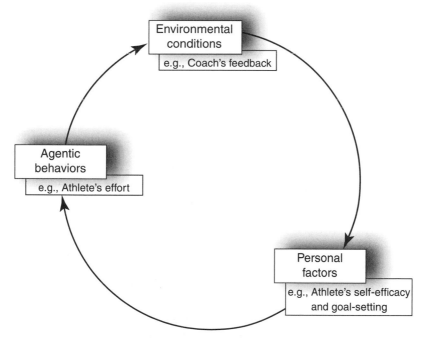

Figure 1.1 Example of athlete's proactive behavior within social cognitive theory.

the treatment of anxiety, it has since been expanded and applied to other domains of psychosocial functioning, including health and exercise behavior (McAuley, 1992b; McAuley & Mihalko, 1998; O'Leary, 1985) and sport and motor performance (Feltz, 1988b, 1994). In the sport and motor performance field alone, there have been over 200 published papers on self-efficacy (Moritz, Feltz, Fahrback, & Mack, 2000).

Self-efficacy is defined as "beliefs in one's capabilities to organize and execute the courses of action required to produce given attainments" (Bandura, 1997, p. 3). These beliefs vary along three dimensions: level, strength, and generality. "Level of self-efficacy" (or magnitude) refers to people's expected performance attainments at different levels of difficulty. For instance, soccer players with different levels of self-efficacy for penalty kicks would judge how many successful goals they could kick consecutively (e.g., 1 out of 10 up to 10 out of 10). "Strength" refers to the certainty of people's beliefs that they can attain these different levels of performance, from complete uncertainty to complete certainty. Thus, two soccer players may believe they can make 6 out of 10 penalty kicks, but one may have more certainty in this belief than the other. "Generality" indicates the number of domains of functioning in which people judge themselves to be efficacious and the transferability of one's efficacy judgments across different tasks or activities, such as across different sports; but this concept is rarely used in studies on self-efficacy (Maddux, 1995; Schunk, 1995b). The paucity of studies on generality of efficacy beliefs in sport may have to do with the fact that athletes and coaches tend to specialize in one sport.

Self-efficacy beliefs are specific to distinct domains of functioning rather than representing an overall global trait. Even within a domain of functioning, such as in the sport of golf, one might lack confidence in one's putting game but have great confidence on the fairway or in the ability to maintain an attentional focus from hole to hole. According to Bandura (1992, 1997), the degree of specificity at which self-efficacy is measured should be determined by the nature of the situation at hand and the nature of the situation or task (or both situation and task) to which one wishes to generalize (or predict).

Regardless of the breadth of the situation or goal domain, efficacy beliefs are not judgments about possessing a set of skills to produce an action, but rather judgments of what can be accomplished with those skills (Bandura, 1997). In other words, self-efficacy judgments are about what one thinks one can do with one's skills (e.g., I think I can return the majority of the tennis serves from my opponent), not about what one has (e.g., I have excellent reflexes in tennis).

As Bandura (1997) notes, there is a big difference between having a set of requisite skills to perform a certain task and having the confidence to be able to integrate those skills into a course of action and perform them under a variety of circumstances and challenges. Thus, an athlete might have the skill to return high-speed tennis serves but may not have the perceived efficacy to predict an opponent's actions, adapt return strategies when needed, or manage the competitive pressure in a tennis match. Likewise, a team might know how to run a particular offense in basketball and have the dribbling, passing, and shooting skills to perform it, but may not possess the efficacy beliefs to notice shifting game situations and adapt strategies accordingly.

Sources of Efficacy Information

How are efficacy beliefs formed? Bandura (1997) theorizes that they are a product of a complex process of self-appraisal and self-persuasion that relies on cognitive processing (i.e., selection, interpretation, and integration) of diverse sources of efficacy information. He categorized these sources of information as

- past performance accomplishments,
- vicarious experiences,
- verbal persuasion, and
- physiological states.

Others have added separate categories for emotional states and imaginal experiences (Maddux, 1995; Schunk, 1995b).

Performance Accomplishments   Past performances have been shown to be the most influential source of efficacy information because they are based on one's own mastery experiences (Bandura, 1997). One's mastery experiences influence self-efficacy beliefs through the self-appraisal of one's performances. If one has repeatedly viewed these experiences as successes, self-efficacy beliefs will generally increase; if these experiences have been viewed as failures, self-efficacy beliefs will generally decrease. Self-monitoring of one's successes can strengthen the appraisal of the mastery experience and enhance self-efficacy more than the self-monitoring of one's failures. One must be careful, however, not to become complacent owing to success. Bandura (1997) suggests that complacency after easy successes and greater efforts after failure are common sequences in competitive struggles. This happens more with proficient performers than with those who are developing their skills. As we discuss later in this chapter, the discrepancies between performance accomplishments and performance standards influence efficacy beliefs and further motivation in complex ways that include how one reacts to the success or failure of the accomplishment and the resiliency of one's efficacy beliefs.

The influence of mastery experiences on self-efficacy beliefs also depends on the perceived difficulty of the performance, the amount of guidance received, the temporal pattern of success and failure, the effort expended, and the individual's conception of a particular "ability" as a skill that can be acquired versus an inherent aptitude (Bandura, 1997). Bandura has argued that performance accomplishments on difficult tasks, tasks attempted without external assistance, and tasks accomplished with only occasional failures carry greater positive efficacy value than tasks that are easily accomplished, tasks accomplished with external help, or tasks in which repeated failures are experienced without any sign of progress. For example, coaches help to arrange efficacy-enhancing situations by avoiding prematurely placing athletes in activities that are likely to bring repeated failures (Bandura, 1997).

The relationship between effort expended on a performance and perceived efficacy is more complicated. Young children interpret the exertion of high effort as an indicator that they have more ability, thus leading to stronger perceptions of efficacy (Bandura, 1997). Bandura notes that the research with adults has shown the relationship to be more individualized. Some adults infer the need for high effort to accomplish a task as indicating that they have low ability, whereas others view effort as a reflection of enhanced ability. Generally, however, as Bandura suggests, people likely judge their efficacy based on a combination of effort and perceived task difficulty. Past successes with minimal effort on tasks that most find difficult imply high ability and enhance one's efficacy beliefs.

Lastly, one's conception of ability as an acquirable skill versus an inherent aptitude also can influence self-efficacy beliefs. Developing athletes, for instance, who see their past performance failures as learning experiences and believe their ability will improve with deliberate practice will have a stronger sense of efficacy than those who interpret their mistakes as physical limitations.

Vicarious Influences   Efficacy information can also be derived through observing and comparing oneself with others. This modeling process involves observing the performance of one or more other individuals, coding the observed information, noting the consequence of the performance, and then using this information to form judgments about one's own performance (Bandura, 1997; Maddux, 1995). Modeling and social comparison can transmit efficacy information in several ways. Observing repeated demonstrations by a proficient model can provide instructional information on how to perform a task correctly and efficacy information that the task can be learned (e.g., Lirgg & Feltz, 1991). A golf coach or teacher who demonstrates the correct mechanics of a chipping swing provides instructional information that the learner might not otherwise have in assessing whether he or she can perform the task correctly. Modeling of coping strategies (e.g., positive self-talk, self-instruction), as well as observing others making progress toward a certain performance level, can also convey efficacy information that a challenging task is surmountable (e.g., Gould & Weiss, 1981). The vicarious influence of television and other visual media is another potential source of efficacy. Girls and women are seeing many more female athletes competing on television, which can raise their beliefs in their own athletic capabilities.

Efficacy information can also be derived through social comparison with others. Just sizing up another individual in terms of physique may help determine whether he or she is a formidable opponent. For instance, in an early study of self-efficacy and competitive persistence, Weinberg, Gould, and Jackson (1979) manipulated participants' efficacy expectations about competing on a muscular leg endurance task by having them observe their competitor (a confederate), who either performed poorly on a related strength task and was said to have a knee injury (high self-efficacy) or who performed well and was said to be a varsity track athlete (low self-efficacy). Results indicated that observing a competent or incompetent competitor differentially affected participants' self-efficacy beliefs and performance. Participants who competed against an injured competitor had higher preperformance efficacy and endured longer than those who competed against the varsity athlete.

One particular mode of modeling influence that has been suggested to enhance one's sense of efficacy and performance in sport is self-modeling (Dowrick, 1991; Franks & Maile, 1991). In self-modeling, the individual repeatedly observes the correct or best parts of his or her own past performance and uses these as a model for future performance (Dowrick & Dove, 1980). Bandura (1997) suggests that self-modeling affects performance through its impact on efficacy belief.

Vicarious sources of efficacy information have been shown to be generally weaker than performance accomplishments; however, their influence on self-efficacy can be enhanced by a number of factors (e.g., Feltz, Landers, & Raeder, 1979; Feltz & Riessinger, 1990; Weinberg et al., 1979). For example, the less direct knowledge that people have about their own capability to perform a task, the more they will rely on the modeled behavior of others in judging their own capabilities. The effectiveness of modeling procedures on one's self-efficacy judgments also is enhanced by perceived similarities to a model in terms of performance or personal characteristics (e.g., George, Feltz, & Chase, 1992; Weiss, McCullagh, Smith, & Berlant, 1998). Perceived performance similarities carry more efficacy weight than perceived similarity based on personal characteristics (e.g., gender).

Within social cognitive theory, people actively seek out models who can provide the most salient information for judging their own capabilities. Bandura (1997) suggests that people who are similar or slightly higher in ability provide the most informative comparative information for judging one's own capabilities. Athletes who want to challenge themselves to attain higher levels than their previous performance will select for comparison others whose performances are slightly above their own to serve as standards to beat. For master athletes, Frey and Ruble (1990) suggest that they may select performance comparisons that buffer themselves from failure and enhance their sense of competence. That is, they may avoid comparisons to their previous performances (temporal comparisons) or younger cohorts if their performance has been declining over time, and instead rely more on age-mate comparisons. Bandura notes that, in competitive environments, people usually consider both social and self-comparison in appraising their capabilities. Thus, modeling can help serve as a goal standard against which one can appraise one's capabilities.

Verbal Persuasion   Persuasive techniques include verbal persuasion, evaluative feedback, expectations on the part of others, self-talk, and other cognitive strategies. These techniques are widely used by coaches, managers, parents, and peers in attempts to influence an athlete's or a team's perceptions of efficacy. Coaches have ranked verbal persuasion techniques as among the most effective for increasing the efficacy beliefs of their athletes (e.g., Gould, Hodge, Peterson, & Giannini, 1989; Vargas-Tonsing, Myers, & Feltz, 2004; Weinberg & Jackson, 1990). Although verbal persuasion by itself is of limited influence, it can help motivate people to persist in their efforts if the persuader's appraisal is within realistic bounds (Bandura, 1997).

The strength of the persuasive influence on self-efficacy has also been hypothesized to depend on the prestige, credibility, expertise, and trustworthiness of the persuader. Coaches are usually believed to be credible information sources of their athletes' capabilities. Coaches can influence their athletes' efficacy beliefs through direct appeal, inspirational messages, evaluative feedback, expectations, and attributions. Vargas-Tonsing (2004) found that coaches' pregame speeches significantly increased athletes' self-efficacy beliefs about the impending game.

Feedback from coaches that emphasizes the progress made tends to raise efficacy expectations, whereas evaluations that highlight the shortfalls lower them. Coaches who encourage their athletes to measure their successes in terms of self-improvement rather than outcome can help in the persuasion process. Coaches' expectations of their athletes and corresponding behaviors also convey subtle efficacy messages (e.g., Horn, 1985). Horn found that coaches gave their low-expectancy athletes more praise for mediocre performances and ignored more mistakes compared to how they behaved toward their high-expectancy athletes. They gave their high-expectancy athletes more criticism and corrective instruction in response to skill errors. These behaviors were interpreted by the low-expectancy athletes as suggesting that they had less ability than those for whom the coaches were conveying higher expectations.

The attributions that coaches provide for their athletes' performance also have persuasory influence. A coach who provides attributional feedback to an athlete suggesting that the athlete's success was the result of ability is more likely to enhance that athlete's future efficacy beliefs than if the success was attributed to luck, an easy task, or even effort (if effort is the only reason offered for repeated success). Similarly, a coach who helps convince athletes that ability is an acquirable skill will instill a stronger sense of efficacy in the athletes than one who emphasizes ability as an inherent aptitude.

Although coaches have the persuasory power to enhance their athletes' efficacy perceptions, Bandura (1997) indicates that the debilitating effects of persuasory information are more powerful than the enabling effects. Individuals tend to avoid challenging activities when they have been persuaded that they lack the capabilities to meet those challenges, or they give up quickly. It is harder for a coach to instill strong beliefs of self-efficacy by persuasory means alone than it is to undo those beliefs. Thus, coaches must have good diagnostic skills regarding their athletes' strengths and weaknesses in order to cultivate a strong sense of efficacy.

In addition to a coach's persuasory influence, societal-level persuasion can influence the efficacy judgments of individuals, especially in negatively stereotyped groups (Milner & Hoy, 2003). Merely introducing a negative belief or stereotype about a social group in a particular task domain can reduce the quality of task performance exhibited by members of that group (Steele, 1997). The term "stereotype threat" has been coined to describe this phenomenon. For instance, framing a sport activity (e.g., balance beam) as indicative of a negative stereotype (e.g., men are poorer at balance tasks than women) can harm the performance of members of the negatively targeted group by undermining self-efficacy judgments (Beilock, Jellison, Rydell, McConnell, & Carr, 2006; Beilock & McConnell, 2004; Stone, Lynch, Sjomeling, & Darley, 1999). This may be especially true for high-level or expert athletes because stereotype threat is most pronounced for domains in which performance is important to the individual (Beilock & Feltz, 2006; Wheeler & Petty, 2001).

Lastly, people also persuade themselves that they can perform or cope with certain tasks. Within social cognitive theory, individuals have the capacity to regulate their own thought processes. Thus, athletes can help convince themselves that they can accomplish a goal through positive self- and task-related statements. Self-talk can include statements to help focus attention on acquiring skill (e.g., "eyes on the ball"), to control emotion (e.g., "stay smooth"), to control effort (e.g., "keep pushing"), to control unwanted thoughts (e.g., "I'm quick"), and to help deal with occasional failure (e.g., "unlucky"). Negative self-talk and irrational thinking can, likewise, undermine one's self-efficacy, and this can carry over to subsequent performances.

Physiological Information　People also cognitively appraise their physiological state or condition to form efficacy judgments in deciding whether they can successfully meet specific task demands. Bandura (1997) addresses physiological and affective states together within the same category of information because they both have a physiological basis, but we have chosen to separate the two because they relate to different aspects of performance in sport. Physiological information includes one's level of strength, fitness, fatigue, and pain. Physiological information has been shown to be a more important source of efficacy information with respect to sport and physical activity tasks than in the case of nonphysical tasks (e.g., Chase, Feltz, & Lirgg, 2003; Feltz & Riessinger, 1990).

According to Bandura (1997), the impact of physiological states on efficacy beliefs will depend on several things, such as situational factors and the meaning given to them. To use his example, speakers who ascribe their sweating to the physical discomfort of the room read their physiology quite differently from those who view it as distress reflecting personal failings. In sport, an athlete's level of autonomic arousal could be associated with fear and self-doubt or with being "psyched up" and ready for performance. Or, those who read their fatigue and muscle soreness as a lack of physical fitness are more apt to lessen their efforts and conserve energy during a performance than those who trust that their physical condition will carry them through. Less experienced athletes also could misinterpret an increased heart rate and breathing rate early in a competition as lack of stamina rather than as competitive excitement, which would lead to similar results. In many physical performances, discomfort and muscle soreness are expected. Some performers dwell more than others on these discomforts. Those who do are more apt to be influenced by their physiological signals than those who have learned to play through them. This does not mean disregarding serious pain signals, but learning to know the difference.

Perceived physical adeptness and maintaining one's fitness may be especially important for master athletes as they adapt to physiological changes brought on by the aging process (Bandura, 1997; Langley & Knight, 1999; Wilson, Sullivan, Myers, & Feltz, 2004). Master athletes who appraise their fitness level changes as related more to training than to biological aging are more inclined to push themselves in training rather than scale down.

Emotional States   Bandura (1997) discusses physiological and emotional states together as a source category of efficacy beliefs. However, as pointed out by Maddux (1995), emotional experiences (which include subjective states of feelings and moods) are not simply the product of physiological arousal, which is why we present them as their own source category. Bandura (1997) postulates that emotions also affect behavior through the cognitive appraisal of the information conveyed by the emotion. He also lists a number of factors that influence this cognitive processing. Among them are appraisal of the sources of emotions and past experiences of how arousal affected one's performance. For instance, emotions, just as perceived physiological arousal, can be associated with fear and self-doubt or with being psyched up and ready for performance. Schunk (1995a) suggested that emotional symptoms that signal anxiety might be interpreted by an individual to mean that he or she lacks the requisite skills to perform a certain task, which in turn influences efficacy judgments. Whether or not emotional states are perceived as facilitative or debilitative is also based on athletes' perceptions of control, specifically whether they believe they have the ability to cope with the symptoms that signal anxiety so as to attain their goals. Thus, emotional arousal can enhance efficacy beliefs that a performance is attainable when people believe that they can bring their anxiety under control. Additionally, positive affect, such as happiness, exhilaration, and tranquility, is more likely to enhance efficacy judgments than are negative affective states, such as sadness, anxiety, and depression (e.g., Maddux & Meier, 1995; Treasure, Monson, & Lox, 1996).

Bandura (1997) also stated that the impact of mood on efficacy beliefs is at least partially mediated by selective recall of past success and failures. Successes achieved under positive moods spawn a high level of efficacy, whereas failures under negative moods breed a low sense of efficacy. This efficacy-biasing impact of mood is especially evident when mood mismatches performance attainments. People who fail under a happy mood overestimate their capabilities, whereas those who succeed under a sad mood underestimate their capabilities. People also tend to recall more successes from events that occurred in happy moods than in sad moods.

Imaginal Experiences Lastly, Maddux (1995) suggested that imaginal experiences be considered as a separate source of efficacy information. However, Bandura (1997) refers to this source as cognitive self-modeling (or cognitive enactment) and describes it as a form of modeling influence. Regardless of the category of sources in which one places imaginal experience, athletes can form efficacy beliefs by imagining themselves or others behaving successfully or unsuccessfully in anticipated performance situations. Imagining oneself winning against an opponent has been shown to raise efficacy judgments and endurance performance (e.g., Feltz & Riessinger, 1990). Other cognitive simulations, such as mental rehearsal strategies, have also been shown to enhance competition efficacy beliefs and competitive performance (e.g., Callow, Hardy, & Hall, 2001; Garza & Feltz, 1998; Short, Bruggeman, et al., 2002).

Confidence in one's imagery ability is also important to being able to use imagery as an effective tool to enhance confidence in one's performance. Short, Tenute, and Feltz (2005) examined whether efficacy in using imagery could mediate the relationship between imagery ability and imagery use with female college athletes. They found that the more athletes were confident in their ability to use a certain image, the more they used it. Also, efficacy in using imagery was found to mediate the relationship between imagery ability and imagery use.

In forming efficacy judgments, these six categories of efficacy information are not mutually exclusive in terms of the information they convey, though some are more influential than others. How various sources of information are weighted and processed to yield judgments on different tasks, in different situations, and regarding individuals' skills is still unknown. Self-efficacy judgments are also modifiable. They are expected to change from experience, modeling, social persuasion, and affect or mood shifts (Zimmerman, 1996). Various interventions, based on one or more sources of efficacy information, can alter self-efficacy beliefs.

Sport-Specific Sources of Efficacy

Vealey and her colleagues extended the sources of information beyond self-efficacy theory to identify the most salient sources of confidence for athletes based on the unique sociocultural aspects of sport competition (Vealey, Hayashi, Garner-Holman, & Giacobbi, 1998). For instance, the distinct social nature of sport suggests that social support, beyond verbal persuasion, may be a salient source of confidence. Vealey and colleagues (1998) developed the Sources of Sport Confidence Questionnaire (SSCQ) to measure sources of confidence information specific to the sport setting. They identified nine sources of sport confidence for high school and intercollegiate athletes:

- Mastery
- Demonstration of ability
- Physical and mental preparation
- Physical self-presentation
- Social support
- Coaches' leadership
- Vicarious experience
- Environmental comfort
- Situational favorableness

With respect to how these sources relate to Bandura's sources, mastery and demonstration of ability are considered to be reflective of performance accomplishments; physical and mental preparation is tied to physiological and emotional states; social support is similar to verbal persuasion; and vicarious experience is the same. Bandura did not specifically refer to physical self-presentation, coaches' leadership, environmental comfort, or situational favorableness in descriptions of his sources. The sources of information that are unique to sport may have important practical applications for enhancing efficacy beliefs with athletes from various age, gender, and ability groups. These sources and corresponding research are described further in chapter 3.

Influence of Efficacy Beliefs on Behavior

Bandura (1977, 1997) proposed that efficacy beliefs are the primary determinant of people's levels of motivation to accomplish a specific goal. This is reflected in the challenges they undertake, the effort they expend in the given activity, and their perseverance in the face of difficulties. Efficacy beliefs influence not only physical proficiency, as Bandura (1997) notes, but all aspects of performance, including reading shifting game situations, selecting effective performance strategies, predicting opponents' likely actions, making in-the-moment decisions, utilizing visualization, managing pressure and setback situations, and managing distractions. Thus, efficacy beliefs are hypothesized to influence certain thought patterns (e.g., worry, attributions) and emotional reactions (e.g., pride, shame, happiness, sadness) as well as behavior.

Choice of Activities and Goals   Research supports the idea that people will choose to undertake physical challenges and set goals that they believe they can master and will avoid those that they think exceed their capabilities (e.g., Feltz, 1982; Feltz & Albrecht, 1986). Selection of activities and goal setting can be considered part of the forethought processes in social cognitive theory (Zimmerman, 2000). According to Bandura (1997), people with reasonably accurate efficacy judgments will undertake realistically challenging tasks and be motivated to take on progressively more challenging tasks as their competence and efficacy beliefs develop. However, people who largely underestimate their capabilities hinder their development in the given area and chance losing out on rewarding experiences. For instance, teenagers who believe that they cannot learn to swim miss out on the potential fitness and social rewards that come from swimming. Some youths who have never played organized soccer before may not even try out for the team if they underestimate their capabilities. These choices foreclose on these youths' options and may have enduring effects. Likewise, inflated efficacy judgments can lead individuals to choose activities that will set them up for failure and possibly discourage further development. Coaches try to influence the challenges that their athletes take on so as not to set them up for overwhelming failure, especially developing athletes. Where it is possible, they choose the competitions or game situations in which they believe their athletes have a reasonable chance of success and gradually add more difficult challenges.

People with higher percepts of efficacy will also choose more challenging goals than those with lower levels of efficacy beliefs (Locke, Frederick, Lee, & Bobko, 1984). The purpose of this chapter is not to provide an in-depth review of goal-setting theory and its relation to motivation (see Bandura, 1997, pp. 128-137; Burton, Naylor, & Holliday, 2001, for further reading). We deal more with goal setting and self-efficacy in chapters 3 and 6. Our intent here is to provide a short description of how efficacy beliefs are posited to influence goal behavior. Thus, athletes set goals based on their perceived self-efficacy. If their performances fall short of their goals, they typically react evaluatively with dissatisfaction. Whether this dissatisfaction serves as an incentive or disincentive for enhanced effort is partly influenced by the athlete's self-efficacy for goal attainment and the degree of the discrepancy (Bandura, 1997; Carver & Scheier, 1981). Bandura predicts that, in general, in the face of negative discrepancies between personal goals and attainments, those who have high self-efficacy beliefs will heighten their level of effort and persistence and those who have self-doubts will quickly give up. For example, a tennis player may react to a difficult loss that fell just short of his goal with great dissatisfaction and decreased self-efficacy that he could ever out-perform against that particular opponent, and thus abandon his goal. It may be that another player is also dissatisfied with his hard-fought failure, but his efficacy beliefs remain high, he views his goal as just within reach, and he uses this discrepancy as motivation. However, if the degree of negative discrepancy is perceived as quite large, athletes' self-efficacy for goal attainment will be undermined. In this situation, research has shown that individuals with high self-efficacy will readjust their goals so as not to further undermine their self-efficacy levels (Bandura & Cervone, 1983).

If athletes match or exceed their previous performances, they typically react with satisfaction and, for those with a strong sense of efficacy, readjust their goals upward to create a new standard for themselves. However, as we noted previously, complacency can also occur after successful performance. For example, Miller (1993) found a negative relationship between high self-efficacy perceptions of competitive swimmers and their motivation when they were given unchallenging goals. However, Feltz and Lirgg (1998) found at the team level that collective efficacy significantly increased for the next game against the same team after a win and significantly decreased for the next game after a loss. As we discuss later in this chapter, these two studies differ in focus on preparatory versus performance efficacy. In addition, teams in the Feltz and Lirgg study may not have viewed their wins as easy and may also have looked beyond their proximal performance in pursuit of more challenging goals, such as postseason tournament play. The continued setting of challenging goals and the positive reactions to substandard performances are hypothesized to help to elevate the intensity and level of motivation (Bandura, 1997). Thus, as Bandura notes, efficacy beliefs have several effects on goal-oriented behavior. "Efficacy beliefs influence the level at which goals are set, the strength of commitment to them, the strategies used to reach them, the amount of effort mobilized in the endeavor, and the intensification of effort when accomplishments fall short of aspirations" (p. 136). As can be seen from this characterization, effort and persistence are influenced by efficacy beliefs and goals.

Effort and Persistence The strength of efficacy beliefs also influences the degree of effort athletes will expend to reach their goals and their persistence in the face of challenges and obstacles. However, testing the effect of effort is not so simple in applied sport settings. Effort is more difficult to operationalize in sport competition compared to other situations. The number of shots attempted in a game, for instance, may be influenced by one's effort but also by the opponent's skill, by opportunities, and by accurate passes from teammates. In exercise physiology laboratories, effort might be measured in terms of one's energy expenditure or number of sit-ups per minute, for instance, when individuals are equated on fitness or strength. The equating is necessary because the more physically fit individuals are, the less effort they need to put forth to accomplish a prescribed task (e.g., run for 30 min at 70% of $\dot{V}O_2$max). In fact, research has shown an inverse relationship between efficacy beliefs and ratings of perceived exertion (RPE: Borg, 1985) on cycle ergometer and treadmill tests for individuals of different fitness levels (e.g., McAuley & Courneya, 1992; Rudolph & McAuley, 1996).

In industry, effort can be measured in terms of rate of work output. In educational settings, effort, as measured by students' rate of solution of arithmetic problems, has been shown to correlate positively with students' perceived self-efficacy for learning (Schunk & Hanson, 1985). In sport efficacy studies, effort is rarely used as a dependent measure. An example of an exception is a study on collective efficacy by Greenlees, Graydon, and Maynard (1999). As explained in chapter 4, these investigators used heart rate monitors to measure effort on team performance in a rowing task in the lab.

The effect of efficacy beliefs on persistence has been examined more typically in sport settings than has effort. Time on a muscular endurance task, for instance, is more easily quantifiable than the energy expenditure involved. In athletic performance, perseverance is strongly associated with high performance results, especially in endurance activities (e.g., Feltz & Reissinger, 1990; Gould & Weiss, 1981; Weinberg et al., 1979). The use of persistence as a dependent variable is unique in sport compared to educational contexts, where self-efficacy has been shown to predict effort and achievement better than persistence (see Lent, Brown, & Larkin, 1984, for review). In educational settings, students may not have the choice to stop working on a task. As Schunk (1995b) states, "as skills develop, higher self-efficacy may relate negatively, rather than positively, to persistence, because students with higher self-efficacy are likely to be skillful and may not have to persist very long to perform well" (p. 131).

Performance More so than persistence, researchers in sport psychology typically examine the predictive strength of efficacy beliefs on performance because improving performance is of utmost importance to athletes and coaches alike. Sport performance is a combination of choice of task (e.g., degree of difficulty in gymnastics), strategy, effort, and persistence. Sport performance is unique from other goal-striving domains in that the performance markers are observable to the performer and others (Feltz & Magyar, 2006). This makes success and failures and goal discrepancies readily available.

As described in chapter 2 on measurement, performance has been quantified in terms of overall competitive measures such as finish times, win/loss percentages, and scores on judged competitions, or in terms of specific contests constructed for research purposes, such as penalty shooting contests in which number of shots made was measured. In fact, as Feltz and Magyar (2006) note, in competitive contexts, self-efficacy beliefs are often based on normative criteria and do not have to be based solely on a mastery-oriented criterion of performance. Feltz and Chase (1998) have labeled this "competitive" or "comparative" efficacy, the belief that one can compete successfully against an opponent. The research on sport performance has supported a consistent positive and moderate relationship with efficacy beliefs from a variety of sport tasks and competitions and with the use of different research designs (Feltz & Lirgg, 2001; Moritz et al., 2000). Given the complex nature of sport performance, efficacy beliefs should not be expected to explain all of the variance in the efficacy–performance relationship, especially when efficacy beliefs are assessed rather narrowly. When final scores in competition are used to measure the effects of self-efficacy, self-efficacy will not be a strong predictor of performance because performance scores are determined by many other factors as well (Feltz, 1992). In addition, as Bandura (1997) states, "performance is rarely, if ever, measured with complete accuracy . . . the magnitude of correlations, therefore, should not be interpreted as though the measure of performance is errorless" (p. 64).

Thought Patterns and Emotional Reactions   Athletes' judgments about their efficacy not only influence their physical behavior—the challenges that they undertake, their effort expended in the activity, and their perseverance in the face of difficulties—but also influence certain thought patterns (e.g., attributions and worry) and emotional reactions (e.g., anxiety and fear). For some athletes, pressure in competition is perceived as a natural part of the event, whereas for others it invokes heightened stress and anxiety. According to self-efficacy theory, perceived self-efficacy influences stress and anxiety through one's beliefs about personal control of actions, thoughts, and affect (Bandura, 1997). Athletes with high self-efficacy focus on the challenge and what they need to do to accomplish their goal. Those with low self-efficacy tend to worry about defeat, possible injury, or the inability to control their stress. These thought patterns lead to anxiety reactions, the aversive feelings of nervousness, distress, and tension that are associated with an athlete's activation or arousal.

Additionally, the emotional arousal involved in performance may not always be perceived as debilitating anxiety. Self-efficacy has been shown to influence a performer's interpretation of emotional arousal (e.g., Treasure et al., 1996). Athletes with higher efficacy beliefs are believed to perceive their emotional arousal as more facilitative than distressing. They may rate themselves as being nervous about the performance, but also report that this is not aversive or distressing. Rather, they consider this high degree of nervousness to be helpful to their performance. Athletes with weaker efficacy beliefs are more apt to perceive their emotional arousal as anxiety arousal and a sign of their inability to prevent, control, or cope with the potential difficulties of the competition. Research has shown little relationship between high arousal and poor performance in sport (Craft, Magyar, Becker, & Feltz, 2003).

Bandura (2001) also stated that efficacy beliefs influence whether people think pessimistically or optimistically and in ways that are self-enhancing or self-hindering. Accordingly, individuals with low self-efficacy tend to believe that things are tougher than they really are, which creates stress and a narrow vision of how best to go about the problem. By contrast, persons who have a strong sense of efficacy focus their attention and effort toward the demands of the situation and press forward with greater effort when faced with obstacles.

In terms of efficacy's influence on anxiety, one's perceived efficacy to cope with competitive pressure and control negative thoughts may be more important to alleviating anxiety feelings than one's perceived self-efficacy as a skillful performer. Athletes and other performers who have a high sense of efficacy in their ability to control anxiety are more able to remain task focused instead of thinking about the pressure. They are also more able to cope with mistakes and failure and not let their performance shortfalls interfere with the performance of the moment.

In terms of predicting performance, research has shown self-efficacy to be stronger than cognitive anxiety. Indeed, in self-efficacy theory, anxiety and impaired performance are considered coeffects of low self-efficacy (Bandura, 1997). Self-efficacy has been shown to predict cognitive anxiety and performance, but anxiety has generally not predicted performance independently (e.g., Feltz, 1982; Feltz & Mugno, 1983).

Relationship Between Efficacy Beliefs and Behavior Over Time

Bandura (1977) has posited that the relationship between efficacy beliefs and performance is temporally recursive. "Mastery expectations influence performance and are, in turn, altered by the cumulative effect of one's efforts" (p. 194). This relationship goes a long way toward explaining the phenomenon of a winning or losing streak in sport and the concept of momentum. If an athlete starts scoring successive points in tennis, she may be more confident that she can keep scoring, which may lead to winning game after game and ultimately the match. Similarly, if players on a basketball team start missing baskets, they may start doubting their shooting capability, which may lead to further failure. These two effects result in potential "spirals" that can be hard to break out of (Lindsley, Brass, & Thomas, 1995). Research using path analyses and structural equation modeling has found support for this relationship in individual and team performance situations (e.g., Feltz, 1982, 1988a; Feltz & Mugno, 1983; George, 1994; McAuley, 1985; Myers, Feltz, & Short, 2004; Myers, Payment, & Feltz, 2004). These efficacy–performance spirals or patterns of momentum can be disrupted through self-correcting adjustments (Lindsley et al.). As noted previously, complacency may occur during upward spirals if individuals are satisfied with their performance and do not believe that they have to continue to work hard for continued success. A downward spiral that is not too steep may lead to intensification of effort to disrupt the spiral or the opponent's momentum.

A recursive relationship can occur between efficacy beliefs and thought patterns as well (Bandura, 1990). Self-doubts about being able to cope with competitive pressure can create feelings of anxiety, which may further lower one's self-efficacy about the performance. Thus, low efficacy beliefs about controlling worry related to competitive anxiety or other emotions can become self-perpetuating because one's lack of efficacy for coping control produces the very emotions one wishes to prevent (Maddux, 1995). Feltz and Mugno (1983) found some support for this relationship for back diving performance. Perceived autonomic arousal significantly predicted self-efficacy perceptions for completing a back dive, which in turn predicted physiological arousal on a subsequent trial. Bandura's (1977, 1997) theory of self-efficacy posits a network of causal and reciprocal relationships. Figure 1.2 presents the relationships between the major sources of efficacy information, efficacy judgments, and consequences as predicted by Bandura's theory and the additional determinants proposed by Maddux (1995).

Qualifiers to the Efficacy-Behavior Relationship

There are qualifiers to the predicted efficacy–performance relationship. Bandura (1997) postulates that self-efficacy beliefs are a major determinant of behavior only when people have sufficient incentives to act on their efficacy beliefs, when they possess the requisite skills, when the tasks or circumstances are unambiguous, when both variables tap similar capabilities (i.e., are concordant), and when both variables are measured in close temporal proximity. Self-efficacy beliefs will exceed actual performance when there is little incentive to perform the activity or when physical or social constraints are imposed on performance. For instance, only when George and his colleagues (1992) used participants who perceived the task to be at least moderately important did they find a self-efficacy–performance relationship.

According to Bandura (1997), discrepancies between efficacy beliefs and performance will also occur when tasks or circumstances are ambiguous or when one has little information on which to base efficacy judgments, such as

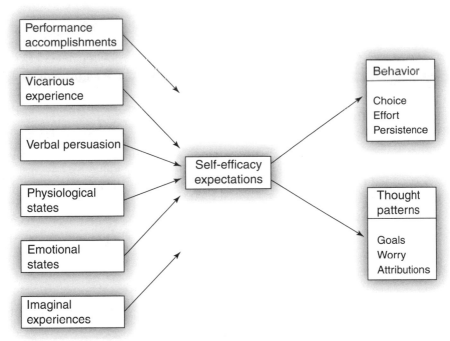

Figure 1.2 Relationship between sources of efficacy information, efficacy judgments, and consequences.

Note. Adapted from Feltz, D.L., and Chase, M.A. (1998). The measurement of self-efficacy and confidence in sport. In J.L. Duda (Ed.), *Advances in sport and exercise psychology measurement* (p 66). Morgantown, WV: Fitness Information Technology. Copyright 1998. Adapted with permission.

when one is first learning a skill. Without some knowledge of the skill to be performed or the conditions under which it is to be performed, one cannot make an accurate judgment of one's capability to perform it. Beginning skiers have only vicarious and instructional information on which to rely in making efficacy judgments about riding a rope tow to the top of a ski slope. They may underestimate or overestimate the task demands or their capabilities (or both) until they gain some experience with the task. Regarding ambiguous circumstances, track runners might overestimate their efficacy concerning the speed with which they can run different events if they assume that they will have adequate recovery time between races but then have to run them back to back. In their meta-analysis of the efficacy–performance relationship in sport, Moritz and colleagues (2000) reported larger correlations for those studies that used performance tasks familiar to the participants ($r = .39$), compared with novel tasks ($r = .31$). The issues of concordance and temporal proximity of measures are addressed in chapter 2.

Types of Efficacy Beliefs

The nature of efficacy beliefs is highly dependent on the research question being studied. In terms of physical skill, a researcher or practitioner might be interested in efficacy beliefs regarding the degree of difficulty of performing a particular task, the number of different tasks a person can perform, the ability to maintain an activity in the face of challenges and impediments, or the ability to cope with stressful conditions or events. Table 1.1 presents the types of efficacy beliefs typically applied to sport and their definitions.

Task Self-Efficacy   Task self-efficacy might be used to examine the beliefs about performing a particular task with graded levels of difficulty, for instance, athletes' beliefs regarding their ability to hit a ball into fair territory from 1 time out of 10 to 10 times out of 10. Task self-efficacy might also be used to examine beliefs about performing a particular task under different situational demands, such as hitting a fastball, hitting a curveball, or hitting to the opposite field. We do not use the term "task self-efficacy" here in the way

TABLE 1.1   *Types of Efficacy Beliefs Used in Sport*

Type	Description	Example in sport
Ameliorative efficacy	Belief regarding one's ability to cope with diverse threats (e.g., stress, unwanted thoughts, difficult situations, or pain)	Athletes' beliefs regarding their ability to control negative thoughts about their performance
Collective efficacy	Beliefs that group members have about their group's capabilities to organize and execute successful group actions	Athletes' beliefs that their team can force more turnovers against opponent team
Competitive efficacy	Beliefs regarding performing successfully against an opponent	Athletes' beliefs regarding their ability to beat various opponents
Coping efficacy	Same as ameliorative efficacy	
Learning efficacy	Beliefs in one's learning capabilities	Athletes' beliefs that they can learn a new golf swing
Performance efficacy	Efficacy beliefs at the time of performance or competition	Athletes' beliefs regarding their ability to perform a successful squeeze bunt in today's baseball game
Preparatory efficacy	Efficacy beliefs during acquisition phase of learning skills or during the preparation time for a competition	Athletes' beliefs regarding their ability to perform successful squeeze bunts in practice (when first learning the skill)
Self-regulatory efficacy	Beliefs in ability to exercise influence over one's own motivation, thought processes, emotional states, and patterns of behavior	Athletes' beliefs about adhering to a weight training program on a regular basis and in the face of competing time demands
Task efficacy	Belief in capability to perform a particular task	Athletes' beliefs regarding their ability to hit a ball into fair territory

that Maddux (1995) defines it, as perceived capability to perform a "simple motor act." The tasks in sport performance can be quite complex. Maddux used the term "behavioral self-efficacy" to refer to what sport psychology researchers call task self-efficacy.

Self-Regulatory Efficacy Self-regulatory efficacy beliefs concern the ability to exercise influence over one's own motivation, thought processes, emotional states, and patterns of behavior. Self-regulatory efficacy might be used to investigate beliefs about tasks that are familiar but that must be performed on a regular basis to achieve the desired results, as in resistance training. In this type of capability, athletes are capable of lifting weights but may vary in their confidence about doing so on a regular basis and in the face of competing time demands.

Ameliorative and Coping Efficacy Ameliorative efficacy (Bandura, 1997) is sometimes used more specifically with reference to perceived ability to manage perceived threats. Ameliorative efficacy, also referred to as coping efficacy, might be of interest to a researcher or practitioner concerned with athletes' beliefs about coping with competitive stress, controlling unwanted thoughts, managing performance slumps, or coping with pain and recovery from injury. Maddux (1995) uses the term "cognitive self-efficacy" to refer to perceptions of the ability to exercise control over one's thoughts, and "emotional self-efficacy" to refer to people's beliefs in their ability to perform actions that influence their moods or emotional states. Regardless of the term ("ameliorative," "coping," "self-regulatory," "cognitive," or "emotional" self-efficacy), the type of efficacy beliefs that we are describing here has to do with beliefs about exercising personal control over thoughts, actions, and affect.

Learning Efficacy Learning efficacy is the belief in one's capability to learn a new skill. A strong sense of learning efficacy can accelerate the process of mastering a skill because people with this sense will invest more effort in practicing the skill than those who doubt their learning capabilities (Bandura, 1997). However, Bandura also notes that this type of efficacy is more effective in fostering learning efforts when the task is challenging, less so when the task is perceived as easy. Efficacy beliefs for learning are related to a belief system known as conception of ability (Nicholls, 1984a). Those who regard ability as an acquirable skill are more likely to also have confidence in being able to learn it and view their mistakes as a natural part of the learning process.

Preparatory Efficacy and Performance Efficacy Bandura (1986b, 1997) also differentiates between preparatory efficacy and performance efficacy, distinguishing between two phases and their effects. The preparatory phase includes the acquisition of skills and the preparation for a competition.

Preparatory efficacy is an efficacy belief about a task or a competition during the preparation phase. It should not be confused with efficacy about one's ability to learn or prepare. In the skill acquisition or preparatory phase, Bandura suggests that some self-doubt is necessary to provide the incentive to invest the time and effort to acquire the knowledge and skill needed to become proficient. If a person has high self-efficacy, especially for a task that he or she perceives as easy, there is little reason to invest much time and effort in practicing that task. Bandura also warns that too much self-doubt can turn into a stressor and debilitator rather than a motivator to practice. This hypothesis implies a curvilinear, or inverted-U, relationship in the skill acquisition phase between self-efficacy beliefs and effort and persistence as the dependent variable. However, to our knowledge this relationship has not been empirically tested. Even with proficient athletes, Bandura (1997) notes that coaches will inflate the capabilities of athletes' opponents and emphasize the deficiencies of their own athletes to try to motivate them to practice hard for the next competition. In addition, as noted earlier in this chapter, complacency can set in after easy successes to affect motivation, and greater efforts can occur after failure.

In the performance phase, however, when one is about to execute a task, a more linear relationship is predicted between self-efficacy beliefs and performance as the dependent measure. As Bandura explains, one cannot execute a task very well while plagued with self-doubt. "Explicit monitoring" theories of choking under pressure would suggest that these self-doubts focus one's attention on motor skills that have become automated or "procedural-ized" and are best executed without conscious awareness (Beilock & Carr, 2001; Beilock, Carr, MacMahon, & Starkes, 2002). A high-level skill that becomes automated with extended practice may be especially susceptible to the negative consequences of performance pressure because high-level, expert performance is thought to operate largely outside of conscious control and can be harmed when explicit attention to it is prompted by self-doubt (Beilock & Feltz, 2006).

Competitive Efficacy As mentioned earlier in this chapter, Feltz and Chase (1998) have defined competitive efficacy as the belief that one can compete successfully against an opponent. Examples include "I am confident that I can win this match," "I am confident that I can beat my opponent to the ball," and "I am confident that I can throw the javelin farther than my opponent." These beliefs are based on normative performance markers, and as we explain later in this chapter, they should not be confused with outcome expectation beliefs.

Collective Efficacy Lastly, Bandura (1982, 1986b, 1997) has discussed efficacy beliefs as they relate to groups. We devote an entire chapter to collective efficacy in sport, but briefly, Bandura (1997) defined collective efficacy as "a group's shared belief in its conjoint capabilities to organize and execute the courses of action required to produce given levels of attainment" (p. 477). Similarly to self-efficacy, collective efficacy is the primary determinant of a group's level of motivation to accomplish a specific goal. This is reflected in the challenges that the group undertakes, the effort they expend in the given activity, and their perseverance, as a group, in the face of difficulties.

Related Measures and Concepts of Self-Efficacy

Terms other than self-efficacy have been used to measure the same construct, self-efficacy, but also different constructs. That is, terms such as "self-confidence" or "sport confidence" (Vealey, 1986) are similar goal-oriented terms that have been used to measure people's judgments about their capabilities to accomplish a particular goal in sport or physical activity. These terms fit with Bandura's (1977, 1997) definition of self-efficacy when they are used to measure what people perceive they can do rather than what they have or what they are (see chapter 2 on measurement). Other terms, such as "perceived competence" and "perceived ability," are goal-oriented terms but have different predictive purposes than self-efficacy, as we describe later in this chapter. Terms such as "self-concept" and "self-esteem" are concepts of the self, but are not measures of perceived capability within a goal-striving context. See table 1.2 for comparisons between self-efficacy and related constructs used in sport.

TABLE 1.2   *Comparisons Between Self-Efficacy and Related Constructs Used in Sport*

Construct	Description	Goal-striving context	Sample item in sport
Self-efficacy	Belief that one can successfully organize and execute a course of action to reach a specific goal	Yes	"How "confident" are you that you can kick a soccer goal in a penalty kick against this goaltender?"
Sport confidence (Vealey, 1986)	Degree of certainty one possesses about the ability to be successful in sport	Yes	"Compared to the most confident athlete you know, how confident are you that you can perform under pressure?"
Self-confidence (from CSAI-2: Martens et al., 1990)	Belief that one can perform successfully in competition	Yes	"In this competition, I'm confident I can meet the challenge."

(continued)

TABLE 1.2 *(continued)*

Construct	Description	Goal-striving context	Sample item in sport
Perceived competence and perceived ability	Belief of one's ability in a certain domain or across a set of behaviors, developed as a result of cumulative interactions with one's environment	Yes	"How likely do you feel that you are better than others your age at sports?"
Outcome expectancy	Belief that a certain behavior will lead to a certain outcome	Yes	"How confident are you that the goals you score will lead to approval from your coach?"
Self-concept	One's self-description profile formed through evaluative experiences and interactions with one's social environment. It can be global or domain specific.	No	"I am athletic."
Self-esteem	Individual's judgment of self-worth and feelings of self-satisfaction. It can be global or domain specific.	No	"On the whole, I am satisfied with myself as an athlete."
Level of aspiration	One's estimation of a given level of performance prior to attempting the task. It is specific to the task.	Yes	"How many targets will you hit in the next trial?"
Response expectancy	One's belief in the effectiveness of a prescribed treatment or strategy. It is specific to the situation.	Yes	"How confident are you that this karate program is effective in deterring assaults?"
Locus of control	One's expectancy that outcomes are within one's control or determined by external forces. It can be global or specific.	Yes	"Winning this event is under my control."
Sport Confidence from CSCI (Manzo et al., 2001)	Dispositional belief that incorporates perceived optimism and competence in sport.	Yes	"I feel that if something can go right for me during sports, it will." (optimism) "In the company of my peers, I feel that I am always one of the best when it comes to joining sports activities." (competence)

Sport Confidence

Vealey (1986) developed a model and instrumentation of sport confidence and a later revision (Vealey et al., 1998) to provide an operationalization of self confidence that could be used across sports and sport situations (see figure 1.3). Sport confidence is defined as the degree of certainty individuals possess about their ability to be successful in sport. In the original model, sport confidence was conceptualized into trait (SC-trait) and state (SC-state) components. In addition, Vealey (1986) included a competitive orientation construct in her conceptual model to account for individual differences in defining success in sport. Competitive orientation is considered a dispositional construct that indicates an athlete's tendency to strive toward achieving a certain type of goal in sport (performing well or winning) that will demonstrate competence and success. Vealey developed state and trait versions of the Sport Confidence Inventory (SSCI and TSCI) and the Competitive Orientation Inventory (COI) to measure the key constructs in her model. Feltz and Chase (1998) consider sport confidence to have commonalities with self-efficacy in that both are conceptualized as cognitive mediators of people's motivation and behavior within a goal context and both are conceptualized as what one can do with one's skills, though the goal in sport confidence is more broadly defined (e.g., performing successfully in one's sport) than is typical with self-efficacy.

The original sport confidence model was based on an interactional paradigm, with SC-trait and competitive orientation (performance or outcome) predicted to interact with objective sport situations and influence SC-state. Specifically, SC-state was hypothesized to be positively related to SC-trait and performance orientation, to be negatively related to outcome orientation, and to be a critical mediator of behavior. Subjective outcomes (e.g., causal attributions, perceptions of success, satisfaction) were predicted to have a reciprocal relationship with SC-trait and competitive orientation. Although Vealey (1986) found that SC-trait and competitive orientation did predict SC-state and subjective outcomes as expected, precompetition SC-state did not predict performance. Contrary to her original model, further studies showed that SC-trait was a better predictor of performance than SC-state (Gayton & Nickless, 1987; Roberts & Vealey, 1992).

Vealey and colleagues (1998) noted the SC-trait and SC-state distinction as a weakness and presented a reconceptualized model based on a social cognitive perspective. As illustrated in figure 1.3, the updated model includes a single sport confidence construct, organizational culture, athlete characteristics, and sources of sport confidence. The biggest change in terms of sport confidence is in the flexibility of its measurement on a continuum from more trait-like to state-like, depending on the temporal frame of reference used (the measurement of sport confidence is addressed in chapter 2). Vealey and colleagues' revised model (1998) predicts that organizational culture of a program (e.g., competitive

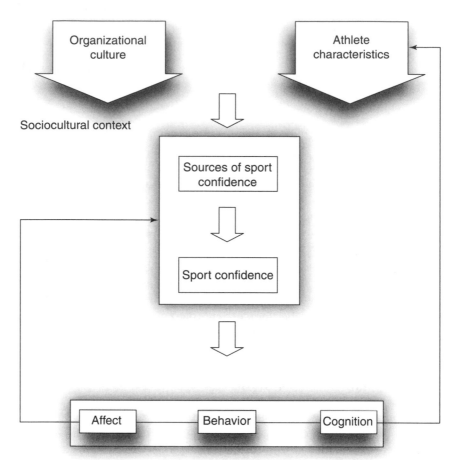

Figure 1.3 Conceptual framework of sport confidence.

Reprinted, by permission, from R.S. Vealey, et al., 1998, "Sources of sport-confidence conceptualization," *Journal of Sport and Exercise Psychology* 20: 56.

level, motivational climate, type of sport) and the characteristics of an athlete (e.g., age, gender, personality) influence sources of sport confidence, which in turn predict sport confidence levels. Sport confidence, in turn, is hypothesized to predict athletes' cognitions, their affective state, and effort and performance. As noted in chapter 2, however, the state version of sport confidence was not found to be as predictive of performance as were task-specific efficacy scales in a meta-analytic study of efficacy and motor performance (Moritz et al., 2000).

Self-Confidence Within the Competitive State Anxiety Inventory-2 (CSAI-2)

Martens and colleagues (1990) discovered a third component in their factor analysis of an instrument designed to measure the cognitive and somatic components of anxiety. They identified this component as self-confidence (the self-confidence subscale is discussed further in chapter 2). The CSAI-2 was designed to measure competitive state anxiety, and self-confidence for competition was not originally conceptualized as being part of competitive anxiety. According to self-efficacy theory, perceived self-confidence influences stress and anxiety through one's beliefs about personal control of actions, thoughts, and affect rather than being a component of anxiety. As Bandura (1997) hypothesizes, "both anxiety and impaired performance are coeffects of a low sense of efficacy to meet competitive demands" (p. 389). Athletes with low self-confidence tend to worry about defeat, possible injury, or the inability to control their stress. These thought patterns lead to subsequent anxiety reactions and impaired performance.

Perceived Competence and Perceived Ability

Two other goal-oriented self-perception constructs are perceived competence and perceived ability (Harter, 1978, 1981; Nicholls, 1984a). These terms are more related to perceptions developed over time (from cumulative interactions with the environment) than to state-specific perceptions that either vary across tasks or vary within the same task at different levels of difficulty and under different circumstances (Bandura, 1997). These terms also focus on the perceptions of abilities that one has developed, not perceptions of what one can accomplish with those abilities, even if they have been adapted for a specific sport. For example, a perceived soccer competence measurement item is "how likely do you feel that YOU ARE better than others your age at soccer" (Feltz & Brown, 1984). A perceived efficacy item, on the other hand, might be "how confident are you that YOU CAN make a soccer goal from the penalty kick line 1 out of 10 to 10 out of 10 times."

Outcome Expectations

Bandura (1986b, 1997) warns that self-efficacy expectations should not be confused with outcome expectations. Outcome expectancies are defined as the belief that certain behaviors will lead to certain outcomes, whereas self-efficacy is the belief in one's ability to perform the behavior successfully. Bandura (1997) describes the three major forms that outcome expectations can take: physical effects, social effects, and self-evaluative effects. "Behavior and the effects it produces are different classes of events" (p. 22). That is, examples of physical outcome effects are positive or negative sensory experiences; examples of social outcome effects are approval or disapproval and monetary compensation or deprivation of privileges; and examples of self-evaluative outcome effects are self-sanctions or self-satisfaction. Outcome expectations depend largely on self-efficacy expectations, and add little if anything to the prediction of performance in sport, where outcomes are tightly connected to the quality of performance. As Bandura (1997) notes, "Athletes who concede that they cannot triumph over formidable opponents do not expect to capture top prizes in contests with them" (p. 24). However, in situations in which coaches provide noncontingent praise to all athletes, regardless of performance, outcome expectancies for praise would be expected to be an additional predictor of behavior.

Some sport psychology researchers confuse performance markers, such as "winning or losing an event," with an outcome expectation (e.g., Dawson, Gyurcsik, Culos-Reed, & Brawley, 2001; Eyal, Bar-Eli, Tenenbaum, & Pie, 1995; Neiss, 1989). Because the term "competitive outcome" has been used extensively in the sport psychology literature to mean the final score, rank, or win/loss, the terms can be easily confused. As Feltz and Lirgg (2001) explain, however, an athlete's final position at the end of a competition or winning does not fit the class of effects that Bandura (1997) defines as outcomes. Rather, an athlete's position at the end of a competition—first, second, third, and so on—is a performance marker. An outcome expectation of winning a competitive event, using Bandura's definition, might be experiencing a high level of self-satisfaction, gaining approval from one's coach, or receiving money or a trophy. The efficacy expectation is the belief about the probability of winning the competition. In essence, outcome expectations are the expected consequences of performance, rather than the performance itself (Bandura, 1997). Thus, the statement by Dawson et al. (2001) that, "an individual may train as hard as she can for a marathon but not achieve the outcome of a first-place performance because her competitors are faster" (p. 342), does not point to an outcome; it is an example of a performance marker.

Response expectations (Rogers, 1983) also should not be confused with outcome expectations. The term response efficacy has been used to define one's belief in the effectiveness of a prescribed treatment or strategy for a particular health benefit. For example, participants may vary in their beliefs about how effective karate is in deterring assaults, or they may vary in their beliefs about the situations in which karate techniques are effective or ineffective (Feltz & Chase, 1998). These are really response expectancy examples.

According to Bandura (1997), response expectations are "concerned with whether a given course of action can produce a particular attainment; outcome expectations are concerned with the consequences that flow from that attainment" (p. 283) and have been described mostly in relation to self-regulatory behavior. Response expectations are not particularly useful in adding to the explained variance of self-regulatory behavior in sport because participants typically unite their personal efficacy beliefs with their belief in the strategy to act on their beliefs.

Self-Concept and Self-Esteem

Self-concept is generally regarded as one's self-description profile formed through evaluative experiences and interactions with one's social environment. Examples might be "I am a skier," "I am a mother," and "I am a professor." Self-concept also incorporates a variety of self-reactions, feelings of self-worth, and general beliefs of competence (Zimmerman & Cleary, 2006). Global measures of self-concept are helpful for understanding one's total outlook toward life and psychological well-being, but not very useful in predicting intraindividual variability in performance situations. Advances have been made in conceptualizing and measuring self-concept in the physical domain (Fox & Corbin, 1989; Marsh, Richards, Johnson, Roche, & Tremayne, 1994). Physical self-concept is one's view of oneself in a physical context and also is helpful for understanding one's outlook toward sport and physical activity and one's physical well-being (see Fox, 1997, for a review).

Another global construct related to self-efficacy, self-esteem, concerns one's personal perception of worthiness. Although self-efficacy and self-esteem can be related, self-efficacy is a cognitive judgment rather than an affective reaction (Pintrich & Schunk, 2002). People can have low self-efficacy and still perceive themselves to be "OK." Likewise, people may have a high sense of efficacy that they can perform a given activity but not "like themselves" very much. Physical self-esteem measures have also been developed to measure people's perception of physical self-worth in the physical domain (Fox & Corbin, 1989).

Other Related Concepts

Other self-referential concepts include level of aspiration; locus of control; and Manzo, Silva, and Mink's (2001) two-factor (dispositional optimism and perceived sport competence) dispositional model of sport confidence as measured by the Carolina Sport Confidence Inventory (CSCI). Level of aspiration was first conceptualized in the 1930s regarding people's estimations of performance on a familiar task. It was specifically defined as "the level of future performance in a familiar task which an individual, knowing his level of past performance in that task, explicitly undertakes to reach" (Frank, 1935, p. 119). Once a level of aspiration was set, the person performed, examined the discrepancy between performance and level of aspiration, and reacted with feelings of success or failure. Success and failure led to corresponding increases and decreases in level of aspiration (Lewin, Dembo, Festinger, & Sears, 1944).

Early investigations on level of aspiration were the precursors to later research on various cognitive aspects of goal setting, self-appraisal, and self-satisfaction in relation to success and failure (Feltz, 1994). Much of the basis for current views on self-regulation within social cognitive theory (e.g., self-monitoring, self-evaluation, and self-reaction) can be traced to the level-of-aspiration paradigm (see Bandura, 1982; Carver & Scheier, 1981). However, Bandura's (1977) self-efficacy construct added a further explanation to people's fluctuations in levels of aspiration. Success does not always lead to increased levels of aspiration, nor do failures to lowered levels. "Having surpassed a demanding standard through laborious effort does not automatically lead people to raise their level of aspiration" (Bandura, 1986b, p. 348).

Rotter's (1966) concept of locus of control concerns people's expectancies about their ability to control reinforcements in life. People who perceive events as more internally controlled tend to behave in more self-determined ways; whereas, those who perceive events as more externally controlled tend to behave in more fatalistic ways (Bandura, 1997). For instance, athletes who believe that jumping ability can be improved through plyometric exercises will be more apt to try to improve their jumping skill than will those who believe jumping ability is controlled by genetics. As Zimmerman and Cleary (2006) note, although perceptions of control and perceived self-efficacy are similar in that they both deal with how individuals can act in agentic ways on their environment, perceived control does not take into account how confident an individual feels about performing specific tasks within a particular context.

The CSCI (Manzo et al., 2001) was first conceptualized as a three-factor model of sport confidence, dispositional optimism, and perceived control. Manzo et al. defined their sport confidence concept as, "A relatively enduring belief system which is the result of the interaction between possessing an expectation that good things will happen (dispositional optimism), believing one's skills and abilities can successfully fulfill the demands of a sport task (sport competence), and a positive estimation of the cause and effect contingency between one's ability and the resultant performance and outcome (perceived control)" (p. 263-264). However, psychometric tests supported only the dispositional optimism and perceived sport competence factors. Although the inventory is titled as a confidence measure, its conceptualization fits better with the dispositional measures of perceived competence and positive expectancies than with self-efficacy. In summary, self-efficacy judgments differ from other related self-belief constructs because they are task and context specific and focus exclusively on measuring one's perceptions of capability (Zimmerman & Cleary, 2006).

Criticisms of Self-Efficacy Theory

The early criticisms of self-efficacy theory focused on the self-report nature of efficacy judgments and the lack of need for a cognitive construct from a behavioristic view. Self-efficacy ratings suffer from the same demand and suggestion problems as self-report measures of fear (Bernstein, 1973). Self-efficacy theory received early criticisms for being so heavily based on self-report measures (Borkovec, 1978; Kazdin, 1978). However, Bandura (1978) argued that in situations in which individuals have no reason to distort their reports, self-reports can be quite representative of cognitions. Thus efficacy judgments are best made when evaluation apprehension has been minimized and when they are recorded privately. Although researchers in sport have found no difference between making public and making private efficacy expectation statements (Weinberg, Yukelson, & Jackson, 1980), critics suggested that even making a private efficacy statement creates a demand or goal to match the performance with the efficacy judgment (Biglan, 1987; Borkovec, 1978). In testing this presumption, Telch, Bandura, Vinciguerra, Agras, and Stout (1982) showed that variation in social demand had little effect on congruence between self-efficacy and performance. It is more likely that social demand encourages conservation in making efficacy judgments and thus reduces the congruence between self-efficacy and performance.

In anxiety-based contexts, self-efficacy theory was also criticized on the grounds that self-efficacy is merely an epiphenomenon of anxiety reduction (Eysenck, 1978; Kirsch, 1990). Anxiety-control theories proposed that fear creates an anxiety drive that motivates subsequent avoidance behavior and leaves one with low levels of efficacy beliefs. However, Bandura (1997) has reviewed several studies that refute this notion and demonstrate the causal superiority of self-efficacy for coping with potential threats as a predictor of both anticipated anxiety and avoidance behavior. Additionally, path-analytic studies in sport contexts that compared anxiety-based and efficacy-based models showed greater support for a self-efficacy-mediating model (Feltz, 1982; Feltz & Mugno, 1983; McAuley, 1985). These studies are addressed in more detail in chapter 3. As Bandura (1997) notes, "It is a good thing that anxiety does not control actions. If people fled from what they were doing or froze every time they felt highly tense or anxious, their lives would be immobilized much of the time" (p. 324).

In addition to these early arguments, Kirsch (1982, 1995) argued that self-efficacy expectations may be more reflective of one's willingness to perform certain tasks than one's confidence. "When you ask people if they could do something that violates their moral standards or that would result in extremely aversive consequences, they are likely to interpret the word 'could' figuratively rather than literally" (Kirsch, 1995, p. 338). To take a sport example, if a pitcher, asked how confident he is that he can throw a bean ball in a game, replies with low confidence, Kirsch would interpret the response to mean that the pitcher would not throw a bean ball, rather than that he is not physically capable of throwing a pitch accurately aimed at the batter's head. However, self-efficacy is not just beliefs about the motor acts. In this example, it is the belief that the pitcher can override his feelings about the moral dilemma he faces, his belief that he can make the throw look unintentional, or that he can stand up to possible retaliation. This belief may not be the type of efficacy that we would want to assess in sport, but it serves to provide a sport example of Kirsch's argument. For people with genuine avoidance behavior, Williams (1995) suggests that the "will" is not what is lacking; people desperately want to overcome their fears. The self-efficacy to approach feared tasks is the belief that is lacking.

Some studies assessing the reciprocal relationship between efficacy beliefs and performance over time have included past performance in the causal analysis and have shown past performance to be a stronger predictor than self-efficacy of future performance (e.g., Ackerman, Kanfer, & Goff, 1995; Feltz, 1982; Feltz & Mugno, 1983; Vancouver, Thompson, Tischner, & Putka, 2002; Vancouver, Thompson, & Williams, 2001). The performance conditions in these studies have been invariant. When conditions are more variant over time, efficacy beliefs are stronger predictors of performance than are previous performances (George, 1994; Lee, 1986; Myers, Feltz, & Short, 2004). However, whether conditions are variant or invariant, Bandura (1997) has argued that "performance is not a cause of performance" (p. 395). Because past performance is a "conglomerate index" that includes efficacy beliefs as well as other sociocognitive factors (e.g., goal effects) operating at the time, Bandura argues that these variables should be partialled out of past performance (i.e., residualizing past performance) when we are testing for its predictive strength on subsequent performance (Bandura, 1997; Bandura & Locke, 2003). This process is explained in more detail in chapter 2.

As noted by Bandura and Locke (2003), many studies have demonstrated that self-efficacy contributes independently to performance after residualizing of prior performance (e.g., Myers, Payment, & Feltz, 2004). However, Heggestad and Kanfer (2005) argue that removing the effects of self-efficacy from past performance before entering it into the analysis is an overadjustment because the procedure also removes common cause variables. More importantly, however, Bandura (1997) argues that to advance the understanding of psychosocial contributors to athletic performance, researchers should shift their attention from past performance as a determinant of future performance to the actual determinants of performance.

Vancouver and his associates also have argued that efficacy beliefs can be self-debilitating when measured on an intraindividual basis across time (Vancouver et al., 2002, 2001). On the basis of Powers' (1978, 1991) perceptual control theory (PCT), they posited that high self-efficacy can result in decreased performance because an individual may become overconfident and allocate fewer resources to the task as it is repeated across time. Without reviewing PCT in depth (see Bandura & Locke, 2003, for a review and critique), it is a cybernetic model that is based on a negative feedback loop wherein people are motivated to reduce the discrepancy between feedback received and internal goals. If the discrepancy is reduced to zero, no further adjustment in performance is needed. As Vancouver and colleagues applied PCT to self-efficacy, when individuals have high self-efficacy they may be overly optimistic about the degree to which they are meeting their goals. This perception would reduce the discrepancy between goal and perceived performance, and thus individuals would apply fewer resources to meeting goals, which in turn would result in lower subsequent performance. The authors argued that past performance has a strong positive influence on self-efficacy beliefs, but resultant self-efficacy has a weak negative influence on subsequent performance.

Vancouver and colleagues (2001, 2002) tested their hypotheses using a laboratory task (a computer-based decision game called Mastermind). This is a task that does not vary in difficulty as perceived by the participants. The investigators found that, at a within-person, across-time level of analysis, performance was positively related to subsequent self-efficacy and that self-efficacy negatively predicted subsequent performance. In addition, inductions of high self-efficacy had a decreasing effect on subsequent performance. In reviewing the studies by Vancouver and coworkers, Bandura and Locke (2003) argued that there were conceptual and methodological problems in these studies that limit confidence in the results and the conclusions. Conceptually, self-efficacy was not a part of PCT. In self-efficacy theory, goals and self-reactive influences play an important role on future efforts. The argument is not that self-efficacy will always have a positive influence on performance, but rather that the direction of influence depends on these self-evaluative reactions and goal adjustments in relation to one's past performance. People with high self-efficacy are expected to set higher goals after reaching a challenging performance standard, which creates a discrepancy rather than reduces one. In activities in which there are no additional challenges to meet and there is little investment in the task (e.g., Vancouver et al.'s computer game), high-efficacy individuals are not expected to intensify their efforts. In sport, when people are first learning new skills, mastery leads to increases in self-efficacy, which leads to further mastery (e.g., Feltz et al., 1979).

Methodologically, Vancouver and colleagues' studies involved lab tasks that were not personally meaningful and did not permit progressive changes in self-efficacy and performance across time. Thus, the results have little generalizability for nontrivial tasks. In sport, athletes look beyond their immediate performance and keep their sights on their goals. For example, Myers, Payment, and Feltz (2004) found collective efficacy beliefs to have a positive relationship with subsequent performance within hockey teams with a task that was constant across time (i.e., the opponent). They reasoned that, unlike tasks in laboratory studies, their task was meaningful to the participants and permitted progressive changes in collective efficacy and team performance across time. Bandura and Locke concluded that "converging evidence from diverse methodological and analytic strategies verifies that self-efficacy and personal goals enhance motivation and performance attainments" (p. 87).

Specifically as self-efficacy relates to sport performance, Roberts (1992, 2001) has been critical of the usefulness of self-efficacy in sport contexts and argues that it fares much better in the exercise achievement arena in predicting choice, effort, and persistence. In terms of sport performance, self-efficacy judgments are a weaker predictor than they are of other achievement behaviors (e.g., effort, persistence, concentration, choice), according to Roberts, because other mechanisms contribute to sport performance (e.g., opponent's ability, external factors) as we have similarly noted in this chapter. However, "athletes of comparable abilities but different self-assurance do not perform at the same level" (Bandura, 1997, p. 358). Furthermore, as we noted at the beginning of this chapter, Bandura (1986b, 1997) places self-efficacy within the broader theory of social cognition, where it is an important, but not the sole, determinant of goal-directed behavior. Knowledge, goals, values, anticipated outcomes, and environmental factors (facilitators and constraints) also contribute to performance. Even so, as Moritz and colleagues (2000) showed in their meta-analytic review, where self-efficacy has not been shown to be a reliable predictor of sport performance, this has had more to do with the way in which performance was measured than with its conceptual usefulness in predicting sport performance.

In addition, Roberts (2001) declared that "research in self-efficacy in sport has come almost to a standstill" (p. 9) and that achievement goal theory is more powerful and appropriate to explain achievement behavior in sport. Far from being at a standstill, as we outline in part II of the book, self-efficacy research in sport has expanded to include investigations of teams, coaches, unique sources within sport, relationships to other social cognitive variables, and the self-regulation of other processes beyond physical performance in sport. Furthermore, Bandura (1997) devotes considerable space to goal theory and its relationship to self-efficacy within social cognitive theory. Achievement goals and self-efficacy are not competing theories.

In summary, the early criticisms of self-efficacy theory focused on the methods by which self-efficacy ratings were made and its usefulness in explaining anxiety (Biglan, 1987; Borkovec, 1978; Eysenck, 1978; Kazdin, 1978; Kirsch, 1982, 1990, 1995). Later criticisms focused on self-efficacy's explanatory power in sport and other performance contexts across time (Roberts, 1992, 2001; Vancouver et al., 2001, 2002). Many of these criticisms have been refuted through empirical research (Bandura, 1995, 1997; Bandura & Locke, 2003). That self-efficacy beliefs are not the only determinant of physical performance is undisputed by Bandura (1997). He distinguishes between social cognitive theory, which encompasses a large set of factors (e.g., knowledge, goals, expected outcomes, attributions, emotional states, and environment) that regulate and motivate behavior, and the self-efficacy component, which operates in concert with these factors and plays an interactive role along with physical endowment and skill to determine athletic performance. Even so, research on self-efficacy in numerous sport contexts has shown a consistently significant relationship between self-efficacy and performance (Moritz et al., 2000). We address this research in part II. In addition, what makes self-efficacy theory so appealing to sport psychologists is that efficacy beliefs are modifiable and have great functional value. Sport psychologists can target strategies to strengthen efficacy beliefs for athletes, teams, and coaches rather than just predict behavior based on personality traits. We describe these strategies in detail in part III of the book.

Measuring
Efficacy Beliefs

> Confidence is a very fragile thing.
>
> *Joe Montana, former NFL quarterback, member of the Pro Football Hall of Fame*

As we mentioned in chapter 1, efficacy beliefs are modifiable. They can be changed by a number of events, thoughts, and worries. They can be, as Joe Montana noted, "fragile." Thus, careful attention is needed to how they are measured. Although the research in sport has supported a consistent positive relationship between efficacy beliefs and performance in divergent sports and participants, and with the use of different research designs, the measurement of efficacy beliefs has not been consistent across research studies, nor has it always been appropriate. Therefore, in this chapter, we review Bandura's (2006) guidelines for constructing efficacy measures and provide sport-specific examples of measures, describe hierarchical and nonhierarchical efficacy scales, describe the microanalytical approach to efficacy-belief assessment, describe how to measure the efficacy-performance relationship over time, and describe and critique the existing assessments. Because efficacy beliefs in the sport world involve athletes, teams, and coaches, we discuss special considerations and issues in measuring efficacy with these populations. Lastly, we provide specific recommendations for the development of efficacy-belief instruments in sport to improve their predictive strength.

Bandura's Guidelines for Constructing Efficacy Measures

Bandura (2006) has provided a set of guidelines for constructing efficacy scales that supplement the issues he describes in chapter 2 of his 1997 book, which we overviewed in chapter 1. In this set of guidelines, Bandura provides recommendations regarding domain specification, gradations of challenge, content relevance, response scaling, phrasing of items, item analysis, minimizing response bias, and validation. We do not review all of these guidelines in detail in this chapter—just those most pertinent to the study of sport. Readers interested in these recommendations are referred to this 2006 work.

Domain Specification

Specifying the content of the activity domain is probably the most important guideline in Bandura's (2006) set of recommendations. Bandura (1997) distinguishes among three levels of domain specification. Measures that assess efficacy beliefs for a particular performance under a specific set of conditions (e.g., confidence in hitting a squeeze bunt against a particular pitcher with a runner on third, bottom of the ninth, and one out) are the most specific. Measures that assess efficacy beliefs for a class of performances within the same activity (e.g., confidence in batting in baseball) under a class of conditions that share common properties (e.g., against different types of pitches) are intermediate in specificity. The most general measures of efficacy beliefs do not specify the activities or the conditions under which they must be performed (e.g., athletic efficacy). Bandura (1997) states, "The optimal level of generality at which self-efficacy is assessed varies depending on what one seeks to predict and the degree of foreknowledge of the situational demands" (p. 49). With that said, he advocates the use of efficacy-belief measures that are specific to particular domains of functioning rather than ones that assess global expectations of performance that are devoid of context.

Although global efficacy measures lack a context, Bandura (1997) warns that the settings in which they are administered may "inadvertently graft a context onto decontextualized items" (p. 40). Using athletic efficacy as an example, he argues that track runners versus gymnasts will think differently about their capabilities if asked to judge their athletic efficacy in general. Thus, if a researcher is truly interested in measuring athletic efficacy, then perceived capabilities across a full range of sport activities should be specified (e.g., running, swimming, soccer, gymnastics). Bandura recommends that these specific activity scores be correlated to obtain the generality of perceived athletic efficacy and the mean of the different domains be used as an integrative index of athletic efficacy.

In addition, domain-linked efficacy scales are more predictive of specific behavior because of the variations in efficacy perceptions that occur across different task domains, different levels of demand within a domain, and different environmental circumstances of performance. Thus, global measures that assess one's efficacy beliefs for sports, in general, would not be as predictive of performance in baseball, for example, as would a baseball-specific efficacy measure. Even with measures such as Vealey's (1986) Sport Confidence Inventory (SSCI) and Martens, Vealey, and Burton's (1990) Competitive State Anxiety Inventory-2 (CSAI-2), which use the stem *"in your sport,"* confidence beliefs were not found to be as predictive of performance as were task-specific efficacy beliefs in a meta-analytic study of efficacy and motor performance (Moritz, Feltz, Fahrbach, & Mack, 2000). Because specific efficacy measures, tailored to a specific study, are recommended for research on self-efficacy in sport, Feltz and Chase (1998) argue for their inclusion as appendixes to the research articles produced.

Gradations of Challenge

As Bandura (1997, 2006) has emphasized, the construction of good domain-specific efficacy measures requires a detailed assessment of the level, strength, and generality of self-efficacy beliefs. As we described in chapter

1, "level of self-efficacy" (or magnitude) refers to people's expected performance attainments. "Strength" refers to the certainty of people's beliefs that they can attain these different levels of performance. "Generality" indicates the number of domains of functioning in which people judge themselves to be efficacious, but it is rarely used in studies on self-efficacy (Maddux, 1995; Schunk, 1995b). However, as Myers and Feltz (2007) note in their chapter on collective efficacy in sport, sport efficacy researchers often assume that they have unidimensional efficacy measures without testing them empirically (e.g., through factor analysis). Multidimensional efficacy scales such as the Coaching Efficacy Scale (CES: Feltz, Chase, Moritz, & Sullivan, 1999) would tap the breadth or generality of efficacy beliefs within a domain.

A detailed assessment of the level, strength, and generality (if appropriate) of efficacy beliefs involves conducting a conceptual analysis of the subskills needed to succeed in the performance area of interest and a contextual analysis of the level of situational demands. A detailed assessment of the subskills does not mean, as some have advocated (Manzo & Silva, 1994), that self-efficacy items must be constructed for minute particulars. As stated previously, the level of specificity of the items depends on the particular level of performance that one is trying to predict. If one is trying to predict overall sport performance in a competition, then a comprehensive assessment of all that is needed to succeed will produce a more predictive efficacy measure than one that involves only one aspect of performance. These measures would include psychological and strategic skills as well as physical skills.

The conceptual and contextual analyses may involve interviews or open-ended surveys with coaches and athletes to identify the appropriate gradations of challenge against which efficacy judgments are made in order to avoid floor and ceiling effects. For instance, Feltz and Lirgg (1998) interviewed collegiate hockey coaches to determine the competence areas for measuring collective efficacy in collegiate hockey. The competence or challenge areas that coaches agreed on included (a) skating, (b) checking, (c) forcing turnovers, (d) bouncing back from performing poorly, (e) scoring on power plays, (f) killing penalties against the opposing team, and (g) having an effective goaltender who could block a high percentage of goal attempts. They also included winning against the opposing team. To assess the situational demands, players were asked to rate themselves on the items just listed against teams varying in difficulty. Feltz and Chase (1998) provide a baseball example with the subskills categorized into hitting, fielding, and baserunning and then into situational demands within each category that vary in degree of difficulty, such as hitting a fastball, hitting a curveball, and hitting to the opposite field for the hitting category.

Bandura (2006) recommends pretesting the items and discarding those for which the vast majority of participants check the maximum efficacy category because this indicates a lack of sufficient difficulty to differentiate among respondents. Bandura's solution is to increase the difficulty level by raising the level of challenge in the item. For instance, George (1994) constructed a hitting efficacy scale in which players rated their efficacy that they could put the ball in play from 1 out of 1 time at bat to 4 times out of 4 at bats and found high ratings among respondents. He might have had less of a ceiling effect if the high end of his scale had been "putting the ball in play 6 times out of 6 bats." However, the challenge must also be realistic to the sport. It would be unrealistic to include the item "putting the ball in play 20 times out of 20 times at bat" because of the improbability that one would ever come to bat 20 times in a game.

In addition to advocating a conceptual analysis of competence areas, Bandura (1997) stated that "the structure of the relationship between efficacy beliefs and action requires that both tap similar capabilities" (p. 62). This means that the efficacy items should be targeted to the factors that affect the performance measure. The self-efficacy assessment and the performance criteria must match. This match is what Moritz and colleagues (2000) have referred to as concordance between assessments. Using golf as an example, if one assessed self-efficacy beliefs only for component skills in golf (e.g., drive, approach shots, putting) and then assessed performance by measuring final scores, there would be a lack of concordance, and efficacy would account for less of the performance variance than if beliefs regarding hazards, competitive pressures, attentional focus, and other aspects of competitive play had been included. If, on the other hand, one is interested only in the efficacy beliefs for the component skills of golf, then assessment of the component aspects of performance should be used. Moritz and colleagues found stronger correlations ($r = .43$) between self-efficacy and performance for those studies that were concordant in assessment methods compared with nonconcordant studies ($r = .26$).

Conducting a conceptual analysis and creating enough gradations of challenge also imply that multiple items should be constructed to tap all of the key competence components. Feltz and Chase (1998) noted that researchers in sport psychology have sometimes used one-item efficacy measures to tap confidence judgments regarding winning against an opponent. They labeled items about winning as reflective of *competitive* or *comparative* efficacy (these are not to be confused with outcome expectations as addressed in chapter 1). Respondents are usually asked to rate their percent certainty (e.g., on a 100-point probability scale) of being able to beat their opponents (e.g., Feltz & Riessinger, 1990; Hodges & Carron, 1992; Weinberg, Gould, & Jackson, 1979). We recommend against using one-item efficacy scales, whether comparative or mastery based. The use of one-item scales to make efficacy assessments reduces self-efficacy's predictive power (Lee & Bobko, 1994).

Feltz and Chase (1998) also note that when one-item scales are used with athletes in competitive situations, they tend to have lower correlations with measures of performance outcome because of other factors beyond one's control that also influence performance (Bandura, 1990). In addition, one-item competitive or comparative efficacy scales have the tendency to create ceiling effects when used with athletes who may not have (or be willing to admit) much diffidence (Vealey, 1986). These points are not intended to imply that researchers should avoid assessing comparative efficacy beliefs, but rather that these beliefs should be assessed in combination with multiple items that tap all of the key components of competitive performance. As noted in chapter 1, in competitive contexts, self-efficacy beliefs are often based on normative criteria and do not have to be based solely on a mastery-oriented criterion of performance (Feltz & Magyar, 2006). Furthermore, in terms of concordance, as Moritz and colleagues (2000) recommend, if one is interested in using win/loss as a performance measure, then the self-efficacy measure should include items that ask respondents how confident they are that they can win the event.

Content Relevance

The content relevance of efficacy items in Bandura's (2006) guidelines has to do with fidelity to the construct of self-efficacy as a "can do" perception. As mentioned in chapter 1, self-efficacy judgments are about what one thinks one can do with one's skills, not about what one has and not about one's intentions. Thus, as Bandura states, items should be written in terms of *can do* (a judgment of capability) rather than *will do* (a perception of intent). In addition, the capability judgments should be assessed for present capabilities, not potential or future ones. That is, they are about what one thinks one can do right now. Self-efficacy items should also not be phrased in terms of *have* or *am*. *I have* and *I am* items are not constructed within a goal-striving context. These phrases do not focus on what one thinks one can do in terms of choice, effort, and perseverance. Marsh (1994) warns that not all scales labeled with the same name necessarily measure the same construct, and different names may be given to measures that assess the same construct. He labels this confusion as the "jingle-jangle fallacy," in which the first condition represents the "jingle" aspect of the fallacy and the second condition represents the "jangle" situation. Thus, when using previously published scales, researchers should carefully examine the scale's items rather than just search for those labeled as efficacy scales.

Feltz and Chase (1998) provide the example of the Physical Self-Efficacy Scale (PSES: Ryckman, Robbins, Thornton, & Cantrell, 1982) as one that resembles more of a self-concept measure than a self-efficacy measure even though it is labeled as an efficacy scale. Sample items include "I have excellent reflexes," "I have a strong grip," and "I am sometimes envious of those better looking than myself." As Feltz and Chase noted, a PSES item pertaining to strength should have been phrased as "I can hang in a flexed-arm position for 20 sec" or "I can hang in a flexed-arm position longer than most people my age," for example, to reflect one's physical efficacy beliefs and to mediate one's goal-striving behavior or to be modifiable through mastery experiences. Hu, McAuley, and Elavsky (2005) supported the view, empirically, that at least one of the subscales in the PSES (Perceived Physical Ability) was more reflective of physical self-esteem than of physical self-efficacy by comparing it to task-specific self-efficacy measures and other self-esteem measures. Not only was the PSES subscale more positively correlated with self-esteem measures than was task-specific self-efficacy, it was less predictive of physical performance.

Response Scale

Once a conceptual analysis has been conducted with a series of tasks listed in varying degrees of difficulty, stressfulness, or complexity, and items have been phrased in *can do* terms, then a response scale is constructed. Participants typically are asked to designate ("yes" or "no") the tasks they believe they can perform (efficacy level). For each task designated as "yes," they rate their degree of certainty (efficacy strength) that they can execute it on a near-continuous scale from total uncertainty to total certainty. Another format that can be used for obtaining efficacy strength is one in which participants simply rate the strength of their efficacy beliefs without designating "yes" or "no." A zero rating would imply a "no" designation. Generally, the efficacy strength scale ranges from 0 to 10, in one-unit increments, or from 0 to 100, in 10-unit increments. One obtains a strength measure by summing the scores across items for which respondents believe they can perform and dividing by the total number of performance items (Bandura, Adams, & Beyer, 1977). See the diving questionnaire on page 44 for an example of how efficacy levels and strength scores are obtained on a diving efficacy scale that was used by Feltz (1982) for a modified diving task. The level score was 3 (modified back dive from 23 in. [0.6 m]) on a possible 0 to 4 scale. The strength score was 4.4 on a possible 0 to 10 scale, which could be thought of as an average of 44% confidence about performing these dives.

In addition to the 0 to 10 or 0% to 100% scales, a visual analog scale (VAS) might be used. Feltz and Chase (1998) reported at least one sport study (Watkins, Garcia, & Turek, 1994) that used a VAS 10 cm (4 in.) in length. On a VAS, the respondent makes a check mark or slash at any point along the line, which is scored in standard unit increments (e.g., centimeters for Watkins et al.). See the example on page 45 of a VAS and how level and strength scores are calculated from this type of scale.

Diving Questionnaire

INSTRUCTIONS: For the following board heights, circle the number for each height that represents how confident you are that you can perform a modified back dive (without spring takeoff).

Diving board heights	RATING OF CERTAINTY										
	Complete uncertainty			Moderate certainty						Complete certainty	
1. Modified back dive from 15 in.	0	1	2	3	4	5	6	7	⑧	9	10
2. Modified back dive from 19 in.	0	1	2	3	4	5	⑥	7	8	9	10
3. Modified back dive from 23 in.	0	1	2	③	4	5	6	7	8	9	10
4. Modified back dive from 27 in. (approximately the height of a 1 m board)	⓪	1	2	3	4	5	6	7	8	9	10

Reprinted, by permission, from D.L. Feltz, 1982, "Path analysis of the casual elements in Bandura's theory of self-efficacy and an anxiety-based model of avoidance behavior," *Journal of Personality and Social Psychology* 42: 764-781.

Level = 3

Strength = 8 + 6 + 3 + 0 = 17 / 4 = 4.25

As can be seen from the two examples, self-efficacy strength measures would probably show stronger predictive validity than self-efficacy level measures. The level of self-efficacy is not as sensitive to one's perceptions. Two respondents could have a 3 on the diving scale and one be 100% confident while the other is only 30% confident. Most researchers in sport psychology have relied solely on the strength measures to assess self-efficacy or have reported both level and strength scores (see Feltz & Lirgg, 2001).

Feltz and Chase (1998) argued that the so-called "composite" score (a composite of self-efficacy level and strength) advocated by Lee and Bobko (1994) was no more than a linear transformation of their strength measure. To calculate Lee and Bobko's strength measure, one summed all items, regardless of whether subjects designated "yes" or "no" to indicate that they could or could not perform the tasks, and divided by the total number of items. In other words, Lee and Bobko's strength measure was a mixture of certainty responses to yes and no items and is, therefore, of questionable utility. Their composite measure, on the other hand, was constructed in the manner recommended by Bandura and colleagues (1977) for strength.

Example of a Visual Analog Scale (VAS)

For each line below, make a slash (/) mark on any point where you feel confident that you can hit a fastball pitch the following number of times:

RATING OF CERTAINTY

Times	Complete uncertainty	Complete certainty
1 out of 6 times	_____/	
2 out of 6 times	_____/____	
3 out of 6 times	_____/_____	
4 out of 6 times	_____/_____	
5 out of 6 times	_____/_____	
6 out of 6 times	/_____	

Scoring is measured in centimeters. To obtain a strength measure, one sums the scores across items and divides by 6 because there are 6 items.

Level = 5

Strength = 10 + 9 + 6 + 4 + 1 + 0 / 6 = 5

Another example of an efficacy scale used in sport is shown on page 46 (see "Skating Appraisal"). This example was taken from a study by Garza and Feltz (1998). Garza and Feltz used an individualized approach to assessing self-efficacy based on each skater's current skating level of ability because of the varying range of abilities. Specifically, skaters were asked "what is the most difficult jump or combination jump, spin or spin combination, and step/connecting move in your skating routine?" Skaters were then asked to indicate the strength of their belief in correctly performing this skill. The skating appraisal on page 46 shows the scale for jumps. Feltz and Chase (1998) suggest that individualized scales could have more predictive validity in sports in which there are many levels of competition with different skills employed by different competitors (e.g., figure skating, gymnastics, diving). The fourth example is a scale that one might use with young children who may not have the cognitive ability to understand the standard efficacy scale format. Research with children 9 years and older has incorporated this type of scale without any reported problems (Chase, Ewing, Lirgg, & George, 1994; Lirgg & Feltz, 1991). Feltz and Chase (1998) noted that some revisions to the format of the questions may be necessary for children under the age of 9 years, such as converting the response format to a Likert scale and using shapes (circles or squares) increasing in size to represent the points on the Likert scale (see "Example of a Self-Efficacy Scale for Children" on page 47). Chase (1995) conducted research with 8- to 9-year-olds incorporating this method without problems. Bandura (2006) warns not to use happy or sad faces because children may think that the scale is measuring their happiness or sadness instead of confidence.

Skating Appraisal

DIRECTIONS: For the skill that you fill in below, please circle one number for each of the 10 items that describes your confidence.

I. What is the most **difficult** jump or combination jump **in your skating routine?**

Fill in element _____

Regarding the skill above, how confident are you that you will be able to perform this element correctly—

	I'm certain I can't do this		I'm moderately certain I can do this					I'm very certain I can do this		
1. at least 1 of 10 attempts?	0	1	2	3	4	5	6	7	8	9	10
2. at least 2 of 10 attempts?	0	1	2	3	4	5	6	7	8	9	10
3. at least 3 of 10 attempts?	0	1	2	3	4	5	6	7	8	9	10
4. at least 4 of 10 attempts?	0	1	2	3	4	5	6	7	8	9	10
5. at least 5 of 10 attempts?	0	1	2	3	4	5	6	7	8	9	10
6. at least 6 of 10 attempts?	0	1	2	3	4	5	6	7	8	9	10
7. at least 7 of 10 attempts?	0	1	2	3	4	5	6	7	8	9	10
8. at least 8 of 10 attempts?	0	1	2	3	4	5	6	7	8	9	10
9. at least 9 of 10 attempts?	0	1	2	3	4	5	6	7	8	9	10
10. at least 10 of 10 attempts?	0	1	2	3	4	5	6	7	8	9	10

Reprinted, by permission, from A.D.L. Garz and D.L. Feltz, 1998, "Effects of selected mental practice on performance, self-efficacy, and competition confidence of figure skaters," *The Sport Psychologist* 12: 1-15.

Example of a Self-Efficacy Scale for Children

How sure are you that you can make a basket from this distance?

Very sure

Not sure

Bandura (2006) has argued that the 11-point probability scale is more sensitive and reliable than scales that use fewer response categories. Pajares, Hartley, and Valiante (2001) compared responses on the 11-point rating scale structure to those on a 5-point Likert scale and concluded that the former structure resulted in greater prediction of the theoretically relevant external variables. However, as Myers and Feltz (2007) have noted, others have argued for fewer response categories because fewer categories are more practical and increase the likelihood of measurement stability, measurement accuracy, and related inferences for future samples (Maurer & Pierce, 1998; Myers, Wolfe, & Feltz, 2005; Zhu & Kang, 1998). For instance, Myers and colleagues, using item response theory (IRT) methodology for analyzing rating scale structures, reported that the functioning of a 10-category CES could be improved if the structure was collapsed to four categories. In a subsequent study, the authors demonstrated confirmatory evidence for a four-category CES rating scale structure using a sample of youth sport coaches (Myers, Feltz, & Wolfe, 2006). Although Bandura's concern regarding less sensitivity with fewer categories may be valid for pre–post intervention studies, in predictive studies, Myers and Feltz (2007) argue that this concern can be allayed in IRT whereby raw scores are typically stretched farther apart by undergoing a nonlinear transformation onto a logit scale (Smith, 2000).

Such transformations of data may be particularly important in sport contexts with athletes who rarely use the lower half of efficacy scales, especially when they are measured close in time to competition (Feltz & Chase, 1998). Because confidence building is a part of preparation for competition, it makes sense that athletes would report fairly high levels of precompetitive efficacy beliefs. Unless one is investigating young or beginning-level athletes, Feltz and Chase recommend that researchers develop scales that can detect subtle differences in confidence with highly skilled performers or use a transformation to normalize the data. They also suggest that the VAS might prove useful in detecting subtle efficacy changes in high-level performers, or that *moderately confident* be used as the baseline anchor, or both. However, the IRT framework that Myers and Feltz (2007) suggest could accomplish the same idea. Myers and Feltz recommend empirical study within the IRT framework to determine optimal rating scale structure(s) for scales intended to measure collective efficacy in sport. We extend that recommendation for self-efficacy measures in sport as well.

Validity

Bandura (2006) argues that efficacy scales should have face validity. Thus, validity is typically inferred from how well the measure predicts the behaviors hypothesized in the study, such as choice of task, persistence, thought patterns, emotional responses, and performance attainments. In sport psychology, researchers often use final performance scores as the dependent measure for determining the predictive validity of their self-efficacy measure. However, when final competitive performance scores are used to measure the effects of self-efficacy, self-efficacy will not be a strong predictor of performance because final performance scores are determined by many other factors as well (Feltz, 1992). Furthermore, as previously mentioned, when efficacy measures tap elements that are not concordant with a final performance measure, efficacy judgments will be less predictive. Even so, in their review of self-efficacy studies that used competitive performance measures, Feltz and Chase (1998) found that most reported significant and moderate relationships.

In addition to predictive validity of the construct, validity of the measurement model that is imposed on the construct is also important (Messick, 1989). That is, whenever responses from multiple items are collapsed into a composite score, a measurement model is imposed on the efficacy construct. Bandura (2006) recommends a factor analysis to verify the homogeneity of items. Myers and Feltz (2007) recommend that evidence for the imposed measurement model for efficacy beliefs (e.g., factor analysis) be reported as well as for the external variable(s) to which one wishes to relate the efficacy measure. If the factor analysis indicates multiple dimensions, then the efficacy measures should be analyzed accordingly.

Additional Recommendations

Bandura (2006) also has some recommendations for phrasing items and minimizing social evaluative concerns. One is that items should be written at the reading level of respondents and in appropriate sport-related terminology. For instance, in baseball, there is a difference between batting average and contact average (e.g., George, 1994). Terminology should be piloted with a sample of participants similar to the study participants. As we mentioned earlier, pictorial representations might be necessary for young children. Also, practice items will help familiarize respondents with how to use the scale, though the items should contain different subject matter from the tasks of interest to the research. As with any type of questionnaire construction, the common problems to avoid include using ambiguous items, technical jargon, double-barreled items, and lengthy items.

As described in chapter 1, basing self-efficacy so heavily on self-report measures was an early criticism of the theory (Borkovec, 1978; Kazdin, 1978). However, Bandura (1978) argued that in situations in which individuals have no reason to distort their reports, self-reports can be quite representative of cognitions. Thus, efficacy judgments are best made when evaluation apprehension has been minimized and the judgments are recorded privately, and a nondescript title (e.g., "Skating Appraisal") has been used to label the questionnaire. As Feltz and Chase (1998) note, however, athletes may still find it difficult to report that they have little confidence to perform in competitive situations in their sport (Feltz & Lirgg, 1998; George, 1994; Vealey, 1986). A summary of recommendations based on Bandura's (2006) guidelines is contained in table 2.1.

TABLE 2.1   *Recommendations for Constructing Efficacy Measures Based on Bandura's (2006) Guidelines*

Guideline area	Recommendation
Domain specification	Scales should be tailored to the level of specificity at which the participant will be performing.
Gradations of challenge	Scales should be constructed to represent enough gradations of challenge or impediments to avoid ceiling effects. Conceptual analyses should be conducted to determine the appropriate challenges involved in performing the task, and a contextual analysis of the level of situational demands should be conducted.
Content relevance	Scale items should be written in terms of *can do* rather than *will do*.
Response scales	Bandura recommends scales with 11 response categories (0 to 10 or 0 to 100 in 10-unit intervals) because they are more sensitive and reliable than those with fewer response categories. However, Myers and Feltz (2007) argue for fewer response categories because this increases measurement stability and accuracy.
Validity	Scales should have face validity. For nonhierarchical scales, validity of the measurement model imposed on the construct should include a factor analysis to verify the homogeneity of items. If the factor analysis indicates multiple dimensions, then the efficacy measures should be analyzed accordingly. Internal consistency reliability should be determined and reported as well.
Phrasing items	Items should be written at the reading level of respondents and in appropriate sport-related terminology. Terminology should be piloted with a sample of participants similar to the study participants.
Minimizing social evaluative concerns	Scales should be administered when evaluation apprehension has been minimized and should be recorded privately; a nondescript title (e.g., "Skating Appraisal") should be used to label the questionnaire.

Hierarchical and Nonhierarchical Scales

Researchers in sport psychology have typically constructed efficacy scales by listing tasks in a hierarchical fashion, according to difficulty. These might include hitting a ball 1 of 6 times to 6 of 6 times, diving from increasingly difficult heights, putting with increasing accuracy or consistency, or pressing increasingly heavier weights. The diving and figure skating scales are examples of hierarchical scales. In early self-efficacy studies in sport psychology in which leg endurance tasks were used (e.g., Feltz & Riessinger, 1990; George, Feltz, & Chase, 1992; Gould & Weiss, 1981), respondents were asked to indicate how confident they were that they could perform the task at each of a certain number of time designations (e.g., 15 time periods ranging from 15 sec to 4 min) that were typically increased by 15 sec intervals, along with their certainty (efficacy strength) at each time designation. Most studies using hierarchically oriented scales show correlations of aggregated self-efficacy level or strength scores with aggregated performance scores. Because the items in hierarchical scales are the same except for degree of difficulty, the reliabilities for internal consistency will be very high (e.g., .88 and .91 for Theodorakis, 1995). In addition, the recommendation for testing the homogeneity of items through factor analysis is unnecessary. The primary concern in constructing hierarchical efficacy scales is that degree of difficulty be high enough so as not to result in ceiling effects but still include realistic performance demands. As Bandura (2001) recommends, pretesting the items with pilot samples from the target populations will help to ensure the adequacy and applicability of the measures.

Nonhierarchical scales do not have items that necessarily vary in difficulty from low to high. As described earlier in this chapter, in constructing nonhierarchical scales, the scale developer should conduct a conceptual analysis of the subskills needed to succeed in the performance area of interest and a contextual analysis of the level of situational demands. An example of a nonhierarchical scale described by Treasure and colleagues (1996) for wrestling includes rating one's confidence for the following moves against an opponent: escape, get reversal, get back points, pin opponent, not get take down, get take down by throw, get take down single leg, ride opponent, get take down double leg, and not be pinned. In addition to Bandura's (2006) recommendation of conducting a factor analysis to verify the homogeneity of items, Feltz and Chase recommend that internal consistency reliability be determined and reported for each study using a nonhierarchical self-efficacy scale, even if it is a scale whose pyschometric properties have been previously published. The past internal reliabilities of these scales cannot be assumed to remain the same with all samples.

Microanalytic Approach

Bandura (1986b, 1997) advocates a microanalytic approach as the strongest test of self-efficacy's relationship to behavior. A microanalytic approach permits an analysis of the degree of congruence between self-efficacy and action at the level of individual tasks (Bandura, 1986b). Analyzing the degree of congruence involves computing the percentage of items for which efficacy judgments and performance agree. The number of congruent tasks is divided by the total number of possible tasks. This quotient is multiplied by 100 to obtain a percent congruence score (Cervone, 1985). The calculation of percentage match-scores, according to Bandura (1977), provides a more precise index of predictive accuracy than does an aggregate correlation between efficacy and performance. As Bandura (1977) noted, respondents may predict and perform the same absolute number of tasks but not have correspondence between predictions and task performance, leading to a high correlation but a low item-by-item match. However, Cervone (1985) argues that when self-ratings and behavior are completely hierarchical, the level of congruence can be obtained from the aggregate scores on the efficacy and behavioral scale because there is no chance congruence. Cervone advocates a microanalytic congruence analysis when the data are not completely hierarchical. Table 2.2 provides an illustration, modified from Feltz and Chase (1998), of how congruent scores are obtained using a hierarchical

TABLE 2.2 Illustration of Congruence Scores on a Nonhierarchical Scale

Performance items	Efficacy scale (level)	Performance scale	Match
Wrestling move items			
1. Escape	yes	yes	x
2. Get reversal	yes	yes	x
3. Get back points	no	yes	
4. Not get taken down	yes	no	
5. Get take down by throw	no	no	x
6. Ride opponent	yes	yes	x
7. Pin opponent	yes	no	
8. Get take down single leg	yes	yes	x
9. Get take down double leg	yes	yes	x
10. Not be pinned	yes	yes	x
Score:	8	7	7

Congruence = 7/10 × 100 = 70%.

Adapted, by permission, from D.L. Feltz and M.A. Chase, 1998, "The measurement of self-efficacy and confidence in sport. *In Advancements in sport and exercise psychology measurement*, edited by J.L. Duda (Morgantown, WV: Fitness Information Technology), 65-80.

scale. In this example, the congruence or item-by-item match (70%) is more than what would be expected by chance (at least 50%).

In reporting congruence values, one needs a statistical procedure to indicate the probability of obtaining such values by chance. The Feltz and Chase (1998) example does not contain calculations of chance congruence because it represents just one respondent. Bandura (1980) has proposed a method for computing chance congruence that is appropriate only in cases in which none of the tasks are hierarchically ordered (e.g., in Kane, Marks, Zaccaro, & Blair, 1996 and Treasure, Monson, & Lox, 1996). Cervone (1985) has also outlined a procedure for computing chance congruence that is not limited to nonhierarchical tasks, but we have not seen this used in the literature.

Few researchers in the psychology or sport psychology literature have actually analyzed the degree of congruence between self-efficacy judgments and performance at the level of individual tasks (Wurtele, 1986). A possible reason is that many of the studies use hierarchical scales, making congruence analysis unnecessary. Another reason may be the difficulty in obtaining behavior measures in field situations in sport.

Measuring the Reciprocal Pattern of Efficacy Beliefs and Performance

A number of sport psychology researchers have been interested in measuring the efficacy–performance relationship over time (i.e., recursively) using path analyses and structural equation modeling (e.g., Feltz, 1982; George, 1994; Myers, Feltz, & Short, 2004). Some of the studies also examine the unique contribution of efficacy beliefs to performance in a network of causal factors. The details of these studies are outlined in subsequent chapters.

Bandura has provided guidelines for testing the contributions of efficacy beliefs to performance recursively (Bandura, 1997; Bandura & Locke, 2003). First, a dynamic environment should be used to test the efficacy–performance relationship rather than invariant conditions, because performance stabilizes when situational conditions do not change and there is no need for reappraisals of efficacy beliefs. Thus, there is little change to explain. In studies in which the performance conditions are invariant (e.g., Feltz, 1982; Feltz & Mugno, 1983), the correlations between prior and subsequent performance simply reflect the degree of commonality of their determinants (Bandura, 1997; Bandura & Locke, 2003). This does not mean that efficacy beliefs and performance should not be measured repeatedly within one setting or competition. If the situational conditions change, which can happen during a competition as scores change and mistakes are made, then reappraisals of efficacy are more apt to occur and the role of efficacy beliefs in predicting performance can be assessed more accurately.

Secondly, in assessing efficacy beliefs and performance recursively, one must consider that the previous performance is a "conglomerate index" that includes efficacy beliefs as well as other sociocognitive factors (e.g., goal effects) operating at the time (Bandura, 1997; Bandura & Locke, 2003). For example, efficacy beliefs are assessed at the beginning of an activity, and then the first performance of the activity is measured. Bandura argues that this performance score now represents, in part, one's efficacy beliefs as well as other factors. As illustrated in figure 2.1, the predictive strength of Performance 1 on Performance 2 will be inflated unless the initial efficacy assessment is partialled out from the variance in Performance 1 (i.e., residualized performance). Myers, Payment, and Feltz (2004) provide an example of statistically controlling for previous efficacy beliefs across hockey games by residualizing past performance.

Heggestad and Kanfer (2005), however, argue that removing the effects of self-efficacy from past performance before entering it into the analysis is an overadjustment because the procedure also removes common cause variables. They state that "the residualization procedure will take out variance in past performance that is due to prior self-efficacy and variance due to any other variable that influences both prior self-efficacy and past performance. If such common cause variables exist, then the residualization procedure is an overcorrection" (p. 94). To resolve this controversy, Feltz, Chow, and Hepler (2006) reanalyzed the Feltz (1982) data set in order to compare the predictive validity of self-efficacy on performance in three different statistical models: raw performance model, residualized performance model, and a model that residualizes both past performance and self-efficacy. Results from the path analyses revealed that self-efficacy was a stronger predictor of performance in the residualized performance and residualized self-efficacy and performance models than in the raw, unadjusted past performance model. Furthermore, the influence of past performance on future performance was

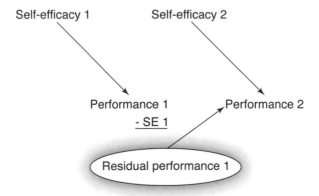

Figure 2.1 Illustration of residualized performance.

weaker when both residualized methods were conducted. Thus, the results support Bandura's argument (Bandura, 1997; Bandura & Locke, 2003) that residualizing performance scores does not appear to be an overadjustment in favor of self-efficacy.

Still, Heggestad and Kanfer (2005) believe that the "raw" performance model is more interpretable. Whether one uses the residualized procedure or the raw model, we recommend that the data first be examined for normality to determine if a transformation is necessary.

Collective Efficacy Measurement

The concept of collective efficacy in sport and the related research are discussed in chapter 4. A number of sport-specific measures have been developed to study collective efficacy (see table 2.3). How these measures were derived is more complicated than may appear. A number of issues involving conceptual approaches, level of measurement, and consensus among team members must be considered in the measurement of collective efficacy. These issues are detailed by Myers and Feltz (2007) but are summarized here.

TABLE 2.3 Sport-Specific Measures of Collective Efficacy

Sport	References
Adventure racing	Edmonds, 2003
Baseball	Sturm & Short, 2004
Basketball	Bray & Widmeyer, 2000
	Heuze, Raimbault, & Fontayne, 2006
Bowling	Moritz, 1998
Football	Myers, Feltz, & Short, 2004
Hockey	Feltz & Lirgg, 1998
Rowing	Magyar et al., 2004
Rugby	Greenlees, Nunn, et al., 1999
	Kozub & McDonnell, 2000
Volleyball	Paskevich et al., 1999

Assessment Based on Conceptual Approaches

The primary issue regarding how collective efficacy is measured in sport psychology is based on the way in which the construct is defined in each study. As described in chapter 4, Bandura (1997) defines collective efficacy as a group's shared beliefs in its capacities to organize and execute actions to produce a desired goal. It is a group-level construct that emerges or is composed from individual perceptions. On the basis of his definition, Bandura suggests two approaches to measuring collective efficacy. The first method involves aggregating team members' individual responses to appraisals of their own capabilities to perform within the team. For instance, in Feltz and Lirgg (1998), hockey teammates were assessed on beliefs that they could outperform their offensive opponent, outperform their defensive opponent, and bounce back from performing poorly and be successful against their opponent. The second method involves aggregating team members' individual responses to appraisals of their team's capability as a whole. The corresponding hockey efficacy questions in Feltz and Lirgg's study using this method were phrased as "rate your confidence that your team can outskate (outcheck, force more turnovers against, etc.) your upcoming opposing team." The responses are still individual perceptions, but they are about the team's capability. Bandura contends that the second method encompasses the coordinative and interactive influences that operate within the group. The majority of the collective efficacy studies in sport have used Bandura's second method (Chase, Feltz, & Lirgg, 2003; Edmonds, 2003; Feltz & Lirgg, 1998; Greenlees, Graydon, & Maynard, 1999, 2000; Greenlees, Nunn, Graydon, & Maynard, 1999; Hodges & Carron, 1992; Kozub & McDonnell, 2000; Lichacz & Partington, 1996; Magyar, Feltz, & Simpson, 2004; Myers, Feltz, & Short, 2004; Myers, Payment, & Feltz, 2004; Spink, 1990b; Vargas-Tonsing, Warners, & Feltz, 2003). These studies are summarized in chapter 4.

Bandura suggests that the method used, and its corresponding predictive strength, depends on the degree of interdependent effort required for successful team performance. The first method may have sufficient power to predict team performance in sports in which interdependence among team members is low (for example, for a golf team). However, where interdependence is high (e.g., for a basketball team), Bandura hypothesizes that an aggregate of individuals' judgments about the team's capabilities is the better predictor. Some evidence, using sport performance, exists to support this contention (Feltz & Lirgg, 1998; Myers, Feltz, & Short, 2004). As Myers and Feltz (2007) point out, though, neither study reported the statistical difference between the two coefficients (one using aggregated individual efficacies, the other using aggregated efficacies about the team) that estimated the relationships between collective efficacy and group performance.

Another group of researchers, Zaccaro, Blair, Peterson, and Zazanis (1995), defined collective efficacy as "a sense of collective competence shared among members when allocating, coordinating, and integrating their resources as a successful, concerted response to specific situational demands" (Zaccaro et al., 1995, p. 309). Zaccaro and his colleagues emphasize the coordination, interaction, and integration components of collective efficacy and argue that these efficacy components should be directly assessed, whereas Bandura (1997) considers perceptions of a team's capability to perform a task to encompass the coordination and interaction influences operating within a team. Zaccaro and colleagues' sense of shared collective competence has been interpreted by some sport psychology researchers (e.g., Heuze, Raimbault, & Fontayne, 2006; Paskevich, Brawley, Dorsch, & Widmeyer, 1999) to mean that individual teammates should rate *their team's beliefs* in its capabilities rather than rate *their belief in their team's* capabilities (Myers & Feltz, 2007). Proponents of this method maintain that a shared, team-level belief emerges from a team member's ability to cognitively consider social entities larger than him- or herself. This method focuses the respondent on the team's belief, and thus the respondent is used as an *informant* of the team's collective efficacy (Moritz & Watson, 1998).

Short, Apostal, and colleagues (2002) conducted a study with football players to determine if collective efficacy ratings varied according to whether the stem read "rate your confidence that your team . . ." or "rate your team's confidence. . . ." Data were collected over three time periods. Both "versions" of the collective efficacy measure for all time periods were reliable. The correlations between the versions for the different time periods ranged from .65 to .90. Repeated-measures multivariate analyses of variance (MANOVAs) showed that there were no differences between these two assessment methods in collective efficacy ratings. The authors concluded that either stem was adequate.

Some researchers (e.g., Prussia & Kinicki, 1996) have argued that the use of aggregation represents surrogates of team-level measures. Instead, they suggest using measures that require team members to provide a single response. That is, the team makes the collective efficacy judgment together (see Moritz, 1998). Thus, a fourth method of assessing collective efficacy is to use the single group response to each item (e.g., Bray, 2004; Moritz, 1998). This approach eliminates the calculation of statistical indicators of agreement and avoids the aggregation issue. Bandura (1997) has noted that team members are rarely of one mind in their appraisal of matters, however, and that having a team form a consensual judgment is subject to social persuasion and conformity pressures. A more prestigious team member, for instance, could influence the judgment in such a way that it does not accurately reflect the team. Or team members could consent to a response without truly believing it (Guzzo, Yost, Campbell, & Shea, 1993). Forced consensus may be highly misleading, especially with large teams, because it masks the within-team variability. In addition, Myers, Feltz, and Short (2004) note the impracticalities in implementing the group discussion method with real sport teams in longitudinal field studies.

Of the two studies in sport that used the discussion method (Bray, 2004; Moritz, 1998), one was a laboratory study (Bray) in which the environment could be controlled and three-member teams were used, and the other (Moritz) utilized two-person bowling teams. Both studies used small team sizes, which may have minimized the time involved for discussion and the opportunity for social persuasion and conformity.

As concluded by Myers and Feltz (2007), there is insufficient evidence that any of the collective efficacy assessment methods produces measures that relate to performance significantly better than the measures produced by the other methods, with the exception of the use of aggregated self-efficacy judgments with highly interdependent team sports. However, we do have a preference. Of the four possible assessment methods, we agree with Myers and Feltz in preferring the "rate your confidence in your team's capabilities" stem due to accessibility of one's own thoughts versus the thoughts of others. Myers and Feltz state,

> People have better access to their own beliefs about a group's capabilities than they do to a group's beliefs about its capabilities. Beliefs, even those about a group's capabilities, reside in human beings and not in inanimate social systems. Groups are not alive in the same way that human beings are alive. If a group were alive in the same way then we could ask it, directly, about its efficacy beliefs or take its blood pressure. There would be no need for informants. (p. 803)

In addition, the "rate your confidence in your team" stem conforms to the way in which Bandura's original conceptualization of collective efficacy was constructed. In opposition to our stated preference, we next describe a questionnaire we developed, the Collective Efficacy in Sport Questionnaire (CEQS: Short, Sullivan, & Feltz, 2005), that uses the stem "rate your team's confidence." This example provides support for using the method that best fits the design characteristics of a study.

Multilevel Assessment Issues

As stated previously, with use of Bandura's (1997) definition of collective efficacy, the group-level construct emerges or is composed from individual perceptions. Team members' perceptions are aggregated to the team level to represent a team-level assessment. This approach represents a multilevel assessment at the individual and team level. Rousseau (1985) suggests that perceptions at the level of the individual can be aggregated to a higher-level construct and the mean used to represent this collective interpretation when the two variables are functionally equivalent. This condition is met when perceptual consensus has been demonstrated (James, 1982; Kozlowski & Hattrup, 1992). Perceptual consensus is discussed in the next section. However, to focus solely on the team-level (aggregated) data while ignoring the individual, within-team perceptions may be misguided because this ignores within-team variability (Moritz & Watson, 1998). In addition, as Raudenbush and Bryk (2002) note, analyzing data at the team level only can result in a loss of power, inefficient estimation of fixed effects when sample size is

CEQS

Although a number of sport-specific collective efficacy measures have been developed to investigate the collective efficacy–performance relationship in specific sports, we (Short, Sullivan, & Feltz, 2005) developed the CEQS to measure team beliefs across sports. To investigate whether some sports exhibit stronger collective efficacy among participants than others requires a measure that can be used with many different sports. In developing the CEQS, we conceptualized collective efficacy in sport as a multidimensional construct based on Bandura's (1997) contention that "efficacy beliefs involve different types of capabilities, such as management of thought, affect, action, and motivation" (p. 45). It was also conceptualized as a state measure, based on current capabilities, not potential capabilities or expected future capabilities.

From a design standpoint, we selected the stem "Rate your team's confidence, in terms of the upcoming competition, that your team has the ability to . . ." even though we have recommended the stem preferred by Bandura (1997). We made this decision in order to match the stem of a correlate team cohesion measure, the Group Environment Questionnaire (GEQ: Widmeyer, Brawley, & Carron, 1985), that we used in the study. The group subscales on the GEQ use phrasing such as "*Our* team is united in trying to reach its performance goals." Furthermore, the previous study by Short, Apostal, and colleagues (2002) showed no predictive difference between the two stems. All items were scored on a 10-point Likert-type scale from 0 *(not at all confident)* to 9 *(extremely confident)* to gauge efficacy strength.

Our research supported a five-factor instrument containing 20 items (four items per factor). The five subscales included *Ability* (e.g., play more skillfully than the opponent), *Effort* (e.g., play to [the team's] capabilities), *Persistence* (e.g., persist in the face of failure), *Preparation* (e.g., mentally prepare for this competition), and *Unity* (e.g., be united). We also found convergent, divergent, and predictive validity for the CEQS by examining correlations among the CEQS subscales and the GEQ. The range of correlations among the CEQS subscales was from .59 to .95, while the range of correlations between the CEQS and GEQ subscales was lower (.20 to .57). The CEQS is contained in the Short, Sullivan, and Feltz (2005) paper.

As we note in our 2005 paper, the majority of items used by previous researchers dealt specifically with the team's ability, whereas the development of the CEQS suggested that other aspects of team functioning were salient in determining collective efficacy. Future research will determine if there is differential predictive strength among the five collective efficacy factors for performance and other team constructs.

unequal within teams, and difficulty in interpreting the amount of variance explained by team-level predictors. Myers and Feltz (2007), who provide an in-depth critique of the multilevel issues in collective efficacy assessment in sport, suggest that, in most instances, multilevel modeling (e.g., hierarchical linear modeling, HLM) is the optimal framework for analyzing collective efficacy data. Even when performance data are collected at the team level only (e.g., goals scored, shots attempted, shots blocked), multilevel modeling can be used to assess the collective efficacy and performance relationship (see Myers, Feltz, & Short, 2004; Myers, Payment, & Feltz, 2004).

The inability to address multilevel issues is another reason that we discourage the group discussion (or single group response) method of assessing collective efficacy. Along with the statistical shortcomings noted earlier, one cannot examine individual perceptions using this method that might provide meaningful insight into how collective efficacy beliefs influence player satisfaction, social loafing, individual performance, and other individual variables.

Consensus Within Teams

When team members perceive the team or their own abilities to function within the team in the same way, then perceptual consensus (also called interrater agreement) exists. Feltz and Lirgg (1998) argued that researchers need to assess the degree of within-group variability of the perceptions of team members' collective efficacy to determine that the beliefs are shared by the members. (This is not a problem with the group discussion method of assessing collective efficacy because there are no individual perceptions.) They noted that failure to consider consensus when aggregating data at the individual level to represent a higher level of analysis may result in aggregation bias (James, 1982). Aggregation bias means that individuals' perceptions are aggregated and used to represent the group's perception without considering the homogeneity of within-group perceptions. However, James did not offer empirical guidelines for what constituted a sufficient level of consensus for the purpose of aggregating scores to the group level; and as Myers and Feltz (2007) have argued, we no longer believe that a particular cutoff level (e.g., .70; Magyar et al., 2004) is necessary in order to aggregate individual-level data to the group level. Multilevel software programs do not require that a certain consensus estimate exist before computing a weighted average of the individual-level responses. Even so, there are still important reasons to calculate and report a consensus index.

As Myers and Feltz (2007) recommend, consensus estimates should be reported for descriptive purposes and used as a team-level variable within multilevel models to explain variance around an average team-level effect. If there is not a high degree of consensus, there will be more within-team variance around the team mean, which could be partitioned and explained in multilevel modeling (Moritz & Watson, 1998). There can be two units of analysis (individual and team) when a significant proportion of variance exists between teams. Myers and Feltz note, "It may be that teams that consist of athletes who have a low degree of consensus on collective efficacy demonstrate a negligible relationship between collective efficacy and subsequent performance because there is so much within team variance around the mean collective efficacy for these teams" (p. 814). A consensus index would be important in explaining such a finding. We also add that analyzing the relationship between consensus of collective efficacy and other variables (e.g., cohesion, performance, team satisfaction) may be an important research question in itself. The method that is most typically used in the literature on collective efficacy in sport, the within-group agreement index, r_{wg} (James, Demaree, & Wolfe, 1984), is described in detail in Myers and Feltz (2007). Myers and Feltz argue strongly that teams should not be eliminated from analysis if they do not show consensus on collective efficacy above a particular cutoff. The use of multilevel modeling has helped eliminate the concern that James (1982) once had about aggregation bias in using group-level means to represent a construct measured at the individual level.

The Coaching Efficacy Scale

The CES (Feltz et al., 1999) is the only published scale to date to measure coaching efficacy within the confines of Bandura's (1977, 1997) theory of self-efficacy. Although Barber (1998) developed the Perceived Coaching Competence Questionnaire, it was not subjected to standard psychometric analyses, nor were the items published. Therefore, it is not reviewed here. As reviewed in chapter 5, coaching efficacy is the extent to which coaches believe they have the capacity to affect the learning and performance of their athletes (Feltz et al.). Feltz and colleagues developed the CES to measure the multidimensional aspects of coaching efficacy for youth, high school, and lower-division collegiate coaches. Unlike many task-specific efficacy scales, the CES was designed to measure efficacy beliefs in coaching across time rather than for a specific practice or competition. In chapter 5, we describe the process involved in the development of the final instrument that contains four dimensions (game strategy, motivation, technique, and character-building efficacy) and employs a 10-point scale (0 = *not at all confident* to 9 = *extremely confident*). A copy of the CES is printed at the end of chapter 5.

A confirmatory factor analysis (CFA) of the CES using maximum likelihood procedures (Joreskog & Sorbom, 1996) was used to test the first-order factor structure (four first-order factors) and a second-order factor structure (representing total coaching efficacy) with a heterogeneous sample of high school coaches. Results indicated an acceptable, but not excellent, fit for the first-order factors using various global indexes (nonnormed fit index = .88; comparative fit index = .89; root mean square residual error of approximation = .08). Marginal support was also found for a total coaching efficacy factor that explained the correlations among the four first-order factors. Accepted criteria for excellent goodness of fit include above .95 on the comparative fit index and other goodness of fit indexes (Hu & Bentler, 1999) and .10 or less for the root mean square residual error of approximation (Browne & Cudeck, 1993). However, Marsh, Hau, and Wen (2004) have argued that Hu and Bentler's proposed cutoff values for testing goodness of fit indexes were intended to be guidelines rather than "golden rules" such as those used in traditional hypothesis testing. Given the consistency of fit indexes across studies, different sample characteristics, and sample sizes, and given the predictive validity of the measure, continued use of the CES is reasonable.

The factor structure is illustrated in figure 5.2 (p. 157), showing that all factor loadings in both the first-order CFA and the second-order CFA were significant at $p < .05$, an indication of convergent validity that each item was significantly related to the relevant latent variables. Disattenuated correlations among subscales ranged from .46 (Motivation and Character Building) to .73 (Technique and Game Strategy), suggesting moderate discriminant validity. Internal consistency analyses revealed standardized Cronbach alphas ranging from .88 to .91 and .95 for total coaching efficacy. Test–retest reliability also showed acceptable coefficients of .77 (Character Building) to .84 (Strategy) and .82 for total coaching efficacy.

Three studies have evaluated the internal structure of the CES using its 10-point scale structure (Lee, Malete, & Feltz, 2002; Myers, Wolfe, & Feltz, 2005; Sullivan & Kent, 2003). Lee and colleagues used data from Singapore youth coaches in a CFA and reported fit indexes that were similar to those found by Feltz and colleagues. Sullivan and Kent (2003) examined the factor structure of the CES using CFA with collegiate coaches from the United States and Canada and also found a similar fit.

Myers, Wolfe, and Feltz (2005) used a different approach to evaluating the internal structure of the CES by examining the item-level fit in a multidimensional item response model (MIRT). Using previously collected data in the United States from high school and college coaches, Myers and colleagues examined the degree of item-level fit, the utility of the rating scale structure, and the degree of precision of the coaching efficacy estimates in addition to the overall fit of the structural model. As in the previous two studies, they found that the four-dimensional model provided the best fit to the data. However, the correlations among the factors suggest limited discriminant validity among subscales, particularly between Game Strategy and Technique efficacy.

Results of the rating scale structure indicated that respondents did not use the rating scale (0 to 9) in the manner that Feltz and colleagues (1999) intended. All categories should have at least 10 observations for minimal precision of threshold estimates when one is examining model fit (Linacre, 2002). Myers, Wolfe, and Feltz (2005) found that respondents were not meeting this criterion in the 0 to 4 categories. Once coaches make the decision to coach, they seem to have at least a moderate level of confidence. Myers and colleagues concluded that coaches were being asked to distinguish between too many levels of coaching efficacy. Thus, they advocated reducing the number of categories to four (i.e., low, moderate, high, and complete confidence). Their recommendation is congruent with previous findings for the optimal structure of an ordered response efficacy scale (Zhu, Updyke, & Lewandowski, 1997) and long-standing recommendations for Likert scales (Likert, 1932). In addition, as described earlier, Myers, Feltz, and Wolfe (2006) demonstrated confirmatory evidence for a four-category CES rating scale structure using a sample of youth sport coaches.

In terms of item fit, Myers, Wolfe, and Feltz (2005) found that the residual for only two items varied more than was expected: *instill an attitude of good moral character* (item 5—Character Building) and *demonstrate the skills of your sport* (item 7—Technique). The moral character item may be more ambiguous than the other three (fair play, good sportsmanship, and respect for others) that compose the Character Building subscale. Myers and colleagues suggested that the demonstration item may tap an unintended source of variance (e.g., age or fitness level or both) because older, more experienced coaches may not feel as confident as younger coaches in demonstrating skills that they once could perform with ease. The authors suggest that future users of the CES consider dropping these items depending on the samples that they intend to use.

The degree of precision of the coaching efficacy estimates refers to the consistency of a coach's estimated efficacy measure from one context to another and was depicted with the corresponding conditional standard error (Myers, Wolfe, & Feltz, 2005). Results indicated some mismatches between the distributions of item difficulties and coaching efficacy estimates. Motivation efficacy provided the most precise measures, while Character Building provided the least. However, as Myers and colleagues conclude, "That rather imprecise measures produce evidence of external validity probably speaks to the robustness of the coaching efficacy model" (p. 156).

Thus, overall, tests of the CES structure have been adequate and consistent. Myers, Wolfe, and Feltz (2005), however, suggest that the instrument could be improved through revising a couple of items that exhibited misfit, revising other items and adding items to create wider ranges of difficulties within all of the subscales and to lessen the overlap among the subscales, and reducing the number of response categories from 10 to four. Apart from improving measurement of the existing CES factors, an additional competency area that the CES does not tap is training and conditioning efficacy. Measuring a coach's training and conditioning efficacy, in addition to assessing his or her motivation, game strategy, technique, and character-building efficacies, is important because this would increase the comprehensiveness of an instrument intended to measure the extent to which coaches believe they have the capacity to affect the learning and performance of their athletes. In fact, a revision is under way to include this dimension in a CES II instrument (N.D. Myers, personal communication, December 2, 2005).

Other Efficacy-Type Measures in Sport

A few other measures have been developed to tap self-appraisals of capability in sport that have a broader focus regarding one's capability to perform successfully in competition. The ones most related to self-efficacy include the State Sport Confidence Inventory (SSCI; Vealey, 1986) and the self-confidence subscale of the CSAI-2 (Martens et al., 1990). The Carolina Sport Confidence Inventory (CSCI: Manzo et al., 2001) discussed in chapter 1 is a dispositional measure, and thus does not meet the modifiability criterion for efficacy measures and will not be described here. Common to the SSCI and CSAI-2 measures is the treatment of self-confidence as a cognitive mediator of people's motivation and behavior within a goal context (Feltz & Chase, 1998).

SSCI

As described in chapter 1, Vealey (1986) defined sport confidence as the degree of certainty individuals possess about their ability to be successful in sport and conceptualized it into trait (SC-trait) and state (SC-state) components. Vealey and colleagues (1998) reconceptualized the sport confidence measure as on a continuum from more trait-like to state-like, depending on the temporal frame of reference used (e.g., how certain you are right now, how certain you were during the last two weeks, how certain you are right now about the upcoming season, how certain you are about tomorrow's competition). However, the more "state-like" references align more closely with self-efficacy theory. The measure of SC-state in the original instrument is the SSCI, which consists of 13 items with respect to which the participants rate their sport confidence on a 9-point Likert scale (1 = low and 9 = high). The SSCI asks athletes to think about how confident they feel "right now" about performing in an upcoming competition in reference to "the most confident athlete" they know. The 13 items address various abilities that an athlete typically displays during competition (e.g., ability to execute skills, perform under pressure, concentrate well enough). To obtain scores, one sums the 13 items.

Feltz and Chase (1998) reviewed the SSCI as a measure of self-efficacy in sport and recommended that it not be used when a researcher is interested in investigating self-efficacy in specific sport situations because it will have lower predictive power with respect to performance. As mentioned earlier in this chapter, Moritz and colleagues (2000) supported this view with evidence from their meta-analysis that the SSCI had lower correlations with sport performance ($r = .28$) than did task-specific efficacy scales ($r = .38$). This most likely occurred because there was more concordance between the task-specific scales and performance than in studies using SSCI. Because of its standard format, the SSCI is most useful when one wants to compare the confidence–performance relationship across sports and across studies. Even within a sport that has different events, such as track and field, swimming, and gymnastics, the sport confidence measures provide a standard format.

However, the comparison-based format of the sport confidence measures has been criticized because participants are instructed to rate their confidence in relation to the most confident athlete they know. Feltz and Chase (1998) believe that this format may produce unsystematic variance, depending upon who the respondents select as their standard of confidence. In addition, if one is using these measures longitudinally, comparison-based measures show a decline over time as an individual increases in skill mastery because the individual's comparison has also gained in skill (Zimmerman, 1996). As Feltz and Chase note, a mastery-based measure avoids this problem. A new, multidimensional sport confidence measure has been developed that is mastery based rather than normatively based, but it has not yet been published (Vealey & Knight, 2003).

Some evidence exists that sport confidence is modifiable, a condition that is requisite for an efficacy construct. Vealey and Sinclair (1987) demonstrated that sport confidence fluctuated over the course of a competitive season in relation to various situational factors. However, we are unaware of any intervention studies aimed at altering sport confidence.

CSAI-2

As noted in chapter 1, Martens and colleagues (1990) developed the CSAI-2 to measure the multidimensional aspects of competitive anxiety. Self-confidence for competition was not originally conceptualized as a part of competitive anxiety, but exploratory factor analysis uncovered three factors: cognitive anxiety, somatic anxiety, and self-confidence. Thus, the final 27-item measure has those three subscales. The self-confidence subscale (nine items) is the only one of importance in this chapter and includes items such as "I feel at ease" and "I'm confident I can meet the challenge." Only four of the items are written in the *I can* format; the other five are about how one feels (e.g., at ease, comfortable, self-confident, secure, and mentally relaxed). Athletes are asked to indicate "how you feel right now" for each item on a 4-point Likert scale ranging from "not at all" to "very much so." The items are summed to yield a score representing the level of intensity that the athlete is feeling for self-confidence about performing in competition.

Although the CSAI-2 has been a popular instrument in sport psychology, and research has shown that the self-confidence subscale is sensitive enough to detect changes in self-confidence due to interventions (Garza & Feltz, 1998), psychometric critiques have called the measure into question. Cox (2000) conducted a CFA using 506 intramural athletes and failed to fit the hypothesized three-factor structure of the CSAI-2 to the data. Meta-analyses of the self-confidence–performance relationship have shown the measure to lack predictive strength (Craft, Magyar, Becker, & Feltz, 2003; Moritz et al., 2000). Craft and colleagues, in a meta-analysis of 69 independent samples using the CSAI-2, found that of the three subscales, self-confidence displayed the strongest and most consistent relationship with performance ($r = .25$), but the correlation was still weak. Their finding was similar to that of Moritz and colleagues, who reported a mean correlation of $r = .24$ for studies utilizing the CSAI-2.

Furthermore, as Craft and colleagues (2003) noted, researchers have failed to consider the interdependency of the three CSAI-2 subscales. In their meta-analysis, Craft and colleagues found that the three subscales were highly intercorrelated and therefore should not be considered independently of one another. As they point out, unless one considers this shared variance it becomes difficult to determine the unique relationship of each subscale with performance. Thus, it would be inappropriate to use the self-confidence subscale alone in research. Craft and colleagues suggest the possibility that the best-fitting pattern among the network of variables is hierarchical or one in which self-confidence mediates the relationships between cognitive and somatic anxiety and performance. Their suggestion is in line with social cognitive theory, in which "both anxiety and impaired performance are coeffects of a low sense of efficacy to meet competitive demands" (Bandura, 1997, p. 389). However, Craft and colleagues caution researchers about using the CSAI-2, and we recommend task-specific efficacy scales for precompetitive self-confidence.

Improving the Predictive Strength of Efficacy Measures

Feltz (1992) suggested that where self-efficacy has not been shown to be a strong predictor of sport performance, this probably has more to do with the way in which efficacy beliefs were measured than with the conceptual soundness of self-efficacy theory. We have made a number of recommendations throughout this chapter and in other publications to improve the predictive strength of efficacy measures. We summarize these recommendations here.

- Most importantly, whether one is assessing self-, collective, or coaching efficacy, efficacy-belief measures that are specific to particular domains of functioning are stronger predictors of performance than those that assess global expectations of performance and are devoid of context. In developing domain-specific scales, a comprehensive assessment of all that is needed to succeed will produce a more predictive efficacy measure than assessment of only one aspect of performance. This also means employing multiple items rather than a single item to measure an efficacy belief. Of equal importance is ensuring that efficacy measures and performance measures are concordant.

- Past research in sport psychology has not considered microanalytic congruence analysis in work on self- or collective efficacy. As Feltz and Chase (1998) suggest, congruence analyses (at least with use of nonhierarchical efficacy measures) provide a more powerful test of self-efficacy's predictive strength than correlational analyses, although they are more difficult to perform in field studies in sport competition. The microanalytic approach might be more useful in intervention studies.

- The time lapse from the assessment of efficacy beliefs to performance is also important (Bandura, 1997). If the time lapse is too long, efficacy beliefs could be altered by an intervening experience (Bandura). Wiggins (1998) found, however, that efficacy expectations for athletes remained very stable over the 24 hr before competition. Thus, in field studies, where access to athletes is often limited, Feltz and Lirgg (2001) recommend that measures be taken at least within 24 hr of performance but as close to the time of performance as possible.

- As we mentioned in chapter 1, efficacy beliefs will have less predictive strength when people have little information on which to base efficacy judgments, such as when they are learning a skill (Bandura, 1997). Moritz and colleagues (2000) found that correlations between self-efficacy and performance were lower when researchers employed tasks that were novel to their participants. In addition, there may be minimal variability, or floor effects in efficacy judgments, among novice learners of a task. Thus, Feltz and Chase (1998) recommend that researchers interested in questions regarding task-specific efficacy make sure that participants have had some prior experience with the given research task. Schunk (1995b) suggests that with novice learners, a measure of self-efficacy for learning also be included. Often measures based on self-efficacy for learning are more predictive of performance and motivated behavior because they compensate for changes in performance due to subsequent learning (Zimmerman, 1996).

- Lastly, a similar problem of minimal variability may occur with high-level athletes at the upper end of efficacy scales, which can create ceiling effects. To improve the predictive strength of efficacy beliefs with high-level performers, Feltz and Chase (1998) recommend that researchers develop scales with enough gradations of difficulty to detect subtle differences in confidence or use a transformation to normalize the data. They also suggest that the VAS might prove useful in detecting subtle efficacy changes in high-level perform-ers, or that *moderately confident* be used as the baseline anchor, or both. Myers and Feltz (2007) suggest as well that IRT models could accomplish the same purpose by stretching the raw scores farther apart.

In this chapter, we have presented Bandura's (2006) guidelines for con-structing efficacy scales and provided a number of examples of different types of scales for different purposes. We described controversies regarding how efficacy beliefs and performance are measured over time, how collective efficacy has been measured, and problems with the use of self-confidence in the CSAI-2 questionnaire. We also described progress in the development of measures of coaching efficacy and sport confidence. In the next three chapters, we describe research on the efficacy beliefs of athletes, teams, and coaches. The research studies discussed in the upcoming chapters have used a variety of measures to assess these efficacy beliefs. Some have followed Bandura's guidelines; some have not.

PART

The Nature of Efficacy Beliefs in Athletes, Teams, and Coaches

In part II of the book, we divide efficacy into the three main areas—self-efficacy, collective efficacy, and coaching efficacy. Each of these areas is represented by a chapter. We present a summary of what is known about the sources of these efficacy beliefs and also what is known about their effects on athletic functioning. In addition we address topics such as gender differences. Together, these chapters provide explanations for why efficacy beliefs are vital in sport and the supporting evidence.

3

Efficacy Beliefs of Athletes

The Person Who Thinks He Can

If you think you are beaten, you are. If you think you dare not, you don't!
If you'd like to win, but you think you can't, it's almost a cinch that you won't.
If you think you'll lose, you're lost. For out in the world we find,
Success begins with a fellow's will; it's all in the state of mind!
If you think you're outclassed, you are. You've got to think high to rise.
You've got to be so sure of yourself before you can win the prize.
Life's battles don't always go to the strongest or fastest man;
But sooner or later the person who wins is the person who thinks he can!

Anonymous

Many factors can influence an athlete's performance in sport. When the psychological factors are considered, however, few would argue against the importance of self-efficacy. Adages such as "You can do it if you have confidence" and anecdotes from athletes regarding the importance of having confidence are abundant in sport literature. A recent search on the Internet using the Google search engine for the terms "sport" and "confidence" yielded over 3 million results, with quotes from athletes about how important confidence was to their success appearing most frequently.

A considerable amount of research has shown that self-efficacy beliefs are related to performance. In their meta-analysis, Moritz, Feltz, Fahrbach, and Mack (2000) showed that the average correlation between self-efficacy and individual performance in sport (based on 45 studies and 102 correlations) was .38. What this result means is that approximately 16% of the variance in athletic performance can be attributed just to self-efficacy. When all the factors that can affect a person's sport performance are considered, this number is very meaningful. Other meta-analysts who summarized the relationship between self-confidence and sport performance reported similar effect sizes (i.e., ES = .25, $Beta$ = .36: Craft, Magyar, Becker, & Feltz, 2003; ES = .24: Woodman & Hardy, 2003). As a comparison, for cognitive anxiety, another psychological factor thought to affect performance in sport, Woodman and Hardy (2003) reported an effect size of –.10, whereas Craft and colleagues estimated it to be .01. As Bandura (1997) points out, the contribution of efficacy beliefs to a particular domain of functioning is probably underestimated given that self-efficacy assessment is rarely inclusive of all the facets in that domain, such as in athletic performance.

In this chapter, we summarize the self-efficacy research on athletic populations. To start the chapter, we present two systematic programs of research on self-efficacy beliefs in a historical fashion. These lines of research addressed several tenets of self-efficacy theory and spawned several other lines of inquiry. In the next section we present the research on the influence of efficacy beliefs on athletic functioning, most notably performance. In the third section we present the research on the sources of efficacy information, which includes key contextual factors such as feedback, attributions, and goal setting. The chapter concludes with a section on gender differences.

Our review of the research on self-efficacy beliefs in athletes was very comprehensive, but given space constraints we describe in detail only exemplary or novel studies. Research summaries for all of the efficacy- or confidence-based studies in sport referenced in this chapter, including those not described in detail, can be found in the annotated bibliography at the end of the book. In this chapter we also include some of the research that has been carried out using tasks with nonathletic populations (i.e., undergraduate students, exercise participants) if they have implications for athletic settings. Only those studies that involved a sport-related task are included in the annotated bibliography, though. Still, this chapter is considerably longer than those on efficacy beliefs for teams and coaches because the bulk of the efficacy research in sport has been conducted at the individual level with athletes.

We have grouped the research studies into the areas we consider most relevant to their primary purpose; however, it was often difficult to classify studies exclusively into one area because many dealt with several components of self-efficacy theory. In addition, we have focused primarily on those studies in which the self-efficacy of athletes was examined with self-efficacy scales rather than other measures (e.g., Competitive State Anxiety Inventory-2 [CSAI-2]: Martens, Vealey, & Burton, 1990; sport confidence measures: Vealey, 1986). We also did not separate the research according to age level except when unique findings were reported. For a comprehensive summary of self-efficacy research in sport and physical activity settings for youths (ages 7-18 years), readers are directed to Feltz and Magyar (2006). For children, key references for sport include articles written by Chase and colleagues (Chase, 1998, 2001; Chase, Ewing, Lirgg, & George, 1994). Unfortunately, there is little research on self-efficacy beliefs in sport for master-aged athletes except for one study on the sources of sport confidence (Wilson, Sullivan, Myers, & Feltz, 2004). Finally, this chapter emphasizes research on efficacy beliefs with athletes. Here we point to areas in which research is lacking; our suggestions for future research appear in chapter 9.

Early Research

The study of self-efficacy beliefs in sport started with two systematic programs of research. One, by Feltz and her colleagues, focused on the causal relationships between self-efficacy and performance across time (Feltz, 1982, 1988a; Feltz, Landers, & Raeder, 1979; Feltz & Mugno, 1983). The other was by Weinberg and his colleagues (Weinberg, 1985; Weinberg, Gould,

& Jackson, 1979; Weinberg, Gould, Yukelson, & Jackson, 1981; Weinberg, Yukelson, & Jackson, 1980). The Weinberg studies were experimental and used competitive tasks.

The Feltz Series

The primary goal of Feltz's program of research was to investigate the causal relationships between self-efficacy and performance. The origins of self-efficacy research in psychology were in approach–avoidance tasks. A high-avoidance task was operationalized as a skill that required some "daring" to complete; that is, participants could experience a withdrawal reaction if they perceived the situation as too unpleasant or dangerous. Fittingly, Feltz used a modified back dive. In their first study, Feltz and colleagues (1979) investigated the effectiveness of different sources of efficacy information (participant, live, and videotape modeling) on efficacy beliefs and the learning and performance of the back dive. Consistent with Bandura's (1977) theory, they hypothesized that performance-based (or participant modeling) techniques would be more powerful than live modeling or videotaped modeling techniques in producing psychological and behavioral change (i.e., participants would be more efficacious in their ability to perform the dives and perform more dives correctly). The participants, 60 college-aged females with no diving experience, were randomly assigned to one of the three conditions. Self-efficacy and performance were assessed prior to the intervention, after the training period of four dives, and after completion of all eight dives (dives 5-8 were considered the testing period). The findings supported Bandura's theory in showing that students in the participant-modeling condition performed better after the intervention and had higher efficacy ratings than the students in the other conditions. However, the study design did not allow the conclusion that self-efficacy beliefs mediated the treatment effects on performance.

In a second study, Feltz (1982) used path-analysis techniques to investigate the mediational predictions of self-efficacy theory. She also tested an alternative model that excluded self-efficacy and instead included the direct influences of self-reported state anxiety, physiological arousal (heart rate), and previous performance on performance. Results confirmed a reciprocal or temporally recursive cause-and-effect relationship between self-efficacy and performance (see figure 3.1). However, as one gained experience on the task, past performance had a greater influence on self-efficacy than self-efficacy had on performance. Feltz also showed that self-efficacy was a more important predictor of performance compared to self-reported state anxiety, physiological arousal, and past related performance accomplishments on the first of four diving attempts. After the first trial, performance on previous trials was the major predictor of performance on the next trials. These results prompted Feltz to propose a respecified model that included both self-efficacy and previous performance as predictors of performance.

McAuley (1985) supported Feltz's findings using a similar path-analytic design for a gymnastics task.

As an update and as described in chapter 2, Feltz, Chow, and Hepler (2006) reanalyzed the Feltz (1982) data set using residualized past performance scores because Bandura has argued that self-efficacy should be partialled out of past performance when one is testing for its predictive strength on subsequent performance (Bandura, 1997; Bandura & Locke, 2003). The reanalyzed results showed support for Bandura's argument. Self-efficacy was a stronger predictor of performance when past performance was residualized, and the influence of past performance on future performance was weaker when it was residualized. However, residualized performance was still a significant predictor of future performance, lending support for Feltz's (1982) respecified model.

Feltz and Mugno (1983) replicated the original Feltz (1982) path-analysis study and examined the additional influence of perceived physiological arousal on self-efficacy and performance. In her earlier study, Feltz (1982) did not look at perceptions of arousal, but used heart rate as an indicator of physiological arousal. The results from Feltz and Mugno supported the respecified path-analysis model found in Feltz (1982). With respect to the value of using perceived physiological arousal over heart rate, the former was a stronger predictor of self-efficacy. Moreover, when participants attempted the dive for the

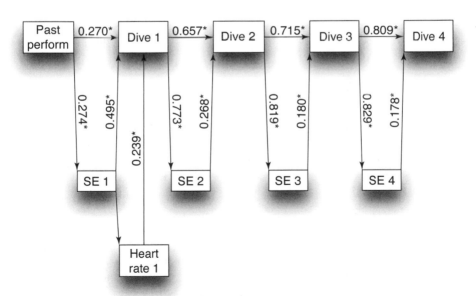

Figure 3.1 Respecified model by Feltz (1982) showing the relationship between self-efficacy and diving performance across trials. *$p < .05$

From "Path Analysis of the Causal Elements in Bandura's Theory of Self-efficacy and an Anxiety-based Model of Avoidance Behavior," by D. L. Feltz, 1982. *Journal of Personality and Social Psychology, 42*, p.776. Copyright 1982 by American Psychological Association. Reprinted with permission.

first time, perceived physiological arousal was actually the most potent source of efficacy information. It did not, however, predict diving performance, but rather influenced performance through its mediating effect on self-efficacy.

In a fourth study, Feltz (1988a) again examined the causal elements of self-efficacy theory using the same high-avoidance task. This time, however, she used 40 males and 40 females as participants, and they were tested on only two dives instead of four. The rationale for the changes was that males and females may respond differently to anxiety in stressful situations, and that the greatest variability would be seen on the initial performance trials. There were no gender differences for efficacy expectations, heart rates, past performance accomplishments, and performance behavior. Males, however, reported lower perceptions of arousal and anxiety than females. Follow-up analyses showed that males and females were biased in their perceptions of autonomic arousal; males underestimated their changes in heart rate and females overestimated their changes. The model (tested by path analysis) fit the data better for females than for males. The reciprocal relationship between self-efficacy and performance was supported for females, but not for males. Past performance and self-efficacy were strong predictors of subsequent performance for both males and females.

Taken together, the results of these studies provided strong support for Bandura's (1977) theoretical premise that self-efficacy is an important predictor of performance, and also for the respecified model that included past performance as a predictor of subsequent performance. The research program also showed that performance accomplishments were a stronger predictor of self-efficacy beliefs than were physiological arousal and emotional states such as perceived autonomic arousal.

The Weinberg Series

In the early Feltz studies on self-efficacy beliefs, the tasks used were high avoidance. These tasks were selected because they were similar to the situations on which Bandura's (1977) self-efficacy theory was based. During this same time period, Weinberg and his colleagues initiated a series of experimental studies that shifted the focus to competitive situations (Weinberg, 1985; Weinberg et al., 1979, 1981, 1980).

In the first of these studies, Weinberg and colleagues (1979) tested whether feelings of self-efficacy were associated with changes in persistence on a competitive muscular endurance task. The task required the participants to extend their leg and hold it for as long as possible in either a high- or low-self-efficacy condition. In the high-self-efficacy condition, participants thought they were performing against a person with weak ligaments and a knee injury who had performed poorly on a related leg strength task. Conversely, participants in the low-self-efficacy condition thought they were performing against a track athlete who lifts weights to increase leg strength, and who, compared to the participant, displayed greater leg strength. To measure self-efficacy, the participants were asked what they thought their chances of winning were and how confident they were in their prediction. Results showed that the high-self-efficacy group was more efficacious and persisted longer than the low-self-efficacy group. In addition, the high-self-efficacy group increased their performance on the second trial, whereas the low-self-efficacy group performed worse on the second trial. This interaction was interesting because it showed that after failing on the first trial, high-self-efficacy participants extended their legs for a longer period of time on Trial 2, whereas their low-self-efficacy counterparts extended their legs for a shorter period of time on Trial 2 (both groups were told they had lost the first trial). Thus, this was the first study to show that self-efficacy affected persistence in the face of failure on a motor task.

Weinberg and his colleagues extended the results of their self-efficacy–performance study by changing a few of the experimental conditions (Weinberg et al., 1980). For this follow-up study, the participants competed against each other in a back-to-back setup and made self-efficacy ratings either out loud (so the person the participant was competing against could hear) or in private (i.e., by writing on a questionnaire). Similar to what had occurred in the previous study, success was manipulated to create high and low efficacy beliefs. The high-self-efficacy males extended their legs longer than the low-self-efficacy males, but there were no statistically significant differences in performance between the high- and low-self-efficacy groups for females. The self-efficacy–performance relationship was stronger for males ($r = .31$) compared to females ($r = .04$). Weinberg and colleagues (1980) speculated that sex-role socialization patterns and sex typing of tasks might explain the gender differences (we discuss this in our section on gender differences in this chapter). No differences resulted from the public versus private efficacy manipulation. Weinberg and colleagues concluded that the face-to-face competitive situation from the first study produced better performance and higher self-efficacy–performance correlations than the back-to-back situation.

In their third study, Weinberg and colleagues (1981) examined the effect of preexisting and manipulated self-efficacy judgments on muscular endurance performance. This time participants were selected for the study based on preexisting levels of self-efficacy (high or low) and then randomly assigned to either a manipulated high- or low-self-efficacy condition. Like the others, the manipulation was successful, and the high-self-efficacy group had higher self-efficacy ratings and performance scores compared to the low-self-efficacy group. The results also showed that variations in self-efficacy had differential motivational effects in response to failure. That is, the high-self-efficacy group responded to failure with greater persistence than the low-self-efficacy group, who had the lowest performance times. The preexisting self-efficacy expectations that an individual brought to the competition were found to influence performance on the first trial, but the manipulated self-efficacy intervention had a greater influence on the second trial. These results showed that self-efficacy beliefs could be modified. This conclusion set the stage for subsequent research on interventions designed to affect self-efficacy beliefs.

In a final study, Weinberg (1985) examined the interaction of self-efficacy and cognitive strategies on muscular endurance performance. Similar to the situation in the previous studies, participants were randomly assigned to a high- or low-self-efficacy condition, but they were also assigned to a cognitive strategy condition (i.e., dissociation or positive self-talk). The manipulation check showed that the high- and low-self-efficacy groups differed in their expectancy of success and were confident in their predictions. Again, participants in the high-self-efficacy group held their legs out longer and tried harder than those in the low-self-efficacy condition. Males outperformed females. The type of cognitive strategy employed did not affect performance.

Historically, the next major contribution to the self-efficacy literature in sport came from Feltz (1988b) with her review paper that summarized all of the self-efficacy research in sport settings. Back then, about 20 studies had been published on self-efficacy in sport and motor performance. This time period seems to have been a turning point because efficacy researchers in sport began to branch off in different directions. Although the relationship between self-efficacy and performance was and still is the most popular one to study, several other research areas on self-efficacy within the sport domain emerged that focused on either the effects of self-efficacy on athletic functioning or the sources of self-efficacy. We present the effects first, followed by the sources.

Self-Efficacy Effects in Athletic Functioning

In this section, we present first the research on the effects of self-efficacy on performance. Then we discuss research on the effects of self-efficacy on behavior (i.e., choice, effort, and persistence), goals and self-regulation, thought patterns (e.g., attributions, decision making, and optimistic and pessimistic thinking), and emotional reactions (i.e., anxiety, worries or fear). Feltz (1988b) commented that much of the sport research on self-efficacy had looked at it in relation to sport performance rather than in terms of the motivational behavior actually specified by the theory, such as persistence or mastery attempts, choice of activities or skills, and effort expended. Although we are writing this book almost 20 years later, the same conclusion can be made. For this reason, the information in other parts of this section may seem a bit light.

Self-Efficacy and Performance

By far the most popular line of inquiry with respect to self-efficacy in sport has been to demonstrate its relationship with performance. These studies, from the early Feltz series and Weinberg series to the present, are diverse in methodologies that demonstrate the generalizability of the positive relationship between these constructs. For example, participants have included various groups, from children to professional athletes to extreme sport athletes to athletes with disabilities. The self-efficacy measures used vary greatly, although most have been constructed for a specific task in accordance with Bandura's recommendations as described in chapter 2. The methods range from descriptive studies to those that use more complex designs involving multiple regressions, path analyses, and multilevel modeling. The number of participants varies as well, from single subjects in case studies to hundreds of participants in survey-based research. The studies are representative of both experimental (i.e., intervention-type studies) and nonexperimental designs. One note of caution, however, is that research on the relationship between self-efficacy and performance on sport tasks does not exclusively involve athletes as participants. On the contrary, several studies have used undergraduate students from kinesiology and other departments (Feltz, 1992).

Taken together, this research shows overwhelming support for the relationship between self-efficacy and performance in the sport domain. Several researchers have used self-efficacy as an independent variable and performance as a dependent variable (i.e., usually with a mean or median split on self-efficacy scores) and have found that the high-self-efficacy groups performed better than the low-self-efficacy groups. In addition, self-efficacy has been shown to be significantly and positively correlated with performance and to be a significant predictor of performance using regression techniques and path analyses. Moritz and colleagues (2000) reported that the positive correlations between self-efficacy and performance have ranged from a high of .79 to a low of .01, which means that a few studies have failed to show a significant relationship between self-efficacy and performance, and some even showed a negative relationship (e.g., Carnahan, Shea, & Davis, 1990; McCullagh, 1987). The studies that showed low correlations or failed to find a relationship either used a nontraditional measure of self-efficacy, had a long time lag between the self-efficacy and performance measures, or had nonconcordant self-efficacy and performance measures. For example, in the Lee (1988) study of collegiate female hockey players, the time period between the self-efficacy and performance measures was unspecified, self-efficacy was not assessed prior to matches, and the self-efficacy measure (based on individual hockey skills) was not concordant with the performance measures (based on team winning percentage). Feltz (1992) suggested that where self-efficacy has not been shown to be related to performance in sport, this probably has more to do with the way the constructs were measured than the conceptual soundness of self-efficacy theory.

One interesting study that exemplifies the comparative strength of self-efficacy in relation to other physiological and psychological variables in predicting performance was done by Burke and Jin (1996). They utilized physiological measures ($\dot{V}O_2$max, adiposity, height, weight), history of performance, and sport psychological constructs (self-efficacy, motivation, sport confidence, cognitive and somatic anxiety) to predict total performance time and individual swim, cycle, and run performance times in an Ironman triathlon event (3.8 km swim [2.4 miles], 180 km cycle [112 miles], and 42.2 km run [26.2 miles]). The results revealed that when all variables were included in the analysis, total performance time was predicted most accurately by self-efficacy, performance history, and weight.

As mentioned in chapter 1, the relationship of self-efficacy beliefs to performance is conditional on the skill development versus execution phases of functioning. In the skill development phase, some self-doubt about one's capability provides motivation and focus to acquire the skill, whereas, in the execution phase, self-doubt inhibits performance execution. Findings by Eyal and colleagues (1995) on motor tasks of various levels of difficulty provide some support for this conditional hypothesis. Although Eyal and colleagues erroneously labeled self-efficacy beliefs as outcome beliefs, they found that the highest performance scores, across tasks, were achieved by participants in the moderate efficacy expectation condition compared to those in the high-expectation condition, with the greatest difference for the intermediate-difficulty tasks. The tasks were competitive and were novel to participants. Participants' efficacy expectations were manipulated via comparison of their performance to that of their opponent (a confederate) as higher, similar, or lower. The authors did not explain their findings in terms of Bandura's (1997) preparatory and performance efficacy conditional hypotheses because the study was published prior to his book, but they did speculate that the moderate uncertainty might have produced higher levels of exertion that resulted in higher performance scores.

The relationship between self-efficacy and performance accomplishments is believed to be reciprocal or temporally recursive. According to Bandura (1977), "mastery expectations influence performance and are, in turn, altered by the cumulative effects of one's efforts" (p. 194). In other words, high self-efficacy leads to enhanced performance, which then leads to high self-efficacy, and so on. In sport performance, self-efficacy has been shown to predict initial performance; and, as one gains experience on the task, performance also becomes a significant predictor of both self-efficacy and future performance (e.g., Feltz, 1982; McAuley, 1985), even when the influence of previous efficacy beliefs on past performance is controlled for (Feltz, Chow, & Hepler, 2006). Thus, although the reciprocal relationship between self-efficacy and performance has been supported in sport performance, past performance cannot be discounted as an important predictor of future performance.

Sport and Motor Behavior: Choice, Effort, and Persistence

In terms of behavior, efficacy beliefs are theorized to influence one's choice of activity, how much effort to expend in the endeavor, how long to persevere in the face of obstacles and failures, and whether failures are motivating or demoralizing. According to Bandura (1986b, 1997), people will avoid situations that they believe they are not capable of handling. Escarti and Guzman (1999) examined the mediating effect of self-efficacy in the feedback–performance and feedback–*task choice* relationships. The experimental paradigm consisted of three sessions. In the first session, participants were shown a task (hurdles), and they completed a self-efficacy measure. The task was then performed individually. One week later, in the second session, participants were given manipulated feedback referring to their previous performance (one group received feedback that exceeded their efficacy expectations, whereas the second group received feedback that failed to meet their efficacy expectations). Participants then estimated their self-efficacy for the hurdle task, which they later performed. In the third session (one day after the second session), the participants were presented with three tasks involving clearing hurdles of progressive difficulty. They were asked to select whichever task they felt capable of completing, then they performed their chosen task. Structural equation modeling confirmed a model in which self-efficacy was related to performance and task choice. Participants with higher self-efficacy performed the task better and chose more difficult tasks. Similar results were obtained by Chase (2001) with children. She found that children with higher self-efficacy chose to participate more and had higher future self-efficacy scores than those with lower self-efficacy.

The relationship between self-efficacy and effort or persistence is also expected to be positive. The stronger the perceived self-efficacy, the more vigorous and persistent are people's efforts (Bandura, 1986b). Support for this part of the theory comes from Weinberg's program of research discussed at the beginning of this chapter. He showed repeatedly that participants with high self-efficacy persisted longer than those with lower self-efficacy. In his 1985 study he asked participants to indicate how hard they tried at the leg endurance task using a scale ranging from 1 *(not at all)* to 11 *(extremely hard)*. The high-self-efficacy group's scores on this scale were significantly higher than those of the low-self-efficacy group. Positive correlations between self-efficacy and performance on other endurance tasks (e.g., Gould & Weiss, 1981; Martin & Gill, 1995) also support this relationship. In his review of the literature on personal beliefs and mental preparation in strength and muscular endurance tasks, Biddle (1985) concluded that positive efficacy expectations increase both effort and persistence in endurance tasks, although effort was not directly measured on these tasks.

Researchers have also demonstrated a relationship between self-efficacy beliefs and perceived effort using non-endurance-type tasks. For example, Moritz (1998) showed that perceptions of efficacy were positively correlated with participants' responses to an item that assessed the amount of effort participants perceived they put into a bowling tournament. Similarly, George (1994) reported path-analysis results showing that higher self-efficacy predicted greater effort in baseball hitting.

Self-Efficacy, Goals, and Self-Regulation

As described in chapter 1, people's choices involve goals, which are based on self-efficacy judgments. People with higher levels of self-efficacy will choose more challenging goals than those who have lower levels of self-efficacy (Bandura, 1997). Boyce and Bingham (1997) showed that the self-efficacy levels of their participants affected their goal setting in terms of difficulty in that those with high self-efficacy set higher goals than those with medium and low self-efficacy. The authors also showed that the self-efficacy levels of participants in the control condition (i.e., a "do your best" with no specific goals communicated to the group) affected their spontaneous goal-setting behavior; that is, participants with high and medium self-efficacy levels were more likely to spontaneously set goals for themselves.

Self-efficacy has also been considered to be a mediator of the goal-setting–performance relationship when goals are assigned (e.g., Kane, Marks, Zaccaro, & Blair, 1996; Lerner & Locke, 1995). For example, Lerner and Locke (1995) showed that self-efficacy mediated the relationship between assigned goals and performance on a sit-up task using undergraduate students as participants. Thus, people set goals based on the strength of their self-efficacy. However, it is important to note that goals that are assigned by others, such as coaches, are also a *source* of self-efficacy beliefs because the goals convey information about the coach's belief in the athlete's abilities (Bandura, 1997). This relationship is covered in the section on sources.

The self-efficacy, goals, and performance relationship has been described as a single theoretical model that characterizes self-regulation. This model emerged after the consistency in research findings regarding these relationships was noted and is based on goal theory (Locke & Latham, 1990) and social cognitive theory (Bandura, 1977, 1986b, 1997). Kane and colleagues (1996) used the term self-regulation to describe the changes in behavior and cognition that occur as people try to reach their performance goals. As described by the authors, self-regulation begins with a person's evaluation of information that bears upon his or her competency in a specific task domain (i.e., a self-reactive influence). On the basis of this information, people form self-efficacy judgments and set goals. The sources of self-efficacy influence both the level of self-efficacy and the goals that are set. The subsequent effects of self-efficacy on performance are both direct and mediated by personal goals: personal goals directly influence task performance, and task performance then serves as additional information that influences subsequent self-efficacy and goal setting. Thus, the self-regulatory processes are dynamic and cyclical, where self-efficacy and personal goals are the key components (see figure 3.2).

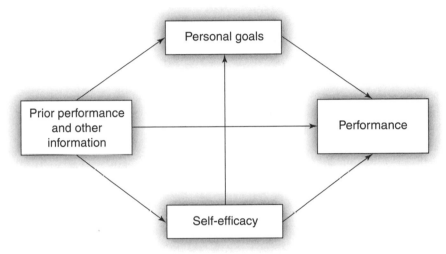

Figure 3.2 Self-regulation model as adapted from Kane and colleagues (1996).

Adapted, by permission, from T.D. Kane et al., 1996, "Self-efficacy, personal goals, and wrestlers' self-regulation," *Journal of Sport and Exercise Psychology* 18: 37.

Kane and colleagues (1996) tested the components of their self-regulation model in competitive wrestling. They hypothesized that significant relationships would exist among prior performance, self-efficacy, personal goals, performance, and performance satisfaction. In addition, they hypothesized that for overtime wrestling matches, self-efficacy, rather than prior ability, would be the best predictor of performance. This hypothesis was based on the assumption that if a match was tied after regulation time expired, the two wrestlers had demonstrated close to equal ability in that match. Participants were high school wrestlers enrolled in a week-long wrestling camp. Measures included win/loss records from previous-season performance records and for performance at the camp (including performance in overtime matches), camp goals, next-season goals, self-efficacy, and satisfaction with camp performance. Results showed that all hypothesized paths of the self-regulation model were statistically significant and in the hypothesized directions except for the direct influence of self-efficacy on performance. However, as pointed out by Kane and colleagues, this lack of direct effect was probably due to the mismatch between how self-efficacy was assessed and how performance was measured. When the analyses were rerun using more concordant assessments, there were stronger relationships between the variables. When only overtime performances were considered, the only significant predictor was self-efficacy.

Thought Patterns

The research in sport on the influence of self-efficacy beliefs on thought patterns has focused on attributions, decision making, and optimistic versus pessimistic thinking. Emotional reactions usually involve thought patterns as well, but because they represent an affective class of responses they are described in a separate section.

Attributions   Bandura (1990) stated that "attributions and self-efficacy appraisals involve bidirectional causation" (p. 141). Those who regard themselves as highly efficacious tend to attribute their failures to insufficient effort or situational impediments, whereas those with a low sense of self-efficacy view their failures as stemming from a lack of ability. These attributions can, in turn, influence one's subsequent efficacy beliefs for future performance. Thus, self-efficacy affects attributions, but the attributions made also affect future self-efficacy. For this reason, attributions are covered in both this section on self-efficacy effects and in the following section on sources of self-efficacy.

The results from several studies (e.g., Cleary & Zimmerman, 2001; Kitsantas & Zimmerman, 1998, 2002; Zimmerman & Kitsantas, 1997) support Bandura's assertions regarding the self-efficacy–attributions relationship. Zimmerman and Kitsantas (1997) showed that girls who attributed their failure to hit a bull's-eye to strategy insufficiency displayed significantly higher levels of self-efficacy, had higher dart-throw acquisition, were more satisfied, and were more interested in the task than those who attributed their failure to inability or inadequate efforts.

Although similar results have been found with children, effort and ability may not be the most salient attributions that children use. Chase (2001) examined children's self-efficacy, motivational intentions, and attributions in physical activity and sport. More specifically, she looked at how differences in children's self-efficacy levels affected choice, persistence, effort, future self-efficacy beliefs, and attributions following perceptions of failure. Only the attributions of effort and ability were selected because they represented the traditional attributions cited in the literature. Results showed that low-self-efficacy children attributed their failure to a lack of ability more than high-self-efficacy children. However, although the predicted differences were found, the actual attribution scores were rather low, prompting Chase to recommend that future researchers try an open-ended type of question to gather more information about the other types of attributions that children make for failure experiences.

Several other researchers have also examined the effect of self-efficacy beliefs on attributions. For example, Bond, Biddle, and Ntoumanis (2001) showed that athletes whose self-efficacy increased over the course of a golf tournament judged themselves to be more successful, and in turn made more stable and internal attributions for their performance than did those whose self-efficacy decreased. The authors suggested that success and failure may moderate the relationship between attributions and self-efficacy, where self-efficacy is related to attribution dimensions differently under conditions of success and failure. This assertion is in line with results from Shaw, Dzewaltowski, and McElroy (1992), who found that failure did not lower self-efficacy beliefs when unstable attributions were made. Gernigon and Delloye (2003) demonstrated a relationship among attributions, feedback, and self-efficacy. More specifically, the authors showed that attributions mediated the relationship between unexpected success or failure feedback and self-efficacy among elite sprinters.

Decision Making In addition to attributions, another thought process affected by self-efficacy beliefs is decision making. Superior functioning in athletics not only is based on the physical execution of motor skills, but also is influenced by the cognitive processing of information, especially in a dynamic environment where split-second decisions must be made. According to Bandura (1997), after proficiency is acquired with cognitive guidance, motor skills are routinized and no longer require higher cognitive control. Thus, the execution of motor skills is largely regulated by lower-level sensory-motor systems, but cognition continues to play an influential role in athletic performance through its strategic function. Bandura considers successful performance to be the result of quality anticipatory decision making as well as motor skill. He recognized that there is much cognitive self-regulation of seemingly routinized skills and stated that "athletes' perceived decisional efficacy is an area worthy of study" (p. 375).

Very little published research has addressed the relationship between decision making and self-efficacy in sports. Using video clips, Hepler and Feltz (2006) examined the relationship between decision-making efficacy and the accuracy and speed with which decisions were made for various infield defensive situations in baseball. Results showed that self-efficacy significantly and positively predicted decision-making performance between individuals and at the intraindividual level when past influences of self-efficacy on decision-making performance were controlled for (i.e., residualized past decisions). Thus, self-efficacy is also linked to making quick and accurate decisions in sport situations.

Optimistic and Pessimistic Thinking As we described in chapter 1, Bandura (2001) posits that efficacy beliefs influence whether people think pessimistically or optimistically and in ways that are self-enhancing or self-hindering. There is some support for a relationship between self-efficacy and optimism in sport. Grove and Heard (1997) administered the Life Orientation Test (LOT: Scheier & Carver, 1985), the Coping Inventory for Stressful Situations (CISS: Endler & Parker, 1990), and the Trait Sport Confidence Inventory (TSCI: Vealey, 1986) to athletes from a variety of individual and team sports. The LOT is a measure of dispositional optimism; the CISS assesses how often athletes use task-oriented, emotion-oriented, and avoidance-oriented coping strategies when confronted with a stressful situation. Because separate samples were used (i.e., one group of athletes completed the CISS and LOT, while the other completed the CISS and TSCI), the authors were unable to report a correlation between optimism and confidence. However, they did show that both optimism and confidence were positively correlated with the use of problem-focused coping strategies and negatively correlated with the use of emotional-oriented and avoidance-oriented coping strategies.

Research from exercise psychology also supports a relationship between self-efficacy and optimism. Kavussanu and McAuley (1995) showed that individuals who were highly active were significantly more optimistic and less pessimistic than inactive/low-active individuals. The highly active group was also higher in self-efficacy and lower in trait anxiety than the inactive/low-active group.

Emotional Reactions

Anxiety, arousal, fear, worry, and depressive moods are the typical emotional reactions that have been studied in relation to one's efficacy beliefs. Of these, the most frequently assessed emotional state in sport is anxiety. In social cognitive theory, anxiety is considered a coeffect of a low sense of efficacy to meet competitive demands as well as a source of efficacy information (Bandura, 1997). For this reason, we include it in this section on self-efficacy effects.

Anxiety The relationship between self-efficacy and anxiety has been researched in many different ways. For example, correlational studies have shown that self-efficacy is negatively associated with anxiety (e.g., Cartoni, Minganti, & Zelli, 2005; Haney & Long, 1995). Regression analyses have been used to show that self-efficacy is a stronger predictor of performance than anxiety (e.g., LaGuardia & Labbe, 1993; Weiss, Wiese, & Klint, 1989). Also, path analyses (e.g., Feltz, 1982; Haney & Long, 1995; McAuley, 1985) have consistently shown that anxiety has a direct relationship to self-efficacy, rather than to performance.

As pointed out by Treasure, Monson, and Lox (1996), researchers and practitioners often assume that athletes' precompetition experiences are limited to negative cognitions and emotions, such as anxiety. In their words, "ignoring potential positive affective experiences prior to competition in favor of assessing the negative (i.e., anxiety) is too limiting of an approach when attempting to understand the antecedents of performance and the relationship between self-efficacy and affect in sport" (p. 76). In their study, they investigated whether self-efficacy was associated with positive and negative affective states prior to participation in a competitive wrestling match. Participants (male high school wrestlers) completed a task-specific self-efficacy measure as well as the CSAI-2 for cognitive and somatic anxiety and the Positive and Negative Affective Schedule (Watson, Clark, & Tellegen, 1988). Performance was assessed using win/loss outcome and points accrued in wrestling bouts. The results showed that self-efficacy was positively related to positive affect and negatively related to negative affect and the anxieties prior to competition. However, given the correlational nature of the results, directionality could not be determined.

Bandura (1997) suggested that researchers in sport psychology focus on assessing how people interpret arousal, how much attention they pay to it, and their perceived coping efficacy and ameliorative efficacy (which reflects belief in one's ability to alleviate arousal through various cognitive strategies). With respect to coping efficacy, Bandura (1988) has argued that people's perceived coping efficacy is more indicative of capability than their perceptions of their physiological arousal. If people believe that they cannot cope with a potential threat, they experience disruptive arousal, which may further lower their beliefs that they can perform successfully. Initial evidence for this argument came from research *outside of sport* showing that it is not fear-evoking cognitions in themselves that account for anxiety symptoms, but rather the perceived self-efficacy to control them (Kent, 1987; Kent & Gibbons, 1987). Within sport, Treasure and colleagues (1996) showed that athletes with higher self-efficacy perceived competitive wrestling situations as less threatening than athletes with low levels of self-efficacy.

Fear and Worry Several recent studies have shown associations between self-efficacy and a negative emotion in sport—namely, the fear of injury. In fact, Magyar and Chase (1996) operationalized fear of injury as existing when athletes lack confidence in their ability to perform successfully in a threatening or taxing situation. Short, Reuter, Brandt, Short, and Kontos (2004) found negative relationships between worry/concern (fear) regarding injury and confidence about avoiding injury, as well as between probability of injury and confidence about avoiding injury, in contact sport athletes. When only those athletes who had been previously injured were considered, their results showed that they perceived the highest probability of reinjury, demonstrated the greatest worry/concern regarding reinjury, and had the least amount of confidence in their ability to avoid reinjury. Reuter and Short (2005) replicated and extended these findings with athletes in noncontact/limited-contact sports. They showed that athletes who had experienced more than one injury in the past 12 months perceived more risk of reinjury and had less confidence in their ability to avoid injury than those who had had only a single injury in the same 12-month time period. Cartoni and colleagues (2005) reported a negative correlation between self-efficacy and fear of injury in gymnasts and showed that the size of the correlation increased with age; that is, the oldest participants in their study showed the strongest negative relationship between confidence and fear of injury.

Before ending this section on the effects of self-efficacy on emotional states, we want to introduce some of the newer research that has addressed the self-regulatory effects of self-efficacy—the notion that a strong, resilient sense of self-efficacy can help one withstand the effects of competitive pressures. Research has shown that athletes who lose a competitive sporting event experience a significant decline in positive affect levels from pre- to postcompetition (Brown, Malouff, & Schutte, 2005). A positive sense of self-efficacy, however, can help prevent the decline in positive affect after a loss in sport. In an interesting study, Brown and colleagues (2005) had participants focus on or imagine for a minute one or more specific thoughts or images that related to three sources of self-efficacy. The items were

- Personal mastery
  - "think about something you did really well during the game," and
  - "think about winning your next game and how you will feel;"
- Verbal encouragement
  - "think about a time when your teammates or coach praised you," and
  - "think about a time when your teammates or coach showed confidence in you;"
- Vicarious mastery
  - "think about a great athlete who failed at first and then succeeded," and
  - "think about a great athlete who works harder after losing so he or she can win in the future."

The participants in the experimental group experienced less decline in positive affect, compared to precompetition affect, after losing than the control group participants.

Sources of Self-Efficacy Beliefs for Athletes

As discussed in chapter 1, judgments of efficacy, whether accurate or faulty, are a product of a complex process of self-appraisal and self-persuasion that relies on cognitive processing of diverse sources of efficacy information. The four principal sources of information according to Bandura (1977, 1986b, 1997) are enactive mastery experiences (or past performance accomplishments), vicarious experiences (comparisons), verbal persuasion and other types of social influences, and physiological states and affective states. Others have added separate categories for emotional states and imaginal experiences (Maddux, 1995; Schunk, 1995b). In this section, we describe the research that has been conducted on these sources of self-efficacy, using the six categories we presented in chapter 1. The research may involve intervention-type studies that addressed the effectiveness of a particular technique (grounded in self-efficacy theory and based on a particular source) as a way to affect efficacy beliefs in athletes. We also present more general information pertaining to which sources athletes indicate they use when forming their efficacy beliefs and provide an introduction to the most recent research on the sources of confidence as advanced by Vealey, Hayashi, Garner-Holman, and Giacobbi (1998).

Past Performance Accomplishments

From a theoretical standpoint, the most important and powerful source of self-efficacy for athletes is derived from their own past performance accomplishments (Bandura, 1977, 1986b, 1997). The primary strategies that researchers have used to examine the effect of performance accomplishments on self-efficacy beliefs include (1) using performance measures to predict self-efficacy beliefs in regression analyses and path analyses, and (2) using success and failure as independent variables in analysis of variance (ANOVA)-type analyses with self-efficacy as the dependent variable. This latter type of research design is popular in natural settings and laboratory settings where self-efficacy beliefs are manipulated. An additional method, described earlier, is the one that Feltz and colleagues (1979) used when they compared mastery-based and vicariously based instructional methods, showing superiority for the former. Studies illustrative of these research methods are included in table A in the Appendix as well as in the annotated bibliography.

Taken together these studies show overwhelming support for the influence of past performance accomplishments on self-efficacy beliefs. But even though the positive relationship between past performance accomplishments and self-efficacy beliefs is robust, from a practical standpoint Bandura (1997) warned successful athletes to be careful not to become complacent because letdowns after easy successes and intensifications of effort after failures are common sequences in competitive struggles in sport. One can cite examples of events in which exceptional athletes who were supposed to win fell short and the "underdog" emerged with victory. In the 2005 U.S. Open tennis tournament, fourth-seeded Andy Roddick lost in the first round to unseeded Gilles Muller of Luxembourg. After the match, Roddick said, "I'm a little bit in shock right now to be honest. I've never felt better going into a slam. This has totally blindsided me." Of his victory, Muller stated, "I have no idea how I did it." Depending on the resiliency of one's self-efficacy beliefs and the degree of discrepancy between the level of performance aspired to and actual performance, failures may actually spur further efforts (Carver & Scheier, 1990b). For example, Weinberg and colleagues (1981) showed that their high-self-efficacy group responded to manipulated failure feedback by exerting greater effort; the authors speculated that this may have been because the high-self-efficacy group saw failure as discordant with their self-efficacy beliefs. The low-self-efficacy group seemed to become demoralized by failure: They were led to believe they would not win, they did not win, and as a result their performance was worse. They did not increase their effort as a result of failure. Chase, Feltz, and Lirgg (2003) showed that athletes often perceive a "bouncing back" or "we're due" effect after previous poor performances as a source of efficacy information.

According to Bandura (1997), the influence of past performance experiences on self-efficacy beliefs depends on several other factors, such as the perceived difficulty of the performance. Theoretically, self-efficacy beliefs are more likely to be enhanced when personal accomplishments are achieved with minimal effort on difficult tasks, but we found no research in sport that addressed the effect of perceived task difficulty on self-efficacy beliefs. One study (Slobounov, Yukelson, & O'Brien, 1997) showed that self-efficacy varied inversely as a function of dive difficulty. Even though self-efficacy beliefs are postulated to increase after performance accomplishments on difficult tasks, this does not mean that athletes should be given only difficult tasks to perform. Successes on difficult tasks could also lower self-efficacy beliefs if performers believe that they will not be able to repeat the same level of effort again (Bandura & Cervone, 1986). Furthermore, tasks that are too difficult for athletes at a given skill level may set them up for failure. Failure has been shown to be debilitating to athletes, especially early in the learning or training process, and may lead to feelings of learned helplessness. For example, Lane and colleagues (2002) showed that self-efficacy significantly decreased following defeat. Similarly, Gernigon, Fleurance, and Reine (2000) showed that failure was associated with less persistence and that perceptions of failure provoked perceptions of learned helplessness.

Theoretically, Bandura (1986b, 1997) has stated that the temporal patterns of success and failure affect self-efficacy beliefs such that performance successes generally raise self-efficacy beliefs and repeated performance failures lower them, particularly if the failures occur early in the course of events and do not reflect lack of effort or adverse external circumstances. That is, failures often undermine self-efficacy beliefs especially if they occur before a sense of self-efficacy is firmly established. Escarti and Guzman (1999) found that success and failure, manipulated through feedback, were related to self-efficacy, performance, and task choice. Those who received positive (success) feedback had higher self-efficacy scores, performed the task better, and chose more difficult tasks than those who had received negative (failure) feedback.

Despite the evidence that performance successes raise efficacy beliefs and performance failures lower them, it is important to note that these effects are not "automatic." Bandura (1997) stated that, "changes in perceived efficacy result from cognitive processing of the diagnostic information that performances convey about capability rather than from the performances per se. Therefore, the impact of performance attainments on efficacy beliefs depends on what is made of those performances. The same level of performance success may raise, leave unaffected, or lower perceived self-efficacy depending on how various personal and situational contributors are interpreted and weighted" (p. 81). Consider, for example, two athletes who start out with the same level of self-efficacy, perform at the same task, and score the same—say they both perform successfully 6 out 10 trials. To one athlete, scoring 6 out of 10 may signify adequate performance and thus not affect his or her self-efficacy beliefs. To the second athlete, scoring 6 out of 10 may signify a better than average performance, thereby raising that athlete's self-efficacy beliefs. To the best of our knowledge, athletes' perceptions of their performance attainments (e.g., subjective ratings of success or satisfaction in relation to goal attainment *after* performance) have mostly been assumed rather than examined in self-efficacy–performance research in sport.

Vicarious Experiences

Modeling and social comparison constitute the sources of efficacy information gained through vicarious experience. McCullagh and Weiss (2001) indicated the importance of modeling in relation to self-efficacy beliefs by noting that "it is apparent that modeling can indeed have profound effects not only on performance but also on psychological variables that may impact physical activity patterns" (p. 212). The authors stated that observational learning and self-efficacy go hand in hand. Observational learning is a key source of efficacy beliefs that, in turn, influence thoughts, emotions, and behaviors (McCullagh & Weiss, 2002).

In sport psychology, models are used as a stimulus for effecting some type of psychological or behavioral change, and in that way, use of models is considered an intervention technique. Researchers have shown the effectiveness of modeling in enhancing self-efficacy beliefs and performance; they have also compared modeling with other interventions in relation to efficacy beliefs. In addition, researchers have examined which characteristics of models were most important to observers. Some of these studies are described next.

With respect to the characteristics of the model, the variables most often studied have been model status, competence, and similarity. This line of research started in 1973, prior to Bandura's (1977) seminal article introducing the construct of self-efficacy, when Landers and Landers (1973) published their study on the effect of model type (i.e., peer or teacher) and model competence (i.e., skilled or unskilled) on children's performances using a balance task. Their results showed that the best performances came from those who viewed a skilled teacher; the next best came from those who viewed an unskilled peer. Thus, both a high-status competent model and a similar-ability peer model were effective in enhancing performance. Landers and Landers reasoned that the unskilled peer demonstration may have provided the students with a challenge to surpass. In a follow-up study, Lirgg and Feltz (1991) sought to determine the more salient model attributes (similarity or competence) with respect to self-efficacy as well as performance as measured by both outcome and form. They showed that model competence elicited higher efficacy beliefs and performance form and outcome than did model similarity. In both studies, however, the skilled teacher elicited the best performance. As Bandura (1997) notes, when observers are trying to learn a new task, model competence has a greater influence than other model attributes such as age, sex, or status.

However, in contexts in which people are uncertain of their capabilities at a task, model similarity adds to the influence of model competence. Gould and Weiss (1981) studied the influence of model similarity on self-efficacy and performance using a muscular endurance task. In their experimental conditions, sedentary females watched either a nonathletic-looking female (similar model) or an athletic male (dissimilar model) endure on a physical task. The similar model led to higher self-efficacy and performance. A follow-up study by George and colleagues (1992) looked at the effects of model similarity cues on motor performance and self-efficacy using the same endurance task. Their study was designed to determine which characteristic of a model (gender or ability) was more salient. For the female participants, there were four different types of models: athletic male, athletic female, nonathletic male, and nonathletic female. The results showed that the model's ability level mattered more than the model's gender for enhancing self-efficacy and performance (nonathletic models had a greater effect than the athletic models).

As the studies just described suggest, different types of models have different levels of effectiveness in different contexts. Coping models are the same as learning models and do not repeatedly display exemplary behaviors (McCullagh & Weiss, 2001). Instead, they demonstrate the negative cognitions, affects, and behaviors that may precede or accompany performance on tasks that are perceived as difficult or that evoke fear. Through repeated trials, coping models gradually verbalize more positive thoughts and show more positive affect and more correct performance. Thus, these models show a progression from low ability to cope with the demands of the task to exemplary performance. Coping models are generally considered most useful in threatening situations, in pain management and injury recovery, or when the task to be learned is difficult. Mastery models, on the other hand, immediately demonstrate exemplary or errorless performance. Weiss and colleagues (1998) examined the role of peer mastery and coping models on children's swimming skills, fear, and self-efficacy. The results showed that coping models had a stronger effect on self-efficacy than mastery models.

In another form of modeling, covert modeling, a participant first imagines a fictional model performing successfully and then imagines him- or herself performing the desired behavior (Rushall, 1988). Using a case study design, Rushall found this to be an effective strategy in raising the self-efficacy level of a wrestler.

As mentioned in chapter 1, self-modeling is yet another form of modeling, which has been defined as the behavioral change that results from the repeated observation of oneself on videotape showing only desired target behaviors (McCullagh & Weiss, 2001). All videotape feedback cannot be considered as self-modeling because in self-modeling, individuals must be shown performing more skillfully than normally. Self-modeling is preferred over video feedback because it is assumed that eliminating errors will enhance self-efficacy and lead to enhanced performance (McCullagh & Weiss, 2001). According to Bandura (1997), self-modeling affects performance through its impact on efficacy beliefs.

There are two forms of self-modeling: positive self-review and feedforward. Positive self-review includes images of adaptive behavior as fine-tuned examples of the best the individual has been able to produce thus far. In sport, these are referred to as highlight videos (McCullagh & Weiss, 2001). Feedforward is used when the learner may already possess the skills but has not executed them in a particular order or in a certain context. In this case, the video is edited to construct a behavior that is possible but has not yet occurred. An example given by McCullagh and Weiss is that of an athlete who can successfully perform behaviors in practice conditions but not in games. Using feedforward, the environment would be reconstructed so that the product is a video in which the athlete sees him- or herself perform the desired behaviors in game situations. For instance, Singleton and Feltz (1999) showed that collegiate hockey players exposed to several weeks of self-modeling videotapes had greater shooting accuracy and higher self-efficacy beliefs for game performance compared to a control group (see figure 3.3).

There seems to be little doubt that self-modeling interventions result in changes in performance and efficacy, but when self-modeling is compared with other types of modeling, the results are less consistent. In their comparison of peer and self-modeling, Starek and McCullagh (1999) did not find any differences between the groups on self-efficacy and performance in adults learning to swim. Self-efficacy did, however, increase across sessions, and the self-modeling group had higher scores in all sessions. Starek and McCullagh also found that the participants who watched themselves as opposed to watching peers had more accurate estimations of their performance, which they suggested was evidence that it was the accuracy of self-efficacy rather than the estimation that influences performance changes.

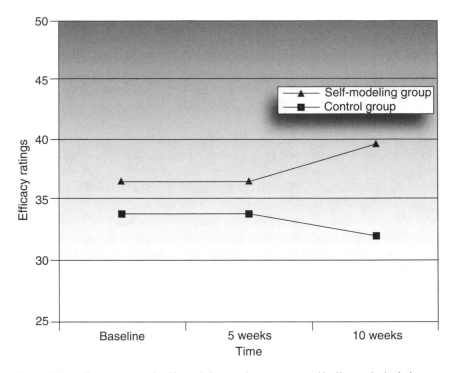

Figure 3.3 Effectiveness of self-modeling videotapes on self-efficacy beliefs for collegiate hockey players.

Reprinted, by permission, from D.A. Singleton and D.L. Feltz, 1999, *The effects of self-modeling on shooting performance and self-efficacy among intercollegiate hockey players.* (East Lansing, MI: Michigan State University). Unpublished manuscript.

When the effectiveness of modeling-based interventions has been compared with that of other interventions, results have supported the superiority of modeling techniques. For example, Hall and Erffmeyer (1983) randomly assigned 10 female basketball players to either a videotaped modeling condition or a progressive relaxation and visual imagery (no modeling) condition. The results offered empirical support for the efficacy of modeling in improving foul-shooting accuracy, but self-efficacy was not assessed. Soohoo and colleagues (2004) showed that a modeling condition resulted in better performances (on free-weight squat lifts) compared to an imagery condition. There were no differences in self-efficacy between the two groups; both imagery and modeling resulted in increased self-efficacy scores. The results showed that modeling led to better acquisition performance and was the preferred intervention for individuals first learning motor skills.

Efficacy information gained through social comparison has also been shown to influence performance on athletic tasks (Eyal et al., 1995; Feltz & Riessinger, 1990; Weinberg, 1985; Weinberg et al., 1979; 1980, 1981). In these examples, confederates posed as formidable or weak opponents to manipulate participants' efficacy expectations about winning the competition. In addition to social comparison, Bandura (1986b) notes that people use normative and self- or temporal comparative information that they weigh and integrate in judging their personal efficacy. The self-comparative information is based on past performance, which is not always the most useful for strengthening one's confidence. For instance, Frey and Ruble (1990) suggest that master athletes may avoid comparisons to their previous performance (temporal comparisons) if their performance has been declining over time and instead rely more on age-mate (vicarious) comparisons with less talented age-mates to judge their capabilities. For athletes whose performances are improving, which is the more typical situation for younger athletes, temporal comparisons may be more important sources of information.

How one integrates past performance and normative information to cognitively appraise efficacy information could also be dependent on one's goal perspective (Feltz & Magyar, 2006). Achievement goal theory (Ames, 1992; Nicholls, 1984a) proposes two major goal perspectives from which individuals evaluate their ability and success: self-referenced and norm referenced. In a self-referenced orientation, one focuses on one's learning accomplishments, effort, and improvement in judging one's ability. In a norm-referenced orientation, on the other hand, one uses social comparison to judge ability and success at a task. Integrating self-efficacy and achievement goal theories, one could say that athletes with a self-referenced orientation would be more apt to use past performance sources of information to assess their efficacy while norm-referenced athletes would rely on social comparisons. Previous research has associated norm referenced sources of information with maladaptiveness because when ability is judged as low compared to that of others, norm-referenced individuals (also labeled ego oriented) may choose easier tasks, not try as hard, or drop out (Magyar & Feltz, 2003). However, as the example with master athletes illustrates, maladaptive behavior can also occur if people judge their ability to be lower than when they were in their prime. Choosing what efficacy information to focus on is strategic in optimizing efficacy beliefs.

Verbal Persuasion

The forms of verbal persuasion as a source of efficacy information are diverse, consisting of feedback; expectations on the part of others; pregame, half-time, or postgame speeches; and other cognitive strategies. These forms of persuasion predominantly come from other people, although verbal persuasion could also come from oneself in the form of self-talk. As described in chapter 1, the extent of the persuasive influence on self-efficacy depends on the prestige, credibility, expertise or knowledge, and trustworthiness of the persuader. Compared to the other sources of self-efficacy already discussed, verbal persuasion has been the subject of considerably less research.

Feedback The most popular line of inquiry on verbal persuasion as a source of efficacy beliefs has to do with evaluative feedback. Within motor behavior, how feedback is given to athletes influences both their learning and performance of a skill. Two types of feedback have been identified: knowledge of results (KR), which consists of externally presented information about the outcome of performing a skill or about achieving the goal of the performance; and knowledge of performance (KP), which is information about the movement characteristics that led to the performance outcome. For example, a coach using KR feedback may tell an athlete that he or she ran the 100 m in 11 sec flat, whereas KP feedback would emphasize technique or form instead of time. Most efficacy studies have focused on KR feedback.

The feedback given to an athlete can either undermine self-efficacy or boost it (Bandura, 1997). Researchers in sport have investigated the effect of feedback on self-efficacy beliefs mostly by using success and failure manipulations in laboratory settings, although a couple studies have looked at how failure affects self-efficacy beliefs in the field (for examples, see the appendix). Typically, informing athletes that they were successful is considered positive feedback whereas conveying failure is negative feedback. The effects of these manipulations on self-efficacy beliefs show that success and failure increase and decrease self-efficacy, respectively. What is noteworthy, however, is that self-efficacy has been shown to be a mediator of the feedback–performance relationship. That is, even when athletes received negative feedback, those who were self-efficacious performed better than those who were less so (e.g., Escarti & Guzman, 1999).

One type of feedback that has been used in self-efficacy research is bogus feedback. In fact, the effect of bogus feedback as a means of verbal persuasion on efficacy beliefs and performance was once a hot topic for researchers. Typical research studies used weightlifting tasks, and the research design involved randomly assigning participants to groups who were told that they had lifted more or less weight than they actually had. Results from Ness and Patton (1979) showed that participants obtained higher strength performances when the actual resistance was greater than the participants believed (i.e., participants lifted 100 lb [45 kg] but were told it was only 80 lb [36 kg]). Extensions of this line of research included investigating self-efficacy beliefs in addition to performance. Fitzsimmons and colleagues (1991) showed that false positive feedback increased self-efficacy beliefs and performance. However, results from Wells, Collins, and Hale (1993) showed that in participants who lifted more weight than they believed, self-efficacy was decreased following the manipulation. Another study, by Yan Lan and Gill (1984), showed that providing participants with bogus feedback, and the suggestion that their elevated arousal levels were indicative of good performance, did not increase confidence. In contrast, Wilkes and Summers (1984) found that persuasive techniques aimed at enhancing efficacy and emotional arousal influenced strength performance but that efficacy beliefs did not seem to mediate the effect. These studies showed that manipulating self-efficacy beliefs through bogus feedback may or may not result in performance changes.

Feltz (1994) offered several explanations for the equivocal findings in these studies. First, she suggested that different results may have to do with differences in the degree of persuasive influence. For example, in the Weinberg (1985) study, described in chapter 1, the participants were not told that the cognitive strategy they were using would enhance their performance, so there was no attempt at persuasion. Wilkes and Summers (1984), on the other hand, instructed their participants to persuade themselves that they were confident. Second, as pointed out by Bandura (1986b), the degree of persuasive influence depends on the believability of the persuasive information. Yan Lan and Gill (1984) tried to lead participants to believe that they had the same heightened pattern of physiological arousal as good competitors. However, there was no manipulation check to show that the participants believed this. Fitzsimmons and colleagues (1991), in contrast, used pilot data to ensure that the deceptive feedback provided was believable. Third, Feltz (1994) suggested that the lack of effects for verbal persuasion in some of the research may also have been due to confounds with actual performance. All of the studies used multiple performance trials; thus participants may have formed perceptions on the basis of their past performances. The effect of past performances on efficacy would have overpowered much of the influence that these other sources had on efficacy beliefs.

Bandura (1997) noted that altering efficacy beliefs by providing bogus feedback is an effective way to test the theoretical propositions regarding efficacy beliefs. However, he recommends against using it to build efficacy beliefs and suggests the use of other methods that genuinely cultivate both skills and a robust sense of efficacy. More specifically, he considers performance gains to be more achievable when people are convinced that they have what it takes to succeed. This self-efficacious thinking fosters effective use of skills.

Attributions There is more to the relationship between feedback and efficacy beliefs. The attributions that one makes regarding previous achievement behavior are often thought of as a source of self-persuasive information in the formulation of future efficacy expectations (as already discussed, self-efficacy beliefs also affect the attributions people make). According to Bandura (1997), the effects of attributions on performance are mediated by perceptions of self-efficacy. In his words, attributions are "conveyors of efficacy-relevant information that influence performance attainments mainly by altering people's beliefs in their efficacy" (Bandura, 1997, p. 125). Attributions of success to ability are accompanied by heightened beliefs of self-efficacy, which in turn predict subsequent performance attainments.

The studies that we have included in this section all deal with interventions in which participants were trained or oriented toward making certain attributions. It is for this reason that we consider attributions in this section on verbal persuasion.

The research on the relationship between attributions and self-efficacy is not as plentiful as one might expect. McAuley (1992a) pointed out that few investigations dealing with these relationships have been conducted in the area of motor tasks, and even fewer in competitive sport (see table A in Appendix). Rudisill (1988) investigated the effect of attributional instructions on self-efficacy beliefs. Participants who were oriented to see their performance on a balance task as due to internal, unstable, and controllable causes had higher self-efficacy and performed better than both those who were oriented to attribute their performance to internal, stable, and uncontrollable causes and those who were provided no instructions. Orbach, Singer, and Price (1999) showed that beginning tennis players who were instructed to attribute their failures in tennis ball returns to unstable and controllable causes developed higher self-efficacy than those instructed to attribute them to stable and uncontrollable causes. Kitsantas and Zimmerman (1998; and Zimmerman & Kitsantas, 1997) showed that participants who were taught to make strategy attributions for poor outcomes had greater self-efficacy than participants who attributed failure to a lack of ability or effort.

Effort Attributions and Conceptions of Ability   Compared to the effect of the other attributions, the effect that effort attributions have on efficacy beliefs is more complex and may vary under different conceptions of ability and differing views of the controllability of effort. As we mentioned in chapter 1, one's conception of ability as an acquirable skill versus an inherent aptitude also can influence self-efficacy beliefs. Bandura stated that high effort will be positively correlated with self-efficacy beliefs for people who consider ability to be acquirable by hard work, but will be negatively correlated with self-efficacy for those who regard ability as an inherent attribute. Jourden, Bandura, and Banfield (1991) first investigated the impact of conception of ability on the acquisition of motor skills. To manipulate conception of ability, participants were told that a rotary pursuit task was indicative of either natural ability (innate conception) or a skill that could be learned (acquired conception). Individuals assigned to the acquired-conception condition demonstrated self-efficacy gains, more positive self-reactions to performance and interest in the activity, and a higher level of skill acquisition than those in the innate-conception condition.

Similar results were obtained by Lirgg, George, Chase, and Ferguson (1996), who also manipulated conception of ability by telling participants that tasks either were dependent on natural ability or could be learned with practice. The study used two tasks that participants had identified as more appropriate either for males or for females (i.e., baton twirling and kung fu). Lirgg and colleagues found that, for females, both the gender appropriateness of the task and the conception of ability had a significant influence on efficacy beliefs. Females were more efficacious than males on the "feminine" task; and when the task was gender appropriate, self-efficacy levels did not differ between the innate-conception and acquired-conception condition. On the "masculine" task, however, females were less efficacious than males, and those in the innate-conception group were less efficacious than those in the acquired-conception condition. The males were equally efficacious on the feminine and masculine tasks, and the conception of ability did not affect their self-efficacy levels. More recently, Solmon, Lee, Belcher, Harrison, and Wells (2003) did a similar study testing for differences in confidence in the ability to learn hockey skills. Male and female participants were divided into three groups: an "innate-conception-ability" group, an "acquired-but-ability-helps" group, and an "acquired-ability" group. Results showed that individuals with an acquired-ability conception had higher levels of confidence than those in the other two groups.

Assigned Goals   Assigning goals and setting goals have been very popular areas of inquiry in sport psychology. We include this section here because the people who do the goal assigning are, in essence, engaging in a form of verbal persuasion. There is little doubt that goal setting works. In their meta-analytic review of goal setting in sport, Kyllo and Landers (1995) summarized the results of 36 studies showing the effectiveness of this technique. Burton, Naylor, and Holliday's (2001) review, focusing only on published research, included 67 goal-setting publications in sport, 56 of which were empirical investigations. Forty-four of the studies, or 78.6%, demonstrated moderate or strong goal-setting effects.

According to Bandura (1997), the goals people set result from their self-efficacy beliefs, not the other way around. We have already covered how self-efficacy beliefs influence goal setting. However, we also discuss goal setting here because of Bandura's belief that goals that are assigned by others can be a source of influence on self-efficacy beliefs when they convey information about the assigner's belief in the performer's abilities. By assigning challenging goals—especially for novices—coaches, teachers, and parents convey their belief that the athlete is capable of attaining that level of performance. Elston and Martin Ginis (2004) conducted an acute controlled experiment examining the effect of self-set versus assigned goals on exercisers' self-efficacy for an unfamiliar task (i.e., grip strength). Participants were randomly assigned to the self-set or assigned-goal group. In the assigned-goal condition, participants were assigned a moderately difficult goal by a fitness expert. Elston and Martin Ginis reasoned that when the fitness expert conveyed the goal to the exerciser, this would instill goal acceptance and confidence in the exerciser by creating the belief "if an expert thinks I can do it, then I must be able to do it" (p. 503). The results showed that participants in the assigned-goal condition reported significantly higher task efficacy than those in the self-set condition. The authors concluded that goals assigned by authority figures can increase self-efficacy.

According to Bandura (1986b, 1997), coaches must do more than convey positive appraisals to build their athletes' self-efficacy. In order to be informative and motivational, they must provide feedback in relation to defined performance standards or goals (Bandura, 1986b). In addition, for athletes who are in the beginning stages of skill acquisition, Bandura (1997) notes that goals help build a sense of efficacy by providing markers for gauging skill development. Goal setting has often been considered a key contextual influence on self-efficacy beliefs. As described in chapter 1, the key to this relationship has to do with a process of cognitive comparison of perceived performance to an adopted personal standard. To Locke and Latham (1990), evaluation is the most critical step in the goal-setting process because only when athletes evaluate goals do the motivational and self-efficacy benefits of goal setting become evident. The evaluation process involves a comparison of current performance with the original goal. Bandura (1986b) considers short-term goals the most effective because they provide more frequent evaluation of success; this stimulates the development of self-efficacy beliefs when goals are attained and stimulates motivation, regardless of the outcome, thereby preventing procrastination and premature discouragement.

To date, the most comprehensive program of research on how goal setting affects self-efficacy beliefs was conducted by Zimmerman and his colleagues. Although the primary purpose of these studies was to examine goal setting as a self-regulated learning strategy, the studies are described here because they yielded results on the goal-setting–self-efficacy relationship. This series of studies (Zimmerman & Kitsantas, 1996, 1997; Kitsantas & Zimmerman, 1998) focused on the effects of the types of goals assigned to participants. Three main types of goals have been identified in sport psychology research (Moran, 2004). Outcome goals (not to be confused with outcome expectancies, see chapter 1) are objective targets such as winning a competition, defeating an opponent, or achieving a desired finishing position (e.g., placing in the top three). Achieving this type of goal is considered to depend heavily on the ability and performance of one's opponents or competitors. An athlete could, for example, set a personal best goal but still lose a match (and therefore fail to achieve that goal). Performance goals, on the other hand, designate the attainment of a personal standard of competence with regard to such aspects as technique, effort, time, distance, or height. Unlike outcome goals, performance goals are considered to be under the control of the athlete. For example, a tennis player could set as her performance goal the task of making a certain percentage of her first and second serves. Regardless of how her opponent plays, she has the potential to achieve her goal. The third type of goal is a process goal. These goals are considered to be behavioral strategies by which an athlete executes a particular skill. For example, a process goal for a figure skater might be to keep her shoulder in while executing a jump.

The Zimmerman studies compared process goals (defined as methods and strategies that can help a person master a particular task) and product goals (defined as goals that specify the outcomes of learning efforts). In their first study, Zimmerman and Kitsantas (1996) randomly assigned high school girls to one of four experimental conditions (process or product goal and self-monitored or not) or a no-practice control group. The task was dart throwing. In the product goal condition, girls were told to try to attain the highest score they could. Those who were in the product goal condition with self-recording were instructed to also write down their scores after each block of practice trials. Girls in the process goal condition were told that in order to do well they should concentrate on properly executing the sighting, throwing, and follow-through steps for every dart throw they attempted. Those who self-recorded in this condition wrote down the steps they had missed at the end of each block of practice trials. The results showed that the group who received the process goal and who self-recorded were the most self-efficacious, had the best performances, were the most satisfied, and had the most intrinsic interest in the activity. The lowest scores on all dependent variables were obtained by the product goal group that did not self record. Zimmerman and Kitsantas reasoned that process goals are more effective in raising efficacy beliefs because they include strategies needed to keep learners focused on key facets that are essential to success, keep track of progress, and evaluate their competence.

In their second study, Zimmerman and Kitsantas (1997) added two more types of goals (coupled with self-recording or not; the result was eight experimental conditions). The four types of goals were process, outcome, transformed, and shifting. The goal-setting intervention was applied during the independent physical practice phase of skill learning (i.e., after initial skill training, which included modeling and imitation). The process and product goal groups were the same as the ones in Zimmerman and Kitsantas' 1996 study. In the transformed goal condition, one of the new goal-setting groups, participants were told that they should determine where the dart struck the target. For instance, if the dart hit to the right or the left of the bull's-eye, they should concentrate on keeping their arm vertical during the next throw. This goal-setting procedure converted throwing outcomes into strategic process adjustments. The girls in the shifting-goal condition were instructed that to do well they should concentrate first on properly executing the final two steps (i.e., throwing and following through) in every throw they attempted and that after achieving automaticity (i.e., after they had thrown three sets of three darts without missing a strategic step), they should shift their goal to trying to attain the highest score.

The results showed that the shifting-goal group had the best performances and highest self-efficacy scores, followed by the transformed goal, process goal, and product goal groups (see figure 3.4). In addition, the scores for each of the goal groups were higher with self-recording compared to no self-recording. Interestingly, when goal setting was converted to a metric variable by ranking of the conditions according to their effectiveness (i.e., 0 = *control group*, 1 = *outcome goal*, 2 = *process goal*, 3 = *transformed goal*, 4 = *shifting goal*), the correlation between goal setting and self-efficacy was .68. The results from this study show that learners need to focus initially on performance processes during practice time instead of outcome or product goals. However, after fundamental processes are mastered, students can benefit from shifting their goals to outcomes. In this order, outcome goals then provide the ultimate criterion by which process attainments can be measured and as such they motivate learners to continue their quest toward higher levels of personal mastery.

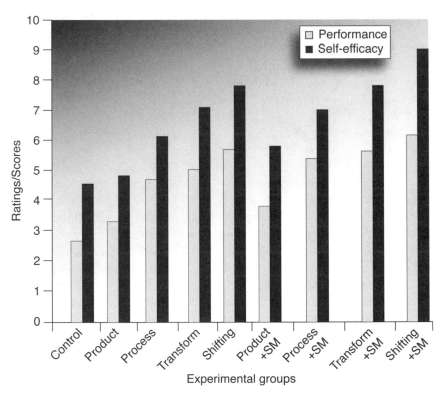

Figure 3.4 Effects of types of goals and self-monitoring on performance and self-efficacy beliefs from Zimmerman and Kitsantas (1997). *Note:* Performance scores range from 0 to 7; self-efficacy scores range from 1 to 10.

Reprinted, by permission, from B.J. Zimmerman and A. Kitsantas, 1997, "Developmental phases in self-regulation: Shifting from process goals to outcome goals," *Journal of Educational Psychology* 89: 29-36.

In a third study, Kitsantas and Zimmerman (1998) again showed the superiority of shifting practice goals during learning compared to unchanged or fixed goals. Compared to their previous studies, in this study performance strategies were added as another independent variable, and the types of goals used were different. Thus, the treatment conditions were based on the type of self-regulatory instructions—either strategy (analytic or imaginal), goal (fixed or dynamic cue), or self-evaluation (present or absent). Those in the fixed-goal condition were instructed to focus exclusively on a single cue, the bull's eye, and told to just throw the dart. Those in the dynamic-goal group were instructed to focus on verticality and follow-through components of the throwing process that were not properly performed during the previous block of trials. Central to our focus on goal setting and self-efficacy, the results extended these authors' previous research by showing that the dynamic process goals designed to help the learners analyze and focus on erroneous response components increased self-efficacy (and performance) more than the unchanging attentional goals.

Overall, the results of Zimmerman's program of research show that the types of goals used by participants influence their self-efficacy beliefs. Thus, these studies show support for assigned goals as a source of self-efficacy. Moreover, the results highlight the differential effectiveness of the types of goals during the various stages of the learning process. Zimmerman proposed a developmental sequence of skill mastery in which process goals precede product or outcome goals. He stated that process goals are more effective as learners begin to practice on their own, whereas product goals assist learners later when they are adapting their routinized performance skills to dynamic naturalistic conditions.

Self-Talk   Self-talk is another form of verbal persuasion. Self-talk has been defined as a dialogue in which an individual interprets feelings and perceptions, regulates and changes evaluations and convictions, and gives him- or herself instructions and reinforcement (Hackfort & Schwenkmezger, 1993). Throughout practices and competitions, athletes often engage in some form of self-talk, although its frequency and content vary from person to person and situation to situation. In their descriptive study on the use of self-talk in sport, Hardy, Gammage, and Hall (2001) showed that athletes engaged in sport-related self-talk outside of practice as well as before, during, and after both practices and competitions, but used it the most during competitions. Self-talk is useful because it serves many functions. For example, Hardy and colleagues (2001) identified 17 cognitive and motivational functions of self-talk; building self-efficacy was included as one of these functions.

The bulk of the research conducted in sport has focused primarily on the effect that positive and negative self-talk have on performance. However, the actual number of research studies is surprisingly low given the number of times self-talk has been suggested as an intervention technique for enhancing self-efficacy. Weinberg (1985) failed to find an interaction between self-efficacy and positive self-talk on endurance performance; however, Hanton and Jones (1999) found that a multimodal intervention strategy that included self-talk led to increases in confidence levels. Lohasz and Leith (1997) showed that male varsity athletes who used a mental preparation strategy consisting of positive self-talk performed better on a complex response timing task than an attentional focus group, and Thelwell and Greenlees (2003) provided qualitative evidence that the use of self-talk aided the confidence of triathletes. Most recently, Hardy, Hall, Gibbs, and Greenslade (2005) found that self-talk was moderately and positively associated with self-efficacy for a sit-up task, and that self-talk valence (i.e., rated from negative to positive) had a stronger relationship to self-efficacy than the directional interpretation of self-talk (i.e., rated from demotivating to motivating).

Pregame Speeches   The final form of verbal persuasion that is pertinent to sport is pregame speeches. Although Bandura (1997) considers verbal persuasion as a source of efficacy to be more than "fleeting pep talks" (p. 106), both coaches and their athletes believe that a coach's verbal boosts help to enhance self-efficacy (Vargas-Tonsing, Myers, & Feltz, 2004; Weinberg, Grove, & Jackson, 1992; Weinberg & Jackson, 1990). There also is evidence for the effectiveness of such talks on efficacy beliefs. Vargas-Tonsing and Bartholomew (2006) showed that athletes predicted larger margins of victory and also had stronger beliefs in their team's ability to win when listening to a speech with confidence-building phrases. These speeches also contained verbal persuasion in the form of emotional pleas reminding the athletes to play with pride and desire. In another study, Vargas-Tonsing (2004) found that the amount of perceived informational content in a coach's pregame speech predicted the athletes' efficacy beliefs to play well, play to the best of their ability, and contribute to the team's victory.

Physiological States

The most salient physiological sources of efficacy information in sport situations relate to athletes' levels of autonomic arousal, fitness, fatigue, and pain. Physiological information has been shown to be a more important source of efficacy information with respect to sport and physical activities than in the case of nonphysical tasks (e.g., Feltz & Riessinger, 1990). Few studies have addressed the perception of one's physiological state as a predictor of efficacy beliefs. Recall that in the study by Feltz and Mugno (1983; Feltz & Albrecht, 1986), perceived autonomic arousal was a stronger predictor of self-efficacy compared to actual autonomic arousal as measured by heart rate. Moreover, the results demonstrated that when participants were attempting a dive for the first time, their perceived physiological arousal was actually the most potent source of efficacy information compared to heart rate and past performance on similar tasks. Perceived physiological arousal did not predict diving performance, but rather influenced performance through its mediating effect on self-efficacy.

The effect of physiological states on efficacy beliefs probably has been studied more by exercise psychologists than by sport psychologists. For example, Rudolph and Butki (1998) showed that fatigue was negatively correlated with self-efficacy levels. In addition, participants who possessed high pre- and postexercise efficacy have been shown to report lower perceptions of effort and physical strain during exercise compared to less self-efficacious participants (Rudolph & McAuley, 1986).

Perceptions of physiological states have been combined with goal-setting strategies to increase efficacy beliefs in athletes. Galloway (2003) taught elite karate athletes how to use Borg's (1998) Ratings of Perceived Exertion Scale for their training sessions and to set goals for each training session as to which level of exertion they wished to achieve. Participants were then classified as overachievers, underachievers, and those who met their rating of perceived exertion (RPE) goals. The athletes who consistently met their goals over a 6-week period showed progressive increases in self-efficacy compared to the overachievers and underachievers, who started high but then decreased in their self-efficacy ratings over time.

Emotional States

Theoretically, positive affect—characterized by happiness, exhilaration, and tranquility—is more likely to enhance efficacy judgments than are negative affective states such as sadness, anxiety, and depression (Maddux & Meier, 1995). Furthermore, the more intense the mood is, the greater its impact on efficacy beliefs (Bandura, 1997). The research in sport has typically examined mood or emotional arousal (frequently referred to as anxiety).

Mood   There is some research to support the relationship between mood and efficacy beliefs. Kavanagh and Bower (1985) observed changes in self-efficacy across a wide range of task domains in response to happy and sad mood inductions and found that efficacy beliefs were raised in a positive affect state and lowered in a negative affect state. However, when more sport-specific tasks were used (i.e., handgrip strength and push-ups), they found that mood had no effect on self-efficacy for the handgrip strength task but did for push-ups; that is, happy participants thought they could perform more push-ups than sad participants (Kavanagh & Hausfeld, 1986). The difference in results was attributed to the type of task: Mood altered efficacy beliefs for the familiar task (i.e., push-ups) but not for the unfamiliar task (i.e., handgrip strength). However, push-ups may also have more of an effort component than handgrip strength, which is not easily influenced by effort.

Using the Profile of Mood States (POMS: McNair, Lorr, & Droppleman, 1971), Prapavessis and Grove (1994) found that competitive rifle shooters, divided into high- and low-confidence groups using the TSCI, were significantly different from each other on mood. The high trait sport confidence group demonstrated more vigor and esteem-related affect, as well as less tension and confusion, than the low trait sport confidence group prior to competition. For total mood disturbance scores, the high trait sport confidence participants exhibited less precompetitive mood disturbance than their lower scoring counterparts.

A more popular measure for assessing emotional states in sport has been the Positive and Negative Affective Schedule (PANAS: Watson et al., 1988). The PANAS consists of two 10-item subscales that assess positive affect (i.e., active, alert, attentive, determined, enthusiastic, excited, inspired, interested, proud, and strong) and negative affect (i.e., afraid, ashamed, distressed, guilty, hostile, irritable, jittery, nervous, scared, and upset). Respondents rate how they are feeling for each adjective on a 5-point Likert scale. Using the PANAS, Treasure and colleagues (1996) found a negative relationship between negative affect and self-efficacy but a positive one between positive affect and self-efficacy in wrestlers prior to a competition. These same relationships have been found in other sport studies (Martin, 2002) and with use of different measures of affect (Mack & Stephens, 2000).

Ryska (2002), however, showed a positive relationship between the negative affect scale and comparative self-efficacy (he used the State Sport Confidence Inventory but modified it to reflect tennis players' confidence in outperforming their opponent). He interpreted these findings as support for a relatively independent relationship between negative mood states and self-efficacy in that it is possible for people to experience precompetitive negative emotions yet remain confident in their specific abilities. He suggested examining the factors that influence the attributional process involving negative emotions and comparative efficacy. For example, athletes might attribute their precompetitive negative mood to low personal ability in comparison to their opponent, or, conversely, believe that they are less able than their opponent to compete successfully due to the negative feelings they experience prior to competition (i.e., attribute their performance to their mood). Of course, direction of influence, if any, cannot be determined by these types of correlational studies.

Emotional Arousal and Anxiety   In sport psychology, anxiety has typically been referred to as an unpleasant emotion, characterized by feelings of worry, apprehension, nervousness, or tension (or some combination of these) associated with physiological activation or arousal. Perceptions of anxiety are, therefore, cognitive appraisals of arousal (i.e., the physiological activation or autonomic reactivity that occurs in the body and varies along a continuum from deep sleep to extreme excitement). In other words, anxiety is an emotional label for a particular type of arousal experience (Hardy, Jones, & Gould,

1996) and, more specifically, refers to negatively interpreted arousal (Gould, Greenleaf, & Krane, 2002). It is important to note that although we are able to provide these differentiations between arousal and anxiety, in the past the terms were often used interchangeably in sport research. More recently, Mellalieu, Hanton, and Fletcher (2006) defined competitive anxiety in sport as a specific negative emotional response to the environmental demands associated primarily and directly with competitive performance.

Emotional arousal is often considered one of the more important emotional states, and its effects on self-efficacy are influenced by athletes' interpretations of it. According to Bandura (1997), whatever effects emotional arousal might have on performance are likely to depend more on how much attention is paid to the arousal and whether it is interpreted as being "psyched up" or being distressed. Furthermore, "to the extent that perceived arousal affects performance, it does so indirectly through the influence of efficacy beliefs" (p. 390).

In the past 10 years or so, there has been a dramatic increase in the number of research studies on athletes' perceptions of arousal or the symptoms of anxiety. We do not review these studies here, but rather emphasize a few key points that are relevant to our focus on anxiety and self-efficacy. For an excellent review of the competitive anxiety literature, readers are directed to Mellalieu, Hanton, and Fletcher (2006).

Most of the research on athletes' perceptions of arousal in sport has used the CSAI-2 (described in chapter 2), which asked athletes to rate the intensity of their anxiety responses. Intensity refers to the amount or level of the symptoms experienced by an athlete (Mellalieu, Hanton, & Fletcher, 2006). More recently, researchers have assessed athletes' directional interpretations of anxiety symptoms as well. Directional interpretation refers to the extent to which the intensity of the cognitive and perceived physiological symptoms is labeled as either positive or negative to performance on a facilitative-debilitative continuum (Mellalieu, Hanton, & Feltcher, 2006). For example, one item from the cognitive anxiety subscale of the CSAI-2 reads "I am concerned about this competition." Traditionally athletes would rate "how they feel right now" on a 4-point Likert scale ranging from *"not at all"* to *"very much so"* for intensity. When assessing the direction component, athletes would also rate the extent to which the experienced intensity of each item was either facilitative or debilitative to subsequent performance from –3 *("very debilitative")* to +3 *("very facilitative")* (Jones & Swain, 1992). A third component has also been assessed—that is, the frequency of cognitive intrusions. This refers to the amount of time (expressed as a percentage) thoughts and feelings about the competition occupy a performer's mind (Swain & Jones, 1993). Thus, when assessing anxiety in sport, researchers now consider not only the intensity of the response but also the frequency with which the symptoms are experienced and their directional interpretations.

An important finding from the direction line of anxiety research has shown that self-confidence is a key variable. In their review, Mellalieu, Hanton, and Fletcher (2006) concluded that one of the most robust findings to emerge from the direction (i.e., facilitative/debilitative) literature is that athletes who interpret their anxiety (arousal) as facilitative (often called facilitators) report greater levels of self-confidence than those who view their anxiety as debilitative (debilitators). In addition, the authors noted that several studies have shown strong correlations between the self-confidence and the direction subscales of the CSAI-2. According to Mellalieu, Hanton, and Fletcher, because of these results researchers are now studying whether self-confidence could act as a resiliency factor and protect against the debilitating effects of anxiety. For example, Hanton, Mellalieu, and Hall (2004) showed that self-confidence influenced the relationship between competitive anxiety intensity and symptom interpretation. In their qualitative study, they found that increases in cognitive symptoms accompanied by low self-confidence were perceived as outside of the performer's control and debilitating to performance, while the presence of high self-confidence and cognitive symptoms led to positive perceptions of control and facilitating interpretations. Similarly, Mellalieu, Neil, and Hanton (2006) found that self-confidence mediated the relationship between athletes' worry symptoms and subsequent directional interpretations. Mellalieu, Hanton, and Fletcher (2006) stated that compared to all other individual difference variables, self-confidence may be the most significant factor in discriminating how athletes manage and interpret stressful situations.

Imaginal States

As we described in chapter 1, Bandura (1986b, 1997) originally considered imaginal experiences as part of vicarious experiences (cognitive self-modeling). However, recent researchers have included this type of experience as a separate source (Maddux, 1995). Imagery refers to all those quasi-sensory or quasi-perceptual experiences that we are self-consciously aware of, that exist for us in the absence of those stimulus conditions known to produce their genuine sensory or perceptual counterparts, and that may be expected to have different consequences from their sensory or perceptual counterparts (Richardson, 1969, p. 2-3). Imaginal experience has been operationalized as

> an experience that mimics real experience. We can be aware of 'seeing' an image, feeling movements as an image, or experiencing an image of smell, tastes or sounds without actually experiencing the real thing. Sometimes people find that it helps to close their eyes. It differs from dreams in that we are awake and conscious when we form an image. (White & Hardy, 1998, p. 389)

Over the years, researchers have provided evidence that the use of imagery in sport can be a highly effective performance enhancement technique for athletes (for meta-analytic reviews see Driskell, Copper, & Moran, 1994; Feltz

& Landers, 1983). Over 200 studies have been conducted, providing a framework of how imagery works; what images are used; and when, where, and why imagery is used in sport (e.g., Hall, 2001; Martin, Moritz, & Hall, 1999; Munroe, Giacobbi, Hall, & Weinberg, 2000). Considered together, these studies provide overwhelming support for a relationship between imagery and self-efficacy.

As with performance, the relationship between self-efficacy and imagery has been studied from multiple perspectives. Self-efficacy has been used as both an independent variable and a dependent variable (see table B in the appendix). For example, in studies using it as an independent variable, athletes have been divided into high- and low-self-efficacy groups and have been shown to differ in their imagery use according to their self-efficacy level. With self-efficacy as a dependent variable, imagery interventions have been shown to increase self-efficacy for certain sport tasks. Similarly, self-efficacy beliefs have been used as a criterion variable in regression-type studies in which the predictive strength of different images has been examined to determine which best predict self-efficacy beliefs. This research has been extended to rehabilitation settings as well, where motivational, cognitive, and healing imagery has been shown to be related to task and coping self-efficacy, albeit to a lesser degree than in sport situations (e.g., Milne, Hall, & Forwell, 2005).

As just mentioned, Bandura (1997) refers to imagery as cognitive self-modeling (or cognitive enactment) and describes it as a form of modeling influence. Consistent with the research and theory on modeling, images, then, should include seeing oneself performing successfully. While research has shown that imaging oneself winning against an opponent can raise self-efficacy beliefs (Feltz & Riessinger, 1990), other images such as seeing oneself as confident, mentally tough, and focused have the same effect (Moritz, Hall, Martin, & Vadocz, 1996). In fact, athletes use a single image for multiple reasons, and a single image can have different meanings for different athletes (Short, Monsma, & Short, 2004). There appears to be less of a concern about what is imaged and more of an emphasis on the function of the image (Short, Ross-Stewart, & Monsma, 2006). Many images can be used for efficacy enhancement as long as they are not considered negative by the imager. Images of poor performances have a debilitative effect on subsequent performance (e.g., Short, Bruggeman, et al., 2002).

The factors that influence whether or not an athlete chooses to engage in imagery are largely unknown. We (Short, Tenute, & Feltz, 2005) showed that athletes' efficacy in their ability to use imagery affected their imagery use. More specifically, the more athletes were confident in their ability to use imagery, the more they used it; and efficacy in using imagery was found to mediate the relationship between imagery ability and imagery use. These results are consistent with Bandura's (1997) position that "those who have a low sense of efficacy to generate and control useful cognitive enactments will abandon the practice or use it haphazardly" (p. 377).

Compared to modeling, imagery was shown to be equally effective in raising efficacy beliefs (Soohoo et al., 2004). However, in that study, modeling led to better acquisition performance and was the preferred intervention for individuals first learning motor skills. Imagery strategies have also been shown to be less effective in raising self-efficacy beliefs compared to analytic strategies for girls learning how to throw darts (Kitsantas & Zimmerman, 1998). The results from these two studies suggest that imagery may be less effective for novices. This finding is actually consistent with Bandura's (1997) views on imagery. He stated that there is little value to using imagery in the early phase of learning before an adequate conception of the skilled activity has been formed; and he warned that without some prior experience in forming the conception of the skilled activity, the likelihood is high that many faulty habits will be imaged.

Research on Multiple Sources of Self-Efficacy

From a theoretical standpoint, Bandura (1977, 1986b, 1997) stated that the categories of efficacy information are not mutually exclusive in terms of the information they provide, although some are more influential than others. Personal performance accomplishments are likely to be most influential, while vicarious experience, verbal persuasion, and physiological and emotional states are generally seen as less reliable but still important sources of efficacy. The informational sources are often present together within particular performance contexts. Research on how people weigh and process the various sources to make judgments on different tasks, in different situations, and with respect to their individual skills is limited. However, researchers have queried athletes about the sources of their efficacy beliefs.

Feltz and Riessinger (1990) were the first researchers to inquire about people's sources of efficacy beliefs, as a part of their experimental study on the effect of imagery and performance feedback on self-efficacy beliefs and performance in a muscular endurance task. After making an efficacy judgment, participants were asked to state the basis for their judgment on an open-ended section of the questionnaire; they then competed against a very athletic-looking confederate. For self-efficacy, frequency results indicated that most participants (86%) used a form of past performance accomplishments as the basis for their beliefs. The second most popular category was physiological states (e.g., "I'm in poor shape right now"), which was followed by persuasion (e.g., "I told myself I could do it") and vicarious experiences (i.e., "my comparison to the other guys"). For comparative efficacy (i.e., the participants' certainty about whether they could beat their opponent), participants used past performance accomplishments the most, followed by vicarious experiences and physical states.

The sources used by athletes were investigated by Chase and colleagues (2003). More specifically, they tested whether the four sources of efficacy information originally suggested by Bandura (1986b) were selected by athletes for self-efficacy and collective efficacy, whether the athletes used more than one of these sources, and if there were patterns of sources among individual players or teams. Female basketball players from three teams were questioned about their sources prior to 12 games spread over the course of a season. The responses were coded as either past performance, persuasion, social comparison, or physiological/emotional states using a deductive method of analysis. An additional category, "outside sources," was also created to account for sources outside the athletic arena. Sources for self-efficacy were ranked as follows: past performance, physiological/emotional states, outside sources, social comparison, and persuasion. This same order of sources was evident for collective efficacy except that social comparison was third and outside sources was fourth. This finding, that self-efficacy was influenced more than collective efficacy by sources outside of basketball, shows that athletes view other events (i.e., personal life problems, relationships with friends, school demands) as influencing their self-efficacy beliefs but do not feel that these things affect their team's efficacy as much. Interestingly, although the analysis was not statistically significant, the results showed that the players used practice situations as a source of efficacy information more often than game situations. Also, negative past performances affected athletes who had high self-efficacy more than their low-self-efficacy counterparts. Additionally, the results showed that some players chose multiple sources for efficacy. In fact, approximately 25% of the responses included at least two sources, with one of these most often referring to past performances.

The influence of the different sources of efficacy information on self-efficacy beliefs was examined experimentally by Wise and Trunnell (2001). In their study, each experimental group received three sources of bench press efficacy information (performance accomplishment, model, verbal message) presented in a different sequence. Bench press efficacy was measured after each source of efficacy information was presented. Results indicated that performance accomplishment information led to significantly stronger bench press efficacy than did observation of a model, which in turn was more effective than hearing a verbal message. Performance accomplishment information also enhanced efficacy ratings even when it followed one or both of the other sources (i.e., showing an additive effect). The verbal persuasion message was the most effective in increasing efficacy scores when it followed performance accomplishment information.

Whether experimental or self-report methods are used to compare the strengths of multiple sources of efficacy information, results show consistently that past performance accomplishments are what athletes rely on most. These findings add support to Bandura's hypothesis that the most important and powerful source of self-efficacy for athletes is derived from their own past performance accomplishments (Bandura, 1977, 1986b, 1997).

Research on the Sources of Sport Confidence

As introduced in chapter 1, the most comprehensive examination of sources of efficacy unique to sport competition has been that of Vealey and her colleagues (1998). They conducted a four-phase research project utilizing over 500 athletes from a variety of sports to identify relevant sources of confidence for athletes and to develop a reliable and valid measure of the sources—the Sources of Sport Confidence Questionnaire (SSCQ). They identified nine sources of sport confidence for high school and intercollegiate athletes, which are described in table 3.1.

Beyond identifying the salient sources of confidence in sport, Vealey and colleagues (1998) examined which sources were most important for athletes. For individual-sport collegiate athletes, the top five sources were physical and mental preparation, social support, mastery, demonstration of ability, and physical self-presentation. Physical self-presentation and social support were more important sources of confidence for females than for males. For high school ath-

TABLE 3.1   Sources of Confidence Proposed by Vealey et al. (1998)

Source	Description ("confidence derived from . . .")
Mastery	Mastering or improving skills
Demonstration of ability	Showing off skills to others or demonstrating more ability than one's opponent
Physical/Mental preparation	Feeling physically and mentally prepared with an optimal focus for performance
Physical self-presentation	Perceptions of one's physical self (how one perceives one looks to others)
Social support	Perceiving support and encouragement from significant others in sport, such as coaches, family, and teammates
Vicarious experience	Watching others, such as teammates or friends, perform successfully
Coach's leadership	Believing coach is skilled in decision making and leadership
Environmental comfort	Feeling comfortable in a competitive environment
Situational favorableness	Feeling that the breaks of the situation are in one's favor

Reprinted, by permission, from R.S. Vealey et al., 1998, "Sources of sport-confidence: Conceptualization and instrument development," *Journal of Sport and Exercise Psychology* 20: 54-80.

letes, mastery, social support, physical/mental preparation, coach's leadership, and demonstration of ability were the top five sources of sport confidence.

Chase (1998) showed that the primary sources of efficacy information for children and adolescents were personal performance accomplishments and feedback from significant others. The 8- to 9-year-olds indicated subjective successful performances and significant others' praise and encouragement as most important to self-efficacy. The 10- to 12-year-olds stressed the importance of praise and encouragement from significant others such as family, coaches, and peers, in addition to practicing hard to improve on a skill. The oldest group in the study, the 13- to 14-year-olds, described significant others' praise and encouragement, emphasizing how the coach's evaluation was central to their confidence, followed by their self-appraisal of successful personal performances. These results were replicated by Magyar and Feltz (2003).

However, the SSCQ failed to hold up through confirmatory factor analysis for a sample of master-level athletes (Wilson et al., 2004). Thus, using a modified eight-factor structure, Wilson and colleagues found that physical/mental preparation and mastery were the highest-ranked sources among master-level athletes (i.e., over 35 years of age) and suggested that the SSCQ needs more psychometric work to be used with this type of population.

One last point regarding the sources of efficacy information concerns the importance of the sources during different stages of learning. In their chapter on self-efficacy and expertise, Beilock and Feltz (2006) raised the point that self-regulatory activities, such as those used in forming efficacy beliefs, may actually affect novices and experts in different ways. Processing information from the various sources may detract from the unskilled performances of novices, yet enhance skill execution at later stages of learning and higher levels of skill expertise. The reason is that the process of forming efficacy beliefs is thought to require attention, and it may "use up" the attentional capacity for successful initiation and execution of skills for novices. For experts, skill performance should be automated, so they may have the attention "left over" to devote to storing information about their previous past performance. Research supports the idea that novices and experts differ in their memories of performance outcomes (Backman & Molander, 1986; McPherson, 2000). Beilock and Feltz suggested that the increased task proficiency and experience that experts have is accompanied by an increased ability to assess and recollect past performances, enabling them to form more accurate efficacy beliefs. Thus, it may be that self-efficacy is a better predictor of performance as skill expertise increases. However, these authors also warn that because expert performance is thought to be automated in a fashion that does not require conscious attentional control, experts may have difficulty introspecting on some aspects of performance, which may affect how they form their self-efficacy beliefs. This "expertise-induced amnesia" was empirically shown by Beilock and Carr (2001), but its effect on the processing of self-efficacy information has not been assessed.

Gender Differences

The last section of this chapter addresses gender differences in self-efficacy beliefs. In 1974, Maccoby and Jacklin published their book, *The Psychology of Sex Differences*. They were the first to suggest that the self-confidence of girls and women in achievement situations was lower than for boys and men. Included in the list of achievement situations was physical activity. Around the same time, Title IX identified lower sport participation rates for girls as well as the lack of sport opportunities for girls compared to boys. These two events provided the impetus for the study of gender differences in self-efficacy beliefs in sport. Nowadays, most researchers check for gender differences in self-efficacy beliefs as "preliminary analyses" before moving on to their main hypotheses. Reviewers and editors of popular sport psychology journals often demand that gender differences be checked for when self-efficacy is a variable of interest. Often when there are gender differences, either gender is included as an additional variable, or the subsequent analyses are conducted on males and females separately. Is gender so important as to warrant this attention?

Research on gender differences in self-efficacy beliefs has been both descriptive and explanatory. The earlier studies were conducted to find out if males were really more confident than females, and the later studies to see what situations gender differences were evident in. Most of this research was conducted in the early 1980s, and reviews of the literature appeared around 10 years later.

There have been several myths surrounding female self-confidence in sport. As identified by Lirgg and Feltz (1989) the myths are that females have lower self-confidence than males in all achievement settings, that all females have low confidence in perceived ability, that females have less confidence because their performances are inferior to those of males, and that females have a fear of success and are therefore less self-confident. Obviously the word "all" is the giveaway that these are myths.

As originally claimed by Lirgg and Feltz (1989), a search of the literature will quickly reveal a number of studies that, on the surface, support these myths. In her meta-analysis of 35 studies, Lirgg (1991) showed an average effect size of .40 favoring males in self-confidence on physical tasks. It is because of this finding that this meta-analysis is one of the most frequently cited journal articles when researchers need to show that males and females differ in self-efficacy in physical activity settings. However, the findings about gender in self-efficacy research are not that "clean." Males do not "always" have higher self-efficacy scores than females. Lenney (1977) was the first to put caveats on this finding. More specifically, she concluded that females would not display lower self-confidence than males when the task involved was "gender neutral," when they were given clear feedback about their performance, and when they were placed in noncompetitive (or noncomparative) situations.

The phrase "sex type" of the task refers to the "stereotyping" of certain sports as more masculine, more feminine, or gender neutral. Society views masculine-type tasks as those requiring strength, power, and competitiveness, and consequently many team sports receive a masculine label. Sex type of task and self-efficacy interact in such a way that self-efficacy beliefs tend to be higher when an activity is perceived to be gender appropriate than when the activity is perceived to be gender inappropriate. However, viewing activities as gender inappropriate generally seems to have a more detrimental effect on females than on males. For example, Lirgg and colleagues (1996) showed that females were more efficacious on feminine-type tasks than on masculine-type tasks, but the efficacy levels of males did not differ based on the type of task. Thus, it appears that the males assumed that if the task was appropriate for females, it must be easy enough that they could perform it too.

Sex type of the task was considered by Lirgg (1991) as a potential moderator in her meta-analysis. Her results showed that the more masculine a task, the greater the difference between males and females whereby females showed less confidence than males. For example, girls displayed lower confidence than boys in football, but they were higher in confidence in ballet (Sanguinetti, Lee, & Nelson, 1985). In swimming (considered a gender-neutral task), there were no gender differences. Similar results have been obtained by Clifton and Gill (1994). The interest in gender differences and sex type of task has persisted throughout the years. In a more recent study, Solmon and colleagues (2003) showed that males expressed more confidence in their ability to learn ice hockey than females, but that the females who perceived the activity to be gender neutral were more confident in their ability to learn ice hockey than females who believed that the activity was predominantly for males. What is interesting about this study is the strong evidence it offered to show that traditional gender-related boundaries for participation in sports viewed as masculine are being challenged and expanded upon. Several women in the study conveyed messages that gender should be irrelevant for sport participation. More women stood firm that the sport of ice hockey was masculine, but eased up when individual skills were considered (e.g., wrist shots). That is, individual skills were more likely to be viewed as appropriate for both sexes compared to the entire sport. It appears that sex type of the task needs to be considered further in self-efficacy studies. Chances are that the results of such studies may also be dependent upon geographical location. Solmon and colleagues conducted their study in the Southwest. If ice hockey were to be considered in hockey-obsessed states like North Dakota and Minnesota, there would likely be less sex typing of it as primarily for boys and men.

With respect to the competitive situation, recall Lenney's (1977) suggestion that gender differences would be seen according to the sport setting. More specifically, females are likely to display lower self-confidence than males when in competitive or comparative situations. The rationale for this statement involves socialization patterns. Men are socialized to be competitive at a very young age, and females often have less experience with competition. However, Lirgg's (1991) meta-analysis showed that the setting did not appear to play a major role in confidence differences between males and females in physical activity. The gender differences for tasks performed in competition versus those performed alone were small, even when only masculine tasks were considered. One point deserving mention here is that in some cases sport tends to be equated with competition. With respect to socialization patterns for males and females, while it may be true that females have fewer experiences with competitive sports, sport is not the only setting where competition occurs. Competition exists in settings such as acting and drama (e.g., competing for parts in a play) and math classes (e.g., multiplication table challenges like "Champ Hat"). As pointed out by Lirgg and Feltz (1989), competition alone will not increase confidence for females, and in fact, placing any individual with low confidence in a competitive situation will probably do more harm than good.

Even though females do not always show lower efficacy scores than males, the bottom line is that gender differences in self-efficacy research in sport are a common finding. One explanation is that females have less confidence than males because their performances are inferior to those of males; if females perform at a lower level than males, it makes sense that their self-efficacy ratings are also lower. As pointed out by Lirgg and Feltz (1989), though, there are problems with this line of reasoning. First, performances by males are not always better, and, second, the relationship between efficacy and performance is not perfect. Even the best athletes sometimes have doubts.

Another explanation for gender differences in self-efficacy has to do with the interaction between the task demands and perceptions of self-efficacy. According to Lirgg (1991), one reason suggested for gender differences in self-efficacy may be that males are boastful and overestimate their performances (i.e., think they will do better than they do), making it appear that females have lower self-efficacy. On a similar note, Bandura (1986b) suggested that males may have high self-efficacy ratings because they underestimate the demands of the task (i.e., they think a task is easier than it really is). Even on tasks they have never performed before, males have been shown to have unrealistically high confidence beliefs compared to females (Feltz, 1988a). Corbin, Landers, Feltz, and Senior (1983) tested this hypothesis and found no evidence for it, suggesting that the differences may be due instead to female modesty (i.e., females think they will do worse than they do). When making comparisons to males, females may expect males to perform better in certain tasks and devalue their confidence in their own abilities, thereby reporting lower self-efficacy scores on questionnaires (Bandura, 1986b). One way to check whether females devalue their abilities or males overestimate theirs is to correlate self-efficacy ratings with actual performance measures separately for males and females (Lirgg, 1991). This statistical procedure will highlight the accuracy of the efficacy ratings.

In this chapter, we reviewed the relevant research on self-efficacy and its influence on performance, motivational behavior, goals, thought patterns, and anxiety. The research shows that when self-efficacy is measured and tested within the confines of the theory, it is consistently and positively related to athletic performance, motivational behavior, and other achievement-related cognitions and affect. We also provided a review of research on the sources of efficacy information pertinent to athletic performance. In support of Bandura's theory, past performance accomplishments or mastery experiences are clearly the strongest source of efficacy information for judging one's capability in the athletic realm. Lastly, we provided a review of the research on gender differences in self-efficacy or self-confidence in athletic functioning and pointed to some myths and explanations regarding these differences. The research discussed in this chapter focuses on self-efficacy and athletic functioning at the individual athlete level. In the next chapter, we focus on these variables within teams.

Efficacy Beliefs
of Teams

> "Confidence shared is better than confidence only in yourself."
>
> *Mike Krzyzewski, coach, Duke University Blue Devils men's basketball team*

Although the study of efficacy in sport has traditionally been understood and studied with respect to the individual athlete, it is not exclusively an individual attribute. Much of sport performance, as well as performance in other contexts, occurs within teams. Consider the example of a baseball team in the World Series—a collection of 25 players attempting to win four of seven games against the same team in the span of 2 weeks. Knowing that confidence can have a tremendous impact on performance, and vice versa, it is not hard to appreciate the notion of *collective* efficacy. How confident the team is should be a significant and dynamic issue. Consider the following situations. What if the team's star player does not feel confident batting against the opposing pitching staff? Would that affect the confidence the rest of the team has in winning the series? What if one team was clearly the best team in the league during the regular season but had a losing record against their opponents in this series—what would we expect their confidence to be?

In this chapter we discuss the notion of collective efficacy, or team confidence, in sport. These two terms are used interchangeably throughout this and subsequent chapters, though we predominantly use "collective efficacy" in discussing research as that is the term used in the research literature. In this first section of the chapter, after discussing the salience of teams in sport, we explore the conceptual nature of collective efficacy. This includes the definitions, operational definitions, and conceptual models. The next section deals with the empirical research on collective efficacy, including studies on the sources of collective efficacy, the collective efficacy and performance relationship, and the interrelations between collective efficacy and other constructs.

The Nature of Teams

In order to discuss the prevalence of teams in sports and sport participation, we must first clarify what we mean by "team." A sport team has been defined as

> a collection of two or more individuals who possess a common identity, have common goals, and objectives, share a common fate, *exhibit structured patterns of interaction and modes of communication* [italics added], hold common perceptions about group structure, are personally and instrumentally interdependent, reciprocate interpersonal attraction, and consider themselves to be a group. (Carron, Hausenblas, & Eys, 2005, p. 13)

Although a complete discussion of the nature of teams in sport would be a book unto itself, several points must be clarified before our discussion of the efficacy of sport teams. Most of the characteristics of sport teams are fairly straightforward. Teams obviously consist of two or more individuals, and the fact that teams have *structured modes of communication* (e.g., use of nicknames) and *structured patterns of interaction* (e.g., a recognized captain and coach) is relatively salient. However, some less obvious features of a team are relevant when one is analyzing collective efficacy.

In particular, Carron and colleagues (2005) state that teams "are personally and instrumentally interdependent" (p. 13). What this means is that teammates depend on each other for both social and task-oriented resources. For instance, it would be typical of athletes in a team sport to interact with and influence each other for social reasons (e.g., develop friendships) as well as more instrumental reasons (e.g., offer tips about performance). However, whereas these processes are understood to operate in all sport teams to varying degrees, how the team is constructed can affect the nature of this interdependence.

For example, consider a basketball team and a track and field team. Both are groups of more than two people with shared goals and structured ways of interacting to achieve those goals, but they are two different types of teams. In performance (and by extension, in training), a basketball team is characterized by very dynamic and fluid interaction. A typical play might see the center on one team defending the other team's center so as to force a low-percentage shot. This missed shot could be rebounded by the forward, who could pass to the point guard. This player would be responsible for bringing the ball up the court and spotting another teammate for the open shot. Now, as one considers a track and field team, the dynamics change. Team performance is determined by the individual achievement of each athlete. A hurdler may earn 10 points for the team by winning an event, while a javelin thrower may earn another 6 points by finishing second in an event. The team would earn a total of 16 points from these two individual accomplishments. Therefore, in some teams, the team product is the composite addition, as opposed to the dynamic interaction, of teammates' contributions. Regardless of the degree of interdependence, both types of teams are characterized by some interdependence and are influenced by the performance of their members, and as such fulfill the criteria for being a team. Figure 4.1 summarizes the degree of interdependence in common team sports.

As we discuss later, the concept of interdependence is an important distinction when one is considering collective efficacy. How does it differ to have confidence in your team when you can interact with your teammates actively to produce performance compared to when you must work on your contribution individually? And how would this affect other behavioral constructs, such as cohesion or satisfaction? These and other topics are discussed later in the chapter.

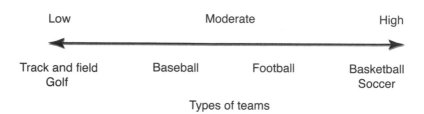

Figure 4.1 Interdependence in team sports.

Teams are an undeniably salient aspect of sport performance. The 2000 United States census summarized participation in high school athletic programs and National Collegiate Athletic Association (NCAA) sports. The most popular high school sports for males were football, basketball, track and field, baseball, soccer, and wrestling. For females, they were basketball, track and field, volleyball, softball, soccer, and tennis. At the university level, the most popular sports for males to participate in were football, baseball, track (indoor and outdoor), and soccer, whereas for females they were track (outdoor), soccer, basketball, track (indoor), and softball. All of these are team sports according to Carron and colleagues' (2005) definition in that the athletes compete as part of a team.

Team sports are important for the sport spectator as well as the sport participant. In 2004, Harris Interactive, a global research firm, conducted a poll of 2,555 adults in the United States (Harris Poll #77, 2004). In response to the question, "if you had to choose, which one of these [sports] would be your favorite," the eight most popular sports (in order) were identified as follows:

- Professional football (30%)
- Baseball (15%)
- College football (11%)
- Men's professional basketball (7%)
- Auto racing (7%)
- Men's golf (4%)
- Hockey (4%)
- Men's soccer (3%)

Of these, only auto racing and golf are not explicitly team sports, and both still contain team elements (i.e., some racing circuits have racing teams, and at least part of the golf season includes team tournaments such as the Ryder Cup). Thus, in terms of participation and spectatorship, sports in North

America are overwhelmingly played as team sports. Therefore it is relevant, if not necessary, to inquire into the notion of confidence in the conjoint ability of members within these teams.

Collective Efficacy

Even the most casual of sport fans is familiar with the notion of a team that is "great on paper" but woefully underperforms. In fact, such teams are so plentiful that, even at the highest levels of competition, examples are surprisingly easy to come by. One notable example is the U.S. men's basketball team in the 2002 world championship. Despite a team consisting of National Basketball Association (NBA) all-stars, the team finished in sixth place in the tournament, held in Indianapolis. Subsequently, the team missed an automatic qualification for the 2004 Olympics, in which the United States has won gold only since professionals were allowed (the team eventually qualified and finished with a disappointing silver medal). Another example is the Washington Redskins of the National Football League (NFL), who over the past five years have set records for team payroll three times, as well as twice signing head coaches to record contracts, and during that time did not make the playoffs once.

Alternatively, some teams perform quite successfully despite the apparent lack of any superstar players. For example, in a recent three-year period, the Detroit Pistons of the NBA reached the finals twice (winning once) and, in the third year, had the best regular-season record in the league. Interestingly, this dominating team success was achieved despite (or, one could argue, because of) a lack of individual success. In fact, during those three seasons, the highest a team player ranked in league scoring was 23rd. There clearly is some truth to the notion that a team is more than a collection of athletes.

The prevalence of underachieving and overachieving teams exemplifies the notion that the whole is greater (but not necessarily better) than the sum of its parts. A team cannot be understood as just the sum total of its individual components. This is reflected in the definition of sport teams, which explicitly includes such factors as interdependence. Such group-level dynamics can do much to enhance or diminish the individual attributes of team members. It was this notion that caused Bandura (2000) to speculate on the nature and importance of confidence of the collective, not the individual. As he stated, "it is not uncommon for groups with members who are talented individually to perform poorly collectively because the members cannot work well together as a unit. Therefore, perceived collective efficacy is not simply the sum of the efficacy beliefs of individual members. Rather, it is an emergent group-level property" (p. 76). However, the extension of efficacy to the group level was not a discrete event, and the process of gradually recognizing, conceptualizing, and defining collective efficacy had empirical ramifications.

Defining Collective Efficacy

The process began when Bandura (1982) introduced the term "collective efficacy." Although he did not define the term precisely, he did note that because much performance occurs at the group level, there should be a group equivalent to self-efficacy. This "collective efficacy" would refer to judgments group members make about the group's capabilities to organize and execute successful group actions. This extension from the self to the collective was deemed important because it would affect what people do as a group and how long they persist in these teams.

In 1986, Bandura referred to collective efficacy as "perceptions of the groups' efficacy to effect change" (1986b, p. 451). But, it was not until 1997 that Bandura defined collective efficacy as "a group's shared belief in its conjoint capabilities to organize and execute the courses of action required to produce given levels of attainment" (p. 477). However, by this time, several studies had been conducted (mostly on collective efficacy and performance), and other researchers had offered their own definitions and measurement. One particularly common alternative definition for collective efficacy was offered by Zaccaro, Blair, Peterson, and Zazanis (1995), who stated that collective efficacy refers to "a sense of collective competence shared among individuals when allocating, coordinating, and integrating their resources in a successful concerted response to specific situational demands" (p. 309).

Both definitions stress that the perception of collective efficacy is shared among teammates. This key conceptual point has practical ramifications for research. Analysis of the data must acknowledge that individual perceptions are nested within teams; the observations of any one athlete cannot be considered independently of those of his or her teammates. Most statistical procedures assume that the individual observations are independent of one another. For certain attributes in sport psychology, it can be assumed that they are independent between people (e.g., personality traits); however, this is not the case for collective efficacy.

The most appropriate type of analysis for such data is multiple-level modeling (MLM). As indicated in chapter 2, this procedure deals with research questions between independent and dependent variables when the data are organized in levels. For the case of collective efficacy, a typical research question would deal with perceptions at the individual level but outcomes at the team level. For such a research question, the data would include several teams. This issue of proper level of analysis of group-referent perceptions is not unique to collective efficacy. Research on cohesion, which has a longer history within sport psychology, has struggled with this as well. Although most of the research has been done before such complicated models as MLM emerged, recent studies have incorporated multiple-level designs. For example, Carron, Bray, and Eys (2002) and Spink, Nickel, Wilson, and Odnokon (2005) used such procedures to support that cohesiveness is a shared perception and is related to team performance and satisfaction, respectively. By utilizing the appropriate statistical analysis, researchers provide more valid support for the conceptual relationships of cohesion. Such research on a similar group perception offers much promise for similar research and conclusions on collective efficacy.

Although Bandura's (1986b, 1997) and Zaccaro and colleagues' (1995) definitions are the most popular ones for collective efficacy in the published literature, they are not the only ones. Table 4.1 highlights the other definitions that have been published.

In a few studies, the researcher(s) developed their own definition of collective efficacy (e.g., Lichacz & Partington, 1996; Spink, 1990a, 1990b) and developed corresponding measurements. However the bulk of research in the field has followed the conceptualizations of either Bandura (1997) or Zaccaro and colleagues (1995). In all but one of the 22 studies listed in table 4.1, collective efficacy was defined in a way that is consistent with Bandura's (1986b, 1997) definitions. Only one study (Paskevich, Brawley, Dorsch, & Widmeyer, 1999) adopted a different definition, that of Zaccaro and colleagues. We briefly discuss the similarities and differences between these two definitions. Although the views are generally similar, there are some important and fundamental differences.

TABLE 4.1 *Definitions of Collective Efficacy*

Source	Definition
BENCHMARK DEFINITIONS	
Bandura, 1986b	Judgments that people make about a group's level of competency
Bandura, 1997	Group's shared belief in its conjoint capability to organize and execute the courses of action required to produce given levels of attainment
Zaccaro et al., 1995	A sense of collective competence shared among members when allocating, coordinating, and integrating their resources as a successful, concerted response to specific situational demands
SPORT RESEARCH DEFINITIONS	
Bray, 2004	Direct quote from Bandura (1997)
Bray & Widmeyer, 2000	"Team members' perceptions of the team's shared confidence in the team's abilities" (p. 3) Cited Bandura (1997) and Zaccaro et al. (1995)
Feltz & Lirgg, 1998	"Group's beliefs in their conjoint capabilities to produce given levels of attainments" (p. 557) Cited Bandura (1986b, 1997)

(continued)

TABLE 4.1 *(continued)*

Source	Definition
	SPORT RESEARCH DEFINITIONS
Greenlees, Graydon, & Maynard, 1999	"Group's shared belief—which emerges from an aggregation of individual group members' perceptions of the group's capabilities—in its ability to achieve a desired goal" (p. 151) Cited Bandura (1982, 1986b, 1997)
Greenlees, Nunn, et al., 1999	"Group's shared belief—which emerges from an aggregation of individual group member's perceptions of the group's capabilities—to succeed in a given task" (p. 431) Cited Bandura (1986b, 1997)
Greenlees et al., 2000	"Group's shared belief, emerging from an aggregation of the perceptions of individual group members of the group's capabilities, in its ability to attain a desired outcome" (p. 451) Cited Bandura (1982, 1986b, 1997)
Hodges & Carron, 1992	Defined as "efficacy manifested by the collective (extension of self-efficacy)" (p. 49) Cited Bandura (1982)
Kozub & McDonnell, 2000	"Involves the individual's perceptions regarding the group's performance capabilities" (p. 121) Cited Bandura (1986b, 1997)
Lichacz & Partington, 1996	"Refers to the judgment by group members of the group's capabilities to organize and execute courses of action required to attain designated types of performance" (p. 148) Cited Bandura (1982, 1986b)
Maclean & Sullivan, 2003	Direct quote from Bandura (1997)
Magyar et al., 2004	Direct quote from Bandura (1997)
Moritz, 1998	Direct quote from Bandura (1997)
Paskevich et al., 1999	Direct quote from Zaccaro et al. (1995)
Myers, Feltz, & Short, 2004	Direct quote from Bandura (1997)
Myers, Payment, & Feltz, 2004	Direct quote from Bandura (1997)
Short, Apostal, et al., 2002	Direct quote from Bandura (1997)
Short, Sullivan, & Feltz, 2005	Direct quote from Bandura (1997)
Spink, 1990a	"Reflects the fact that groups often have collective expectations for success" (p. 302) Cited Bandura (1982)
Spink, 1990b	"Terms used reflect the fact that groups often have collective expectations for success" (p. 381) Cited Bandura (1982, 1986b)
Watson et al., 2001	Direct quote from Bandura (1997)

Conceptual Similarities

The first similarity between Bandura's definition of collective efficacy and that of Zaccaro and colleagues (1995) is that both are rooted in Bandura's (1977) notion of self-efficacy as a situationally specific confidence. Paskevich and colleagues (1999) went so far as to state that this was one of the four essential characteristics of Zaccaro and colleagues' conceptualization. Like Bandura, Zaccaro and colleagues stress the importance of the interdependence of team members, acknowledging that the greater the interdependence, the greater the distinction between collective efficacy and aggregated self-efficacy. Thus, both camps agree that a team with an additive task, such as a track and field team, may possess a collective efficacy that does not differ from the composite of the self-efficacy of its members. And there is further agreement that in an interactive sport such as soccer, this would be more unlikely. A second similarity is that, like Bandura, Zaccaro and colleagues note that specificity of group tasks must be taken into account in discussions of collective efficacy. Because individual athletes act on teams in order to accomplish goals that cannot be met as individuals, we must acknowledge that these goals are part of how one determines perception of confidence (whether individual or group).

A third similarity is that both Bandura (1997) and Zaccaro and colleagues (1995) define collective efficacy as a *shared* belief regarding the collective competence of the group. Although unanimity of belief is rare, both camps believe that any analysis of collective efficacy should ensure greater variation between groups than between members within any one team. Thus any measurement of collective efficacy must address how *shared* this attribute is between teammates. Chapter 2 describes how within-team interrater agreement (e.g., r_{wg}; James, Demaree, & Wolfe, 1984) could be used to determine the consensus within a team (Moritz & Watson, 1998; Myers & Feltz, 2007). In this way, the researcher would be able to statistically ascertain if the individual responses of team members are consistent enough to be considered a team perception. However, we also note in chapter 2 that multilevel software programs do not require that a certain consensus estimate exist before computing a weighted average of the individual-level responses. And, if the degree of consensus is not high, this within-team variance could be partitioned and explained in multilevel modeling (Moritz & Watson, 1998). The relationship between consensus of collective efficacy and other variables (e.g., cohesion, performance, team satisfaction) may be an important research question in itself.

Conceptual Distinctions

The major distinction between Bandura's (1997) and Zaccaro and colleagues' conceptualizations has to do with the stress that the latter place on the team's belief in "allocating, coordinating, and integrating their resources." As described in chapter 2, Zaccaro and his colleagues emphasize the coordination, interaction, and integration components of collective efficacy and argue that these efficacy components should be directly assessed, whereas Bandura (1997) considers that team members' perceptions of the team's capability to perform a task automatically encompass the coordination and interaction influences operating within a team. In addition, although Bandura and Zaccaro and colleagues have a similar conception about collective efficacy as a *shared* belief, proponents of Zaccaro and colleagues' definition differ from Bandura on how to measure such a collective belief.

Measuring Collective Efficacy

In chapter 2, we described four methods of measuring collective efficacy: (a) aggregating team members' individual responses to appraisals of their own capabilities to perform within the team; (b) aggregating team members' individual responses to appraisals of their team's capability as a whole; (c) aggregating team members' individual responses regarding *their team's beliefs* in its capabilities rather than *their belief in their team's* capabilities; and (d) using a single response to each item from team members who make the collective efficacy judgment together. The first two methods are based on Bandura's (1997) definition. Bandura hypothesizes that an aggregate of individuals' judgments about the team's capabilities is the better predictor for team sports that are characterized by high interdependence. Proponents of Zaccaro and colleagues' (1995) sense of shared collective competence prefer the third method. The fourth method is rarely used in sport. As we declare in chapter 2, we prefer the second method, aggregating team members' responses when asked to rate "your confidence in your team's capabilities," due to the accessibility of one's own thoughts versus the thoughts of others. In addition, this method conforms to the way in which Bandura's original conceptualization of collective efficacy was constructed.

In 1999, Maddux suggested the need for a consensus opinion on how to define collective efficacy (and thus, how to measure it). It now appears that this consensus has been reached. The bulk of studies to date in sport psychology have defined collective efficacy as a "group's shared belief in its conjoint capability to organize and execute the courses of action required to produce given levels of attainment" (Bandura, 1997, p. 477). In endorsing Bandura's definition, researchers in the field have utilized his assessment recommendations. They also subscribe to his basic rationale for why collective efficacy deserves empirical attention—because a team's efficacy beliefs are important in sport in that they influence what people choose to do as team members, how much effort they put into their team endeavors, and their persistence when collective efforts fail to produce quick results or encounter forcible opposition. The bottom line is that highly efficacious teams should perform better than teams having lower collective efficacy.

Although collective efficacy is typically composed from individual perceptions and then aggregated to the team level to represent a team-level assessment, some researchers have examined collective efficacy and its correlates only at the level of individual perceptions without aggregation. Others have used only aggregated data at the team level. In chapter 2 we noted the problems with using only one level of analysis. Only a few studies have examined collective efficacy at multiple levels to capture both between-team and within-team influences.

Related to the issue of levels of analysis in collective efficacy research are sample size and the difficulty of conducting research on teams. While 25 individuals may compose a hockey team, if one were doing research at the team level of analysis, these 25 individuals would form an n of 1! With respect to dealing with teams, there are often a limited number that play in the same league. For example, there are 30 teams in the National Hockey League (NHL); and if a researcher collected data from even half of these teams, the n, at the team level, would be a mere 15. If one were interested in conducting a standard regression analysis predicting team performance (adopting a 5:1 subjects/teams to predictor ratio; Tabachnick & Fidell, 2001), that n would result in three predictors. The point of this example is to show how difficult it is to do team research. Our review shows that seven studies included team-level analyses of collective efficacy (e.g., Edmonds, 2003; Feltz & Lirgg, 1998; Moritz, 1998; Myers, Payment, & Feltz, 2004; Myers, Feltz, & Short, 2004; Paskevich et al., 1999; Watson, Chemers, & Preiser, 2001). The ns for the field studies ranged from a low of 6 teams (Feltz & Lirgg, 1998) to a high of 26 teams (Watson et al., 2001).

One way to overcome the difficulty of conducting research on teams is to employ a more heterogeneous population in sport research. Instead of concentrating on one sport, researchers could collect data from a number of teams from a number of sports and use a more general measure such as the Collective Efficacy Questionnaire for Sports (CEQS: Short, Sullivan, & Feltz, 2005). As described in chapter 2, Short and colleagues (2005) developed the CEQS to measure team beliefs across sports. We are not asserting that researchers should stop using task-specific measures of collective efficacy. However, using a measure like the CEQS may provide more power to investigate the network of variables that correlate with collective efficacy beliefs among sport teams because a single study could use more than one sport, thus permitting the use of a greater number of teams and permitting comparisons by type of sport. For example, Short (2006b) examined the relationship between team size, type of sport, time of season, and gender on collective efficacy beliefs using CEQS scores as the dependent variable.

Sources of Collective Efficacy in Teams

Theoretically, the efficacy of the team is based on many of the same sources that affect the efficacy of the individual. These primarily are mastery experiences or past performance accomplishments, vicarious experiences, verbal persuasion, and physiological states. No studies in sport have specifically examined the influence of vicarious experiences, such as team modeling, or the influence of physiological states, such as team fatigue, though these two sources could have important effects on collective efficacy beliefs. It is also worth noting that, because of the close relationship between team and self-efficacy, collective efficacy can be influenced indirectly by sources of self-efficacy of the team members (Bandura, 1997). Finally, there is some speculation about some sources unique to collective efficacy because of the more complex socially and situationally mediated interactions involved with teams.

Past Performance Accomplishments

Both Bandura (1997) and Zaccaro and colleagues (1995) noted that the primary source of collective efficacy is mastery experiences (or past performance accomplishments). As discussed in previous chapters, people are more confident regarding those tasks they have successfully executed in the past. Likewise, they are more likely to be less confident in tasks they have been unsuccessful at in the past. There is support for this relationship in teams. Research has supported that in teams organized just for laboratory experiments, collective efficacy can increase or decrease based on their performance (Hodges & Carron, 1992; Lichacz & Partington, 1996).

Further evidence for the relationship between past performance and collective efficacy exists with intact teams. For instance, Watson and colleagues (2001) used multilevel modeling to examine individual- and team-level predictors of collective efficacy over the course of a season with a sample of male and female intercollegiate basketball players. Collective efficacy was assessed at two different points in time—the beginning and end of the season. Team performance was measured by both offensive (i.e., points scored per game) and defensive (i.e., points allowed per game) statistics, as well as overall success (i.e., end-of-season team rank) and players' perceptions of team performance (e.g., subjective ratings of the recent play of the team). Overall team success predicted collective efficacy at the end of the season.

Similar research on intact sport teams has shown that the team's confidence is significantly affected by prior wins and losses (Feltz & Lirgg, 1998; Myers, Feltz, & Short, 2004; Myers, Payment, & Feltz, 2004). Because of the cyclical nature of this relationship (i.e., mastery influences efficacy, which influences mastery), these studies are presented in greater detail later in the chapter in connection with the consequences of collective efficacy. Still, one must not underestimate how profound an impact prior results can have on the efficacy of a team.

Past performance also may indirectly influence collective efficacy through self-efficacy. The confidence in a team's ability to achieve some goal is intimately linked to the confidence of each member in his or her own abilities to contribute to that goal, which is based on past performance. In addition to examining past performance, Watson and colleagues (2001) examined self-efficacy and several other individual- and team-level variables as predictors of collective efficacy. They hypothesized that self-efficacy would be positively related to individual perceptions of collective efficacy at both time points: beginning and end of season. Counter to their hypothesis, self-efficacy was negatively associated with collective efficacy at the beginning of the season. At the beginning of the season, athletes with higher perceptions of personal ability tended to have lower confidence in their team's capabilities to perform successfully. However, at the team level of analysis, self-efficacy was positively related to collective efficacy in teams with high average self-efficacy. At the end of the season, the authors found that self-efficacy beliefs predicted collective efficacy at the individual and group levels. These findings imply that the relationship between individual perceptions about self and team changes with experience within the team across the season.

Similarly, Magyar, Feltz, and Simpson (2004) investigated the relationship between self- and collective efficacy beliefs using multilevel analyses in a sample of rowers. At the individual level of analysis, they hypothesized that athletes who were more confident in their personal ability to row successfully would be more confident in their crew's ability to row successfully. Participants competed in teams ranging in size from two to eight rowers. The authors found that self-efficacy was a significant predictor of individual perceptions of collective efficacy and that "differences in individual perceptions of collective efficacy may be partly explained by differences in task self-efficacy" (Magyar et al., p. 11).

A variable related to self-efficacy within the context of interdependent teams is role efficacy (Bray, Brawley, & Carron, 2002). Bray and colleagues considered role efficacy to represent an athlete's confidence in his or her capabilities to successfully carry out formal interdependent role responsibilities within a group. The authors found that athletes' role efficacy beliefs were distinct from self-efficacy and were significantly related to their collective efficacy beliefs.

In addition to self- and role efficacy, Magyar and colleagues (2004) suggested that goal perspectives may provide a filter used by individual athletes to evaluate their progress and their team's past performance. They hypothesized that goal orientations of athletes (task and ego), in addition to self-efficacy judgments, would predict individual perceptions of collective efficacy (see chapter 3 for a brief description of goal orientations). Specifically, they posited that task orientation would positively predict individual perceptions of collective efficacy, while ego orientation would negatively predict individual perceptions of collective efficacy. They reasoned that a strong disposition in ego orientation may counter the concept of collaboration that is needed for collective achievement, while a strong disposition in task orientation may facilitate a firm sense of collective efficacy. Using the Task and Ego Orientation in Sport Questionnaire (TEOSQ; Duda & Nicholls, 1992), they found that although task orientation (but not ego orientation) demonstrated a significant positive relationship with individual perceptions of collective efficacy, it was not a significant predictor of collective efficacy when compared with task self-efficacy. In speculating, they suggested that the influence of goal orientations on collective efficacy may be partially mediated by task self-efficacy. In essence, goal orientations may influence task self-efficacy, which in turn influences individual perceptions of the crew's ability to row successfully.

Verbal Persuasion

Another source of efficacy noted by Bandura (1997) is verbal persuasion. Again, anecdotal evidence (Haberl & Zaichkowsky, 2003) and empirical research (Vargas-Tonsing & Bartholomew, 2006) have supported this source of collective efficacy. For instance, Vargas-Tonsing and Bartholomew showed that athletes can display greater confidence in their team after listening to a motivational talk from the coach compared to their confidence prior to the talk. This research is discussed in greater detail in chapter 7 on enhancing collective efficacy in teams.

Related to intentionally persuasive sources of efficacy information, such as a coach's feedback or motivational messages, is the motivational climate that the coach sets. Perceptions of the motivational climate reflect athletes' evaluation of the goal structures that are being emphasized by the coach (Magyar et al., 2004). In a mastery climate, coaches provide positive reinforcement to athletes on the basis of hard work, improvement, and good teamwork. They help individual athletes feel that they provide an important contribution to the success of the team. Coaches who emphasize a performance climate punish mistakes and poor performance, give high-ability athletes greater attention and recognition, and encourage competition between team members. Magyar and colleagues also investigated perceived motivational climate at the team level as a source of collective efficacy beliefs in age-group rowing teams. They hypothesized that, at the team level, crews that perceived a stronger mastery climate would report greater confidence in their crew. Using the Perceived Motivational Climate in Sport Questionnaire-2 (PMCSQ-2: Newton, Duda, & Yin, 2000), the authors found support for their hypothesis. Aggregated perceptions of mastery climate significantly predicted aggregated perceptions of collective efficacy. Thus, the greater the extent to which teams perceived that their coach emphasized a mastery-oriented climate focused on learning, improving, and working together, the higher the rowers' collective beliefs in their team's ability to row successfully.

In addition, a coach's sense of coaching efficacy can be an indirect source of collective efficacy through his or her coaching behavior (see chapter 5). For instance, Vargas-Tonsing and colleagues (2003) found a positive relationship between a coach's sense of character-building efficacy and the team's sense of collective efficacy in girls' high school volleyball. There may be other qualities about coaches that also predict a team's collective sense of being successful that have not yet been investigated, such as communication style, athletes' perceptions of the coach's competence, or perceived support.

Further, research has supported that collective efficacy is related to players' perceptions of the ability of team leaders (i.e., captains). In addition to past success and self-efficacy as significant predictors of collective efficacy, Watson and colleagues (2001) found that athletes' confidence in captains was significantly related to collective efficacy at the onset of the season, but was unrelated at the end of the season. Although the study was correlational, the results suggest that team captains also may have an influence on the collective efficacy of the team, especially at the beginning of the season. The results of these two studies are consistent with Vealey's (1986) conceptualization of sources of sport confidence. Vealey noted that the coach's leadership is a source of confidence. Thus, having confidence in the leadership abilities of a coach should be related to the confidence of the team members in their team as a whole. This effect of captains and leaders on collective efficacy beliefs may be due to the attributes or behaviors of the leaders, as well as athletes' perceptions of these competencies. Bandura (1997) also suggests that the modeling of both effective and ineffective behaviors by team leaders may influence the team's collective efficacy in a contagious sense that spreads from teammate to teammate.

Unique Sources of Collective Efficacy

In terms of unique sources of collective efficacy, Zaccaro and colleagues (1995) hypothesized that group size would be related to collective efficacy. Borrowing from Steiner's (1972) framework, Zaccaro and colleagues (1995) stated that members of smaller teams are generally better able to coordinate their activities than their counterparts in larger teams—that as team size increases, individuals participate less, exhibit greater disagreements and dissension, and are absent more often. As these factors enter in, the team's sense of collective efficacy would be expected to decline, accompanied by decreases in individual contributions to the team. Support for this proposition is found in studies of social loafing demonstrating that as team size increases, individual effort and performance decline (Hill, 1982; Latané, Williams, & Harkins, 1979).

Alternatively, however, Zaccaro and colleagues (1995) stated that team size could be positively associated with collective efficacy. More resources may be available to a large team; and the greater the number of different resources teams can apply to a task, the stronger would be the probability of success and the greater would be perceptions of collective efficacy. In such circumstances, team size may be positively associated with members' perceptions of collective efficacy.

Only three studies have considered the effect of team size on collective efficacy beliefs in sport. Watson and colleagues (2001) showed that group size negatively predicted collective efficacy at the end of the season in basketball teams. However, Magyar and colleagues (2004) did not find this effect with boat size in crew teams. They reasoned that due to the unique coordinative dynamics in rowing (e.g., everyone performs the same skill at the same time), the coordination efforts may be no more difficult for athletes in larger boat sizes as compared to smaller ones, and thus group size may not function as a determinant of collective efficacy in this type of sport. Also, no one was "sitting on the bench" in the crew teams. In addition, as Chow and Feltz (in press) note, crews competed only against crews of the same size so there was no advantage to having a smaller or larger team, whereas Watson and colleagues used basketball teams of various sizes where differences in coordination and motivational processes were apparent and could influence team efficacy beliefs. Further, Short (2005b) found a positive relationship between team size and collective efficacy scores across sports—except for "unity efficacy," with respect to which smaller teams were more efficacious. This result makes sense given that unity efficacy is most closely related to team cohesion, and team cohesion has been consistently shown to be higher in smaller-sized groups and teams (Carron et al., 2005; Mullen & Cooper, 1994).

The primary difference between Short's study and the others is that both Watson and colleagues and Magyar and colleagues looked at variation of team size within *one* sport. Short sampled athletes from multiple sports. Short also used the CEQS, which allowed for the study of multiple dimensions of collective efficacy (i.e., ability, effort, persistence, preparation, and unity). The measures used by Watson and colleagues and Magyar and colleagues were both unidimensional and sport specific. Practically speaking, it makes little sense to continue to study the effect team size may have on collective efficacy beliefs because this is typically one aspect of team functioning that is limited by sport rules. Coaches are usually mandated by governing bodies concerning the number of athletes they may have on their playing and practice rosters. What is important to recognize in terms of research is that team size should be a control variable in studies that include varying team sizes.

Another "within-team" factor that may influence collective efficacy beliefs is the length of time the team has been together. From a theoretical perspective, collective efficacy beliefs need time to develop. That is, the team members need to share a significant number of performance experiences in order to develop a coherent and consistent sense of efficacy. Results from research in the sports of hockey (Feltz & Lirgg, 1998) and basketball (Watson et al., 2001) provide support for this. The effect of time of season (beginning, middle, end) on collective efficacy beliefs was also part of Short's (2005b) study. Short showed that the pattern of efficacy scores increasing across the season was evident for the CEQS subscales of effort and unity, as well as the total CEQS scores. For ability efficacy, the highest scores were also reported at the end of the season (but the lowest scores were reported for the middle of the season). For persistence and preparation efficacy, however, the values at the middle of the season were the highest.

The different "across-season" patterns for the efficacy subscale scores raise some interesting questions. It is possible that other variables, perhaps more important than the time of season, are influencing these particular results. For example, efficacy ratings may depend more on the stage of team development. Several theories reflect the stages of team development: for example, the linear perspective (forming, storming, norming, performing, and adjourning, proposed by Tuckman, 1965; Tuckman & Jensen, 1977), the cyclical "life cycle" perspective (Garland, Kolodny, & Jones, 1965); and the pendular perspective (Carron et al., 2005; Schutz, 1966). Using the linear model as an example, it seems reasonable to hypothesize that members of a team in the forming stage may overestimate their team's ability (i.e., perceptions of collective efficacy) due to a generalized sense of optimism. When a team hits the storming stage, tension, conflict, and so on occur, which may lead to feelings of frustration and helplessness (i.e., perhaps resulting in low collective efficacy ratings—"how are we ever going to work together to accomplish the task?"). In the norming stage, in which cohesiveness and team harmony develop, it is likely that collective efficacy ratings will be higher. There is a positive relationship between collective efficacy and cohesion (Carron et al., 2005; Paskevich et al., 1999), so if cohesion is high at this stage, it is likely that collective efficacy ratings will be too. The final stage, performing, may result in high or low collective efficacy ratings, likely dependent on the team's successes and failures (cf. Bandura, 1997).

This line of inquiry—the effect of stage of team development on collective efficacy beliefs—is a topic for future research. As previously suggested, another variable that would be important to consider in this area is the degree of variability among team members' beliefs; it seems reasonable that less variability among team members' collective efficacy ratings would be evident in the performing stages, regardless of actual collective efficacy levels.

One way of getting at the unique sources of collective efficacy is to assess these sources directly from the athletes. As mentioned in chapter 3, Chase, Feltz, and Lirgg (2003) examined the sources of efficacy information that female basketball players selected in making personal and collective efficacy judgments. Players were asked to rate their confidence regarding how well they thought they and their teams could play in an upcoming game, and then completed two open-ended questions indicating the reason(s) behind their individual and team efficacy ratings. Past performance was the most important source of information for both personal and collective efficacy, and players referred to previous practice performance more often than previous game performance. However, there were some differences in reported sources between individual and collective efficacy. Sources outside of sport (e.g., "We just finished exams week.") were more important than social comparison sources for self-efficacy. Social comparison sources were more influential than sources outside of sport for collective efficacy.

Chase and colleagues (2003) suggested that players, as individuals, view events outside of sport (i.e., personal life problems, relationships with friends, school demands) as influencing their individual efficacy beliefs but not as much their team's efficacy. It stands to reason that players would have more insight into their own personal life issues than they would their teammates'. In addition, in relation to past performance, the results showed that sometimes failures spurred further efforts. After a poor performance, athletes reported that they had confidence in themselves and their teams because of a "bouncing back" or "we're due" effect. As we described in chapter 1, the discrepancies between performance accomplishments and performance standards influence efficacy beliefs and further motivation in complex ways that include how one reacts to the success or failure of the accomplishment and the resiliency of one's efficacy beliefs. These reactions logically extend to beliefs about the team as well.

George and Feltz (1995) speculated on other possible sources of collective efficacy, noting that additional outside sources, such as spectator or media influences, may affect the confidence of a team (either positively or negatively). Thus collective efficacy would be a moderating variable in the phenomenon of the home field advantage. For example, a team playing in front of its home crowd may have its efficacy enhanced through the positive messages sent from parents, friends, and fans. Bray and Widmeyer (2000) showed that female basketball players perceived the collective efficacy of their teams to be greater at home than when playing away.

The Effect of Collective Efficacy Beliefs on Team Functioning

"Mastery expectations influence performance and are, in turn, altered by the cumulative effect of one's efforts" (Bandura, 1977, p. 194). There is probably no simpler or more powerful principle with respect to confidence. Whether Bandura's statement refers to individuals or teams, it is generally the case that the more confident athletes are, the better they will perform, and, generally, the more successful they are the more confident they will be. However, it is important to recognize that Bandura's statement deals with *performance* and efficacy, not success and efficacy. Confidence is a very dynamic thing—it can range from high to low, and a poor performance will probably result in a lowering of confidence. Likewise, low confidence should lead to poor performance. As we stated in chapter 1, however, how athletes react to their performances, the perceived difficulty of the task, and their perceived efforts in relation to their goals can also influence the efficacy–performance relationship.

Research has consistently shown that the relationship between performance and confidence is a real and robust one. Within sport, Moritz and colleagues (2000) found a consistently significant relationship between efficacy and performance; however, this research focused on self-efficacy. In 2002, Gully, Incalcaterra, Joshi, and Beaubien conducted a meta-analysis of the efficacy–performance relationship in organizational settings, including sports. In analyzing the results of 67 studies (which comprised 256 effect sizes), they found a significant, positive relationship between the two variables (mean $r = .36$). They also found that this relationship was moderated by the degree of interdependence in the team; the relationship between collective efficacy and performance was stronger when the team was interdependent than when it was not. The authors concluded that "when the task and context encourage coordination, communication, and cooperation among members, team efficacy is related more strongly to performance than when interdependence is low" (p. 827). Sports are a prime setting for such highly interdependent groups.

Although the total number of studies investigating collective efficacy in sport settings is lower than the number on self-efficacy, there are some encouraging signs regarding the nature and vigor of the design of these studies. In particular, a high proportion were field studies. Thus, as a whole, the research on the relationship between team performance and efficacy possesses strong internal and ecological validity, as well as the benefit of diverse valid and reliable operational definitions. Although Bandura's (1997) collective efficacy construct has provided the impetus for current lines of research on the efficacy–performance relationship in sport teams, it should be noted that some studies predate his conceptualization but followed the first presentation of the topic in sport at a meeting of the North American Society for the Psychology of Sport and Physical Activity in Knoxville, Tennessee (Feltz, Bandura, Albrecht, & Corcoran, 1988). It is this literature that we summarize first.

The research literature on collective efficacy and performance shows a clear distinction between studies conducted in laboratories versus studies on real-life teams, and *most* of the early studies were lab studies. We retain this distinction between early (lab) and recent (real world) studies here. This will also help in the following discussion of the importance of interdependence among teammates, as most real-life teams are more interdependent than lab teams.

Laboratory Studies

A few studies on collective efficacy in sporting tasks were conducted in the time frame between the presentation by Feltz and colleagues (1988) and when Zaccaro and colleagues and Bandura stated their operational definitions of collective efficacy in 1995 and 1997, respectively (Greenlees, Graydon, & Maynard, 1999, 2000; Hodges & Carron, 1992; Lichacz & Partington, 1996). Two of these studies were laboratory studies using mainly ad hoc groups. The studies by Greenlees, Graydon, and Maynard also followed the same basic protocol, and are included in this section for that reason.

The lab studies all followed the same basic protocol, similar to the protocol used in the Weinberg series on self-efficacy effects that we described in chapter 3 (see figure 4.2). Basically, after groups were randomly formed, they participated in a series of tasks. Between tasks, they were given bogus feedback so as to manipulate their collective efficacy into one of two conditions—high efficacy and low efficacy. Performance after this manipulation was compared either to the prior premanipulation performance (within-group comparison) or between groups, or in a 2 × 2 analysis of variance design.

The first of these studies was by Hodges and Carron (1992), and we can consider this experiment a prototype for the other studies. The teams comprised three people who did not know each other. Their task was to hold a medicine ball in the air for as long as possible using one arm each, first their dominant arm, then their nondominant arm. Each team competed against another team to see who would win by enduring the longest. Thus, performance was measured in terms of persistence. Prior to working as part of a team, each individual participated in a hand dynamometer task for measurement of their strength.

So, prior to the team task, the groups had information on how strong each member was and hence how good the team should be. Teams were randomly assigned to one of two conditions: high and low efficacy. Groups in the high- and low-efficacy conditions received bogus feedback on their team's strength so as to increase and decrease their efficacy expectations, respectively. A check revealed that this manipulation was successful, as high-efficacy groups had significantly higher efficacy than low-efficacy groups after the feedback was given. Both efficacy groups then competed against a confederate group that held a foam-filled medicine ball. In both conditions, the confederate group "won" the competition by holding the ball aloft for an additional 5 to 10 sec compared to the experimental groups.

Efficacy was measured through two items, both given before each medicine ball trial. Participants responded to "what do you think your group's chances are of wining" and "how confident are you of your prediction"; responses to both could range from 0% to 100%. To obtain a total score of confidence, the two scores were multiplied and scores were aggregated to the team level. The measure was weakly constructed judging by Bandura's

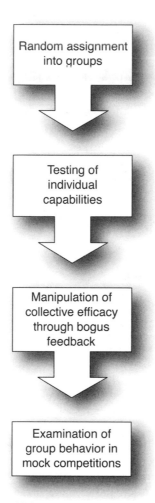

Figure 4.2 Basic paradigm of laboratory collective efficacy studies.

(1997, 2001) guidelines for constructing efficacy scales, and although Myers and Feltz (2007) recommend against using such measures for collective efficacy, this one was sufficient to detect a significant interaction. Participants in the high-efficacy group increased performance from Trial 1 to Trial 2 (the confederate team always "won" on the first trial), but those in the low-efficacy group decreased performance. Thus, the researchers showed that collective efficacy could be affected by previous performance (handgrip dynamometer results) and that this confidence in the team, in turn, would affect team performance.

Although the other laboratory studies further supported these linkages between efficacy and performance, each also added important information. Lichacz and Partington (1996) included some groups of participants with a previous history as a team (i.e., some participants were members of the university's men's rowing and basketball teams, whereas other groups comprised individuals with no prior history together). Perceptions of collective efficacy were measured at the individual level but aggregated to group scores for analysis. Consistent with the results of Hodges and Carron (1992), Lichacz and Partington (1996) found a significant main effect for feedback; groups in the high-confidence condition outperformed those in the low-confidence condition. Further, there was a significant main effect for group history; the groups of rowers outperformed all other groups. Bray (2004) replicated Hodges and Carron's (1992) medicine ball task with same-sex groups, but he also focused on the group's goal level (i.e., "the level of performance [in seconds] the group agreed they should strive for," p. 233). Bray found that collective efficacy explained variation in performance at Time 2 after the initial group performance was statistically controlled for. Further, no gender differences in collective efficacy, goal level, or performance were found. With respect to the effect of goal level, Bray found that groups high in collective efficacy set higher performance goals, and that goal level significantly mediated the relationship between collective efficacy and (postmanipulation) performance.

Greenlees and his colleagues (1999, 2000) conducted a series of experiments that measured and analyzed collective efficacy at the individual level. In both studies, participants competed in teams on rowing machines with two confederates. Conditions were manipulated so that individuals were placed into either high- or low-efficacy groups. In the 1999 study, the authors measured not only efficacy and performance (in rowing time) but also effort, as measured in heart rate. They found that while groups in the two conditions did not differ in perceptions of collective efficacy or in performance prior to the experimental manipulation, those in the low-efficacy condition responded to failure by performing significantly worse. This result was replicated in the 2000 study, as the high-efficacy participants continued to perform at high levels while the low-efficacy participants significantly decreased in performance. This later study also included goal selection as a variable of interest. Those in the low-efficacy condition responded by setting significantly slower time goals whereas the high-efficacy participants made no change in goal selection after having experienced failure.

Thus, consistently in these studies, researchers found that highly efficacious teams outperformed less confident teams in tasks of a sporting nature. But however efficient laboratory studies have been at supporting the theoretical link between collective efficacy and performance, it is somewhat artificial to call three strangers who have never met before, and who have to hold up a medicine ball together, a "team." As was clarified earlier in the chapter, a true sport team possesses many more characteristics than a collection of two or more individuals with a common goal. A true team must also have an identity, have an agreed-upon structure and patterns of communication, and be interdependent in social and instrumental ways. Although there is undeniable convenience in studying these ad hoc groups, and it is useful to be able to manipulate perceptions of collective efficacy and control for extraneous variables, these are not truly the types of teams Bandura was commenting on when he stated that groups may sometimes underperform.

Field Studies

There is ample anecdotal evidence that performance and confidence are intertwined in actual sport teams at any level; for example, consider the comments made by Paul DePodesta, general manager of Major League Baseball's Los Angeles Dodgers. In a 2005 article in *Sports Illustrated,* DePodesta talked about the performance of his team despite the loss of several key players due to injuries. "We could have felt sorry for ourselves, but we didn't. The other thing is, we got quite a lot out of some of those wins, not just a W. There was psychological impact there, and it's given us a lot of confidence" (Farber, 2005, p. 43). Obviously, in this complicated, real-life scenario, DePodesta believes that winning boosts collective efficacy and intimates that winning under such trying circumstances may have a particularly potent effect.

Several studies have been aimed at examining the collective efficacy–performance relationship in real sport teams within their natural competitive settings. Although the laboratory studies established the theoretical link between performance and collective efficacy on sport tasks, they did not allow for examination of the network of dynamic relationships that occur over time, such as over the course of a season.

To this end, Feltz and Lirgg (1998) investigated the relationships between self- and collective efficacy and performance in six collegiate hockey teams over the course of an entire season. Measures for self- and collective efficacy were constructed specifically to be understandable and meaningful to the players. Collective efficacy measures rated players' perceived confidence in the team's ability to (a) outskate, (b) outcheck, (c) force more turnovers, (d) bounce back from performing poorly, (e) score on power plays, (f) kill penalties against the opposing teams, and (g) have an effective goaltender who could block a high percentage of goal attempts. Self-efficacy measures tapped perceived ability to (a) outperform the defensive opponent, (b) outperform the offensive opponent, and (c) bounce back from performing poorly. Performance measures included whether the game was won or lost and the score differential, as well as shots attempted, scoring percentage, power play shots attempted, power play percentage, and shorthanded defense percentage.

These confidence measurements clearly reflect the situational specificity of efficacy beliefs. This conceptual characteristic of efficacy was further aided by the design in that teams played each other on successive days (e.g., Friday and Saturday). Further, consistent with Bandura's notion of efficacy beliefs as a state construct, participants completed the measures within 24 hr of each game.

The authors found that aggregated collective efficacy scores were a better predictor of team performance than aggregated self-efficacy scores. In terms of past performance influence on subsequent efficacy beliefs, past performance was a stronger predictor of collective efficacy than player efficacy. Prior to Friday games, teams showed no significant differences in collective efficacy, but after that game, winners had significantly higher collective efficacy going into Saturday's games; winners' collective efficacy significantly increased while losers' remained the same.

Since the Feltz and Lirgg study on the collective efficacy of true sport teams, subsequent research has further clarified the relationship between collective efficacy and performance, as well as examined the relationships between collective efficacy and such variables as team cohesion, motivational climate, and affective responses. These studies have also incorporated the temporal aspect of the collective efficacy–performance relationship that Feltz and Lirgg (1998) investigated. In one such study, Myers, Feltz, and Short (2004) assessed collective efficacy of 10 football teams. They measured both collective efficacy and aggregated self-efficacy and examined the relationships among these confidence levels and performance over a period of eight consecutive games. They found strong relationships whereby collective efficacy was a significant predictor of subsequent offensive performance. Further, they found this effect both within teams across weeks (i.e., the confidence of a given team from week to week would predict performance), and within weeks across teams (i.e., at any one point in time, confident teams would be more likely to perform better offensively than less confident teams).

Myers, Feltz, and Short (2004) also found that prior performance positively predicted subsequent collective efficacy within weeks across teams but that the opposite was the case for a given team from week to week (within teams across weeks). They speculated that the negative within-team relationship was probably spurious and due to design limitations in the study. In collegiate football, games are played only once per week, on Saturdays, and the time between performance and the next efficacy questionnaire (the following Friday) was longer than the 24 hr within which collective efficacy was measured prior to performance. In addition, the opponent was not constant as in the Friday-Saturday design of the Feltz and Lirgg (1998) study. Thus, performance against a weak opponent on the first weekend would not necessarily predict collective efficacy for performance against a strong opponent on the second weekend.

An interesting extension of this research pertains to gender differences in the confidence–performance relationship in real-life sport teams. As we note in chapter 3, research has consistently shown that males tend to be more self-confident than females on male-related tasks (Lirgg, 1991), and the bulk of the research on collective efficacy, including Feltz and Lirgg's (1998) study, used male participants. One is left to wonder if the collective efficacy–performance relationship is similar for teams of female athletes. With this in mind, Myers, Payment, and Feltz (2004) replicated Feltz and Lirgg's (1998) study with female hockey players. The authors used the same basic design and collective efficacy measurement that Feltz and Lirgg (1998) had except that they statistically removed the contribution of Friday's collective efficacy from Friday's performance (i.e., residualized performance). As described in chapter 2, the studies prior to the investigation by Myers, Payment, and Feltz (2004) did not statistically control for the influence of previous collective efficacy on past performance when measuring the efficacy–performance relationship across time. Because past performance is itself affected by beliefs of personal efficacy, controlling for it allows one to examine a less confounded index of performance as a predictor of future perceived efficacy and future performance. As illustrated in figure 4.3, the authors found that the team's residualized Friday performance significantly predicted subsequent collective efficacy for Saturday's game, and also found that Saturday's collective efficacy was a significant and stronger predictor of Saturday game performance than was residualized Friday game performance.

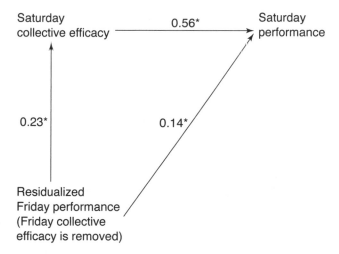

Figure 4.3 Relationship between team performance and collective efficacy using residualized past performance. **p < .05*

Adapted, by permission, from N.D. Myers, C.A. Payment, and D.L. Feltz, 2004, "Reciprocal relationships between collective efficacy and team performance in women's ice hockey," *Group Dynamics: Theory, Research, and Practice* 8: 182-195.

Additionally, they found that the influence of collective efficacy on team performance was positive and moderate, whereas the influence of team performance on collective efficacy was positive and small.

In a follow-up study using the same data set, Myers, Paiement, and Feltz (2007) sought to determine whether collective efficacy was a stronger predictor of performance after the first, second, or third period of play. They reasoned that although collective efficacy judgments are typically based on summative team performance capabilities (e.g., how confident are you that your team can score more goals than the opposing team) and performance is also summative, collective efficacy judgments may predict early performance better than cumulative (or summative) performance because of the changes that can occur over the course of a competition. Performance in period 1 might change collective efficacy judgments, which in turn might influence performance in period 2, and so on. However, they found that collective efficacy was a significant predictor at all three of the performance intervals and that the magnitude of the relationship did not differ among the cumulative time periods. Thus, collective efficacy exerted a similar and moderately sized effect across the game. Myers and colleagues suggested that although a team's collective efficacy likely fluctuates during a game, it may vary only within a relatively narrow band based on its starting point. That is, preperformance assessments of collective efficacy may remain resilient over the ups and downs of performance within a competition. Still, the authors were unable to reassess teams' efficacy beliefs once the competition started.

The question of whether collective efficacy beliefs change within a competition is difficult to assess in sport given its dynamic nature. Many coaches will not allow researchers to disrupt a team's attention and focus by administering questionnaires during a competition. Edmonds (2003), however, found a way, using small groups (ns of 2 to 4) in adventure team racing. Such races consisted of a variety of activities (e.g., canoeing, running, mountain biking, climbing) conducted over a series of stages. The race totaled over 100 miles [160 km] of land. Collective efficacy was assessed both prior to the race and between stages. Collective efficacy was significantly related to performance throughout the race. Further, collective efficacy consistently discriminated between higher- and lower-ranked teams.

By and large, a pattern appears in the studies on collective efficacy and performance whereby the lab studies focus on additive tasks (e.g., rowing) and the field studies focus on interactive team performance (e.g., hockey). This trend was noted by Moritz (1998), who conducted an experiment in which bowlers participated in either an additive or an interdependent team bowling tournament. Bowlers participated in pairs. In the additive condition, the dyad's performance was the sum of each individual bowler's performance. In the interactive condition, teammates could play the pins remaining from their partner's turn; the total performance was the interaction of both team-mates' efforts. Moritz found that collective efficacy (as measured conjointly) was a significant predictor of team performance in the interactive condition, but not in the additive condition.

These studies offer much support to the robust nature of the efficacy–performance relationship in sport teams. Unlike the previous lab experiments, these studies incorporated actual preexisting sport teams in real-life performances. They repeatedly showed that collective efficacy predicted performance and that performance predicted collective efficacy. Further, these studies incorporated both male and female teams and different sports, although all highly interactive and interdependent.

Several conclusions can be drawn from the collection of laboratory and field studies. First, there is a strong, reciprocal relationship between collective efficacy and performance. This is consistent with the notions of Bandura (1997), as well as the results of the meta-analyses both within (Moritz et al., 2000) and outside of sport (Gully et al., 2002). Further, these results are consistent regardless of the type of measurement used or whether the team analyzed was a bona fide team or a collection of individuals placed into groups for the purpose of experimentally testing theoretical predictions of causality.

Finally, it is apparent that the degree of interdependence between team-mates influences how significant collective efficacy is. With respect to the experiments and quasi-experiments on collective efficacy and sport performance, most of the studies incorporating real-life teams dealt with more highly interdependent tasks (e.g., hockey, rugby, football) than the lab studies (e.g., tug of war). Thus far, the sole exception appears to be Moritz's (1998) field experiment on bowling teams. Table 4.2 summarizes some of the landmark findings in the research on collective efficacy and performance.

TABLE 4.2 Key Findings in the Collective Efficacy–Performance Relationship

Study	Implications
Hodges & Carron, 1992	Manipulated collective efficacy can affect team performance in artificial teams.
Feltz & Lirgg, 1998	Collective efficacy is related to self-efficacy and performance in true teams.
Moritz, 1998	Collective efficacy is related to performance in interactive but not additive teams participating in the same task.
Greenlees, Graydon, & Maynard, 1999	Collective efficacy–performance relationship in artificial teams is supported with individual assessment of collective efficacy.
Myers, Payment, & Feltz, 2004	Collective efficacy is related to performance in true teams after statistically controlling for previous performance.

Effects of Collective Efficacy Beliefs on Other Team and Individual Variables

Although the most salient factor associated with collective efficacy is performance, it is not the only one. Confidence in abilities, efforts, and other team attributes and dynamics can influence emotional and behavior outcomes, at both individual and collective levels. These include variables such as anxiety, goals, social loafing, and player satisfaction at the individual level, and factors such as team cohesion, team goals, and team attributions at the team level.

Individual Variables

One individual variable that has been examined in sport in relation to collective efficacy is anxiety. Greenlees, Nunn, and colleagues (1999) studied the relationship between precompetitive state anxiety and collective efficacy in a sample of rugby players whose collective efficacy had been experimentally manipulated to be increased or decreased. Collective efficacy assessments incorporated both confidence in winning the upcoming match and confidence in specific aspects of the game (e.g., fitness, ball handling, defense). Precompetitive anxiety was measured through the Competitive State Anxiety Inventory-2 (CSAI-2), as well as a separate scale to ascertain the interpretation of this anxiety (i.e., debilitative or facilitative). The authors found that collective efficacy was capable of significantly predicting both the intensity of anxiety and the positive affect.

Goal selection has also been linked to collective efficacy. Greenlees, Nunn, and colleagues (1999), prior to and after the efficacy manipulation, monitored both the difficulty of goals participants set and commitment to these goals. They found that individuals in the low-collective-efficacy condition responded to the manipulation by selecting less difficult performance goals than they had previously held. Further, while there was no significant effect of efficacy manipulation on goal commitment, there was a significant correlation between collective efficacy and goal commitment. Thus, it appears that how confident members are in their team could affect both selection of team goals and the degree to which they hold to the attainment of that objective at the level of the individual team member. As mentioned previously, Bray (2004) also found support for the effects of collective efficacy on goal setting.

Bandura (1986b, 1997) has hypothesized that collective efficacy is related to collective effort and perseverance. However, perceptions of collective efficacy can also affect individual effort within a team. A team member may put forth less effort at a task when performing within the team than when performing alone; this phenomenon is called social loafing. Among a number of possible reasons for social loafing, one is an individual's assumption that the other team members are better qualified and the individual can therefore reduce his or her effort (Carron, Hausenblas, & Eys, 2005). In other words, the individual has higher confidence in the team's capabilities than in his or her own. As Feltz (1994) noted, social loafing may represent the dark side of collective efficacy if it undermines contributions to team performance.

However, another reason individuals loaf within teams may be low motivation in combination with low confidence in the team. Lichacz and Partington (1996), who conducted the only study to examine collective efficacy and social loafing in sport, found that members of teams with low collective efficacy, induced through negative performance feedback, were less interested in the rope-pulling task and loafed more during team performance than members in the induced high-collective-efficacy condition. There was one exception. Members of intact rowing teams responded to the negative performance feedback with greater effort during group performance than when performing alone. The authors reasoned that when the task is highly salient to team members, collective efficacy is less likely to influence social loafing. We also suggest that the rowers may all have had high self-efficacy beliefs, and thus each felt he was the important contributor necessary for team success. We suggest that when one examines social loafing in relation to collective efficacy, it is necessary to include self efficacy judgments as well.

Whether or not perceptions of collective efficacy are related to subsequent levels of satisfaction with the team has yet to be investigated within sport teams. However, research outside of sport suggests that collective efficacy is related to member satisfaction (Caprara, Barbaranelli, Borgogni, & Steca, 2003). It makes sense that if a team member has confidence in the team, he or she will be more satisfied with the experience of being on the team.

Collective Variables

Aside from performance, the only team-level attribute repeatedly researched in conjunction with collective efficacy has been team cohesion. Cohesion is in itself quite a well-researched team dynamic. Cohesion has been defined as "a dynamic process which is reflected in the tendency of a group to stick together and remain united in the pursuit of its instrumental objectives and/or for the satisfaction of member affective needs" (Carron, Brawley, & Widmeyer, 1997, p. 3). This is a very powerful, if dynamic, team attribute, and a wealth of literature shows how it is related to team performance, individual satisfaction, leadership, and communication processes, among other factors (Carron et al., 2005).

As a group attribute, cohesion has been recognized to both affect and be affected by collective efficacy (Paskevich et al., 1999; Sullivan & Feltz, 2005). The conceptualizations of both cohesion (Carron et al., 1997) and collective efficacy (Bandura, 1997; Zaccaro et al., 1995) have included the idea that these constructs should be interrelated. Several separate papers have addressed this relationship (Heuze, Raimbault, & Fontayne, 2006; Kozub & McDonnell, 2000; Paskevich et al., 1999; Spink, 1990b). For instance, Paskevich and colleagues (1999) examined the relationship between collective efficacy and team cohesion in volleyball players. They used a collective efficacy scale constructed specifically for the study; this measure tapped perceptions of competence in the team interactions that are specific to successfully playing volleyball more generally (i.e., it was not intended for use just prior to a competition). Cohesion was measured by the Group Environment Questionnaire (GEQ: Carron, Brawley, & Widmeyer, 1985). This scale measures four factors of team cohesion. Two refer to social cohesion (Individual Attraction to Group—Social; Group Integration—Social), and two measure task cohesion (Individual Attraction to Group—Task; Group Integration—Task). The authors used efficacy scores to separate groups of high- and low-confident teams. They found that task cohesion scores were capable of significantly discriminating between these two groups.

Kozub and McDonnell (2000) used a scale for collective efficacy similar to the one used by Feltz and Lirgg (1998) for the hockey study, adapted for rugby. The authors used one sum total collective efficacy score as a dependent variable in a regression analysis, with cohesion factors as predictor variables. Both task cohesion scores emerged as significant predictors of collective efficacy. These two studies confirm the conclusions of one of the first studies on collective efficacy in the sport setting, conducted by Spink (1990b). Spink found that in female volleyball teams, players' perceptions of collective efficacy were highly related to task cohesion. Thus, it seems that how united a team is around instrumental objectives is very closely related to the confidence that they have in their conjoint abilities with respect to their team sport.

Most recently, Chow and Feltz (2006) examined the predictive strength of collective efficacy on team attributions with high school track relay athletes. Efficacy measures were administered prior to the competition while causal attributions for team performance were completed following the race. Results showed that collective efficacy was positively related to individual perceptions of team controllability. Players who held strong perceptions of collective efficacy believed that the cause of their team's performance was controllable by their team as a whole.

Although the research on collective efficacy in teams is not as well established as the research at the individual level, a number of sources and consequences have been examined in relation to the construct at both the individual-athlete level and the team level. These relationships are illustrated in figure 4.4. It remains for future research to determine additional sources and consequences of collective efficacy in sport teams. As Bandura (1997) suggests, however, the greatest progress in advancing knowledge in this area will come from studying the development, decline, and restoration of collective efficacy. Further, Bandura argues that such studies will require multifaceted measures of collective efficacy that are tied to valid indexes of team performance. Myers and Feltz (2007) have outlined some recommendations for measuring collective efficacy in sport. We turn our attention next to coaching efficacy and how coaches' beliefs in their effectiveness interact with athletes and teams.

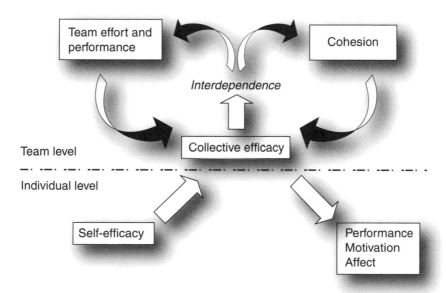

Figure 4.4 Conceptual diagram of the major antecedents and consequences of collective efficacy. *Note:* The arrows are not assumed to represent causal relationships.

Efficacy Beliefs
of Coaches

> "I think the most important thing about coaching is that you have to have a sense of confidence about what you're doing. You have to be a salesman and you have to get your players, particularly your leaders, to believe in what you're trying to accomplish on the basketball floor."
>
> *Phil Jackson, "The NBA at 50" (2003)*

Coaches play a significant role in the motivation and performance of their athletes and teams. They provide instruction, guide the practice of skills, and give feedback. Coaches are concerned with the learning and performance of their athletes and must perform multiple roles to be effective (e.g., teacher, motivator, strategist, organizer, character builder; cf. Gould, 1987). Although they may employ different styles of leadership to accomplish their objectives, their perceptions regarding their coaching abilities (i.e., coaching efficacy) as well as their own behavior will influence the behavior and performance of the athletes. Feltz and her colleagues (Feltz, Chase, Moritz, & Sullivan, 1999) developed a model of coaching efficacy to provide a framework for studying the relationships among coaching efficacy, coaching behavior, and the motivation and performance of athletes. In this chapter, we provide an overview of the model of coaching efficacy developed through Feltz and colleagues' research on sources of coaching efficacy information, the influence of coaching efficacy beliefs on coaching behavior, and the influence of coaching efficacy beliefs on athlete and team outcomes. We also review work on the strategies that coaches use in building the efficacy beliefs of their athletes and teams. We conclude with a special section on women and coaching.

Conceptual Model of Coaching Efficacy

Almost a decade ago Feltz and colleagues (1999) noted that the concept of coaching efficacy had been largely unexplored despite its potential influence on the sport experience of athletes. They argued that although a conceptual model existed for teacher efficacy, leadership effectiveness, and managerial efficacy, these frameworks were not suitable in their entirety for studying coaching efficacy. Coaching efficacy is influenced by different organizational variables than teacher or managerial efficacy, and coaches have unique objectives in the development of athletes' performance. Thus, the authors developed a sport-oriented conceptual framework that was adapted and logically formulated from Bandura's writings (Bandura, 1977, 1986b, 1997) and the teacher efficacy literature (Denham & Michael, 1981; Fuller, Wood,

Rapport, & Dornbusch, 1982; Ramey-Gassert, Shroyer, & Staver, 1996; Smylie, 1988).

Coaching efficacy was defined as the extent to which coaches believe they have the capacity to affect the learning and performance of their athletes (Feltz et al., 1999). Performance in this sense was also meant to include the psychological, attitudinal, and teamwork skills of athletes. The definition and conceptual model focused on high school and lower-division collegiate coaches rather than those at the elite and professional levels. Thus, the model does not apply to Division I and professional-level coaches. The concept of coaching efficacy comprised four dimensions: game strategy, motivation, technique, and character-building efficacy. Game strategy efficacy was defined as the confidence coaches have in their ability to coach during competition and lead their team to a successful performance. Motivation efficacy was defined as the confidence coaches have in their ability to affect the psychological skills and states of their athletes. Technique efficacy was defined as the belief coaches have in their instructional/diagnostic skills. Lastly, character-building efficacy involved the confidence coaches have in their ability to influence a positive attitude toward sport in their athletes.

The dimensions and model were developed during a five-week seminar involving 11 coaches who had varying levels of experience in coaching and were graduate students in sport psychology. The *National Standards for Athletic Coaches* (National Association for Sport and Physical Education, 1995), preliminary work on a coaching confidence scale (Park, 1992), and a review of the coaching education literature (e.g., Brown, 1992; Hargreaves, 1990; Martens, 1987; Seefeldt, 1987) provided a framework for group discussions on the key components of coaching efficacy, its potential sources of information, and its potential outcomes.

In line with Bandura's concept of self-efficacy, Feltz and colleagues (1999) proposed a model of coaching efficacy in which coaches' efficacy beliefs are influenced by their past performance and experience (e.g., coaching experience, coaching preparation, previous win/loss record), the perceived ability of their athletes, and perceived social support (e.g., faculty, student, administrative, community, and parental support). The first set of sources, based on previous experiences, is directly related to Bandura's conception of performance accomplishments. The source of perceived skill of athletes was based on research results from teacher education showing that teacher efficacy was based, in part, on the teachers' perceptions of their students' academic ability (Smylie, 1988). The last set of sources of coaching efficacy information, based on social support, is similar to verbal persuasion.

Feltz and colleagues (1999) also proposed that coaching efficacy in turn should have an influence on how one coaches (e.g., type of feedback used, management strategies, coaching style), how players perform, how confident and motivated the athletes are, and how satisfied one is with one's coaching. High-efficacy coaches, compared to low-efficacy coaches, were hypothesized to demonstrate more effective tactical skills, use more effective motivational and corrective feedback techniques, demonstrate more commitment and time to coaching, have players who are more satisfied with their coach, lead their teams to more successful performances, and have more efficacious and motivated players. The researchers did not make specific dimension-based hypotheses except for character-building efficacy. They hypothesized that coaches who were high in their efficacy for character building would display more character development coaching behavior, as well as have players who exhibit more positive attitudes about good sporting behavior and who demonstrate better sporting behavior, than coaches low in efficacy for character building. Figure 5.1 illustrates the model of coaching efficacy as conceptualized by Feltz and colleagues.

Although Feltz and colleagues did not make further dimension-specific hypotheses, several could align with their model and measure of coaching efficacy. For instance, coaches who are high in technique efficacy should detect more skill errors when analyzing performance, display more corrective feedback, and provide more individualized instruction in their coaching. High

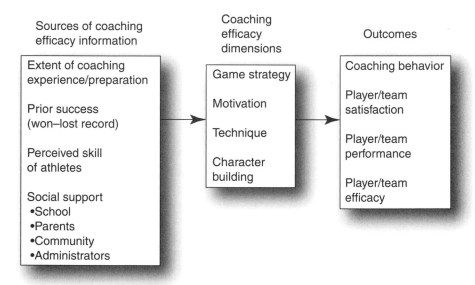

Figure 5.1 Conceptual model of coaching efficacy.

Reprinted, by permission, from D.L. Feltz et al., 1999, "A conceptual model of coaching efficacy: Preliminary investigation and instrument development," *Journal of Education Psychology* 91: 766.

strategy efficacy beliefs should predict the use of more effective tactical skills in competitions. In addition, coaches high in motivation efficacy, compared to those with low motivation efficacy, should have players and teams who feel more confident, feel more mentally prepared, and have more team cohesion. Feltz and colleagues considered their model a preliminary one that probably contained fewer sources, dimensions, and outcomes than actually exist; but the model provided a starting point for future extension or tightening via novel corroborations or falsifications through research. We present extensions to the model later in this chapter.

In addition to the model, Feltz and colleagues (1999) developed the Coaching Efficacy Scale (CES) to measure the multidimensional aspects of coaching efficacy. The graduate students/coaches generated 41 items based on the four dimensions of coaching efficacy. The items included the stem, "How confident are you in your ability to . . ." The rating scale was a 10-point Likert scale with categories ranging from 0 *(not at all confident)* to 9 *(extremely confident)*. Nine collegiate and scholastic coaches evaluated the relevance of the items on a scale that ranged from 1 *(essential)* to 3 *(not essential)*, and all items were potentially important indicators of coaching efficacy.

On the basis of exploratory factor analysis (EFA) results, the final instrument was reduced to 24 items reflecting the four dimensions proposed in the model. For administration purposes it is titled "Coaching Confidence Questionnaire" (see p. 156). The CES contains seven items from the game strategy dimension, such as ". . . recognize opposing team's strengths during competition"; seven items from the motivation dimension, such as ". . . motivate your athletes"; six items from the teaching technique dimension, such as ". . . detect skill errors"; and four items from the character-building dimension, such as ". . . promote good sportsmanship."

The correlations among the factors suggested that the CES may constitute a hierarchical factor model representing four first-order factors and a second-order factor representing total coaching efficacy. A confirmatory factor analysis (CFA) tested these models with a new sample of coaches, which indicated an acceptable fit for the first-order factors using various global indexes (nonnormed fit index = .88; comparative fit index = .89; root mean square residual error of approximation = .08). Marginal support was also found for a total coaching efficacy factor that explained the correlations among the four first-order factors. Greater detail on the psychometric properties of the CES was presented in chapter 2; the factor structure is shown in figure 5.2. Feltz and colleagues (1999) noted that while the means on each of the four subscales were fairly high in their original sample, individuals would probably not enter or remain in this career field if they had little or no confidence in their coaching ability.

Coaching Confidence Questionnaire

Coaching confidence refers to the extent to which coaches believe that they have the capacity to affect the learning and performance of their athletes. Think about how confident you are as a coach. Rate your confidence for each of the items below. Your answers will be kept completely confidential. How confident are you in your ability to—

	Not at all confident							Extremely confident		
1. maintain confidence in your athletes?	0	1	2	3	4	5	6	7	8	9
2. recognize opposing team's strengths during competition?	0	1	2	3	4	5	6	7	8	9
3. mentally prepare athletes for game/meet strategies?	0	1	2	3	4	5	6	7	8	9
4. understand competitive strategies?	0	1	2	3	4	5	6	7	8	9
5. instill an attitude of good moral character?	0	1	2	3	4	5	6	7	8	9
6. build the self-esteem of your athletes?	0	1	2	3	4	5	6	7	8	9
7. demonstrate the skills of your sport?	0	1	2	3	4	5	6	7	8	9
8. adapt to different game/meet situations?	0	1	2	3	4	5	6	7	8	9
9. recognize opposing team's weakness during competition?	0	1	2	3	4	5	6	7	8	9
10. motivate your athletes?	0	1	2	3	4	5	6	7	8	9
11. make critical decisions during competition?	0	1	2	3	4	5	6	7	8	9
12. build team cohesion?	0	1	2	3	4	5	6	7	8	9
13. instill an attitude of fair play among your athletes?	0	1	2	3	4	5	6	7	8	9
14. coach individual athletes on technique?	0	1	2	3	4	5	6	7	8	9
15. build the self-confidence of your athletes?	0	1	2	3	4	5	6	7	8	9
16. develop athletes' abilities?	0	1	2	3	4	5	6	7	8	9
17. maximize your team's strengths during competition?	0	1	2	3	4	5	6	7	8	9
18. recognize talent in athletes?	0	1	2	3	4	5	6	7	8	9
19. promote good sportsmanship?	0	1	2	3	4	5	6	7	8	9
20. detect skill errors?	0	1	2	3	4	5	6	7	8	9
21. adjust your game/meet strategy to fit your team's talent?	0	1	2	3	4	5	6	7	8	9
22. teach the skills of your sport?	0	1	2	3	4	5	6	7	8	9
23. build team confidence?	0	1	2	3	4	5	6	7	8	9
24. instill an attitude of respect for others?	0	1	2	3	4	5	6	7	8	9

Reprinted, by permission, from D.L. Feltz et al., 1999, "A conceptual model of coaching efficacy: Preliminary investigation and instrument development," *Journal of Educational Psychology* 91: 765-766.

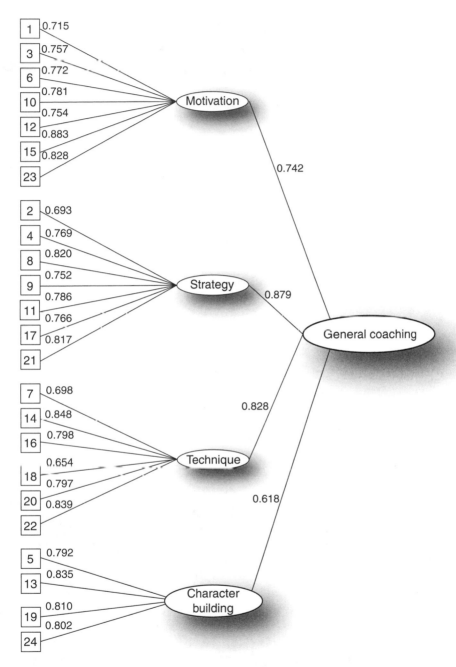

Figure 5.2 Factor loadings of the Coaching Efficacy Scale on first- and second-order factors.

Reprinted, by permission, from D.L. Feltz et al., 1999, "A conceptual model of coaching efficacy: Preliminary investigation and instrument development," *Journal of Educational Psychology* 91: 771.

Research on Sources of Coaching Efficacy Information

The model of coaching efficacy is still relatively new, and only a handful of research studies have been published so far on the sources of coaching efficacy (Chase, Feltz, Hayashi, & Hepler, 2005; Feltz et al., 1999; Lee, Malete, & Feltz, 2002; Malete & Feltz, 2000; Marback, Short, Short, & Sullivan, 2005; Myers, Vargas-Tonsing, & Feltz, 2005; Sullivan, Gee, & Feltz, 2006; Tuton & Short, 2004). Feltz and colleagues provided the initial examination of the proposed sources of CES using high school male basketball coaches. They found support for their model of coaching efficacy in that canonical loadings showed years in coaching ($r = -82$), perceived community support ($r = -.61$), perceived team ability ($r = -.51$), perceived parental support ($r = -.44$), and past winning percentage ($r = -.43$) to be significantly predictive of the dimensions of coaching efficacy. The strongest predictors of coaching efficacy were years of coaching experience and community support for these high school coaches. These sources were most predictive of the game strategy and motivation dimensions of coaching efficacy. Technique efficacy provided a significant but less important contribution to the relationship, and character-building efficacy contributed very little. Thus, coaches who had more years of coaching experience, higher perceptions of their team's ability, and greater perceived support from the community and parents for their teams, and who had had a more successful season the year before, were more confident in their strategic abilities in games, motivational skills, and to a lesser extent their instructional and diagnostic techniques.

Support for the sources of coaching efficacy also has been found using intercollegiate male and female Division II and III coaches (Marback et al., 2005; Myers, Vargas-Tonsing, & Feltz, 2005; Short, Smiley, & Ross-Stewart, 2005). Myers and colleagues examined the same sources of coaching efficacy as Feltz and colleagues (1999) but used years as a collegiate coach instead of total years coaching, as well as using career winning percentage instead of just previous year's percentage. Results were similar in that all of the sources were significant predictors of all of the dimensions of coaching efficacy; and perceived team ability, parental support, and community support were most predictive of the coaching efficacy dimensions. However, the strongest predictor was perceived team ability, and the strongest efficacy dimensions were motivation and character-building efficacy. As Myers and colleagues noted, perhaps the major influence of perceived team ability has to do with the more competitive nature of collegiate compared to high school sports. They also explained that the importance of character-building efficacy may have been due to the overriding mission of the private, often religiously affiliated, institutions that make up Division III colleges where many of these coaches were employed.

Myers, Vargas-Tonsing, and Feltz (2005) also found a difference in the strength of sources for male and female coaches. Although most sources had similar correlations with coaching efficacy for men and women, female coaches reported social support from the community as a stronger source of character-building efficacy than did male coaches. Thus, women who felt supported by the community had more confidence in their striving to instill attitudes of fair play and respect for others in their athletes than those who did not perceive that support. For men, there was very little relationship between these two variables. If small college athletics programs value character-building development in their athletes, they may want to make sure that the community is supporting their female coaches in that developmental aspect. For male coaches, these athletics programs may want to explore what antecedents coaches rely on for building character efficacy.

Marback and colleagues (2005) found slightly different results using coaching preparation, coaching experience, won/lost record, and gender as predictors of coaching efficacy. Coaching experience was the strongest predictor of three of the four dimensions: game strategy, motivation, and character building. Gender also predicted game strategy and character-building efficacy. Male coaches had stronger perceptions of game strategy than female coaches but weaker perceptions of character-building efficacy.

Expanding the Sources of Coaching Efficacy

Other studies have explored sources of coaching efficacy information other than those proposed in the original model. Sullivan and colleagues (2006) assessed the relative importance of previous playing experience (while controlling for coaching experience) as a predictor of coaching efficacy in a sample of curling coaches. The authors reasoned that while coaching education and experience in coaching may provide coaches with the pedagogical (coaching) knowledge and pedagogical-content knowledge (sport-specific coaching knowledge) needed to be effective and feel confident, the content knowledge—knowledge of how the sport is played—is best learned by playing it. In having participated in their sport as players, coaches should have experienced a wide variety of sport-specific content knowledge on which to base their confidence with respect to skill, knowledge of rules, vocabulary, strategy, equipment, motivation, and all aspects of the game. However, as Sullivan and colleagues indicated, playing experience by itself is not enough to influence effective coaching. There are great athletes and scientists who are ineffective coaches and teachers, respectively. To be effective, coaches must connect their playing knowledge to knowledge for coaching.

Beginning-level coaches who were once accomplished athletes but have little coaching knowledge may have an inflated sense of their coaching abilities until they find that coaching involves a different set of skills (e.g., diagnostic and prescriptive) than playing. Thus, playing experience may influence some dimensions of coaching efficacy less than others. For instance, playing experience may not influence a coach's character-building or diagnostic efficacy as much as years of coaching experience. In order to determine the predictive strength of playing and coaching experience on the various dimensions of coaching efficacy, Sullivan and colleagues (2006) conducted four hierarchical regression analyses with each factor of coaching efficacy as a dependent variable. For each of the four analyses, coaching experience was entered into the model first, followed by playing experience. Sullivan and colleagues found that coaching experience was a significant predictor of coaching efficacy in all four analyses. However, for game strategy, playing experience provided a significant improvement in the predictive strength of coaches' responses, accounting for an additional 9% of the variance. Playing experience was also a stronger predictor of game strategy efficacy than was coaching experience. Thus, playing experience may be a significant independent source of coaching efficacy, particularly for those aspects of coaching that involve the application of practical game skills and knowledge. Even for future coaching prospects, still in high school, perceived playing ability predicted their efficacy beliefs for future coaching (Lirgg, Dibrezzo, & Smith, 1994). However, for those already in the coaching ranks, coaching experience seems to be a powerful source of efficacy information with respect to coaches' responsibilities to teach techniques, motivate, and build the character of their athletes.

Short and colleagues (2005) focused on the use of imagery as a preparatory source of efficacy information. Phil Jackson (Jackson & Delehanty, 1995), in his book *Sacred Hoops,* expressed how important imagery was to him as a tool. One of Jackson's strengths as a coach, for instance, was his ability to visualize ways to short-circuit opponents' offensive schemes, which may have influenced his coaching efficacy as a superb game strategist. Short and colleagues hypothesized that imaging strategies would predict game strategy efficacy, imaging skills would predict technique efficacy, imaging goal-oriented responses would predict motivation efficacy, and mastery imagery or imaging being confident would predict character-building efficacy and general coaching efficacy. Using a modification of the Sport Imagery Questionnaire (SIQ; Hall, Mack, Paivio, & Hausenblas, 1998), which measures how often coaches use these different types of imagery (i.e., strategy, skills, goal-oriented responses, mastery, arousal), they found support for their hypotheses but also found mastery imagery to predict motivation efficacy. Thus, coaches who frequently use these multidimensional forms of imagery in their coaching have corresponding efficacy beliefs about them.

Although support has been found for the predictive strength of the sources in Feltz and colleagues' (1999) model, much variance has been unaccounted for in coaching efficacy scores. Chase and colleagues (2005) decided to use a different approach—a structured interview format—to identify possible additional sources of coaching efficacy from the coaches' perspective. Using a subsample of the coaches who had participated in Feltz and colleagues' study, the authors asked the coaches, in individual phone interviews, to identify the information they use to form their coaching efficacy beliefs. Results indicated that, in addition to the sources proposed in Feltz and colleagues' model, coaches relied on evidence of player improvement and development, support from their players, and their own previous playing experience to judge their coaching efficacy. A coach's past success or performance accomplishments may be more related to player development, which is more under the coach's control, than to win/loss records. The findings were replicated with female softball coaches at the collegiate level, although these coaches also considered success an important source of efficacy, especially near the end of the competitive season (Tuton & Short, 2004). These findings plus the results from Sullivan and colleagues (2006) suggest that the sources of coaching efficacy from the coaching efficacy model by Feltz and colleagues (1999) may need to be more specific. Chase and colleagues proposed an extension to the sources in the original model, outlined as follows:

- Extent of coaching experience and preparation:
  - -Knowledge to prepare team
  - -Past experience in coaching
  - -Playing experience
  - -Leadership skills
  - -Coach's development
- Prior success (win/loss record)
- Perceived skill of athletes
- Player improvement
- Support from the following:
  - -School students and teachers
  - -Community
  - -Parents
  - -Athletic director
  - -Players

On the basis of Chase and colleagues' (2005) findings, Feltz, Hepler, Roman, and Paiement (2006) included perceived team improvement and player support as sources of coaching efficacy at the volunteer youth coach level. Because many youth sport programs de-emphasize winning and many volunteer coaches have little experience or formal training in coaching (American Academy of Pediatrics, 2001; Weiss & Hayashi, 1996), they may rely on different sources of efficacy information than those found in previous research. Feltz and colleagues (2006) sampled 400 youth coaches of children aged 7 to 12 years across numerous sports on the CES and seven sources of coaching efficacy: coaching experience, perceived athlete ability, perceived team improvement, years of playing experience, perceived support from the organization, athletes, and community support. The new predictors, based on Chase and colleagues' work, were perceived team improvement, years of playing experience, and player support.

Feltz and colleagues (2006) found, in addition to earlier findings, that perceived team improvement, along with coaching experience, was a significant predictor of motivation, strategy, and technique efficacy. Similarly to findings in the study by Sullivan and colleagues (2006), years of playing experience was a significant predictor of strategy efficacy; but in contrast to Sullivan and colleagues' study, it additionally predicted technique efficacy. Perceived player support significantly predicted motivation and character-building efficacy. Interestingly, perceived parental support was not a significant predictor of any of the dimensions of coaching efficacy. Based on canonical correlation analysis, technique and strategy efficacy were the most important dimensions of coaching efficacy as predicted by these sources. Given that these coaches had relatively little coaching experience, it makes sense that they would rely additionally on their playing experience regarding how to teach the skills of their sport as well as game strategy knowledge. It also makes sense that the basics of the sport—skills and strategies—would be most important at this level.

Research on Coaching Education as a Source of Coaching Efficacy

A few studies also have addressed the role that formal education programs play in the development of coaching efficacy (Corcoran & Feltz, 1993; Lee et al., 2002; Malete & Feltz, 2000). These programs may include college-level coaching education programs, specific coaching education workshops and seminars offered by athletic organizations, and nationally required certification programs. The programs vary greatly in content and length; however, an effective, well-designed coaching education program should enhance the level of one's coaching efficacy if it increases one's knowledge about the skills of coaching.

Corcoran and Feltz (1993) demonstrated that coaches who received educational information about chemical health and use among athletes had higher levels of efficacy about incorporating that information into their coaching than coaches who did not receive this training. Malete and Feltz (2000) compared a group of high school coaches participating in the Program for Athletic Coaching Education (PACE: Seefeldt & Brown, 1990) with a control group of coaches who had not undertaken any formal education programs on pre- and postmeasures of the CES. The 12 hr PACE program, designed by faculty at the Institute for the Study of Youth Sports, covered legal responsibilities of the coach; emergency procedures for injuries; prevention, care, and rehabilitation of sport injuries; role of the coach; effective instruction and game strategy; motivating athletes; personal and social skills; positive coaching; and maintaining discipline. PACE coaches, compared to control coaches, significantly improved their confidence in their coaching abilities as a result of the program. They improved most in their game strategy and technique efficacy, though improvements were relatively small given the short duration of the program. This finding was also supported with a sample of Singapore coaches (Lee et al., 2002). Using a nonexperimental design, Lee and colleagues found that certified coaches reported significantly higher scores on strategy and technique efficacy than uncertified coaches. There was also a main effect for gender; males had higher strategy efficacy compared to females. This result was also supported with intercollegiate coaches (Sullivan & Kent, 2003). Similarly, Campbell and Sullivan (2005) found that in Canada's National Coaching Certification Program, participating coaches showed a significant increase in all factors of coaching confidence after completing the course; however, females showed higher scores on motivation and character-building confidence than did male coaches.

The CES has also been used as a tool to diagnose coaches' needs in order to promote more effective coaching education content. Fung (2003) administered the scale to a sample of high school coaches to ascertain their relative inadequacies and found that coaches felt most confident about character building and least confident about game strategy. Thus, the CES can be used pre–post to determine how effective the educational content of a program is on the various dimensions of coaching efficacy and can be used diagnostically to create educational content that best meets the needs of a particular set of coaches. Preliminary evidence suggests that educational programs enhance the game strategy and technique aspects of a coach's confidence, which may be due to the characteristics of the coaches that those programs target—mostly high school coaches at beginning levels of coaching. More experienced coaches might benefit from educational programs that focus more on motivation skills.

Although the research reviewed supports the sources of coaching efficacy and their influence on coaching efficacy beliefs, the specific sources and the dimensions of coaching efficacy influenced appear to be dependent on the level of coaches involved (e.g., youth, high school, or collegiate), organizational factors (e.g., local vs. travel leagues, competition divisions, size of school), and, to a certain extent, gender of the coach. The association between years coaching and playing and technique and game strategy may be more important at the youth level; years in coaching and game strategy and motivation efficacy may be more important at the high school level; and the association between perceived team ability and motivation and character-building efficacy may be more important at the small college level. Very little research has been conducted using female coaches, but some of the differences found on game strategy efficacy suggest that more research is needed to determine the sources of information that influence this dimension in female coaches. A separate section on gender in coaching is provided later in this chapter. More research is needed that addresses the additional sources of coaching efficacy at different organizational levels of coaching and with more female coaches. In addition, the research on sources of coaching efficacy does not provide evidence for coaching efficacy as a determinant of coaching effectiveness as Bandura's (1997) theory and Feltz and colleagues' (1999) model would suggest. However, in the next two sections we review research on the influence of coaching efficacy on coaching effectiveness in terms of coaching behavior and athlete and team outcomes.

Research on the Influence of Coaching Efficacy on Coaching Behavior

In addition to examining the potential sources of coaching efficacy, Feltz and colleagues (1999) investigated the coaching behaviors and commitment of high- and low-efficacy coaches. Using the total coaching efficacy measure, they hypothesized that coaching efficacy would predict coaches' behavior in terms of positive feedback to players, time spent coaching, and commitment to coaching. They used the Coaching Behavior Assessment System (CBAS: Smith, Smoll, & Hunt, 1977) to observe 15 coaches with the highest and 15 with the lowest CES scores on 12 categories of coaching behaviors such as "positive reinforcement in response to desirable player performance," "mistake-contingent encouragement in response to player mistakes," and "general technical instruction."

Feltz and her colleagues found, as predicted, that higher-efficacy coaches used more praise and encouragement behaviors and fewer instructional and organizational behaviors than lower-efficacy coaches. The fact that high-efficacy coaches demonstrated less instructional and organizational behavior was explained in terms of less efficiency among lower-efficacy coaches who spent more time on organizing players for drills and practice.

The other two predicted outcomes of coaching efficacy, commitment to coaching and perceived coaching effort, were not at all related to the construct. The authors reasoned that because coaching is not a full-time job at the high school level, coaches who are not dedicated to coaching may have already quit. However, Kent and Sullivan (2003), surveying U.S. and Canadian intercollegiate coaches, found a relationship with organizational commitment, defined as the extent to which workers in an organization are committed to the organization, its goals and values, and its processes (Chelladurai, 1999). Rather than use single-item methodology, they measured commitment in terms of *affective commitment* (i.e., attachment to, identification with, and involvement in the organization), *continuance commitment* (i.e., an awareness of the costs to self associated with leaving the organization), and *normative commitment* (i.e., a feeling of obligation to continue employment) (Meyer & Allen, 1991). In a path analysis, they found a significant and strong relationship between coaching efficacy and affective commitment ($r^2 = .99$) and a lesser but still significant relationship with normative commitment ($r^2 = .33$). Thus, coaching efficacy appears to significantly predict intercollegiate coaches' identifications with their current positions and perceptions of obligation toward their positions. Bivariate correlations revealed that this commitment was most consistently related to coaches' efficacy beliefs as motivators and character builders.

Related to coaching commitment is the other side of the continuum—coach burnout. Haugen and Short (2006) assessed high school basketball coaches, pre- and postseason, on the CES and a measure of coaching burnout. They found that although all coaches had higher burnout scores and lower efficacy scores by postseason, low-efficacy coaches were more burned out compared to the high-efficacy coaches. A high sense of one's coaching efficacy may have an insulating effect against the large number of stressors that have been associated with the coaching profession.

Another coaching behavior not specifically addressed in Feltz and colleagues' (1999) model is leadership style, though Smoll and Smith's (1989) model of leadership effectiveness in youth sport is based on the approach to feedback that coaches use, which is included in Feltz and colleagues' model. Sullivan and Kent (2003), using the same sample as in the Kent and Sullivan (2003) study, investigated the predictive strength of specific coaching efficacy dimensions on Chelladurai and Saleh's (1980) five dimensions of self-reported leadership behavior: teaching and instruction, social support, positive feedback, democratic behavior, and autocratic behavior.

Chelladurai and Saleh (1980) conceptualize training and instruction leadership as a task-oriented dimension of coaching behavior aimed at improving athletes' performance through an emphasis on training, teaching specific skills, and coordinating activities. Social support leadership, a motivationally oriented dimension, captures coaching behavior that demonstrates a care for the personal welfare of the athletes and includes the creation and maintenance of a positive group atmosphere and emphasis on interpersonal relations. Positive feedback leadership, another motivationally oriented dimension, refers to coaching behavior that reinforces the athlete by recognizing and rewarding good performance. The last two dimensions, democratic and autocratic behavior leadership, are decision-style factors; the former characterizes behavior that allows athletes greater participation in various decisions, and the latter describes coaches who make most decisions independently. Coaches are asked to compare themselves in their responses to their perception of what would be their *ideal* coach.

Sullivan and Kent (2003) hypothesized that teaching and game strategy efficacy would predict training and instruction leadership behavior, that motivation and character-building efficacy would predict social support and positive feedback behavior, and that game strategy efficacy would also predict democratic and autocratic behavior. Previous studies had not addressed how specific dimensions of coaching efficacy predicted specific dimensions of self-reported coaching styles. Because the social support and autocratic subscales lacked internal reliability in this study, they were eliminated from analysis. However, results using the other three dimensions showed that motivation and technique efficacy beliefs predicted teaching and instruction and positive feedback leadership behaviors. Thus, as coaches were more confident in their roles as motivators and teachers, they were closer to their image of the ideal leader with respect to using positive feedback and appropriate training and instruction.

The positive relationship between technique efficacy and teaching and instruction leadership behavior may appear inconsistent with Feltz and colleagues' (1999) finding that less confident coaches displayed more instructing and organizing behaviors. However, as Sullivan and Kent (2003) explain, these two coaching behaviors are not conceptually the same or operationally measured in the same way. Chelladurai and Saleh's (1980) training and instruction measure has to do with how effective coaches *perceive* themselves as teachers, while Smith and colleagues' (1977) instructional and organizational behavior refers to *observed* general technical instruction, as well as punitive and correctional instruction. Sullivan and Kent further point out, however, that these two patterns are not mutually exclusive. Inexperienced and less confident coaches may rely more on rote instruction and organization skills. As they become more confident (e.g., through experiences and success), they may change their leadership style so as to focus more on the actual improvement of athletes' performance (i.e., training and instruction). More research is necessary to test these assumptions.

Research on the Influence of Coaching Efficacy on Athlete and Team Outcomes

As outlined in Feltz and colleagues' (1999) model, coaching efficacy influences not only coaching behavior but also the behavior, performance, and perceptions of the athletes and teams. The model has not specified whether these athlete and team outcomes are directly influenced by the coaches' efficacy beliefs or are mediated through the coaches' behavior, but the few studies that have been conducted support a significant association between coaching efficacy and athlete and team variables (Feltz et al., 1999; Myers, Vargas-Tonsing, & Feltz, 2005; Short & Short, 2004; Vargas-Tonsing, Warners, & Feltz, 2003). For instance, Feltz and her research teams (Feltz et al., 1999; Myers, Vargas-Tonsing, & Feltz, 2005) found that athletes and teams of higher-efficacy coaches were more satisfied with their coach (i.e., liked playing for the coach, wanted to play for the same coach next year, thought the coach liked them, and liked the sport) and performed better in terms of win/loss records than those of lower-efficacy coaches. This occurred at both the high school and small college coaching levels with male teams. At the collegiate level, where the dimensions of coaching efficacy also were examined, Myers and colleagues found that motivation and character-building efficacies were the most predictive of winning percentages within teams and that technique efficacy was most predictive of team satisfaction.

Myers and colleagues (2005) also examined these relationships within women's teams by gender of coach. When they looked at coaching efficacy by dimensions, they found that none of the coaching efficacy dimensions for male or female coaches predicted winning percentage for women's teams. In terms of team satisfaction, character-building efficacy was negatively related to team satisfaction in female teams with male coaches; in contrast, motivation efficacy was positively related to team satisfaction in female teams with female coaches, even though there was no difference in level of satisfaction between male-coached and female-coached teams.

Myers and colleagues (2005) speculated that this unexpected finding in team satisfaction could be due to athletes' gender bias in preference for same-sex coaches or athletes' preferences for more democratic coach decision styles, which are more prevalent among female coaches (Chelladurai & Arnott, 1985). However, the athletes may have perceived that female coaches gave more attention to teaching them and helping them to improve as a way to motivate them. For instance, Barber (1998) found that high school female coaches placed greater importance than male coaches on the improvement of athletes' skills. In addition, Vargas-Tonsing (2004) found that male coaches of elite girls' soccer teams spent significantly less time giving pregame speeches than male coaches of elite boys' teams (by 93 sec). Thus, it may be that female coaches' motivation efficacy translates into more motivational coaching behavior as perceived by female athletes, which in turn is more satisfying to them.

Although the authors did not speculate on why there was no relation between coaching efficacy and women's teams' winning percentage, we suggest here that the athletic administrators' expectations for coaches of women's teams to produce winning seasons may not be as high as they are for coaches of men's teams. Thus, coaches of women's teams may not be as focused on wins and losses as they are on other aspects of team performance. Research has shown that male and female coaches differed on their perceptions of what it takes to be a good coach (Molstad, 1993). Female coaches ranked being a good role model and understanding athletes' feelings as high priorities. Male coaches ranked relating well to athletes and producing winners as top priorities. Research also has shown a slightly higher ranking by male coaches for the importance of competition in coaching (Lirgg et al., 1994; Molstad, 1993). Further research is needed to examine these speculations.

Other athlete and team variables that have been examined in relation to coaching efficacy are player and team efficacy beliefs and athletes' perceptions of their coach's confidence levels (Short & Short, 2004; Vargas-Tonsing et al., 2003). Vargas-Tonsing and colleagues were interested in whether the dimensions of coaching efficacy were more predictive of efficacy beliefs of athletes or of teams within girls' high school volleyball. As defined in chapter 4, team or collective efficacy is a team's shared judgment on how members think they can perform as a team. Results showed a positive relationship between the coach's character-building efficacy and team efficacy, but no relationship with player efficacy. However, the sample size was too small to permit a hierarchical linear modeling (HLM) analysis to examine player efficacy at the individual level or examination of all of the predictors simultaneously.

How much confidence athletes perceive their coaches to have is important to the athletes' sense of confidence. According to the findings of Vargas-Tonsing, Myers, and Feltz (2004), athletes believed that "the coach acting confident" was one of the most effective strategies that coaches can use to increase athletes' feelings of efficacy. But there can be a discrepancy between how confident a coach believes he or she is and how confident the athletes perceive that coach to be. A coach's positive efficacy beliefs will not be as influential on an athlete if the athlete does not perceive the coach to be very confident. Thus, Short and Short (2004) wanted to compare how much coaching efficacy athletes thought their coaches had in comparison to the coaches' own assessments of their coaching efficacy. Using nine Division II collegiate football teams and coaches, the authors compared the responses of coaches and their athletes on the CES and a modified version of the CES for the athletes. They calculated 95% confidence intervals around the athletes' ratings to determine if the coach's rating was within the confidence interval and therefore considered similar. Unfortunately, with such a small sample, it is difficult to draw any generalities; however, these coaches and athletes mostly considered coaches to have high coaching efficacy on all four dimensions of the CES. Two of the nine coaches rated themselves higher than their athletes' confidence intervals on game strategy, motivation, and technique efficacy, and one coach rated himself lower on all four dimensions. Given that all of the mean ratings were higher than the midpoint of the scales, these differences probably do not have any practical significance with respect to the athletes' seeing their coaches as lacking confidence.

From the few studies conducted on athlete and team variables, the dimensions of coaching efficacy that appear to have the greatest predictive strength on these dependent variables are motivation and character-building efficacies. Technique efficacy was related to team satisfaction on men's teams in the Myers, Vargas-Tonsing, and Feltz (2005) study. Game strategy efficacy was noticeably absent in these studies as a significant predictor of team satisfaction, team efficacy, and even team winning records. From the athletes' point of view, it may be, as Phil Jackson indicated, more important for coaches to have confidence in their ability to convey to teams what they want to accomplish with them—the motivational and whole-player aspects of the game—than just to be a game strategist.

Strategies and Expectancies of Coaches in Building the Efficacy Beliefs of Athletes and Teams

In addition to the influence of a coach's own efficacy beliefs on athletes' self- and team efficacy beliefs, coaches' motivational strategies and expectations influence efficacy beliefs in athletes and teams. A few studies have investigated the strategies that coaches use to try to build the efficacy beliefs of their athletes and teams (Gould, Hodge, Peterson, & Giannini, 1989; Vargas-Tonsing et al., 2004; Weinberg, Grove, & Jackson, 1992; Weinberg & Jackson, 1990). At the collegiate and national coaching levels, wrestling coaches reported encouraging positive as opposed to negative self-talk, modeling confidence oneself, using instruction and drills to ensure performance improvements, and using rewarding statements liberally as the most effective ways to enhance self-efficacy in their athletes (Gould et al., 1989). High school and age-group tennis coaches reported using similar techniques to enhance self-efficacy and also reported using verbal persuasion (Weinberg et al., 1992; Weinberg & Jackson, 1990). Probably unbeknownst to most coaches, these strategies are all based on the major sources of efficacy information as identified in Bandura's (1977) theory: performance accomplishments, vicarious experiences (modeling), and verbal and self-persuasion.

Although coaches may believe that the strategies just mentioned are the most effective for enhancing the efficacy beliefs of their athletes, athletes may not concur. The effectiveness of strategies is mediated by the meaning that athletes give to them, and therefore the athletes' perceptions of the effectiveness of these strategies may be more important than the coaches' with respect to enhancing athletes' motivation, confidence, and performance (Horn, 2002). Vargas-Tonsing and colleagues (2004) examined athletes' perceptions of coaches' efficacy-enhancing techniques and compared them to their coaches' perceptions using 78 Division II and III collegiate teams of various team sports. Athletes reported that encouraging positive talk, the coach's acting confident, instruction and drilling, and verbal persuasion were the most effective efficacy-enhancing techniques. This was also what coaches reported.

However, in examining the congruence of beliefs between athletes and their specific coach, Vargas-Tonsing and colleagues (2004) found that coaches' perceptions were generally incongruent with their teams' perceptions in terms of effectiveness of efficacy-enhancing techniques. Some coaches perceived their techniques to be more effective than their teams did, while others perceived them to be less effective. The authors suggested that athletes' preexisting levels of efficacy may have affected their perceptions of the effectiveness of coaching behaviors; that is, athletes with lower levels of efficacy may be more likely than high-efficacy athletes to evaluate coaching behaviors negatively. However, the authors used team as the unit of analysis and therefore could not determine the extent of incongruence on an individual athlete basis. They acknowledged that there was only mediocre agreement within the teams in regard to a coach's efficacy-enhancing behaviors with athletes. The strength of this study was its inclusion of athletes' perceptions, which supported earlier findings from coaches. Coaches' actions in the form of encouraging positive self-talk, modeling confidence themselves, using instruction and drills to ensure performance improvements, and using verbal persuasion are helpful, as perceived by athletes, for enhancing athletes' efficacy beliefs. In addition, Myers, Vargas-Tonsing, and Feltz (2005) found that the higher the coach's coaching efficacy, the more that coach employed these techniques.

As all the authors of these studies have noted, observations of coaches were not conducted to determine the actual use of the self-efficacy techniques or to determine whether these techniques were effective in enhancing the confidence of athletes and improving performance. Further observational research is needed to advance this line of research.

Verbal persuasion and encouragement are popular techniques and readily available to coaches who wish to try to motivate and enhance the efficacy of athletes. Perhaps the most noticeable use of this technique is in the pregame speech. The pregame speech is the last opportunity the coach has to try to influence a team's pregame confidence. To determine whether verbal persuasion through pregame speeches influenced athletes' efficacy beliefs, Vargas-Tonsing conducted a couple of studies of the effects of pregame speeches on athletes' and teams' efficacy beliefs (Vargas-Tonsing, 2004; Vargas-Tonsing & Bartholomew, 2006). First, using a hypothetical soccer competition scenario, Vargas-Tonsing and Bartholomew randomly assigned college-aged recreational soccer players to one of three pregame speeches: strategy based, motivation or emotion based, or an etiquette-based control. Those receiving the motivational speech reported significantly stronger beliefs that their hypothetical team would win than players in the strategy or control speech groups.

Vargas-Tonsing (2004) followed this study with her dissertation using real soccer coaches who provided real pregame speeches. She obtained somewhat different results with this second study. She studied the pregame speeches of 10 youth soccer coaches of premier-level teams before critical games, as well as the athletes' efficacy and emotional changes as a result of the speech. She found that the coaches' pregame speeches significantly increased athletes' self-efficacy beliefs about the impending game for players who perceived the speech as informational and strategic. The perceived emotional content of the speeches was not related to after-speech perceptions of efficacy. Thus, a coach's persuasive attempts to heighten a team's strategic ability had a more potent effect on players' self-efficacy beliefs than did attempts to heighten a team's emotional arousal. There are several possible explanations for the different results in the two studies. The youth soccer players and their coaches perceived more informational than emotional content in the speeches. The speeches in the contrived study were controlled for content. Premier-level players and coaches may perceive informational or strategic content as more important than recreational players do. One variable not investigated was coaching efficacy. Whether coaches' efficacy levels influence the type of pregame speeches employed is a question for future research with a larger number of coaches.

The coach's efficacy expectations regarding the athlete or team may also play a role in determining the efficacy beliefs of the athletes. Horn (1985) found that middle school coaches gave their low-expectancy athletes more praise for mediocre performances and ignored those athletes' mistakes compared to the way they behaved toward their high-expectancy athletes. They gave their high-expectancy athletes more criticism and corrective instruction in response to skill errors. Low-expectancy athletes interpreted this feedback as suggesting that they had less ability than those for whom the coaches were conveying higher expectations. Although the efficacy expectations of the athletes in this study were not measured, perceptions of ability strongly influence perceived self-efficacy (Bandura, 1997). Solomon (2001, 2002) also found that collegiate coaches' judgments of their athletes' sport confidence significantly predicted individual athletic performance while athletes' own sport confidence judgments showed no relationship. Solomon did not report the correlations, however, and multicollinearity is suspect.

At the team level, Chase, Lirgg, and Feltz (1997) examined the relationship between coaches' efficacy regarding their teams and team performance. With use of a method similar to assessment of collective efficacy, coaches of four intercollegiate women's basketball teams were asked before 10 of their games to rate their confidence in their teams' abilities to perform specific basketball skills (i.e., shoot field goals and free throws, rebound, commit turnovers, etc.).

Coaches were also asked to rate the importance they placed on these skills, the perceived control they felt over the outcome, and opponent ability. Coaches who had higher efficacy beliefs for their teams perceived themselves to have higher control over their teams' outcomes. Also, the higher the perceived ability of the opponent, the lower the coach's efficacy regarding her team. In terms of coach's efficacy regarding the team and team performance, only free throws and turnover performance could be predicted ($R^2 = .12$).

A second purpose of Chase and colleagues' (1997) study was to determine what coaches used as a basis in forming their efficacy judgments of their teams. Inductive content analysis was used to identify sources of both high and low efficacy. Factors that resulted in high efficacy expectations included good past game and practice performances, favorable comparison with opponents, return of an injured player, and negative comments from an opponent. Coaches also identified good performance preparation by either themselves, their staff, or their players as contributing to high efficacy expectations for their teams. Chase and her colleagues also noted that many coaches cited past poor performance as a reason they were confident in their teams because they believed in their teams' ability to bounce back. Low-efficacy factors were analogous to high-efficacy factors: past poor game and practice performance, injured or tired players, and comparison of the team to good opponents. Other factors included low perceived efficacy of players and a team's inconsistent performances. The researchers reasoned that if indeed players were aware of the efficacy expectations coaches had for their teams, a situation similar to the Pygmalion effect might have occurred, wherein coaches first form expectations of their teams and then act in ways that are consistent with those expectations. Athletes, in turn, perceive and interpret those actions and respond in ways that reinforce the original expectations. If this happens, coaches with low efficacy expectations for their teams may inadvertently be contributing to low collective efficacy while those who believe their teams are capable may convey that attitude to their teams.

Since the development of Feltz and colleagues' (1999) model of coaching efficacy, Horn (2002) has formulated a working model of coaching effectiveness (see figure 5.3). The center point of Horn's model is coaches' behavior (box 5) and coaches' expectations, values, beliefs, and goals for their athletes (box 4) as the central mediator of various antecedent factors, including coaches' self-efficacy for coaching (box 3), on coaching behaviors. In contrast, Feltz and colleagues' model has coaching efficacy as the cornerstone and central cognitive mediator of coaching behavior. Also, in Feltz and colleagues' model, perceived ability of athletes might be considered similar to a coach's expectations of his or her athletes; in Horn's model, however, these expectations are considered a consequence of a coach's efficacy beliefs rather than a source of information. In teacher efficacy research, Bandura (1997) portrays these expectations of students as both a source of teachers' efficacy beliefs

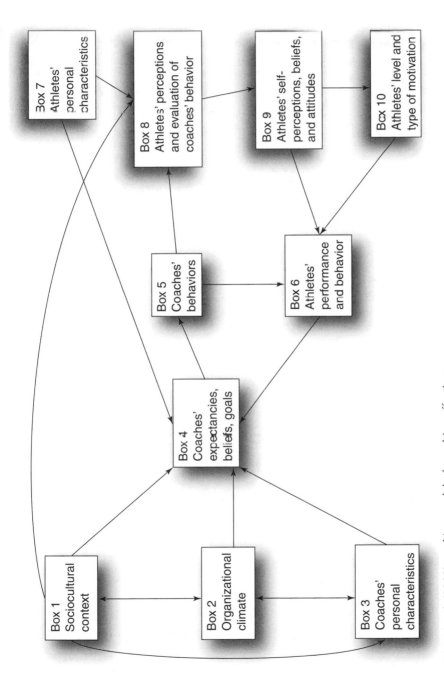

Figure 5.3 Horn's (2002) working model of coaching effectiveness.

Reprinted, by permission, from T.S. Horn, 2002, Coaching effectiveness in the sports domain. In *Advances in sport psychology*, edited by T.S. Horn (Champaign, IL: Human Kinetics), 313.

and a consequence of those beliefs. That is, teachers with low efficacy beliefs in their ability to help students learn are more apt to use low student ability as an explanation for why they cannot be taught. In addition, teachers who are continually assigned students of low ability will have a lower sense that they can affect students' learning (Smylie, 1988). Horn's model also suggests that coaches with high coaching efficacy will have a low expectancy bias that some athletes are less capable than others. Thus, in Feltz and colleagues' model, perceived ability of one's athletes could be viewed as an antecedent and as a consequence of coaching efficacy.

Coaching behavior is one of several consequences of coaching efficacy in Feltz and colleagues' model, and coaching efficacy is hypothesized to directly influence coaching behavior rather than to be mediated by expectancy beliefs, values, and goals of the athletes. The consequences of coaching behavior in Horn's model focus solely on athletes' psychosocial growth and development and not on other coaching factors such as coaching commitment and burnout. However, other variables on the consequence side of coaching behavior are similar to those on the consequence side of coaching efficacy, such as athletes' performance and behavior (box 6), athletes' self-perceptions and beliefs (box 9), and athletes' level and type of motivation (box 10). These consequences are probably more accurately mediated through the coach's behavior rather than directly influenced by the coach's self-efficacy beliefs.

Even with these differences, the Horn (2002) model can contribute to the antecedents and consequences of the coaching efficacy model. For instance, the organizational climate (box 2) includes pressure to win, which could be a source of coaching efficacy information. Coaches' expectancies and expectancy bias for their athletes could be a consequence of coaching efficacy. Athletes' evaluation of the coach's behaviors (box 8) has recently been considered within the coaching efficacy model (Myers, Feltz, Maier, Wolfe, & Reckase, 2006). Myers and colleagues assessed athletes' perceptions of their coaches' competency to affect the learning and performance of athletes using a scale developed to match the dimensions of the CES. They hypothesized that athlete and team measures of perceived coaching competencies would be positively related to athlete and team measures of satisfaction with the head coach, respectively, as predicted within the Horn (2002) model. They found support for the hypothesized relationships for perceived motivation competence within teams. Thus, the more athletes perceived their coach to be motivationally competent, the more satisfied they were with the coach.

Women and Coaching

Much has been written about the decline in the number of female coaches since the passage of Title IX in 1972 (e.g., Acosta & Carpenter, 1985; Fink,

1995; Hart, Hasbrook, & Mathes, 1986; Knoppers, 1987; Pastore, 1991). Researchers have advanced several reasons for this decline in the face of increased participation of female athletes at all levels of competition. These have included lack of experience, competing obligations of family, lack of support systems, the old boys' network, preference for male coaches on the part of female athletes, institutional discrimination, and males' increased attraction to the coaching of females (Everhart & Chelladurai, 1998; Lirgg et al., 1994)

One social cognitive variable that may influence women's decisions to enter and remain in a coaching career is their sense of efficacy to be a successful coach (Everhart & Chelladurai, 1998). However, several studies addressing gender differences in coaching efficacy have shown few differences (Barber, 1998; Lee et al., 2002; Malete & Feltz, 2000; Marback et al., 2005; Myers, Vargas-Tonsing, & Feltz, 2005; Sullivan & Kent, 2003). The few gender differences found had weak effects for game strategy (Marback et al.; Lee et al.) and motivation (Marback et al.), but only Lee and colleagues controlled for coaching experience. Given that male coaches typically have more years of experience than their female counterparts (e.g., Lee et al.), gender differences may have more to do with differences in years of experience. Even with controlling for years of experience, Lee and colleagues found that male coaches reported stronger perceptions of confidence in game strategy and motivation. However, research has also reported that female coaches perceived themselves to be more capable at teaching sport skills (Barber, 1998) and character building (Marback et al., 2005) compared to male coaches. The game strategy differences, though weak, corroborate Weiss and colleagues' (1991) finding that novice women coaches reported strategy and tactical knowledge as their weakest area of coaching competence.

These results are for women who have already entered the coaching ranks—who have already decided that they have the skills to meet the job requirements. Everhart and Chelladurai (1998) examined the role of self-efficacy in career choice to coach among university athletes. Research on occupational self-efficacy has shown gender differences for occupations that are traditionally considered more masculine (Hackett & Betz, 1981; Lent, Brown, & Larkin, 1984, 1986). Coaching has also been considered a male-dominated activity (Coakley, 2004). Everhart and Chelladurai surveyed male and female collegiate basketball players regarding their confidence in their capacity to perform coaching tasks effectively, preferred occupational valence (desired outcomes, for example autonomy, challenge, growth, security), valence of coaching (expected outcomes), perceived barriers to coaching, and desired level of coaching. Using college basketball players, they found no gender differences in perceived efficacy to coach in the future, and women who were coached by women had higher expected outcomes and reported less concern with perceived discrimination if they were to coach than did women who were coached by men. This finding was also supported by Lirgg and colleagues (1994) with high school female athletes.

Thus, even for those who have not yet joined the coaching ranks, if they have collegiate playing experience there appear to be no gender differences in perceived coaching efficacy for the future. The authors refute the "female deficit" model as the explanation for the presence of fewer women in coaching. Although coaching efficacy has been high among the female athletes studied, there has not been a great desire to choose coaching as an occupation (Cunningham, Sagas, & Ashley, 2003; Everhart & Chelladurai, 1998; Lirgg et al., 1994). In Everhart and Chelladurai's study, even though there was a significant relationship between efficacy and coaching desire, perceived number of working hours as a barrier to coaching was the most significant predictor regarding desire to coach among men and women. Barber (1998) obtained similar results for time demands with high school coaches. Although Barber reported low perceived coaching competence as more of a reason for high school female coaches to withdraw from coaching than for male coaches, upon closer inspection the variable resembled outcome expectations rather than perceived competence (e.g., "inability to accomplish personal goals in coaching").

The push to hire more women into coaching positions at all levels may have important benefits to female athletes. Female coaches appear to be important role models for the level of coaching aspirations of female athletes at the high school and collegiate levels (Everhart & Chelladurai, 1998; Lirgg et al., 1994). Female coaches rank being a good role model and understanding athletes' feelings as higher priorities than do male coaches (Molstad, 1993), and they place greater importance than male coaches do on the improvement of athletes' skills (Barber, 1998). In addition, female athletes of female coaches find their coach's confidence-projecting behavior, verbal persuasion, and reward statements more effective in enhancing their own confidence than female athletes of male coaches (Vargas-Tonsing et al., 2004).

In summary, the research on coaching efficacy has shown that it is multidimensional; it has sources that conform to self-efficacy theory plus some that are unique to coaches (e.g., perceived skill of athletes, one's own playing experience); and it is a significant predictor of coaching behavior and athlete and team outcomes. In addition, the CES is, thus far, the only instrument designed to measure coaching efficacy, although revisions are under way to strengthen some of the dimensions. Thus, we have made a good start in understanding the nature of coaching efficacy, but much more is needed in terms of dimension-specific hypotheses, understanding of sources of coaching efficacy at different organizational levels, and understanding of how gender and coaching efficacy interact to influence female athletes and teams.

III

PART

Building, Maintaining, and Regaining Efficacy Beliefs in Sport

In this section, we offer suggestions for efficacy interventions and future research ideas. Our suggested interventions are based on theory and research findings for building and maintaining efficacy in novice and experienced athletes (chapter 6), teams (chapter 7), and coaches (chapter 8). There is often a time lag between research and practice, and the contents of this section bridge the gap in a format that is easy to understand for those who are looking for practical advice. These chapters can be considered "stand-alone" in that understanding the information provided is not necessarily dependent upon previous sections of the book. In chapter 9, we direct attention forward to areas for future research. We describe ideas for research projects that correspond to measurement and to athletes, teams, and coaches, as well as ideas that cut across these three groups.

6

Enhancing Efficacy Beliefs of Athletes

> "You gain strength, courage and confidence by every experience in which you really stop to look fear in the face. . . . Do the thing you think you cannot."
>
> *Eleanor Roosevelt, First Lady of the United States (1933-1945)*

Often in sport people talk about "natural" athletes. Examples range from Wayne Gretzky (who is considered the greatest hockey player of all time) to Alice Coachman (who was the first African American athlete to win an Olympic gold medal), to Tiger Woods (arguably one of the greatest golfers ever). In the case of Tiger Woods, "natural athlete" is apparently written in his astrological chart; he is simply living out his destiny! It is tempting for some people to believe in the notion of the "natural athlete," but it is a myth. That there is a single, global motor ability related to the performance of a variety of motor skills (Magill, 1998), and that through genetics one is born highly athletic, have been refuted in the sport science literature. Instead, there is support for the specificity of motor *abilities* (i.e., plural) hypothesis, which holds that individuals have many motor abilities that are relatively independent of each other. When people excel in certain sports it is likely that they are at the "high end" of the rating scale for the abilities required for that specific task. Moreover, it is likely that these skills were perfected through countless hours of intensive and purposeful or *deliberate practice.* In domains ranging from music to sport, thousands of hours of deliberate practice are thought to be necessary for exceptional skill development (Ericsson & Charness, 1994; Ericsson, Krampe, & Tesch-Romer, 1993; Hodges & Starkes, 1996). However, although dedicated practice may be an important catalyst of exceptional performance, it is also widely recognized that success in athletic competitions requires more than physical skill and sport-specific knowledge, that a firm sense of confidence is essential for optimal performance as well. In Bandura's (1997) words, athletic skills must be cultivated through intensive training and orchestrated by efficacious self-belief.

In this chapter we present methods to build, maintain, and regain self-efficacy based on information from the six sources outlined in chapter 1: (a) performance accomplishments, (b) vicarious experiences, (c) verbal persuasion, (d) physiological states, (e) emotional states, and (f) imaginal experiences (Bandura, 1977, 1986b, 1997; Maddux, 1995). Rather than divide the chapter into sections corresponding to each source, we highlight those techniques that we think are best for novice and elite athletes. Although the techniques sometimes overlap, our assumption is that novice athletes are generally concerned with building confidence, whereas more experienced athletes are focused on maintaining or regaining confidence. In our view, building confidence occurs when an athlete is trying to establish, increase, or strengthen his or her confidence level, likely concomitantly with skill development in novices. Maintaining confidence occurs when one has developed a strong sense of confidence and is focused on keeping it at that level. Regaining confidence occurs when one is trying to recover or get one's confidence level back again. When a technique is applicable to both novice and experienced athletes, we present it in both sections because there are often subtle differences. Overall, it is surprising that so few intervention studies have used self-efficacy as a dependent variable (Feltz & Lirgg, 2001). However, as Feltz and Lirgg stated, this is probably the case because performance is typically emphasized in sport research. At the end of the chapter we address the optimal level of confidence for athletic performance.

Although we use the words self-efficacy and confidence interchangeably throughout this chapter, the interventions described are based on self-efficacy theory. Confidence is a catchword in sport rather than a construct embedded in a theory (Bandura, 1997). Bandura states that advances in sport psychology are best achieved through use of constructs, like self-efficacy, that fully reflect the phenomena of interest and are rooted in theory that specifies their determinants, mediating processes, and multiple effects. Although these theory-based constructs are invaluable in terms of the understanding they afford and the guidance they provide, the term "self-confidence" has more meaning to practitioners and nonpsychologists.

Because this chapter concerns ways to build, maintain, and regain confidence for novice and elite athletes, it is important to first point out that few theories or models used in and out of sport provide explicit step-by-step guidelines for developing interventions (Kanfer, 1984; Maddux & Lewis, 1995). However, good theories do provide the practitioner with a conceptual framework that serves as a general guide for interventions. This is precisely what self-efficacy theory does. The theory may be most useful not in suggesting specific techniques for behavior change but in emphasizing the importance of arranging experiences designed to increase the athlete's sense of efficacy (Maddux & Lewis, 1995).

Social cognitive theory distinguishes between mechanisms of change and procedures for change (Bandura, 1986b). Mechanisms of change are mediating explanatory processes and are primarily cognitive (Maddux & Lewis, 1995). Self-efficacy is believed to influence behavior through four mediating processes: goal setting and persistence, affect, cognition, and selection of environments and activities (Bandura, 1986b, 1997; Maddux & Lewis, 1995). Procedures for change are primarily behavioral in that they provide opportunities for people to engage in new and more effective behaviors (Maddux & Lewis, 1995). According to Maddux and Lewis, these behavioral changes initiate cognitive and affective changes that support the behavioral changes and encourage their durability.

Start With Assessment

When one designs any intervention to produce behavior change, assessment is always important. Without it, how does one know which areas to target? Self-efficacy is not a personality trait, nor is it a global entity or a general disposition (Bandura, 1997). According to Bandura, efficacy beliefs are multifaceted, representing many diverse capabilities. That is, self-efficacy perceptions vary across different activities, different levels of the same activity, and different circumstances. For example, Wayne Gretzky was extremely confident in his ability to perform the skills that were required for his success in ice hockey. However, he has acknowledged that he lacked confidence in his ability to score on breakaways. In fact, when Gretzky played for Team Canada at the Olympics in 1988, memorably, during the shootout in the semifinal match against the Czech Republic, Canadian coach Marc Crawford opted to have defenseman Ray Bourque shoot in the shootout instead of NHL all-time leading scorer Gretzky. Hockey commentators alternatively criticized Crawford's decision (Bourque, like the other four Canadian shooters, failed to score) and praised it on the grounds that Bourque was one of hockey's most accurate shooters at the time and Gretzky had always been surprisingly mediocre on breakaways. The Czech Republic went on to win the game and the gold medal.

There are many reasons why assessment is crucial. It can assist in targeting specific areas, predicting areas of potential difficulty, tailoring interventions to meet athletes' specific needs, and monitoring the effectiveness of intervention techniques (Maddux & Lewis, 1995). Although we addressed ways to assess efficacy beliefs in chapter 2, we want to highlight two points pertinent to this chapter. First, assessment should include behaviors as well as thoughts and feelings (Maddux & Lewis, 1995). These areas correspond to how a person performs, thinks, and feels. Maddux and Lewis defined behavioral self-efficacy as the belief in one's ability to perform the specific actions needed to be successful in particular situations. This is similar to the original definition of self-efficacy as a belief about behavior (Bandura, 1977), and what we labeled as "task self-efficacy" in chapter 1. Although Maddux and Lewis separated cognitive and emotional (or coping) efficacy, as we stated in chapter 1, the type of efficacy beliefs we are describing here has to do with the belief to exercise personal control over unwanted thoughts and emotions. Social cognitive theory assumes that behavior is largely guided by forethought and the anticipation of consequences, so facilitating control over thoughts is important (Maddux & Lewis, 1995). This type of efficacy belief may be most important when athletes start to think of what is at stake and the consequences of fouling up, which is also related to subsequent emotions (Bandura, 1997). In some cases, people seek the services of a psychologist because they are in a state of distress (or slump) and they expect the distress to continue (Maddux & Lewis, 1995).

This exemplifies how a person can believe that his or her worries and feelings are out of control. Taken together, these distinctions between behaviors and thoughts or emotions may be useful when one is designing or selecting a particular intervention strategy. Effective interventions may lead to changes in both behaviors and cognitions, but the technique should correspond most closely to the intended outcome (Maddux & Lewis, 1995).

Assessment is also vital when it comes time to evaluate the effectiveness of interventions. The key is to have some sort of baseline measure that can be used to track changes across time. Usually, in research, assessment techniques provide a baseline measure so that pre–post designs can be used to evaluate the effectiveness of the intervention. Similarly, in more applied settings, some sport psychologists administer psychological tests before starting performance enhancement programs to evaluate athletes' strengths and weaknesses. We are not advocating the use of only standardized questionnaires with demonstrated validity and reliability for assessment purposes in performance enhancement situations. Sometimes when one is working with athletes, it is clear that they have no confidence, have low confidence, or have lost the confidence they once had. Informal assessment techniques such as simply asking athletes how confident they are in their ability to perform, think, or feel in a certain way may be all that is needed. According to Maddux and Lewis (1995), "a self-efficacy approach to psychological interventions is based on the assumption that the individual seeking assistance is experiencing a low and ineffective sense of personal control and that one of the major goals of the intervention is its restoration" (p. 55). This assumption shows how self-efficacy is considered the heart of the broader social cognitive theory.

Techniques for Building Self-Efficacy of Novice Athletes

When people think about building confidence, the statement "Success builds confidence" often comes to mind. This statement is generally supported by research, and Bandura (1997) has identified past performance accomplishments as the most powerful source of efficacy information and has stated that the experience of mastery or previous performance accomplishments are the strongest and most durable determinant of self-efficacy beliefs. Successful experiences generally increase self-efficacy, whereas failures generally tend to undermine efficacy beliefs (Feltz, 1994). Knowing this, it seems like an understatement to suggest that in order to build self-confidence, one needs to structure the sport experience so that athletes experience success. However, this is an effective strategy.

Before we get into the techniques that can be used to build self-efficacy in beginning-level athletes, one caveat is in order. Success does not always lead to enhanced self-confidence. The increases in self-confidence are a result of how successes are interpreted and processed. As we indicated in chapter 1, successes that are interpreted as easily obtained, accomplished with external aids, or attributed to luck will not lead to enhanced confidence. Thus, the sense of "earned" success is required for the development of confidence. In tennis, for example, athletes have been known to withdraw from tournament play due to injuries or other factors. The athletes who advance because of the withdrawals of their opponents seldom report gains in confidence stemming from these incidents. Furthermore, if a success is "earned," but at a highly taxing cost, it may not build an athlete's confidence to be able to sustain future efforts.

There also are novice athletes who, despite early success, tend to focus only on their weaknesses and remember only their failures. Thus, in some situations, the most successful athletes may not be the most confident ones, and it is therefore a misconception that success always builds confidence. Some athletes may not have the level of confidence that their accomplishments would suggest (Zinsser, Bunker, & Williams, 2006).

Regardless of these special situations, there is overwhelming support for the influence of past performance accomplishments on efficacy beliefs. Earned successes build a robust belief in one's self-confidence. Failures undermine it, especially if failures occur before a sense of efficacy is firmly established (Feltz, 1994). The key issue related to building confidence, then, is "How can the sport experience be structured so that athletes can earn success?" The answer to this question lies in how skills are first taught to novice athletes.

TECHNIQUE 1: Instructional Strategies and Performance Aids

One way of facilitating performance mastery is through instructional strategies (Schunk, 1995b). Athletes report that a coach's use of instruction and drills is one of the most effective ways to enhance athletes' self-confidence (Vargas-Tonsing, Myers, & Feltz, 2004). In instructional situations, one must develop not only a person's physical skills (behavioral change) but also the person's confidence in the ability to perform the skills (cognitive change). Instructional sequences of developmental or modified activities in sport may involve breaking the skill into parts. When teaching a person to serve in tennis, for example, instructors could break the skill into the following components: proper stance, grip, ball toss, backswing, point of contact, and follow-through. Often in dance, instructors teach one movement at a time, leading up to a sequence of steps. If one is going to use a series of progressions, progress must be made in small enough steps to ensure intermediary successes ultimately leading to mastery of the complete skill (Feltz, 1994).

Providing performance aids and using physical guidance are also effective strategies (Feltz, 1994). For example, instructors can physically guide learners through the movements, much as one sees golf pros do with novice golfers. Feltz, Landers, and Raeder (1979) did this in their diving study and found this form of guided mastery particularly effective. More specifically, they investigated the effectiveness of participant, live, and videotaped modeling on learning the back dive. Participant modeling involved an expert's demonstration plus guided participation with the learner. On the first four performance trials (the training period), participants in the participant-modeling group were guided through the dives to ensure successful performance. On the second four trials (the testing period), the physical guidance was removed. The participant-modeling group had the most successful dives and had the highest diving efficacy scores compared to the live and videotaped modeling groups.

Many pieces of equipment are also available as performance aids that are designed to improve the execution of specific sport skills. Monsma and Feltz (2006) describe the use of harnesses in figure skating. These harnesses are designed to support the skater's weight by suspending the skater in the air during a jump. Coaches pull the harness to assist the skater with the additional height required to make the necessary revolutions, thereby providing the skater with important kinesthetic feedback involving timing, force, and proper mechanics involved in the jumps.

If any of these instructional strategies or performance aids are used, it is important to remember that the ultimate goal is to facilitate self-directed mastery experiences for the learner, so the aids should be gradually removed (Feltz, 1994). The downside to using techniques such as performance aids or physical guidance is that, as we stated previously, learners could become reliant upon such forms of assistance to an extent that they attribute their successes to them instead of feeling that they earned the success.

The use of performance aids played a major role in the intervention used by Stidwell (1994) to treat a sport performance phobia. Recall from chapter 1 that Bandura's theory was originally designed to help people overcome phobias. As described by Stidwell, the participant was a 21-year-old female athlete. Her phobia began when at 12 years old she was struck in the head with a bat while playing the position of catcher during an organized game. She stopped playing after that, but she decided to resume playing with the intent to overcome her fear of being hit (by a bat or batted ball). She enrolled in a baseball course at the university she attended. Her feelings of anxiety began during the first practice. Her fear was highly specific, directed only to catching a ball being hit from a bat and not to a ball being thrown to her. She repeatedly chose to pitch because she thought she would always have someone else backing her up to catch balls that were hit to her. Stidwell's intervention was based on several sources of self-efficacy, but performance of the desired activity was emphasized. More specifically, Stidwell did the following:

1. Demonstrated the feared activity by hitting the ball off a wall to himself
2. Had the athlete hit the ball off the wall to herself

3. Hit the ball to the athlete

4. Had the athlete pitch to him

5. Had the athlete pitch the ball, but used a real ball and bat (the previous tasks were done using a plastic ball and bat)

6. Hit the ball to the athlete on the field

7. Had the athlete pitch the ball on the field

8. Had the athlete pitch the ball in a game in typical situations with Stidwell present

9. Had the athlete pitch unassisted in an actual game under typical situations

The rationale for using these steps was to progress from demonstrating the feared activity, to affecting the athlete's sense of control, to simulating desired behavior, to achieving desired behavior. Ultimately, the participant reported decreased symptoms of her phobia and displayed less avoidance of the ball in the subsequent games. Increasing the athlete's self-efficacy was clearly the key.

In addition to performance aids, simulation training can be used to facilitate performance mastery. We include virtual reality technology and computer graphics in this broad category. As Orlick (2000) notes, simulation training allows athletes to practice their desired performance responses and coping strategies in situations made as real as possible. Simulations can help prepare athletes physically by replicating the physical conditions in which they expect to compete (e.g., performing particular skills when physically tired). Orlick also suggests that simulations can help prepare athletes mentally by replicating competitive conditions and potential distractions. He suggests that athletes think about the things that happen or might happen in key competitions (e.g., bad weather, false starts, bad calls from officials, come-from-behind situations) and introduce those things into the practice setting. Doing so helps athletes' confidence in knowing that they can stay calm, focused, and in control through these distractions.

One last technique that should be mentioned here involves modifying equipment. For example, lowering the height of basketball nets and using oversized rackets are considered among the easiest and most useful ways to reduce the difficulty or complexity of a task and consequently foster success in learning new skills (Harrison, Blakemore, Buck, & Pellett, 1996; Rink, 1992). Several studies have shown positive effects for equipment modifications on performance measures (e.g., Gruetter & Davis, 1985; Pellett, Henschel-Pellett, & Harrison, 1994; Pellett & Lox, 1997; Satern, Messier, Keller-McNulty, 1989). Furthermore, when self-efficacy was assessed, Chase, Ewing, Lirgg, and George (1994) showed that lowering the height of a basketball net had positive results on children's shooting performance and self-efficacy. These positive effects are not limited to children; Pellett and Lox (1998) showed that undergraduate college students taking a beginning tennis course also performed better and had higher self-efficacy scores when they used a racket with a larger head.

TECHNIQUE 2: Providing Feedback

When one is teaching novice athletes new skills and even refining already learned skills in more experienced athletes, communication is important. All behavioral change interventions involve communication of some sort, whether it be intracommunication (a person talking to her- or himself), inter-communication (talking with someone else), or nonverbal communication (body language). Bandura (1986b, 1997) considers most communication-based confidence-building strategies under the source "verbal persuasion." It is often difficult for a person to evaluate his or her own progress, and therefore credible and expert observers play an influential role in developing confidence beliefs (Feltz, 1994). To be effective, the persuasive information must be believable. In some cases, minimizing or exaggerating performance accomplishments has been used to influence confidence beliefs. For example, a few intervention studies have shown that strength training coaches can improve athletes' maximum press and increase efficacy scores in weightlifting by persuading them to think that they are lifting less weight than they actually are (e.g., Fitzsimmons, Landers, Thomas, & Van der Mars, 1991). In our opinion, if this type of strategy is used, the difference between the false information and the reality should be small. It stands to reason, then, that giving bogus feedback would be most appropriate for learners who lack experience with the task, are in the early stages of their skill acquisition, and are not accurate judges of their own capabilities (Feltz, 1994). If deception is used as a technique to enhance confidence, it should be used sparingly, as continually deceiving athletes may undermine trust (Bandura, 1997). For this reason, most feedback should not involve deception. Although Bandura (1997) recognized that bogus feedback strategies were one way to test his theoretical propositions, he recommends that for interventions, modes of influence that genuinely cultivate both skills and self-efficacy beliefs should be used.

Effective feedback is vital to building confidence. According to Feltz (1994), different types of performance feedback should be used depending on the athletes' expertise or phase of skill acquisition. During the early phases of skill acquisition, progress feedback (information on an individual's progress without regard to others) should be given. Comparisons to other athletes should not be used for novice athletes because the process of making comparisons (and the results of some of the comparisons) may actually lower their confidence beliefs (Short & Vadocz, 2002).

Schultz and Short (2006) used the Trait Sport Confidence Inventory (Vealey, 1986) to examine who college and high school athletes select for "standards of comparison." This questionnaire requires respondents to rate their confidence in their ability to do various tasks (like bounce back from performing poorly) "compared to the most confident athlete they know." Schultz and Short found that all athletes compared themselves to someone who played at or above their level, except for college females, who sometimes compared themselves to high school athletes. The higher the comparison athlete, the lower the confidence score. Thus, it seems that making certain comparisons can undermine a person's confidence, probably because of the negative information the comparisons provide (i.e., "I am not as good as she is"). Clearly, these situations are avoidable, as positive progress feedback could be used instead.

In addition, positive feedback can reduce the negative affect that most people feel in failure situations. Many athletes feel discouraged and ashamed when they do not perform well and need assurance and encouragement with regard to their abilities to promote a sense of self-confidence (Feltz, 1994). However, in providing positive feedback, one must still make it performance contingent. Noncontingent positive feedback in high amounts can be detrimental to self-efficacy and motivation because it implies low ability (Horn, 1985). It suggests that the coach or instructor has low expectations regarding what the athlete can perform. Also, positive feedback that does not acknowledge mistakes is not informative to the athlete. Positive communication focuses on the positive aspects of the performance, but it also acknowledges mistakes, provides instructional feedback, and stresses the learning nature of skill development (Jourden, Bandura, & Banfield, 1991). Feltz (1994) outlines four steps in the positive approach to mistakes:

1. Acknowledge the person's distress about the mistake.
2. Compliment the individual about what was correct with the performance. The compliment should be related to an important and relevant aspect of the skill so as not to be discounted by the performer.
3. Provide instruction on how the person can improve with respect to the mistake.
4. End on a positive note by encouraging the individual to continue the effort.

So, for example, in the sport of bowling, one could say, "Mike, I can see you are getting frustrated by your inability to pick up this split. Your approach is fantastic, you just need to make sure that your starting position is correct. The key is to hit it exactly in between the remaining pins. Remember, the ball is wide enough that it can knock down two pins with a full empty pin space in between. Keep working, you'll get this." Constructing feedback using these four steps promotes a sense of confidence that mistakes can be conquered and that progress can be made.

Related to feedback are attributions—the reasons people give for their successes and failures (Weiner, 1985). Attributions have been grouped on three dimensions representing causality, stability, and controllability. Most attributions can be classified as relating to ability, effort, luck, or task difficulty. Although Technique 9 deals with attributions for experienced athletes, we bring them up here because there is an interaction between the difficulty of the task and the learner's actual efforts (Feltz, 1994). When working with athletes, one should *not* tell novice athletes who expended a lot of effort that their failure on a difficult task was due to a lack of effort. As in providing too much noncontingent praise, feedback pointing to lack of effort may convey to people that they do not have the ability needed to be successful, and it could damage the trust between the athletes and coaches or instructors (i.e., "You said I didn't give 100% when I really did, how well do you know me?"). In situations in which learners are expending great effort at difficult tasks and still not succeeding, one is better advised to acknowledge the difficulty of the task and set up modified challenges that the learner can accomplish to help build self-efficacy.

TECHNIQUE 3: Modeling

Bandura (1997) considers modeling (also referred to as observational learning) one of the most powerful means of transmitting values, attitudes, and patterns of thoughts and behaviors. In this section, we focus on modeling for skill development that occurs concomitantly with building self-efficacy. In the section on the experienced athlete, we focus on the use of coping models. For athletic development, proficient modeling is considered the most effective way of transmitting information about a skill (Bandura, 1997). Four conditions are necessary for effective modeling—attention, retention, production, and motivation (Bandura, 1997)—and have been described by others (Cumming, Clark, McCullagh, Ste-Marie, & Hall, 2005; McCullagh & Weiss, 2001). First, the person must pay attention to the model being observed. The extent to which this happens will depend on the specific characteristics of the model as well as the person's cognitive ability, arousal level, and expectations. Second, the observer must be able to remember the behavior that has been observed. Methods to help retain the observed information include using imagery, analogies, and verbal cues. For example, auditory information or verbal cues appear to enhance rhythmic and ballistic movements and those highly contingent on timing (see McCullagh & Weiss, 2001). Third, people must have the ability to replicate the behavior that the model has demonstrated by coordinating their muscle actions with their thoughts. Teachers and coaches facilitate this process by providing practice time, lead-up skills, and progressions. And fourth, learners must have the motivation to want to perform what they have learned.

Models can be used for a variety of functions. In a recent study, Cumming and colleagues (2005) created a "functions of observational learning questionnaire" showing that observational learning can serve three functions—for skill, strategy, and performance. They suggested that modeling should be promoted as a skill acquisition technique as well as a technique for improving psychological responses and performance enhancement in competition. Compared to the situation with several other techniques suggested in this chapter, there is considerably more research showing the effectiveness of modeling on self-efficacy beliefs. This research was described in detail in chapter 3 and is included in our annotated bibliography at the end of the book.

The performance enhancement technique of watching models perform successfully has been commercially marketed in the form of SyberVision. SyberVision programs were introduced to the public in 1985, and several forms are now available (sport-specific programs have been created for golf, tennis, and skiing). We use the sport of golf for descriptive purposes. SyberVision for golf is a video-based training system involving neuromuscular programming. As described on the SyberVision Web site, using SyberVision involves sitting back, relaxing, and watching an expert model perform thousands of perfectly executed golf swings. The key fundamentals of the swings are also isolated and explained. The swings are apparently executed at mathematically precise tempos and rhythms, and this format is posited to enable the viewer's brain to convert what it sees directly to performance memory. According to the Web site, SyberVision uses a mathematical model as a guide to present golf images in such a way that the swing memory is stimulated nearly 1,000 times per 60 min viewing session. SyberVision has been endorsed by several well-known golfers, and testimonials provide evidence that during the viewing process people can feel their bodies subtly go through the motions. Ultimately, after watching the videos, when people physically practice golf skills, these stored memories are drawn upon, resulting in improved performance and lowered scores. The performance effects of SyberVision are marketed as immediate, and multiple viewings are said to result in continual skill improvement.

In terms of research on SyberVision, the Committee on Techniques for the Enhancement of Human Performance of the National Research Council of the United States (Druckman & Swets, 1988; Druckman & Bjork, 1991) provided a report on evidence for the effectiveness of the SyberVision tapes. In their first report, they found no research evidence addressing the efficacy of the tapes (Druckman & Swets). By the time of their second report, two studies had investigated the use of these tapes. McCullagh, Meriweather, and Siegel (1990a; as cited in Druckman & Bjork) examined the effectiveness of using SyberVision sport training videotapes as a learning tool for the tennis serve. The results showed that the groups that used SyberVision had significant improvements in form scores (not for accuracy) but did not differ from a physical practice or control group. The sample size in this particular study was small, however.

In a second study, McCullagh, Evans, Morrison, and Petersen (1990b; as cited in Druckman & Bjork) again showed that groups that used Syber Vision improved their form scores. In other research, Austin and Miller (1992) showed that although using SyberVision did not result in significant improvements in performance compared to that of a physical practice group, the participants in the SyberVision group did improve more than the non-SyberVision group. In our review of the literature we found only one study (i.e., Maddalozzo, Stuart, Rose, & Cardinal, 1999) that included self-efficacy as a dependent variable. Maddalozzo and colleagues reported that neither form nor accuracy self-efficacy changed significantly during the acquisition or retention phases in their study, in which participants were learning to perform a chip shot in golf via one of two instructional strategies (SyberVision, and SyberVision plus verbal cues). The mean self-efficacy scores did increase between the first day of acquisition and the final retention day, particularly for both the novice and intermediate skill-level groups who watched the Syber Vision videotape augmented with verbal cues. Thus, it seems that most of the supporting evidence for the beneficial use of SyberVision comes from the athletes' testimonials. At this point in time, we conclude that the confidence-boosting modeling benefits of SyberVision are no better than those of other techniques that use proficient models for novice athletes. "Contrary to the extravagant claims, novices gain little if anything from such videos over and above what they already learned about the form of the skill from numerous naturalistic observations" (Bandura, 1997, p. 379).

Recall from chapter 3 that there are a number of types of models and that their effectiveness on self-efficacy and performance varies. Novice athletes may learn how to execute a particular technique better from observing a proficient model than from observing a nonskilled peer; this can provide more confidence in learning the skill (Lirgg & Feltz, 1991). However, similar models and coping models provide more confidence information about one's ability to persist at a task and overcome fear in threatening tasks (George, Feltz, & Chase, 1992; Weiss, McCullagh, Smith, & Berlant, 1998). Bandura (1997) notes that it is easier for people to persuade themselves of their physical abilities if they see people similar to themselves perform difficult physical feats than if they observe those with superior ability. For example, women with little athletic experience have been shown to increase their self-efficacy and performance after watching a nonathletic female model compared to observing a nonathletic male, athletic female, or athletic male (George et al., 1992; Gould & Weiss, 1981). Selecting a model is very important, as evidence suggests that upward comparisons can have unwanted evaluative effects; more specifically, presumably superior athletes have the power to undermine the efficacy beliefs of people who are uncertain (Bandura, 1997). One reason for the lack of SyberVision's effects on self-efficacy may be this disregard for the negative effects that can come from comparative evaluation with the use of superior models.

The use of peer modeling can avoid some of the negative effects of comparisons to superior models. One example of how peer modeling techniques were used to help a person overcome a sport-specific fear was provided by Feltz (1980). In this study, a combination of peer modeling, performance aids, and graduated tasks was used to help a young boy overcome his fear of diving. Thirteen steps were involved, starting with a kneeling dive from the side of the pool and ending with a standing forward dive from a 1 m diving board. Each step involved the following:

1. The action was verbally explained.
2. An adult model did a demonstration.
3. A peer model who was held in high esteem by the learner did a demonstration.
4. Learner was asked to verbally repeat the instructions.
5. Learner was asked if he felt he could perform the task unassisted or whether he desired assistance.
6. If assistance was requested, the adult instructor physically guided him through the dive.
7. Guidance was gradually removed until the learner could perform the task unaided four consecutive times.

Each session was 30 min long. At the beginning of each new session, the task last completed was reviewed prior to continuing on to the next level. Similarly, other research has shown that these types of progressive mastery models lead to higher self-efficacy than mastery models in sport settings, especially when the task is somewhat threatening (e.g., Weiss et al., 1998).

TECHNIQUE 4: Imagery

Another way for novice athletes to experience performance success and thereby build self-efficacy is through mental imagery. Actually, all athletes can have as much success as they want in their minds, but using imagery for building confidence in novice athletes may differ from how experienced athletes use imagery for maintaining or regaining confidence. The topic of imagery has fascinated many people in sport settings for years. Imagery is among the most popular performance enhancement techniques or psychological skills because of its versatility in effecting several different outcomes. Imagery has been referred to by a number of names: visualization, mental rehearsal, mental practice, and cognitive enactment, to name a few. Sometimes researchers use one term over another based on slight differences in meaning. For example, "visualization" implies modality—that the images are visual in nature (i.e., "seeing" yourself do something). However, imagery can (and should) involve all the senses (i.e., seeing, feeling, touching, hearing, and tasting) (Vealey &

Greenleaf, 2001). The terms mental rehearsal and mental practice are from motor learning and are most often used when the images involve specific physical skills and skill learning. However, the content and types of images used and the functions of imagery are more varied than this in that they can be both physical and psychological. Bandura (1997) uses "cognitive enactment" to refer to imagery, and suggested that many facets of athletic skills can be imaged. His suggestions included cognitive images (i.e., plans and strategies), motor images (i.e., movements and the subsequent kinesthetic sensations), and emotive images (i.e., affective emotions like stress and anxiety, as well as perceptions of physiological activation like muscle tension).

The specific relationship between efficacy and imagery use has been studied quite often. Considerable research evidence shows that imagery can be used to build confidence. These studies are included in the annotated bibliography at the end of the book. Although several theories relate to how imagery works in general (e.g., symbolic learning theory, psychoneuromuscular theory, bioinformational theory, dual coding theory, triple code theory), we will not describe these here. Rather, we present two general pathways relating efficacy to imagery. First, having a person image her- or himself successfully performing a specific sport skill can ultimately improve performance of that skill, and that successful performance can lead to feelings of confidence related to performing the skill. For example, if a diver images herself successfully executing a dive, this will increase the probability that she will successfully perform the dive. Once the dive has been successfully performed physically, the diver is likely to develop confidence in her abilities to do it again. These types of images, based on sport skills, are referred to as cognitive images (Paivio, 1985) and seem to be what novice athletes who are learning and perfecting sport skills use (Hall, 2001). It is extremely important that if athletes image themselves doing things that they have either never been able to do or have had difficulty doing, they image themselves performing successfully. Research has shown that negative images like seeing oneself miss a shot cause performance failures (i.e., the shot is missed!) (e.g., Short, Bruggeman, et al., 2002; Woolfolk, Parrish, & Murphy, 1985; Woolfolk, Murphy, Gottesfeld, & Aitken, 1985).

The second pathway relating to how imagery works is a direct one—from imagery to confidence, rather than from imagery to performance to confidence. Recent research has shown that certain images affect confidence more than others. In particular, images such as seeing oneself appearing self-confident, focused, and mentally tough have been shown to increase self-efficacy (Short, Bruggeman, et al., 2002). These images are most often used by elite and more experienced athletes, who are less concerned with mastering specific sport skills and more concerned with psychological states such as confidence (Hall, 2001). We discuss this kind of imagery in more depth in the section on techniques for experienced athletes.

Unfortunately, some of the more recent imagery research has been plagued by conceptual confusion (Short, Ross-Stewart, & Monsma, 2006). For this reason, it is vital to clarify the constructs of imagery type, imagery content, imagery function, and imagery outcome. In alignment with Murphy, Nordin, and Cumming (2006), *imagery type* should be used to denote the actual *content* of an image (e.g., seeing oneself performing a dive, feeling oneself executing a penalty kick). *Imagery function* should refer to the purpose or reason for which an athlete employs an image (e.g., to build confidence, to learn a skill). *Imagery outcome* should indicate the end result of the imagery process (e.g., increased confidence, improved skill level). The bottom line is that different athletes use the same image for different functions, and a single image can have multiple functions for a single athlete (Short, Monsma, & Short, 2004). Short and colleagues found that when questioned as to what images "mean" to them, many athletes reported that images serve a more motivational (confidence building) than cognitive (skill and strategy learning) function. So, in selecting the images to include in imagery interventions, it is advisable to have athletes list several images that they think about when they are performing in their sports, as well as the function that the images serve. To develop confidence, those images identified as confidence building should be used.

Another point about using imagery concerns athletes' confidence in their ability to use imagery. Even though imagery can be a tool to develop one's confidence, some athletes may first need to develop confidence in their ability to use imagery (Short, Tenute, & Feltz, 2005). Everyone has the ability to image, but some are better at it than others (Paivio, 1985). Bandura (1997) stated that those who have a low sense of efficacy to generate and control images will not use imagery or will use it haphazardly. Our research (Short, Tenute, & Feltz, 2005) has shown that the more confident athletes are in their ability to use imagery, the more they use it. In terms of application, this means that the same techniques used to build confidence associated with physical performance can be used to develop confidence in one's ability to use imagery. For example, starting with easy images (i.e., having a swimmer see the pool, or feel the cold water) and progressing to harder images (i.e., imaging races) may provide performance accomplishments in successful use of imagery, similar to what happens with the learning and development of physical skills. When using imagery, athletes should be advised to try it out for about 10 to 15 min at a time, three to five times a week. Imagery is an effective intervention strategy. There are often many constraints on when one can practice physically, but imagery can be used with no sweat at any time and place (Bandura, 1997).

One more thing to remember about imagery-based intervention strategies for efficacy and skill development is that there is little value to using it in the early phase of learning (Bandura, 1997). According to Bandura, the reason is that the learner may not have formed an adequate conception of the skill to be learned. He believes that skill learning is best promoted by first structuring the behavior cognitively and then perfecting it by physical practice and imagery. This does not mean that novice athletes cannot benefit from imagery, just not in the early phase of learning.

One unique form of imagery that combines other strategies and is used in figure skating is "blueprinting" (Monsma & Feltz, 2006). Blueprinting combines a paper "model" or diagram of the skater's routine on the ice with visual imagery. Skaters draw diagrams of elements and connecting steps in their skating programs while using cue words and visualization of their program as their music plays. Monsma and Feltz outlined the following steps for use with skaters. These steps could be tailored for any sport that involves a routine.

1. Skaters list all of the elements of their program in a workbook, writing them on a sheet of paper. Coaches and choreographers can be involved in initial trials of this technique, helping skaters develop their program blueprints.

2. Skaters develop cue words designed to help increase concentration and avoid distraction.

3. Skaters visualize themselves in a high-stakes setting to make the simulation as real as possible. This includes seeing their coaches at the boards, seeing themselves in their skating costumes, and seeing the judging panel before them.

4. Skaters "feel" themselves performing their program from beginning to end.

5. Skaters then draw their programs on paper while their program music is played, placing each element in the correct location on the paper as it would be on the ice and saying their cue words aloud. The music helps skaters keep the timing of elements congruent with the time or speed it takes to skate the program on the ice.

6. Skaters then go back through their program focusing on key features of presentation, or artistic impression. These program features on the blueprint should be reviewed prior to subsequent mental practice sessions.

According to Monsma and Feltz (2006), this strategy can be practiced by skaters daily at home in a quiet place and then one final time just prior to performance to help them relax, improve concentration, and enhance their sense of efficacy.

TECHNIQUE 5: Goal Setting

Another way to build self-efficacy is through goal setting. In sport, athletes often think about where they want to be at the end of the season; however, what they should spend more time thinking about is what they are going to do physically and mentally in order to get there. Goal challenges are ingrained in most athletic activities (Bandura, 1997). The typical goal heard across sports by many athletes is "to win." In sport psychology, winning is considered an outcome goal because it is directed at the final result. However, outcome goals should not be confused with outcome expectancies as defined within social cognitive theory (Bandura, 1997) and as we described in chapter 1. We wish the sport psychology community would choose another term for outcome goals, such as competitive goals, of which final performance is just one of several performance markers. However, given that "outcome" is familiar language to the sport psychology community, we have stuck with this terminology. Other outcome goals may include attaining a specific place at a meet, achieving a time standard or a personal best, or beating a teammate in practice. The problem with outcome goals is that they are the hardest type of goal to control. They depend on the performer's skills, but also on the skill level of opponents or competitors. If athletes set goals to win and perform their best but still lose, they will not have reached their goal and may view their performance as a failure. For this reason, task goals (sometimes called performance or process goals) are recommended because they are more focused on what athletes have to do (physically and mentally) in order to accomplish the outcome goals. Task goals may be related to effort, form, or strategy or some combination of these (Feltz, 1994). Examples of task goals for a swimmer may include being aggressive in and out of each turn, holding a specific stroke count, and maintaining splits through an event.

The importance of differentiating task and outcome goals and their effects on self-efficacy is illustrated by comments that an exceptional collegiate athlete made. Jeff was a kicker for his football team. During one game he went a perfect 4-for-4 in field goal attempts, converting from 52, 48, 26, and 29 yd (48, 44, 24, and 27 m). The 52 yd field goal represented the second longest of his career. A few days after the game (which was also after he received the special teams player of the week award for his performance), Jeff intimated that although he was happy with how things had gone in that game, there were still some technical things that he could do better. Thus, although we more often refer to the possibility that the self-efficacy levels of athletes who set only outcome goals could be negatively affected when those goals are not met, it is also possible for athletes to have exceptional performances (i.e., achieve outcome goals) and still suffer hits to their confidence as a consequence of nonperformance indicators. Notwithstanding this example, the research generally shows that athletes who set task (rather than outcome) goals experience less anxiety and more confidence and satisfaction (Burton, 1989).

The effectiveness of goal setting has been demonstrated in research studies with over 40,000 participants, using more than 90 different tasks and across 10 different countries (Weinberg & Gould, 2003). Meta-analyses (statistical reviews of the literature) show that goal setting works (Kyllo & Landers,

1995). However, although goal-setting techniques seem simple, they are actually quite complex. If you have ever tried to set goals with athletes and teams, you certainly know what we mean! Almost all athletes set goals, and intuitively they know goals can help, but they seem to have trouble figuring out how to best set goals to maximize their effectiveness (Burton, Naylor, & Holliday, 2001).

Table 6.1 contains some important information about setting goals. Rather than reiterate that information here, we elaborate on a couple of additional points concerning goal setting. In terms of how far ahead goals should be set, the general guidelines are to set both long- and short-term goals. These help athletes identify where they are going and how they are going to get there. Many athletes dream of playing professional sports, making an Olympic or national team, or winning championships. The key is to map out the future by using long- and short-term goals. USA Swimming does an excellent job teaching coaches and athletes how to set goals in the "Mental Toolbox" section on their Web site. They suggest having athletes ask themselves a series of questions in order to progress from dream goals to long-term goals to short-term goals to daily goals. For example, athletes could determine a good long-term goal by asking themselves, "Where do I want to be at the end of the season (or the end of high school or college)?" Examples of the answer to this question might be making a specific time standard or earning a starting spot on the top line. To make the long-term goal seem less daunting, one should set short-term goals

TABLE 6.1 *Guidelines for Setting Goals*

Goals should be:	Explanation
Specific	Setting specific goals instead of general "do your best" types of goals is the most effective. A general goal would be "I want to be a better golfer." A more specific and better goal would be "To be a better golfer I will improve my short game by practicing chipping for an extra 15 minutes three days a week."
Measurable	There should be criteria (expressed numerically if possible) for measuring progress toward goals. Questions to consider include "How much?"; "How many?"; and "How will I know when it is accomplished?"
Action oriented	Goals should refer to something that needs to be done.
Realistic	Goals should be tied to skill and motivation levels. A goal should be something that the athlete is able to do and will want to work hard toward because attaining the goal will give him or her great satisfaction. Goals should also be possible to achieve with hard work. Goals that are too hard will lead to discouragement, and goals that are too easy serve no real function. Moderately difficult goals are recommended.
Time bound	A specific time frame should accompany each goal. It may be a week, a month, or longer.

as well. USA Swimming recommends that athletes ask themselves, "Where do I want to be at the end of this month?" Examples might be increasing the number of shots on goals or improving the quality of performances. Because even the short-term goals can sometimes feel far off, people often need something more within reach to maintain focus and motivation. Thus, daily goals or practice goals can be set for both physical training and psychological skill development. The question here is, "Why am I going to practice today?"

Bandura (1997) considers practice goals to be the most effective because they provide more frequent evaluation of success. In his words, frequent evaluations stimulate the development of self-efficacy beliefs when goals are attained and stimulate motivation regardless of the outcome, thereby preventing procrastination and premature discouragement.

Goals and feedback are related. And research shows that both are needed to enhance performance (e.g., Bandura & Cervone, 1983; Feltz & Riessinger, 1990; Locke & Latham, 1990). In order for feedback to be effective, it must be provided in reaction to a defined goal or standard (Bandura, 1997). According to Bandura, without a performance standard, there is no basis on which to form an internal comparison to evaluate a performance. However, once this standard is met, athletes typically set new ones. Even in the face of performance that is short of the goal, Bandura (1997) suggests that one's motivation and self-efficacy may not be undermined if the discrepancy is only moderate and the individual is given knowledge of the discrepancy.

Another thing about goals that is worth mentioning concerns the difficulty of the goals. For complex tasks, goals should be specific and challenging but attainable. For easy or routine tasks, the harder the goal, the better the performance. Assuming that an athlete has the requisite skills and commitment, working toward difficult goals can build a strong sense of confidence because difficult goals offer more information about one's capability to acquire knowledge and skills than do easier goals (Bandura, 1997). By setting goals and achieving them, athletes are able to structure success into their training.

The key to the relationship between goal setting and confidence has to do with the effect of reaching one's goals. When people attain their goals they should experience enhanced feelings of efficacy (Bandura, 1997). Athletes should take some time after every game or practice to identify their successes of the day and pat themselves on the back for their efforts. No matter what happens, athletes should always be able to take something positive home. Being proud of their accomplishments, especially the small ones, is important because they really add up. If the athlete cannot experience enhanced feelings of confidence when goals are attained, then goal setting is not the best technique for that athlete (Feltz, 1994). One way to ensure goal-setting success is to teach athletes how to set goals and readjust them according to their rate of improvement so that the goals are motivating rather than debilitating (Bandura, 1997).

Techniques for Maintaining and Regaining Self-Efficacy of Experienced Athletes

Once novice athletes have mastered physical skills and built up a sense of confidence, the next challenges involve ensuring that they maintain their confidence and even regain it when it drops. In this section, we present techniques that can be used to maintain and regain confidence.

Maintaining confidence seems to be easy when things are going an athlete's way. For example, when athletes are winning more than they are losing, or when they are consistently improving, they are probably not even thinking about their confidence. Although a strong sense of self-efficacy is developed through repeated successes, occasional failures are unlikely to have much effect on judgments of one's capabilities (Bandura, 1997). The key is developing what Bandura calls "mental toughness" or a resilient sense of self-efficacy so that the occasional loss or bad performance does not shatter one's belief. Everyone has ups and downs. According to Bandura, failures that are overcome by determination and effort can instill robust perceptions of confidence because they show that one can eventually master even the most difficult obstacles.

It would seem that the key to maintaining confidence is to have self-efficacy in the exercise of thought control (Bandura, 1997). Bandura stated that athletes need to be able to block out distractions, control disruptive negative thinking, and develop the efficacy to cope with failure because failure is a natural part of competition. However, he also pointed out that much of the distress athletes experience over failure is usually self-inflicted when they dwell on failures instead of savoring successes. In his words, the cognitive control task is for athletes to stop thinking about mistakes and failures and to rid themselves of disruptive thinking by concentrating their attention on the task at hand and generating helpful thinking. "Development of efficacy in self-management of thought processes is vital to success" (Bandura, 1997, p. 392). Bandura stated that without a strong sense of efficacy to exercise cognitive control, athletes' responses to adverse events can deteriorate so that they may tend to dwell on their mistakes, belittle themselves, and engage in negative imaging about future performances. This low sense of self-efficacy can lead to a downward spiral of lower performance and lower self-efficacy (Bandura, 1997).

In this section on experienced athletes, we focus on those techniques that are critical for athletes in maintaining and regaining confidence. It is important to note, however, that even though these confidence-enhancing techniques, like the others already presented, may help in other areas of the athlete's physical or mental preparation, our focus is on their relationship to confidence.

For example, there is no doubt that uncontrollable thinking can impair concentration. However, in self-efficacy theory, gaining mastery over unwanted thoughts increases one's sense of efficacy to manage them (Bandura, 1997). This is the most powerful way to direct concentration away from disturbing trains of thought. Those who are assured of their capabilities to cope with threats have little reason to ruminate about them (Bandura, 1997).

TECHNIQUE 6: Blocking Out Distractions

As previously noted, Bandura (1997) believes that mastery over threats and stressors is vital to athletic functioning. In sport, one of the more popular techniques thought to help athletes block out distractions and concentrate on the task at hand is to develop preperformance routines. Many athletes become anxious or stressed on the day of a competition. They may wake up feeling nervous or start the day with thoughts that create worry and concern about their performance. This time—from the moment they wake up in a hotel room or at home to the moment they step out on the playing surface—is a potentially hazardous time period for experiencing self-doubt. A preperformance plan may help to direct athletes' thoughts and behaviors by concentrating their attention on the task at hand and generating helpful, efficacious thinking. Although novice athletes can develop preperformance plans at the same time they are learning skills, we discuss the technique here as a way to develop the cognitive control over thoughts that is essential to maintaining confidence.

According to Moran (2004), three types of routines are common in sport. Pre-event routines are preferred sequences of actions in the run-up to competitive events. Included are stable preferences for what to do the night before and on the morning of the competition. Preperformance routines are characteristic sequences of thoughts and actions that athletes adhere to prior to skill execution—as in the case of basketball players bouncing the ball before shooting a free throw. Postmistake routines are action sequences that may help athletes leave their errors behind so that they can refocus on the task at hand. For example, a golfer may "shadow" the correct swing for a shot that led to an error. This last type of routine is very important, as according to Bandura (1997), proficient athletes have the efficacy to put mistakes behind them and to continue as though a mistake had never happened.

Postmistake routines seem to be especially important to the maintenance of self-efficacy beliefs of experienced athletes. All athletes make mistakes from time to time. According to Bandura (1997), these mistakes and defeats create cognitive carryover problems with which experienced athletes must constantly struggle. In his words, the athletes who have difficulty ridding themselves of distressing thoughts are more likely to carry them over to subsequent performances, which will likely breed only further mistakes.

According to Moran (2004), preperformance routines improve concentration for a number of reasons. First, they encourage athletes to develop an appropriate mental state by helping them focus on task-relevant information. Second, they enable athletes to concentrate on the present moment rather than on past events or on possible future outcomes. Third, they may prevent athletes from devoting too much attention to the mechanics of their well-learned skills—a habit that can unravel automaticity (Beilock & Carr, 2001). They also often involve the use of additional psychological skills (e.g., self-talk, imagery, relaxation, affirmation statements, goal setting) that assist athletes in feeling physically and mentally prepared.

To develop a routine plan, athletes should take some time to figure out how they are going to execute the given skills and strategies, as well as how they need to be, physically and mentally, in order to perform well in their next competition. The easiest way to do this is for athletes to think about their best performance ever. What did they eat the night before? How many hours of sleep did they get? What time did they wake up? What did they have for breakfast? What did they do for warm-up? How did they feel in warm-up? What other things did they do before the event? How did they feel right before the event? It may also be useful for athletes to recall one of their poorer performances and make comparisons to good ones. Once athletes have reflected on all the thoughts, feelings, and actions that contributed to their successful performances, they should try to incorporate these into a routine that they can use before their next event (see our example in table 6.2). The outcome of this process should be a plan that outlines specific tasks and behaviors for the athlete to engage in prior to, during, and after a competition. These plans help athletes ease their minds by keeping things predictable regardless of where and when they are competing. Effective routines are consistent and keep the same pace regardless of conditions (Moran, 2004). When athletes direct their attention toward a consistent pattern of routine tasks and positive thoughts, they are keeping their attention away from thoughts that may create worry or from activities that may be energy draining.

Even within a competition, preperformance routines can help maintain focus and confidence. Chase (2006) outlined a preshot routine for a free throw in basketball that involved taking the ball from the official, dribbling three times, placing the shooting hand on the ball, looking at the basket, inhaling and exhaling a deep breath, saying the cue words "over the rim," mentally imaging the ball going in, and shooting the ball. When athletes use these preperformance routines, it is important to regularly review them and perhaps revise them. As noted by Moran (2004), it is possible for an athlete to perform a preperformance routine so "automatically" that it no longer serves the purpose it was designed for. More specifically, if an athlete's mind starts to wander while he or she is performing a routine—perhaps to a thought like

TABLE 6.2 Competitive Routine for a Track Athlete

Time	Action
Night before 6:00 p.m.-7:00 p.m.	Eat a meal with a high carbohydrate content and medium protein.
Night before 7:00 p.m.-8:00 p.m.	Listen to favorite music to calm nerves and get mind off competition.
Night before 8:15 p.m.-8:30 p.m.	Take time to image myself successfully competing.
Night before 9:00 p.m.	Pack competition bag.
Night before 10:00 p.m.	Go to bed, read for 30 minutes before turning off the lights.
Morning of 7:00 a.m.	Get dressed in competition clothes and warm-up outfit.
Morning of 7:30 a.m.	Eat breakfast.
Morning of 8:00 a.m.	Check competition bag to make sure everything is packed.
Morning of 8:30 a.m.	Listen to music depending on perceived level of activation (calm music if feeling nervous, dance music if feeling too relaxed).
Morning of 9:30 a.m.	Leave for sports venue.
Morning of 10:30 a.m.	Meet with coach to go over the race strategy.
Morning of 11:00 a.m.	Find quiet area of the venue to image what I want to do in competition.
Morning of 11:30 a.m.	Warm up using regular routine. Rehearse cue words. Check in after first call. Continue warm-up.
Morning of 12:00 p.m.	Set my starting blocks. Rehearse cue words in the starting block. Practice three starts. Take a deep breath, repeat cue word. Compete.

"What am I going to eat after this competition?"—then it is obvious that the routine is no longer serving its purpose and should be revised.

A final point concerns the differences between routines and superstitions. In general, routines and superstitions are distinguished on control and purpose (Moran, 2004). The essence of superstitious behavior is the belief that one's fate is governed by factors outside one's control—for example, "I have to wear my lucky socks in order to play well." Routines, on the other hand, allow athletes to exert complete control over their preparation. Moran pointed out that athletes often shorten their routines in adverse conditions but that the opposite is the case for superstitions, which tend to grow longer over time as athletes "chain together" more and more illogical links between behavior and outcome. With respect to the purpose of routines and superstitions, each part of a routine should have a rational basis, whereas the components of a superstitious ritual may not be justifiable objectively (Moran, 2004).

TECHNIQUE 7: Controlling Disruptive Negative Thinking (Including Self-Talk)

According to Bandura (1997), when people have a strong sense of efficacy to control their own thinking, they are less burdened by negative thoughts. In sport, negative thinking is often referred to as a form of negative self-talk. Self-talk has been defined as a dialogue in which an individual interprets feelings and perceptions, regulates and changes evaluations and convictions, and gives him- or herself instructions and reinforcement (Hackfort & Schwenkmezger, 1993). Throughout practices and competitions athletes often engage in some form of self-talk, although the frequency and content vary from person to person and situation to situation (Zinsser et al., 2006). In their descriptive study on the use of self-talk in sport, Hardy, Gammage, and Hall (2001) showed that athletes used self-talk the most during competitions.

Much of the emphasis in sport psychology has been on alleviating negative self-talk, probably because of its apparent debilitative effects on performance. However, a first step for all athletes should be to take the time to think about what they typically say to themselves when training and competing. In order for a self-talk intervention to be effective (or even necessary), athletes must first be aware of what they are saying to themselves and what effect it has on them. Bandura (1997) stated that the difficulty of controlling thought does not seem to be a function of its content. In his words, pleasant intrusive thoughts are just as difficult to control as unpleasant ones. Moreover, he stated that perceived inability to exercise control over pleasant intrusive thoughts is just as depressing as perceived inability to control unpleasant intrusions because both signify a sense of powerlessness and can disrupt performance.

Williams and Leffingwell (2002) listed four techniques for identifying self-talk: retrospection, imagery, observation, and self-talk logs. Regardless of which method is used, the purpose is to raise awareness and enable the person to self-regulate. Athletes could be encouraged to write down their self-talk on paper. A typical list of negative thoughts might include phrases like "How could I miss that?"; "I'm the worst player out here"; and "Can't I ever do anything right?" Even during competitions some athletes say things to themselves like "I have to score tonight"; "I can't hit the ball into the water"; or "I can't walk this batter." Athletes who have difficulties recalling their thoughts are not alone. Sometimes athletes think that they do not say things to themselves when in fact they do. This is why learning to monitor thoughts is the first step to controlling one's thoughts.

One exercise that has received considerable attention in sport psychology is the "paper clip" technique—a way in which athletes can become aware of their negative self-talk. A golfer, for example, would empty a box of paper clips into her pocket before the beginning of a round. Every time she became aware of a negative thought, she would move one of the paper clips to the other pocket. At the end of the day, she would count the paper clips representing the negative thoughts. On the basis of the outcome of this exercise, some practitioners recommend setting goals (using the techniques described earlier) to reduce the number of negative thoughts, or consistently replacing negative thoughts with positive ones (discussed later), or both.

The fact is that sometimes athletes do not understand just how hard on themselves they really are. There is truth to the saying that we are our own worst critics. Another exercise used in sport psychology involves drawing attention to the debilitating effects of negative thoughts. After making a list of all their negative thoughts, athletes are instructed to apply the thoughts on the list to a teammate or friend (with the same emotion as when they say the thoughts to themselves). For example, if an athlete has told himself "I suck and I will never score again," he should look at his teammate and tell the teammate "You suck and you will never score again." The likely outcome is that an athlete will feel uncomfortable saying such things to another person, and typically the other person will feel bad or have feelings of doubt about her- or himself. Making athletes aware that their words probably have the same debilitative effect on their confidence and performance is important. Many athletes (and even some coaches) berate themselves during a game or competition and are harder on themselves than on others.

The techniques described thus far are popular in sport psychology as ways to have athletes become aware of their self-talk and its potential debilitating effects. According to Bandura (1997), "theories about intrusive thought typically center on the negative valence of the thoughts" (p. 150), and "people struggle to rid themselves of such thoughts because of their aversiveness or because they fear that their thoughts will trigger foolish, detrimental, or dangerous action" (p. 151). However, in social cognitive theory, it is not the frequency of negative thoughts that is considered the source of distress to people, but instead the sense of an inability to control them.

There are several performance enhancement techniques based on cognitive thought control strategies. Descriptions can be found in most applied sport psychology textbooks. It is generally accepted that thought suppression strategies are ineffective (Don't think of a pink elephant or white bear!) (Wegner, 1989); therefore "cognitive restructuring" strategies are often suggested as ways to deal with irrational or distorted thinking and negative self-talk. Examples of cognitive restructuring techniques include thought stopping, changing negative thoughts to positive ones, countering, and reframing. Thought stopping consists of using a key or cue word to interrupt unwanted thoughts as soon as they occur. Changing negative thoughts into positive thoughts involves rewriting the list of negative thoughts so that the phrasing becomes ability based and positive. For example, the statement "I always hit the water on this shot" could be reformulated to something like "I have a powerful, smooth swing that will produce a solid straight drive." Unfortunately, changing negative thought to positive ones is not particularly effective if the athlete believes the negative thoughts. For this reason, countering is sometimes used. To counter a negative thought is to challenge it; for example, if an athlete is feeling too excited before performing, he or she may want to say something like "This happens to all great performers, its natural, and if I follow my routine I'll perform fine." Reframing could also be used (Williams & Leffingwell, 2002). The rationale for reframing is that athletes can change negative self-statements to positive ones by changing their perspective. For example, athletes concerned about competing against a much higher-ranked opponent ("I'm going to really embarrass myself") can reframe the concern as an opportunity to assess their skill ("I'm going to see how good I've gotten and where I need improvement").

If one is set on using cognitive restructuring techniques for thought control, our best advice for alleviating negative self-talk is to have the athlete change his or her thinking. For example, "I have to make this shot" could be rewritten to "I've made this shot 100 times in the past, I can do it again with ease." Using "I can" statements, rather than "I need to . . ." is important because the latter can be pressure building, and the former are efficacy building (Bandura, 1997). Athletes should also be encouraged to use positive outcomes; "I can't believe I missed that shot" should be rewritten to "I can make this shot" or "Everybody misses sometimes, I've made more shots than I have missed." The mind works more effectively when it is told what to do rather than what not to do (Bandura, 1997). The key is to make self-talk instructional and motivational rather than judgmental, negative, and filled with doubt. All athletes have moments when they come down on themselves and when things are not going in the expected direction, but being confident involves believing in oneself even in the worst of times. Confident athletes consistently think that they can and will achieve their goals.

One other strategy for dealing with negative thoughts that has been relatively unexplored in sport psychology research is based on the principles of "Zazen," more popularly known as "Zen." Zazen is a Buddhist practice used to settle one's mind into its original pure and clear state, thereby allowing one to see everything in the world as it is. In the Shambhala tradition, meditation is the medium through which the state of being is trained so that the mind and body become synchronized. It is beyond the scope of this book to cover these principles in detail; briefly, in Zazen practice, people are taught that if any random thought or feeling arises in their mind, they should just let it come and go as it does and not try to stop it, get rid of it, or analyze or judge it. Thoughts are just thinking. They are viewed as indicators of a loss of awareness, and signal the need to regain awareness. So, rather than trying to stop the thought, change the thought, counter the thought, or reframe the thought, athletes simply acknowledge the thought, identify it as a break in concentration, and refocus. The ultimate goal is "action with awareness," and the qualities that accompany this experience include expansive vision, effortless focus, feelings of equanimity and timelessness, abundant confidence, and complete freedom from anxiety or doubt (Parent, 2002).

Confidence has long been associated with Zen and Buddhism. In his book *Shambhala: The Sacred Path of the Warrior,* Chogyam Trungpa, a teacher of Buddhism, differentiated between two types of confidence. First, for the *amateur* warrior, he wrote that "sometimes confidence means that, being in a choiceless state, you trust in yourself and use your savings, information, strength, good memory, and stiff upper lip, and you accelerate your aggression and tell yourself that you're going to make it" (1984, pp. 85-86). For the warrior, however, he wrote this about confidence:

> Confidence does not mean that you have confidence in something, but it is remaining in the state of confidence, free from competition or one-upmanship. It is an unconditional state in which you simply possess an unwavering state of mind that needs no reference point. There is no room for doubt; even the question of doubt does not occur. This kind of confidence contains gentleness, because the notion of fear does not arise; sturdiness, because in the state of confidence there is ever-present resourcefulness; and joy, because trusting in the heart brings a greater sense of humor. This confidence can manifest as majesty, elegance, and richness in a person's life. (p. 86)

Understanding the meaning of "unconditional confidence" or "ziji" (which is the Tibetan word for confidence) is considered part of sacredness, which is the warrior's world.

With the exception of Zazen techniques, the thought control strategies presented here generally involve some form of cognitive restructuring. In his section on methods to control thoughts, Bandura (1997) concluded that "intractable ruminations are more effectively eradicated by personal enablement than by trying to combat unwanted thought with competing thought" (p. 150). The cognitive thought control strategies that receive the greatest attention, Bandura stated, are the ones that usually meet with limited success. Central to the social cognitive view on thought control is the importance for athletes of remembering that they are in control. Athletes can choose whether or not to act, think, and be confident. If an athlete's confidence goes away during a game or event, it is not because the opponent took it away. Rather the athlete gave it away when he stopped believing in himself. Thus, one of the keys to maintaining confidence is for athletes to develop the ability to discipline themselves so that they are always thinking in ways that give them the best opportunity to perform well and achieve their goals.

TECHNIQUE 8: Fostering Coping Efficacy

Coping efficacy (also referred to as ameliorative efficacy) was defined in chapter 1 as one's belief regarding one's ability to cope with diverse threats (e.g., unwanted thoughts, difficult situations, pain, or injury). In this section we focus on the relationship between coping efficacy and fear, pain, and injury.

In general, Bandura (1997) considers threat a relational matter concerning the match between perceived coping capabilities and potentially hurtful aspects of the environment. In his words, "to understand people's appraisals of external threats and their affective reactions to them, it is necessary to analyze their judgments of their coping capabilities. Efficacy beliefs determine, in large part, the subjective perilousness of environmental events" (Bandura, 1997, p. 140). Thus, to him, coping efficacy beliefs affect the degree of awareness and severity of potential threats and the way in which they are perceived and cognitively processed (e.g., manageable or unmanageable). If athletes have a strong belief in their capability to exercise control over threats, they are not likely to imagine disastrous events or feel a sense of panic. Those who have less confidence in managing potential threats are more likely to worry about them and experience feelings of distress, which in turn can impair their level of functioning. As shown in chapter 3, research has supported that higher self-efficacy ratings are related to lower perceptions of the fear of injury.

In addition to coping with fear, athletes have to learn to play through fatigue and pain. "This does not mean playing with injury or disregarding serious pain signals, but rather playing with the soreness and aches that are part and parcel of any strenuous physical activity" (Bandura, 1997, p. 393). According to Bandura (1997), "dwelling on physical discomfort detracts from effective performance" (p. 393). According to his research, the belief that pain is controllable to some extent makes it easier to manage, and the stronger one's perceived coping efficacy, the higher the pain tolerance and the less dysfunction pain produces. Thus, Bandura concluded that the ameliorative effects of some pain control techniques operate partly through self-efficacy beliefs.

Similarly, Bandura (1997) stated that coping efficacy beliefs also enter into other aspects of recovery from physical injury. In rehabilitative settings, athletes have to deal with the injury itself, as well as "tedium, pain, and discouragement over slow improvement" (Bandura, 1997, p. 393). In support, research has shown that one of the major cognitive responses following injury is the decrease in athletes' self-efficacy about returning to full participation (Heil, 1993; Taylor & Taylor, 1997; Wiese-Bjornstal, Smith, Shaffer, & Morrey, 1998).

The role of efficacy beliefs during the rehabilitation process has been a popular topic in sport research, although the study of coping efficacy specifically is relatively new. Quinn and Fallon (2000) showed how important efficacy beliefs were across four phases of injury rehabilitation (ranging from as soon as the injury occurred to full recovery). Confidence was most important at recovery, although it was a predictor of recovery at several of the other stages as well. On a similar note, Theodorakis, Beneca, Malliou, and Goudas (1997) showed that self-efficacy increased over the course of rehabilitation. Research by Taylor and May (1996) was also supportive of the role of efficacy beliefs in motivating athletes to comply with rehabilitation programs. Participants who had stronger beliefs in their ability to complete the prescribed modalities, as well as those with greater expectancy of the benefits of doing so, were more likely to be compliant with the rehabilitation program. The results showed that the compliant athletes were not initially higher in self-efficacy compared to the noncompliant athletes; this also supports the previous studies showing that efficacy beliefs change over time.

In the most specific study to date, Milne, Hall, and Forwell (2005) developed the Athletic Injury Self-Efficacy Scale consisting of task and coping efficacy dimensions (i.e., barrier and scheduling efficacy based on research from exercise psychology). Task self-efficacy was a significant predictor of rehabilitation adherence; coping self-efficacy predicted frequency of exercise during rehabilitation; and both task and coping self-efficacy predicted exercise duration in rehabilitation. One interesting finding from this study was that those participants who had had three or more previous injuries were significantly more confident than those who had been injured for the first time. The authors reasoned that because of this experience, previously injured athletes were better able to master the initial feelings of fear and anxiety and focus on the rehabilitation program. They concluded that although athletes were fairly efficacious in their injury rehabilitation, they lacked some confidence in their ability to perform their exercises when faced with challenges. Milne and colleagues suggested that therapists need to employ techniques geared toward augmenting coping self-efficacy. Introducing treatment goal setting, creating a rehabilitation buddy system, and allowing more flexible scheduling were suggested as potential options that may supplement the athletes' confidence about overcoming challenges in following their rehabilitation program.

According to Bandura (1997), a powerful way to alter coping efficacy beliefs is through modeling. "Coping modeling is more likely to contribute to resilience in personal efficacy under difficult circumstances where the road to success is long and full of impediments, hardships, and setbacks, and where evidence of progress may be a long time coming" (Bandura, 1997, p. 100).

Modeled performances that are designed to alter coping behavior and that are conducive to the enhancement of coping efficacy emphasize two factors: predictability and controllability (Bandura, 1997). Modeling behavior in threatening situations provides predictability by reducing the uncertainties that an individual might have. In Bandura's words, "Predictability reduces stress and increases preparedness for coping with threats" (p. 88). In modeling controllability, however, "the model demonstrates highly effective strategies for handling threats in whatever situation may arise" (p. 88). For the person viewing the models, there are two potential effects. On the one hand, Bandura stated that for those who are inefficacious, seeing similar others fail will make them accept their own subsequent failures as indicators of personal deficiencies, and they will behave in ways that confirm their inability. Conversely, for those who are efficacious, the modeling will weaken the impact of direct failure experiences and sustain effort that supports performance in the face of repeated failure.

Bandura (1997) suggests that coping models voice hopeful determination and the conviction that problems are surmountable and goals are achievable. In his words, models should display decreasing distress as they struggle with difficulties or threats, and they should demonstrate strategies for managing difficult situations. Applied to sport, this suggests that athlete models who struggle with fears similar to those of the observers, and then show confidence in the face of difficulties, should instill higher efficacy beliefs and perseverance in athletes than models who show no struggles or models who start to doubt themselves as they encounter problems. In relation to this point, one particularly effective technique may be for models to describe, and even show, how they experienced similar problems in the past but overcame them through determined effort. This would be a form of progressive mastery of problems described historically rather than enacted presently (Bandura, 1997). Another technique, particularly effective in injury rehabilitation, is to pair up an athlete with another who has recently been through the stage of rehabilitation the injured athlete is currently in. The athlete model can describe problems, explain how she overcame them, and also show that the next stage of the recovery can be reached. Many athletes report that this form of support is essential to their recoveries.

Up to now in this section, we have focused on maintaining confidence. When things are going well, athletes are performing at their best, their times are dropping, their production is increasing, their coach thinks they look good (and they feel this too), it is likely that athletes are feeling very confident. It would be nice if these experiences could last throughout the athlete's entire lifetime. Unfortunately, most athletes hit rough times when things do not feel right and may even experience a performance slump or injury. Even though there are multiple ways to quantitatively assess levels of self-confidence, most athletes report that losing self-confidence is just that, a feeling, something that is hard to describe. It is difficult for athletes to believe in their abilities to perform well (to be successful) when they are not performing well. It is during these times that it is challenging for athletes to remain confident. In this last section we offer a few strategies that can help experienced athletes regain their confidence when things are not going their way or when they have to rehabilitate from an injury.

Before we deal specifically with ways to regain confidence, we note that a first step is for athletes to carefully examine their environment and their own thoughts, feelings, and behaviors. Often athletes think they are in a "slump" when they have had one poor game. This is not a slump. Bandura (1997) considers a slump to be a sustained collapse in performance. Slumps have also been defined as unexplained drops in performance that extend longer than would be expected owing to normal ups and downs of competition (Taylor, 1988). To be in a slump, an athlete should show an uncharacteristic drop in performance for which there is no obvious cause (such as fatigue, minor injuries, illness, or changes in technique or equipment). If this is the case, then psychological factors should be considered. Of all the psychological factors, decreased confidence tends to be most associated with performance slumps. Slumping athletes maintain a lot of inner negativity and self-doubt, which of course affect their confidence and performance. This is why it is essential for athletes to change their thoughts and feelings, which should ultimately affect their behavior.

TECHNIQUE 9: Attributions

Attributions are the reasons people give for their successes and failures (Weiner, 1985). Mistakes, failures, and losses are inevitable in sport; and there is a relationship between the attributions athletes make and their levels of confidence (Kitsantas & Zimmerman, 1998; Orbach, Singer, & Price, 1999; Rudisill, 1989). According to Bandura (1997), by construing performance difficulties as simply unlucky aberrations, efficacy beliefs can serve as a protective factor against slumps or their prolongation. Thus, he recommends attributing performance difficulties to the unstable, external factor of luck. He also recommends that athletes attribute their performance slumps to some minor fault in the mechanics of execution because doing so should hopefully persuade them that all is well again and help them regain their sense of efficacy. Another possibility is to tell athletes that past failures were due to insufficient effort rather than a lack of ability. The rationale is that this can help foster a more resilient sense of confidence because a lack of effort can be rectified more easily than a lack of ability. According to Bandura (1997), athletes who are assured of their capabilities (i.e., confident) are more likely to look to situational factors, insufficient effort, or poor strategies as the causes of their failure. While we agree that these types of attributions are appropriate if protecting one's self-confidence is the goal, we caution that "blaming" all performance setbacks on external sources (such as the officiating, weather, bad luck) can be a serious mistake if done too often (Feltz, 1994). In these cases, athletes may end up perceiving that the outcome of their performances is out of their control and they will not take responsibility for their actions.

TECHNIQUE 10: Relaxing Performance Standards or Goals

Another slump recovery strategy suggested by Bandura (1997) is for athletes to relax their performance standards or goals. The thinking is that this will help athletes view progress toward future performances, rather than attainment of previous performances, as successes. In batting slumps, for example, players can be informed that they are on the road to recovery if they make good contact with the ball even though the placement and power of their hits fail to get them on base (Taylor, 1988). Athletes involved in sports in which goal scoring is important can be told to focus on taking quality shots on goal rather than worrying about the outcome or scoring. Relaxing performance standards is definitely related to goal setting. As pointed out by Weinberg and Gould (2003), one of the common problems in goal setting occurs when athletes fail to adjust their goals. In his research, Burton (1989) showed that swimmers who previously had no difficulty adjusting goals upward found it extremely difficult from a psychological perspective to adjust goals downward after an injury or illness. As suggested by Weinberg and Gould (2003), there are two ways to deal with this problem. First, athletes should be informed from the outset that goals will need to be adjusted upward and downward depending on the circumstances. That way, they will view adjustments as a normal part of the process rather than reflective of a problem on their part. Second, if goals need to be adjusted downward, the adjustment could be reconfigured into a new "staircase" of goals that ultimately surpasses the original goal. This will show the athlete that the lowered goal is only a temporary setback to ultimately be overcome.

TECHNIQUE 11: Reliving Past Successes

Another technique to help athletes regain confidence is based on performance accomplishments as a powerful source of efficacy information. Athletes can relive their past experiences of success using recordings or imagery. This form and use of imagery is different from what we discussed for novice athletes. Novice athletes do not usually have enough proficient performances to "relive." Technique 4 focuses more on imagery for skill development.

In today's world, many sporting events are recorded. The recordings may vary—some are professional productions for television, others are film for coaches, and still others are "family" movies. Many sports are also broadcast on the radio. Having athletes watch or hear about themselves "in action" should serve as proof that they have done in the past whatever it is they are lacking in confidence about today; this reminds them that they can do it again in the future.

In chapter 3 we discussed video as a form of self-modeling and described the two types. In positive self-review, athletes are taped as they perform a given skill or behavior multiple times; and with use of selective editing, a self-modeling tape is produced that shows the successful performances. In feedforward, the video shows a level of performance that the athlete has so far not achieved. To create these videos, skills are staged and edited together to present the desired performance. Research has shown that self-modeling is an effective strategy for producing behavior change as well as for enhancing self-efficacy beliefs (e.g., Singleton & Feltz, 1999; Starek & McCullagh, 1999).

Clearly, creating videos can be a time-consuming task. However, the goal is to create a focused and short (typically only 2 to 5 min in length) video that can be watched over and over again. As mentioned in chapter 3, the effectiveness of the videos, and of modeling in general, depends on whether the desired changes are realistic and desirable for the athlete to achieve. Given that physical skills do not vanish overnight, it is more likely that performance slumps are due to psychological factors. For this reason, we believe that using video can be especially helpful for athletes in performance slumps. Halliwell (1990) showed that such videos were very successful in enhancing the confidence levels of professional ice hockey players.

TECHNIQUE 12: Thinking and Acting Confident

Being positive is also a key to regaining confidence. Similarly to what happens with disruptive thinking (the focus of Technique 7), when athletes are not performing well they tend to be attuned to negatives, to key in to all the negative things that will confirm they are not performing well. For example, a swimmer who is struggling will get out of practice and remember the two missed intervals and how heavy his legs felt on the kick set. Thinking about past mistakes or failures will only breed further mistakes (Bandura, 1997). Athletes need to force themselves to acknowledge the positive, good things that have occurred, such as improvements in technique or feeling better than the day before. Doing so requires that athletes concentrate and put their mistakes behind them (Bandura, 1997). Athletes should carry the positive thoughts with them to competitions to give them the confidence that things are turning around.

Acting confident is also important. Even if an athlete does not feel confident inside, no one needs to know this, and certainly not the athlete's opponent. One's body posture can have a significant effect on one's opponent (Greenlees, Bradley, Holder, & Thelwell, 2005; Greenlees, Buscombe, Thelwell, Holder, & Rimmer, 2005). Greenlees and his colleagues researched the sources of information that athletes used to make judgments of their potential opponents (i.e., impression formation). More specifically, in terms of body posture, they examined the influence of a potential opponent's body language (an amalgam of posture, movement, and gaze) on several "descriptors." The results showed that models who displayed positive body language were rated as more assertive, aggressive, competitive, experienced, *confident,* positive, focused, relaxed, and fit than individuals displaying negative body language. Furthermore, the study participants were more confident about defeating individuals who displayed negative body language.

The results of these studies make it clear that body language matters. How athletes present themselves to their opponent can affect the opponent's impressions of them. Athletes can be taught to display positive body language, even when they are not feeling 100% confident. Moreover, athletes' thoughts, feelings, and behaviors are all related; perhaps if athletes act confident, they can enhance their feelings of confidence. However, the effect of body posture on an athlete's own confidence level has not been assessed. The bottom line has to do with the question, Are we suggesting to athletes, "fake it 'til you make it"? The answer is yes when it comes to presenting themselves to opponents, and maybe when it comes to their own confidence levels. We suggest that behaving with confidence will trigger thoughts and feelings associated with confidence.

We also suggest that in addition to acting confident in warm-ups, acting confident during competitions is very important. Athletes should be taught to keep their heads up even after making a critical error or when a goal is scored against them. Just as acting confident will lead to increases in confidence, acting unconfident is likely to lead to decreases in confidence. It is vital for athletes to become aware of how they handle and respond to adverse situations. One thing athletes do not want to do is to have their opponents recognize their loss of confidence, because this will increase the opponents' confidence.

TECHNIQUE 13: Efficacy by Proxy

It is probably easier for athletes to think and act confident when they are surrounded by people who believe in them. For this reason, athletes should take a look at the people around them and choose their companions well. They should associate with the people who support and accept them. Social cognitive theory distinguishes between three modes of agency: personal agency, with self as the agent; collective agency, with a group as the agent; and proxy agency, in which a third party is empowered to act as one's agent (Bandura, 2001). Efficacy beliefs are the key factors of all these forms of human agency.

Bandura (1997) recognized that in many areas of life, individuals do not have direct control over the mechanisms of change and therefore must turn to proxy control to alter their lives for the better. He stated that people use proxy agents for three main reasons: (a) They have not developed adequate personal means to reach their desired outcomes; (b) they believe that a third party can better help them achieve their desired outcomes; and (c) they do not want the personal responsibility of direct control over possible outcomes. As pointed out by Bray, Gyurcsik, Martin Ginis, and Culos-Reed (2004), this notion of proxy efficacy may conjure up negative images of people's relinquishing control and responsibility over their lives when they lack the skills or motivation to take care of matters on their own. However, it may also be an adaptive strategy when people are acquiring new skills or when they find themselves unable to manage aspects of their lives that were once under their personal control (Bray et al., 2004). Clearly, when athletes are slumping and needing to regain their confidence, they may feel unable to manage certain aspects of their lives and therefore proxy agency may be relevant. An athlete's confidence in his or her coach (i.e., proxy efficacy) may be especially important. We refer to proxy efficacy and its role in the tripartite view of efficacy beliefs more fully in chapter 9.

TECHNIQUE 14: Patience and Rest

Finally, athletes should remember to be patient. Their confidence will not rebound "in the blink of an eye." Undoubtedly perseverance, persistence, and patience on the part of the athlete will be needed to work through this challenging time. Bandura (1997) has suggested that prescribing a short rest is a good strategy to help athletes restore efficacy beliefs. He stated that barring any physical impairment, the benefits of a brief rest probably stem more from expectational changes than from the inactivity or the temporary removal from pressure situations.

Levels of Efficacy

Before ending this chapter, we believe it is necessary to address optimal levels of confidence. Bandura (1997) has suggested that there is an optimal level of confidence, but it seems to depend on the circumstances. Some researchers (Weinberg & Gould, 2003) have illustrated the confidence–performance relationship using an inverted "U" with the highest point biased toward the right (see figure 6.1). This depiction, however, is probably too simplistic. Recall from chapter 1 that Bandura (1986b, 1997) differentiates between preparatory efficacy and performance efficacy. He suggests that, in the preparatory phase, some self-doubt about the ensuing performance is necessary to provide the incentive for athletes to invest the time and effort needed to acquire the knowledge and skill to become proficient. However, Bandura also warns that too much self-doubt can turn into a stressor and debilitator rather than a motivator to practice. This hypothesis implies a curvilinear, or inverted-U relationship in the skill acquisition phase between self-efficacy beliefs and effort and persistence as the dependent variable (see figure 6.2). Bandura (1997) predicts a linear relationship between efficacy and performance in the

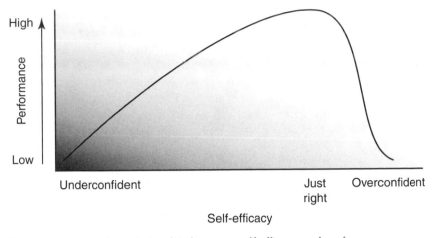

Figure 6.1   Inverted-U relationship between self-efficacy and performance.

Adapted, by permission, from R.S. Weinberg and D. Gould, 2003, *Foundations of sport and exercise psychology*, 3rd ed. (Champaign, IL: Human Kinetics).

performance phase. To our knowledge, though, this relationship has not been empirically tested. Even with proficient athletes, Bandura (1997) notes that coaches will inflate the capabilities of athletes' opponents and emphasize the deficiencies of their own athletes to try to motivate them to practice hard for the next competition. In addition, complacency can set in after easy successes to affect motivation, and greater efforts can occur after failure.

Although most researchers have not differentiated between preparatory and performance efficacy, they have acknowledged that too little or too much

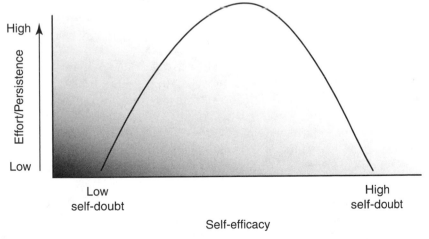

Figure 6.2   Inverted-U relationship between self-efficacy and effort and persistence in the prepatory phase.

confidence can be detrimental. "Overconfidence," "inflated confidence," or "false confidence" are terms that have been used to refer to situations when athletes' confidence levels are greater than their abilities warrant (Martens, 1987; Weinberg & Gould, 2003). Martens proposed two forms of false confidence. In one form, athletes honestly believe they are better than they really are; in the other, athletes act confident yet underneath are actually low in confidence and worried about performing poorly (i.e., an athlete "fakes" confidence to hide actual feelings of self-doubt). Martens proposed that both of these forms of overconfidence would have corresponding effects on performance. More specifically, he stated that the first form of overconfidence would be seen frequently in situations in which athletes take their opponent for granted and think all they need to do to win is to show up. They underestimate the task or opponent. Martens noted that the performance decrements would be caused by the belief that one does not have to prepare oneself or exert the effort needed to get the job done. This emphasis on underpreparation as a causal factor of poor performance is consistent with Bandura's notion of preparatory efficacy.

For the second form of overconfidence, however, Martens emphasized the performance effects. When athletes fake confidence, there is the potential for disaster; especially when two players of different ability are competing against each other. If the better player approaches the situation with fake confidence, he or she may fall behind early in the competition. This may result in the opponent's gaining confidence, thereby making it harder for the better player to bounce back from performing poorly. This scenario is consistent with Bandura's notion of performance efficacy. The key is that the athlete, although projecting outward signs of confidence, is actually low in self-efficacy. Bandura (1997) predicts a more linear relationship between self-efficacy beliefs and performance as the dependent measure (see figure 6.3). As Bandura explains, one cannot execute a task very well while plagued with self-doubt.

Regardless of the distinction between preparation and performance, there seems to be an optimal level of efficacy (Bandura, 1997). In the media, this optimal level has been referred to as "swagger" despite the fact that the dictionary definition of swagger has to do with being boastful or conceited. Former basketball player and Hall of Famer Larry Bird described his swagger when he said, "This game is all confidence and, you know, sometimes it's scary. When I'm at my best, I can do just about anything I want, and no one can stop me. I feel like I'm in total control of everything."

Swagger is mentioned repeatedly in sport coverage. For example, the writer of an article about the Kansas City Chiefs football club notes that "the Chiefs are beginning to develop a bit of attitude. A little swagger. The confidence is there." Similarly, when Andre Rison moved to the Kansas City Chiefs, his coach said, "Rison brings us something—he brings us swagger

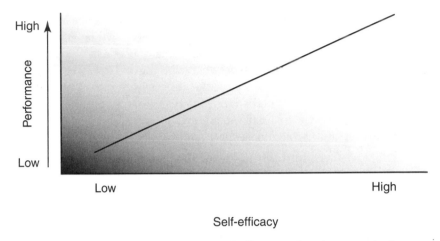

Figure 6.3 Linear relationship between self-efficacy and performance in the performance phase.
Adapted from A. Bandura, 1997, *Self-efficacy: The exercise control* (New York: W.H. Freeman and Company).

and juice and confidence, and he brings us experience. He brings us a guy that, in the clutch, has been able to step up and make plays, and we need that from him for our club to have a chance to move on." Others have recognized the importance of swagger as well. For example, the athletic director at the University of Kansas said, "I think the University of Kansas has lost its swagger. I don't mean cockiness or arrogance. I mean swagger. We have to develop that swagger of confidence." Even though there are times when sport psychologists and the media have different meaning for words (e.g., "choking"), we like the use of the term swagger and for that reason we suggest equating swagger with an optimal level of confidence. Swagger, then, is seen when one's high level of confidence is based on an accurate assessment of skill and ability, with proper credit to the opponent if there is one. Individuals who have swagger have the abilities to get the job done and the belief in themselves that they can do so.

Most athletes and coaches acknowledge that success in sport comes down to psychological factors—depending on who is asked, the percentage varies. There are claims that 40% to 90% of success in sport is due to mental factors (Williams & Krane, 2001). Yogi Berra, the former baseball player and member of the National Baseball Hall of Fame, offered several estimates of the importance of mental skills. A couple of the more popular "Yogi-isms" are "Half the game is 90% mental" and "Baseball is 90% mental, the other half is physical." Now, Berra also said that "90% of the putts that are short don't go in," which shows that he was not a mathematical genius; but the point is that he, like many others, clearly acknowledged the importance of psychological skills.

The importance given to psychological characteristics varies across skill levels. It seems that the higher one's skill or competitive level, the more important these characteristics, such as self-efficacy, become. When all other things are equal and the difference between winning and losing comes down to fractions of a second or single points, the athletes who are more confident are likely to be more successful than the athletes who lack confidence. Stated another way, athletes of comparable abilities who have different levels of confidence do not perform at the same level (Bandura, 1997). However, as pointed out by Bandura, gifted athletes who are plagued by self-doubts can perform far below their potential, and less talented but highly confident athletes can outperform more talented competitors who distrust their capabilities.

Of course, self-efficacy cannot be a substitute for a lack of skill. On the contrary, confidence and physical talent are best considered as codeterminants of athletic performance (Bandura, 1997). Moreover, confidence without the requisite skills and motivation is not enough. Athletes must also possess the physical skills and commitment to perform well. The key is to have a firm and resilient sense of efficacy (popularly called "mental toughness"; Bandura, 1997). In the next chapter on enhancing efficacy beliefs in teams, the same issue of codetermination applies, and we describe similar techniques for raising collective efficacy. The issues are just more complicated because of individual variation in requisite skills and motivation.

7

Enhancing Efficacy Beliefs of Teams

> You need to play with supreme confidence, or else you'll lose again, and then losing becomes a habit.
>
> *Joe Paterno, head coach, Penn State University Nittany Lions football team.*

Having already described the nature and workings of collective efficacy or team confidence in chapter 4, in this chapter we elaborate on how (and why) this perception may be enhanced. Similar to the format in chapter 6, we present methods to build, maintain, and regain collective efficacy based on information from various sources. However, rather than highlighting techniques for novice and elite athletes separately, we highlight techniques that are best for new and more established teams. Granted, novice teams also are fairly new, but elite teams could be newly formed as well and may still need to build their collective efficacy. Before we describe these strategies, we review some of the basic tenets of the collective efficacy concept and describe situations in which intervention strategies might be needed.

Brief Review of Tenets of Collective Efficacy

The following headline, from the May 22, 2005, edition of the *Arizona Republic,* serves as a guide to this brief recap. As the Phoenix Suns were participating in the third round of the NBA's playoffs, the paper's headline read, "Confidence not lacking, despite Spurs' history." A few things are noteworthy regarding this comment on the team's confidence. The first is that collective efficacy is important enough in and of itself to warrant headline attention. In addition to the anecdotal evidence offered by athletes and coaches, research supports that collective efficacy is a valid and significant concept in team functioning. A second point about the headline is that confidence is related to history. As we have already described, collective efficacy is deeply tied to history, or past performances, whether or not they were successful. A third point is implied, namely that confidence is related to future success, because the article focused on the Phoenix Suns' confidence for the upcoming game. A team must be confident to perform well. Fourth, and finally, the headline explicitly named the opponent. In fact, the (San Antonio) "Spurs' history" was one of great success—two recent league championships. And despite this, the Suns were confident. Perhaps against a lesser opponent, the team's confidence would not have warranted attention, or perhaps the team was overconfident. However, in this upcoming series, against one of the best teams in the league, the team was not lacking confidence. Further, the statement suggests that teams size each other up. They use social comparison sources of information as well as their own past performance to form judgments about their team's capabilities to succeed.

Thus, collective efficacy, or "a group's shared belief in its conjoint capabilities to organize and execute the courses of action required to produce given levels of attainment" (Bandura, 1997, p. 477), is a powerful team dynamic. It is involved in an intense, reciprocal relationship with performance. It is based on behavioral, social, and cognitive sources of information. Further, it is an attribute of the team, not one individual, and is a situationally specific perception. Confidence, whether of an individual or a team, is a very dynamic attribute, and it is only natural that teams experience times during which they find their confidence lacking. Considering how important efficacy is and its relationship to such consequences as performance and satisfaction, it is important to know how to increase or enhance the confidence of a team.

Situations Requiring Collective Efficacy Interventions

Before discussing how to increase collective efficacy, we will portray some conditions in which this would be desired by a team. These conditions can include those in which teams are newly established and need to build a sense of team confidence. Alternatively, there are cases of teams that are established and are suffering from a crisis of confidence.

As an example of an existing team wanting to increase its confidence, consider the case of the Murray State University women's volleyball team. In the fall of 2004, the team was dealing with the loss of three key players when they played against the team from Morehead State University. They lost 3 games to 1; and while they were preparing for the next match, it was apparent that the team had lost some of its swagger. Head Coach David Schwepker was quoted as saying that "the team lost confidence after playing Morehead. We went into the weekend knowing it would be rough" (Renfro, 2004). And rough it was, as the team lost the next competition 3 games to 0. Here is the stereotypical example of a team whose confidence has been shaken. The coach and players of this volleyball team would reasonably want to rebuild its state of collective efficacy and subsequently improve performance.

What techniques would be useful to this team in this situation? Would different techniques be more applicable if this had been a team of seniors who had played together for 4 years than if the team had been a group of rookies still in the process of team formation? Finally, note that this example, like the example of the NBA's Phoenix Suns mentioned earlier, reflects an interactive team sport, in which teammates must interact to produce the team outcome. Collective efficacy and its sources are just as applicable to coactive teams in which teammates perform relatively independently of one another (e.g., track and field).

Whether a case involves developing team confidence in new or established teams, the sources are still rooted in Bandura's (1997) framework of collective efficacy. In this chapter, we use this framework by discussing how mastery experiences or performance-based techniques, vicarious experiences, verbal persuasion, and the building of team cohesion, as well as some other methods, may be used to increase team confidence. Many of the techniques are similar to those we described in chapter 6 but are focused at the team level. Others are unique to enhancing collective efficacy in teams. Although most of the techniques discussed would theoretically be valuable for both new and established teams, we differentiate them according to when they would be more typically used.

Building Team Efficacy of New Teams

There are several viable techniques for enhancing the collective efficacy of a new team. These may be based in Bandura's (1997) conceptual tenets or deduced from various empirical studies. Here we expand on several influential methods. One consistent theme related to all these sources of collective efficacy is the definition and interpretation of success in these teams.

TECHNIQUE 1: Defining Success in Mastery Terms

As in all instances of efficacy beliefs, the most powerful way to increase team confidence is for the team to experience success. However, two issues must be first addressed. First, experiencing success is easier said than done. Second, team confidence is a collective attribute, and therefore for mastery to be experienced, it must be a shared sense of mastery. If half of the players believe the team has played well and half believe they have not, this could not be considered a mastery experience for collective efficacy.

The effect of mastery depends on the perception of what it means to be successful. Sport psychologists and athletes recognize that successful performance is not always synonymous with winning. A team may play to the full extent of their abilities and still lose; alternatively a team could play quite poorly and still win. The outcome may be influenced by such factors as the quality of the opponent, the state of the officiating, the weather, and lucky bounces.

In the literature on goal orientation, a distinction has been drawn between ego and task orientations (Nicholls, 1984b, 1989). This is similar to the competitive orientation concept in Vealey's (1986) model, described in chapter 1. As we also have described in chapter 3 in the context of self-referenced and norm-referenced goals, and again in chapter 4, individuals define achievement in two primary ways—task involvement and ego involvement. Ego involvement entails perceiving achievement in terms of demonstration of superiority. Ego involvement is rooted in social comparison (norm referenced); according to this orientation, athletes can achieve success only if they have shown themselves to be the best, relative to others. In the zero-sum situation of most sports, ego involvement equates success with winning. Alternatively, task involvement defines success in terms of the development of one's abilities. Here, instead of the social comparison of an ego orientation, self-comparison is key. A successful performance is defined in terms of how well one did relative to how well one could do (self-referenced). Success equals doing as well as possible, regardless of whether the person or the team won or lost. As we mentioned in chapter 4, a strong disposition in ego orientation may counter the concept of collaboration that is needed for collective achievement, while a strong disposition in task orientation may facilitate a firm sense of collective efficacy through its influence on individual members' self-efficacy beliefs (Magyar, Feltz, & Simpson, 2004).

Thus, especially for newly formed teams or teams that are not highly skilled yet, helping individual team members define success in mastery terms will give them successes over which they have more control and will help develop the concept of collaboration. When success is defined in mastery terms at the team level, the climate is considered a mastery climate, which we address next. A coach, for instance, could define success in terms of having more shots on goal than in the previous game or against the opposing team. For the season, a coach could define success as having more shots on goal than in the previous season. There can be multiple definitions of success for a team, and coaches (of at least high school-aged athletes or older) might sit down with their athletes and form a list of what they will consider as successes.

TECHNIQUE 2: Mastery Climate

The coach's style and leadership dictate the operative motivational climate. Motivational climates reflect the goal structures and feedback that a coach emphasizes and can also be ego oriented (performance climate) or task oriented (mastery climate). A coach who emphasizes a performance climate defines success and failure in terms of wins and losses, punishes mistakes and poor performance, gives high-ability athletes greater attention and recognition, and encourages competition between team members. A coach who emphasizes a mastery environment defines success and failure in terms of mastery goals and provides positive reinforcement to athletes when they work hard, show improvement, and show good teamwork. Each athlete is made to feel that he or she makes an important contribution to the success of the team. Athletes who perceive the team environment as commanding and not under their direct control are less likely to demonstrate firm efficacy in their ability (Bandura,

2000). Improvement and effort, on the other hand, are more directly controllable. Magyar and Feltz (2003) found that volleyball athletes who perceived a mastery climate attended to sources of confidence that were within the athletes' control (i.e., personal mastery, learning, and effort) to form their confidence beliefs in sport. In addition, in Magyar and colleagues' (2004) study, rowing teams that perceived a motivational climate had higher levels of collective efficacy. And in Vargas-Tonsing and colleagues' (2004) study, collegiate athletes reported that the coach's encouragement of positive talk was one of the most effective efficacy-enhancing techniques for them. Thus, coaches can help to develop their athletes' team confidence by emphasizing a mastery environment characterized by reinforcement for effort, improvement, and hard work, and one in which each team member is respected for his or her contributions to the team.

A more detailed example of how a team, even at the elite level, can benefit from a mastery climate with respect to their success can be seen in the case of the U.S. women's ice hockey team as they prepared for the 2002 Winter Olympics in Salt Lake City. The team was clearly one of the two best in the world, although newly formed as a team, and had aspirations of winning the gold medal on their home ice. However, their chief rival, Canada, was the prohibitive favorite, having won the last seven consecutive world championships. Haberl and Zaichkowsky (2003) provide some in-depth commentary on the psychological state of the U.S. team as they prepared for the Olympics. Worth noting is that after the team was finalized, they played Canada 15 times in the year leading to the Games, and the players came to focus on other issues besides the outcome of the game.

> With each win that we had against Canada, and even each loss, because it was a one-goal loss, you know, or it was a really close game . . . so each victory or each close loss kind of built that confidence up. (Haberl & Zaichkowsky, 2003, p. 224)

Here we see an explicit statement by one of the players on the team that a loss, as long as it clearly involved an improvement, could be seen as a successful performance and subsequently a source of team confidence. In this case, the team seems to have clearly endorsed the use of self-comparison in defining success. Confidence grew even with a close loss. This increase in confidence was undoubtedly important as the U.S. team closed the gap between themselves and Canada and eventually won the gold medal in the Winter Olympics in Salt Lake City. If the coach had promoted (and the team had endorsed) an ego-oriented climate, confidence would have been increased only when the team beat Canada. Losses, even close ones, would have resulted in a decreased collective efficacy. To say that if the team's confidence had decreased they might not have beaten Canada in the gold medal game does not seem to be too much of a stretch. Here the difference between a mastery and ego climate may have been the difference between an Olympic gold and a silver medal.

As we mentioned in chapter 6 (Technique 2), the feedback that a coach provides for an individual athlete also applies to teams. That is, during the early formation of a team or with beginning skill teams, progress or improvement feedback (information on the team's progress) should be emphasized. Only during the later phases of skill acquisition or with experienced teams is normative feedback (information based on team progress relative to that of other teams) recommended. Notice that in a mastery-oriented climate, within-team normative feedback is not used. Further, when team mistakes are made, the same four-step positive approach that Feltz (1994) outlined for individual athletes and that we outlined in chapter 6 applies to teams: The coach should (a) acknowledge the team's distress about the mistake, (b) compliment the team on what they did right, (c) provide instruction to correct the mistake, and (d) end with a positive, energizing statement.

TECHNIQUE 3: Team Goal Setting

The concept of goal setting has been defined as "attaining a specific standard of proficiency on a task, usually within a specified time limit" (Locke, Shaw, Saari, & Latham, 1981, p. 145). This is a well-researched psychological process that has been found to be significantly linked to behavior and performance (Kyllo & Landers, 1995). With respect to collective efficacy, we must discuss the use of *team* goals, as well as the process of how they are determined.

Setting team goals does not, by itself, enhance team efficacy. The goals, if realistic yet challenging, allow the team to achieve standards that influence efficacy information and a sense of satisfaction. Gould (2001) organized the numerous suggestions regarding goal setting for teams into three primary components: (a) the planning phase, (b) the meeting phase, and (c) the evaluation phase.

In the planning phase, the coach reviews the team's strengths and weaknesses. From this list of weaknesses, the coach can assess the team's needs. A coach would then list what the team needs to do to improve in these areas by writing down specific, measurable goals. The goals should be realistic but challenging. For teams that are low in confidence, these must be goals that the coach is certain are attainable. For teams with high confidence, setting goals that are just beyond the team's reach may help sustain team goal striving.

In the meeting phase, the coach must consider how to involve the athletes in the goal-setting process to foster a sense of shared responsibility and commitment and how the goal-setting process will be monitored. Endorsing task-oriented goals for a team implicitly means that the team should be involved in some sort of team-based goal-setting procedure. This requires some proactive steps—some reflection and discussion—to define what success is. The coach might start with reflecting upon last season's performance and expectations for the current season. The concept of goal setting can be introduced if it is new to the team. This is the time to explain the differences between outcome-oriented and process-oriented goals and long- and short-term goals. The coach can present the team's strengths and weaknesses and indicate where improvement needs to take place. The team goals, therefore, define the success for the team.

There is independent support for Gould's proposals. Widmeyer and DuCharme (1997) presented a series of suggestions on team goal setting, with collective efficacy specifically noted as a primary outcome of this process. These authors noted that involving the entire team in the goal-setting process will facilitate commitment to the goals and optimize any effect on team confidence. Like Gould, they endorsed the setting of long-term goals, followed by short-term goals. In this way, the goal-setting process is very realistic, a sense of ownership can be derived among the team, and evaluation toward goal attainment is more obvious and coherent.

Evaluation of progress should occur after every practice, after competitions, and at the midpoint and end of the season. Team statistics should be kept that are based on the team goals. The coach should provide this feedback to the team on a regular basis. If the goals appear to be too easy or too difficult, they can be adjusted to keep the team motivated and confident in their performance. These practices were also endorsed by Widmeyer and DuCharme (1997) in their paper on team goal setting.

In order to explain this process more fully, we apply it to a real-life example. A prime example of the goal-setting process lies in the competition between the United States and Mexico in men's soccer. The international rivalry has been noted as the most intense in the history of North America. Although Mexico has traditionally been the dominant team, recent years have seen the Americans gain the upper hand in the competition, including eliminating the Tricolores (Mexico's national team) during the 2002 World Cup. In examining this shift in the fortunes of the two national sides, Grant Wahl (2005) discusses several possible reasons before concluding the following:

> Yet perhaps the most fascinating explanation is that the Tricolores have somehow lost the confidence they once had when facing their northern neighbor. Rare is the discussion that doesn't include the word *metalidad*. 'I think it's a psychological game now,' says Guillermo Cantú, a former player for Mexico who now directs its national teams. 'The mentality is on the American side, and we have to steal it.' (Wahl, 2005, p. 55)

Even though this example is of an established team, it has relevance to the team goal-setting process for a team lacking in confidence. Adhering to the suggestions of Gould (2001), we would suggest the following steps to utilize team goal setting to enhance the collective efficacy of the Mexican soccer team. First, in the planning stage, the coach would conduct an assessment of the team's capabilities and target specific goal areas. This would be a comprehensive process and would involve such activities as detailed analysis of game film, comparisons to other teams, and discussions with other members of the coaching staff and perhaps other coaches. The coach should also solicit the opinions of the team members regarding what are the most relevant issues for the subsequent goal-setting procedure to address. Such interactions could be one-on-one or team based, perhaps during a team retreat. At the end of this planning stage, the coach would have ascertained what aspects of team functioning are most applicable for this goal-setting process. In the Mexican soccer team, this could be many things (e.g., team discipline, set play execution, team cohesion). For the purpose of our discussion, we will pretend that this process has culminated in identification of time of possession as the most important factor for team goal setting. Specific, measurable goals, then, could include a statement of the current situation regarding time of possession (e.g., in the past six games, the team has had possession of the ball for only 40% of the game).

In the meeting phase, the coach and the team would discuss such practical issues as the choice of task or process goals, as well as the exact time frame of goal attainment. We would encourage the team to focus on goals based on self-comparison, starting with a long-term goal and using short-term goals as incremental and measurable steps toward that end. For example, the players and coaches could agree that they need to improve on their time of possession, and that for the next time they face the United States, this should increase from 40% to at least 55%. They could then specify related short-term goals for the team. They might determine a target of ball possession for each of the upcoming games that increases in a challenging but realistic fashion. These stated targets should be objective, clear, and measurable (e.g., a time of possession of 45% for the next game, 50% for the one after that . . .). A fully developed team goal-setting procedure would also focus on those processes that contribute to time of possession (e.g., individual skills to shield the ball, smart and timely passing, and ways to steal the ball during play). Discussion of goals on these processes would also follow the protocol we have outlined.

Finally, the evaluation phase would incorporate these specific, objective, and measurable statements about ball possession into everyday team functioning. The coach and team would make sure that these goals are explicitly attended to during practices, simulated games, "friendlies," and ultimately the next international game against the United States. In this way, the team would experience the mastery (with respect to time of possession) necessary to build confidence to compete with the United States.

TECHNIQUE 4: Modifying the Task

Another mastery-based technique for building team efficacy is to simplify a team strategy or a team drill. This is similar to the instructional technique described in chapter 6 (Technique 1); but instead of modifying the task at the individual level, a team drill, game strategy, or team system can be simplified until the team gets the concept. Then, more aspects of the play can be added. A prototypical example here would be a pick and roll in basketball. This situation begins when a player supports a teammate who has the ball and is being defended by an opponent. The player (without the ball) sets a pick on the defender so that the ball carrier can get free. Then he can move off this pick to a nearby open area, receive a pass from the ball carrier, and have a high-percentage shot. This is a basic team play in the sport of basketball, and confidence in the players' ability to successfully execute it in games can be achieved through modification of the task. This can begin with each player's being taught the basic skills of executing his or her role in the play, as well as the awareness to recognize the appropriate situation when it arises in the game. Practices can begin to execute the drill unopposed, then work up to an active defense. Such a progression of task management would result in incremental mastery experiences, culminating in the team's having confidence to successfully execute the play in a game situation. Similarly, using strategies that capitalize on a team's strengths can help develop the team's confidence (Bandura, 1997). For instance, a basketball team that is fast, but not relatively big and tall, might be more successful using fast breaks and developing their outside shots.

There are times when coaches, especially at the youth levels, try to introduce new systems of play that are too advanced for the players to carry out successfully. They either cannot comprehend the strategy or lack the skills to coordinate the plays. Coaches in these situations would be more successful sticking with the basic and simple systems of play whereby athletes can work on perfecting their skills before moving to more advanced systems of play.

TECHNIQUE 5: Simulations

Researchers have found that participating in a simulation, such as a mock competition or practice session, can have a positive effect on athletes' confidence in their abilities to successfully execute skills (Tenenbaum, Levy-Kolker, Sade, Liebermann, & Lidor, 1996). The use of simulations has proven particularly effective with respect to injured athletes (Evans, Hardy, & Fleming, 2000), novice performers (Starek & McCullagh, 1999), and the evaluation of officials (Mascarenhas, Collins, & Mortimer, 2005; Rainey, Larsen, & Williard, 1987). Unfortunately, there is a lack of empirical research on the effectiveness of simulations with regard to collective efficacy. However, ample theoretical evidence and practical use of simulations in sport provide a sufficient basis for discussion.

A collectivity-based simulation would entail the replication of team performance contexts in a controlled setting. This is a typical component of most team practices. For instance, a soccer team may develop a new play on a corner kick. After players have learned this strategy and practiced the skills, a practice may typically end with performing this skill under game-like circumstances. Some players on the team may practice as members of the opposing team, the corner kick may be set up exactly as it would be in competition, and the coach or another nonplaying team member may act as an official, perhaps even with the clock running close to the end of the game. The coach may even put worthwhile contingencies on successful and unsuccessful performances to replicate the impact of scoring or missing a scoring chance. Simulations can also include practicing set plays with crowd noise piped in over the sound system, with the opposing practice team wearing the same colors as the upcoming opponents and with time-outs called by the opposing practice team. In basketball, some coaches have their athletes practice free throws with hecklers waving Styrofoam "noodles" behind the basket. Such simulations serve as the equivalent of a group-level vicarious experience in that the team as a whole could benefit from the experience of having successfully performed. These simulations provide experiences for the team on which to base a realistic assessment of their collective efficacy before they get to the official competitions.

The best example of such structured simulation experiences toward enhancing team confidence may be in the typical progression seen in the off-season programs of NFL teams. These teams, after having set their playing rosters, progress through a fairly standardized schedule of activities that will more and more closely approximate team performance. For any team following this NFL model, the first step would include physical training and developing and memorizing the particular plays that the team runs. These activities would be the building blocks of vicarious experiences. Teams would develop a set of confidence expectations in their basic physical and cognitive abilities to play well. After this, clubs would move on to practices and scrimmages. In these practices, as described earlier for the soccer team, teams would begin to perform under simulated game conditions and derive the subsequent benefits in collective efficacy.

From this point on, the simulations would become even more realistic. Teams routinely schedule scrimmages with other clubs. Although such a scrimmage would not be an official game, it would have players from different clubs performing in a gamelike competitive situation and include real officials. From these sessions, clubs would move on to preseason games against the full rosters of other teams in full gamelike conditions, although these would not count in league standings.

With use of this progression, teams would begin the regular season after a series of simulations that increasingly approximate "real" games. Again, in the absence of true mastery experiences, the team would still have ample opportunity to develop realistic assessment of the likelihood that their conjoint abilities may be successful. Further, because all activities in this progression of simulations are team activities, this perception of efficacy should be a shared belief. Thus, teams could gradually become more and more confident without ever having won (or lost). The increase in team confidence should result in a variety of team and individual effects (e.g., increased team performance).

TECHNIQUE 6: Manipulating Schedules

The scheduled simulations that we just described are the lead-up to managing schedules. Since a team that experiences success will be more confident, and since scheduled games are more of a performance experience than the simulations just discussed, a coach can explicitly manage the schedule to maximize the probability of the team's experiencing success. For example, the coach of a team could choose to create a team schedule that includes several weaker teams so that her own team would be more likely to experience success and gain confidence before facing more difficult opponents.

This is a relatively common practice in certain levels of sporting competition. For example, at the collegiate level, it is typical of football and basketball teams to schedule weaker opponents in their preconference season. In this way, when the teams begin their conference schedule, they will have already reaped the efficacy-enhancing benefits of (most likely) having repeatedly performed successfully as a team. Similarly, high school and collegiate teams may host a tournament to which weaker opponents are invited. This would potentially achieve the same effect.

There are levels of competition where schedule manipulation is not possible or practical. The schedules of professional leagues are overseen by central agencies that endorse parity among the leagues' teams. The example of the Murray State University volleyball team would be a more appropriate one because in that case the schedule can be changed. If the team had continued to perform poorly for the rest of the year, the coach could have applied this source of collective efficacy by manipulating the schedule for the next season to include weaker teams. The team would then have begun the season by experiencing the mastery of success that they had not perceived the previous season, and accordingly their confidence would have been strengthened as they approached games with more skilled rivals.

It is worth noting that this strategy could backfire, resulting in complacency (see chapter 1), leading to failure and a subsequent loss of team confidence. A team may manipulate their schedule so that early-season games (e.g., the preconference schedule in NCAA football and basketball) are against only weaker opponents. By performing successfully against these weaker opponents, a team might develop an inflated sense of their collective efficacy. They have never been challenged in preseason play. Thus, when faced with a difficult opponent in the regular season, their confidence might crumble the first time they were behind in the score. Alternatively, a coach may choose to schedule strong opponents in the preseason, ostensibly to prepare the team to play against the country's best teams, in hostile environments. Such schedule manipulation could also result in the team's performing poorly and losing confidence that they can put successful plays together. As we mentioned in discussing Technique 5, simulations, progressive manipulations would be best, in which some difficult opponents are introduced strategically during the preseason.

Building Team Efficacy of Established Teams

Efficacy is a dynamic construct. Although established teams have a recognized structure and history, it does not follow that the sense of confidence in such teams will be stable. The following techniques focus more on the dynamic interactions within teams, for example, behaviors and choices that coaches can alter from day to day so that they can have an optimal impact on collective efficacy.

TECHNIQUE 7: Verbal Persuasion

Just as with self-efficacy, maintaining team efficacy seems to be easy when the team is winning more than they are losing, or when they are consistently improving. Developing "team" mental toughness or resilient team efficacy is as important as developing mental toughness in athletes individually. To maintain a robust sense of collective efficacy, teams may need to be convinced that they have the mental toughness and focus to persevere through failures and setbacks. One way in which coaches can help to maintain a team's confidence is through persuasive techniques.

According to Bandura (1986b, 1997) verbal persuasion is a significant source of efficacy information. If a team can be convinced that they can successfully attain a given performance, they are more confident in their ability to do so. Most of the research on the effect of verbal persuasion on efficacy beliefs has occurred at the individual level. The dearth of research on verbally increasing collective efficacy is intriguing considering the wealth of anecdotal evidence on the effectiveness of the "win one for the Gipper" types of speeches common in sport. In fact, there is rich evidence to support the validity of such talks. In 1994, the New York Rangers of the NHL won the Stanley Cup. Prior to the seventh and final game of the championship series against the Vancouver Canucks, Coach Mike Keenan gave what the team captain, Mark Messier, called "the most intense, emotional, greatest speech I've heard in 16 years of hockey" (Farber, 1994, p. 1). The Rangers proceeded to win the game, claiming the cup for the first time in 54 seasons. And this was after losing two straight games in a series they had led 3 games to 1.

So do these "fire and brimstone" speeches work? Did Coach Keenan's talk have a direct effect on the team confidence of the Rangers? Was it the spark the team needed after having lost two potentially clinching games (losses that should have had a detrimental effect on team confidence)? Some research has addressed the validity of such claims. Gallmeier (1987) noted how a coach would time a speech endorsing the themes of readiness, courage, and pride to begin approximately 5 min prior to the game. The responses of the athletes were quite emotional, leading to the conclusion that the coach was capable of manipulating the emotional state and efficacy of the players through such verbal messages so as to optimize team performance. Further, Vargas-Tonsing and Bartholomew (2006) noted that positive emotional pregame speeches were associated with higher self-efficacy and estimated margins for victory in a simulated game situation.

Building on this research, Vargas-Tonsing (2004) investigated this effect of coaches' pregame speeches within a sample of soccer teams. As described in chapter 5, her sample consisted of 151 soccer players (roughly half were female and half were male) and 10 coaches. She measured the efficacy and emotional states of the athletes prior to and immediately after the coaches' pregame talk, specifically looking at the players' confidence about playing well and contributing to the team's victory. After statistically controlling for the athletes' perceptions of the emotional content of the speech, she found that their self-efficacy significantly increased from before to immediately after the speech; thus the informational content of the coaches' speeches appeared to have increased the efficacies of the individual athletes. Considering the strong relationship between self- and collective efficacy, which is supported both theoretically and empirically, one can infer that by increasing the self-efficacy of the athletes, a coach's pregame speech could be a tremendous source of collective efficacy.

In other research on verbal persuasion by Vargas-Tonsing and colleagues (2004), collegiate athletes reported that encouraging positive talk was an effective efficacy-enhancing strategy, and the coach's verbal persuasion was also perceived as an effective technique. Haberl and Zaichkowsky (2003) noted in their study of the American women's ice hockey team that verbal persuasion by the team captain could be as effective as that delivered by the coach.

In helping a team maintain its sense of efficacy, coaches and team captains may need to differentiate between preparatory and performance contexts in their use of persuasive strategies. As mentioned in chapter 1, Bandura (1997) describes different approaches to efficacy beliefs in preparatory practice versus performance. According to a new concept of *collective efficacy dispersion* (DeRue, Hollenbeck, Ilgen, & Feltz, 2005), which we explain in detail in chapter 9, coaches and team leaders may need to create some self-doubt about the team's capabilities in order to motivate them to plan, adapt, and practice for an upcoming game. If the team thinks that they can easily triumph over their upcoming opponents, they have little reason to practice hard, especially when the team already has high confidence through past success. Here the persuasion should be oriented toward reducing the complacency and should reorient the team to focus on their longer-term goals. At the time of the competition, however, coaches and captains should use persuasion to instill a sense of confidence that their practice efforts have paid off, and that they have what it takes to play their best.

TECHNIQUE 8: Positive Team Talk

Related to verbal persuasion is positive self-talk (Technique 7 in chapter 6), or team talk at the team level, which has also been referred to as affirmations. Haberl and Zaichkowsky (2003) noted the effectiveness of the use of positive self-talk by players. Positive self-talk, which includes the use of reaffirming, nonjudgmental comments made to oneself, has been noted as a source of self-confidence (Landin & Hebert, 1999; Mamassis & Doganis, 2004). Haberl and Zaichkowsky's (2003) case study may be evidence that positive self-talk among teammates is a way of enhancing team efficacy.

In using positive team talk or team affirmations to maintain team efficacy, the coach should meet with the team and have them come up with positive phrases that will remind them to stay focused, stay coordinated, or generate greater energy in the competition. These should be positive and process-oriented messages. The team should come to consensus on these affirmations, which can then be posted in strategic locations. Examples of team affirmations include "We cooperate, communicate, and congratulate," "When the going gets tough, we rock," and "We control the game."

TECHNIQUE 9: Building Team Cohesion

An additional technique to help maintain team confidence centers on the cohesion among teammates. Research has repeatedly shown that collective efficacy and team cohesion, particularly task cohesion, are highly interrelated (Kozub & McDonnell, 2000; Paskevich, Brawley, Dorsch, & Widmeyer, 1999). That is, the degree of unity perceived within a team regarding task-oriented issues tends to go hand in hand with the confidence in the team regarding achieving their goals.

This would lead to the conclusion that a way to enhance or maintain collective efficacy would be to do so indirectly through promoting a team's task cohesion. Ample literature on team building in sport clarifies ways to build a team's cohesion (Burke, 2006; Carron, Hausenblas, & Eys, 2005; Hodge, Lonsdale, & McKenzie, 2006), and some of the more notable methods have already been discussed (i.e., team goal setting, experiencing success). To complete the discussion on maintaining team confidence, we consider one more, involving role clarity and acceptance. The purpose is to use the role states within a team to maintain collective efficacy through task cohesion.

Role clarity and acceptance are complementary team dynamics that are both rooted in the responsibilities an individual has to fulfill on a team. Role clarity refers to the precision and starkness with which the duties of a given team member are defined. Role acceptance refers to how clearly that team member accepts those duties (Carron, Hausenblas, & Eys, 2005). Both are of vital importance to team cohesion, particularly task cohesion. To optimize team cohesion, Carron and colleagues suggest that coaches clearly define the duties of every member of the team and also have open discussions to make sure the role is acceptable to the player. Because taking these steps should make a team more united with respect to task objectives, and because task cohesion is related to collective efficacy, this may be a further way to maintain or rebuild collective efficacy.

Beauchamp, Bray, Eys, and Carron (2002) presented a conceptual framework for how roles affect team effectiveness. In their model, role clarity, which they deem the most influential factor with respect to role states in sport, is composed of different role contexts (i.e., offensive context, defensive context). In each of these contexts, various aspects are associated with a given role. For example, players must understand the behaviors required to fulfill a given role and the consequences of not filling these responsibilities. Research has shown that investing in role clarity on behalf of team members contributes to team functioning. Specifically, enhancing role states in a team can result in enhanced task cohesion (Eys & Carron, 2001). Thus, steps to enhance role clarity may be capable of making a team more confident through improved task efficacy.

Similarly, there is ample research on the use of team-building interventions to affect the performance and functioning of sport teams. Although the bulk of this literature has focused on performance and team cohesion as outcomes, Carron and colleagues (2005) note that such programs may potentially increase collective efficacy. Dunn and Holt (2004) reported on a team-building program for a male ice hockey team, designed in accordance with the established team-building principles of Yukelson (1997). Although the primary outcomes were to increase cohesion, the authors also noted that the program resulted in increased confidence in teammates and "feelings of invincibility." There is every reason to believe that team-building programs, well supported as a way of making a team more cohesive, should be just as instrumental in making a team more confident and helping to maintain that confidence. Research is needed, however, to provide empirical evidence for the potential of team building as a source of collective efficacy.

TECHNIQUE 10: Team Attributions

As we noted in chapter 6, attributions are the reasons people give for their successes and failures (Weiner, 1985). Most attributions at the team level also can be classified as relating to ability, effort, luck, or task difficulty. Individuals may make attributions regarding the outcomes of events in a logical or an illogical fashion. One pattern of illogical attributions follows a self-serving hypothesis in that athletes could attribute all failure to external sources and all success to internal sources. This has direct relevance to players in a team sport: Players could attribute loss to the efforts of the team as a whole as opposed to internal factors (e.g., their own effort or ability). Feltz and Lirgg (1998), in their season-long investigation of efficacy in hockey teams, found that collective efficacy was more affected by a loss than self-efficacy (Feltz & Lirgg, 1998). The reason could be a diffusion of responsibility after losses whereby players attribute an outcome to the team, resulting in a detriment to team confidence while self-confidence remains secure.

Although it appears reasonable that such processes occur, little research has been done on the relationships between collective efficacy, causal attributions, and performance; and the studies that do exist have yielded contradicting results. Bird and Brame (1978) and Gill, Ruder, and Gross (1982) found that athletes could be self-serving in that they blamed the team, not themselves, for poor play. However, Taylor and Doria (1981) found that athletes would attribute responsibility for team success to teammates and attribute blame for a failure to themselves. Following up on these results, Taylor, Doria, and Tyler (1983) investigated the role of subgroups within teams (i.e., offense and defense in hockey) and found similar patterns of attributions—that participants consistently attributed more responsibility for failure to in-subgroups than out-subgroups. In other words, defensemen would not blame the forwards for team losses.

It is difficult to draw a conclusion from these results, except to say that causal attributions regarding performance appear to interact with collective efficacy. This is still a rich area for potential research that may be applicable to team confidence. Coaches can help their teams make appropriate attributions during postcompetition debriefings. Martens (1987) has outlined four basic debriefing categories based on the contest outcome and the quality of the performance. These categories are reprinted in figure 7.1. When athletes

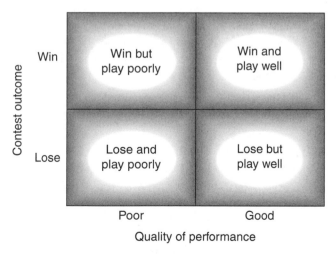

Figure 7.1 The four categories used in making team attributions based on the outcome of the contest and the quality of performance.

Reprinted, by permission, from R. Martens, 2005, *Coaches guide to sport psychology* (Champaign, IL: Human Kinetics), 180.

have won and played well, they are not in confidence trouble. In this situation, the coach wants to maintain the team's confidence by having them attribute their success to their abilities and effort, but not so much that future efforts are jeopardized. However, in the other three categories (win but play poorly, lose but play well, lose and play poorly), team confidence is vulnerable.

In the win-but-play-poorly category, some team members might be excited about their win while others realize that they fell short of meeting any number of team goals, including maximum effort. Thus, the coach should focus team attributions for the win on the weakness of the opponent and maybe lucky breaks, whereas attributions for the poor play should focus on lack of effort and perhaps lack of concentration. Here the coach may need to help athletes see their own role in the team's performance. As Martens (1987) notes, the approach should not be punitive, but informative and constructive.

When a team plays well but loses, their tendency is to decrease their confidence in the team (Feltz & Lirgg, 1998) and attribute the loss to the team's lack of ability. As Martens (1987) suggests, this is one of the most difficult situations for a coach. The coach must convince the team that although they lost to an opponent who played better than they did, the opposing team was superior on that day only. The coach can emphasize the successes within the team. Scapegoating should be avoided for the sake of team unity. If the team was clearly outplayed, however, the coach may need to shift the focus toward adjusting team goals to rebuild the confidence of the team.

In the last category, a loss and a poor performance, the coach needs to make attributions to internal but correctable causes, such as lack of sufficient effort or mistakes in execution, and emphasize everyone's responsibility. The coach should also reward players who displayed good effort, but again avoid scapegoating of individuals. All teams can have a bad game, and they should be encouraged to learn from the game and move on. However, right after the game is not the time to critique the team's play; constructive criticism is best left to the next practice.

TECHNIQUE 11: Videotaping Successes

One example of a team's rebuilding its confidence mentioned by Bandura (1997) is rebuilding confidence between games. Bandura points to the case of an underdog Stanford University football team as they prepared for their game against Notre Dame. The coach had his team watch a videotape of a game in which another team was losing to Notre Dame 31-7 but came back to win. Stanford began their game with some costly mistakes and generally poor play. However, they did not lose composure and eventually won the game.

Bandura argued that the persistence and confidence that the Stanford team displayed, which contributed to their victory, was the result of the videotape they had watched. Thus, videotapes of success can be a source of collective efficacy. This source is a vicarious one, with the team's response a group-level equivalent to the increased confidence of a figure skater as a result of watching tapes of her previous successful performances. As with use of the technique described in chapter 6, teams could watch positive highlights of games in which they came from behind or made successful plays at critical points, and these could be viewed several times to remind teams that they can perform similarly in the future. The pragmatics of watching videotapes means that this activity can occur only between games. Thus it would be very useful in maintaining or rebuilding confidence to stop losing streaks or to prepare for a particularly intimidating opponent.

Such videotapes could either incorporate previous performances of the team, or, as in Bandura's (1997) example, portray other teams for a proxy effect. Either case would relate to the situational specificity of collective efficacy, through reference either to the team itself or to the opponent that they will be facing.

The feedforward type of self-modeling technique described in chapter 3, whereby video is edited to construct an outcome that is possible but has not occurred, can also be used with teams. For instance, a video could be edited to show the team successfully completing a set play in the final seconds of a basketball game to win against a rival who has always beaten them in the past. We are not aware of studies or sport organizations that have used this technique, but the results should be similar to those with self-modeling.

TECHNIQUE 12: Coach Modeling Confidence

A coach's confidence cuts across building, maintaining, and regaining a team's collective efficacy, but can be particularly helpful when a team starts doubting themselves. As we described in chapter 5, athletes reported that the "coach acting confident" was an important strategy in enhancing their sense of efficacy. The coach's modeling of self-confidence is a form of vicarious experience for the team. The coach is part of the team, and when athletes sense that their coach is confident in his or her coaching knowledge, skills, and decisions, that transfers to the team. Chapter 8 deals with the various ways of enhancing coaching efficacy. It is worth noting here that these methods may be an effective, if indirect, way to increase team confidence. With respect to the interpersonal dynamics between the coach and the team, research on leadership style and coaching efficacy supports the view that with increased confidence, coaches tend to use more positive feedback and training instruction styles (Sullivan & Kent, 2003) and fewer organizational techniques (Feltz, Chase, Moritz, & Sullivan, 1999).

In addition, as we noted in chapter 5, the coach's efficacy expectations of the team may play a role in determining the team's efficacy beliefs. From their study on coaches' expectations of teams, Chase and colleagues (1997) suggested that coaches' confidence expectations can create a Pygmalion effect whereby coaches first form expectations of their teams and then act in ways that are consistent with those expectations. Teams, in turn, perceive and interpret those actions and respond in ways that reinforce the original expectations. If this happens, coaches with low efficacy expectations for their teams may inadvertently be contributing to low collective efficacy whereas those believing in their teams' capabilities may convey that attitude to their teams. As Bandura (1997) notes, "by maintaining confidence in their players' ability to do the job, coaches help to relieve some of the disruptive pressure in tense situations" (p. 398).

TECHNIQUE 13: Controlling Group Size

Group size is related to collective efficacy (Magyar et al., 2004; Watson, Chemers, & Preiser, 2001); and although it is not technically a "technique," manipulating the size of the operational units within a given sport team can feasibly influence the group's collective efficacy. Theoretically, the number of players on a team would affect the nature and efficiency of group interactions (Zaccaro, Blair, Peterson, & Zazanis, 1995). There is a curvilinear relationship between team size and group functioning in sport and exercise settings (Carron, Brawley, & Widmeyer, 1990; Widmeyer, Brawley, & Carron, 1990). In small groups, one or two dominant individuals may have a disparate and dysfunctional effect on group dynamics. In larger groups, process losses result in the inefficient production of team outcomes (which would include collective efficacy). Further, larger groups allow for the formation of smaller within-group cliques.

To date, two separate studies have investigated the relationship between collective efficacy and team size in sport. As we reported in chapter 4, Watson and colleagues (2001) found that group size was negatively related to team confidence at the end of the season in a sample of basketball players. Magyar and colleagues' (2004) study on collective efficacy included group size as a variable. All participants in this study were rowers, whose sport includes participation on teams of different sizes (i.e., two, four, or eight rowers per crew). The authors hypothesized that, as in Watson and colleagues' study, larger crews would have significantly less collective efficacy; but this hypothesis was not supported. Magyar and coworkers argued that the reason may have been the difference in interdependency within performance in basketball and rowing. Chow and Feltz (in press) also noted that crews competed against crews of the same size (four vs. four or eight vs. eight). Watson and colleagues, in contrast, used basketball teams of various sizes; differences in coordination and motivational processes were apparent and could have influenced team efficacy beliefs.

These results suggest that if group size has a significant effect on collective efficacy, the effect may depend on the nature of the sport. With respect to maintaining or regaining collective efficacy for larger, interactive teams, one might suggest breaking the group down into smaller units to help boost confidence. If a team of 25 hockey players is going through a losing streak and suffering from a lack of confidence, it may be beneficial to have subteams of defensemen, forwards, and goalies practice their respective skills and strategies. Or the team could be broken down into lines that will perform together and practice as small, inclusive teams. Following these suggestions should make it likely that any coordination difficulties would be minimized and that the smaller units would experience a corresponding boost in confidence, ultimately helping the team as a whole to regain confidence.

TECHNIQUE 14: Shifting the Focus Off the Score

There are times near the end of a competition when it becomes clear that there is no way to make a comeback and win the game. In order to keep the team from giving up and losing their confidence in themselves and their teammates, Bandura (1997) suggests that coaches shift the focus from winning and losing. Instead the time remaining can be used as a learning opportunity.

This process could be a smaller-scale application of many of the concepts discussed in connection with Technique 3, goal setting. For example, during a time-out in the later stages of a blowout loss in a basketball game, a coach could emphasize particular processes that the team could focus on for the remainder of the game. These might include out-rebounding the opposition, generating more high-percentage shots, or outscoring the opposition for the remainder of the game. Goals should be process oriented, objective, and measurable. In this way, the team could refocus from the outcome of the game to more specific process-oriented indicators of team performance. Such procedures could be seen as another way to define success—in precise, self-defined steps.

Self-Efficacy as a Source of Collective Efficacy

Inasmuch as a team is composed of various individuals, a team's confidence is undoubtedly rooted in and affected by confidence on the part of individuals. This has been supported both theoretically (Bandura, 1997; Zaccaro et al., 1995) and empirically (Feltz & Lirgg, 1998). Further, Bandura (1997) has stated that under certain circumstances, for example when interdependence among members of a team is low, collective efficacy may not be very distinct from the sum of self-efficacies. Therefore, we have to recognize that team efficacy may be boosted by efforts aimed at either the team as a whole or those individuals who comprise the team.

Thus, any of the steps outlined in chapter 6 for increasing self-efficacy (e.g., individual mastery, imagery, modeling) may be quite effective at indirectly enhancing collective efficacy. By creating a team of more confident individuals, one would create a confident team. To avoid redundancy with chapter 6, we refer readers to that chapter, on the basis that any mechanism that can enhance the confidence of an individual athlete should, if used at a collective level, correspondingly affect the confidence of a team. However, two points should be made clear.

First, these procedures will be influenced by the degree of interdependence on the team. The less interdependence among team members, the more closely collective efficacy approximates the sum of self-efficacies within the group. Thus, in a highly additive sport, such as track and field, steps to enhance efficacy on an individual level should be quite influential on collective efficacy. Alternatively, for a highly interactive sport like basketball, it would most likely be more fruitful to focus on collective efficacy directly.

A second point to consider with respect to enhancing team confidence through self-confidence is that team confidence appears to be more precarious than self-confidence. As Feltz and Lirgg (1998) showed in their study of hockey teams, team efficacy is more significantly affected by team performance than individual efficacy; self-efficacy seems to be more resilient to poor performance. Thus, particularly when the purpose is to regain collective efficacy, as opposed to building it, self-efficacy as an indirect pathway may not be very effective. In these situations, a focus on team-based interventions (e.g., group goal setting) may be of greater benefit than steps directed toward enhancing the cumulative self-efficacy of players.

However, although collective efforts—such as group goal setting and verbal persuasion aimed at the team—are more likely to be effective ways to enhance team confidence, a variety of less direct efforts could achieve the same goal. Clarifying roles and thus enhancing task cohesion, and having a team-wide imagery intervention to build each member's self-efficacy, are among direct and indirect ways to build or rebuild the confidence of a team. These are summarized in table 7.1. As indicated in this summary, techniques to build collective efficacy with novices or newly established teams are based on building team mastery. Once a team has some history of working together and has a sense of mastery as a team, persuasive techniques become more prominent. These might be direct verbal persuasion or indirect persuasion through the coach's selective use of vicarious information.

TABLE 7.1 Summary of Techniques for Enhancing and Maintaining Collective Efficacy

Technique	Source
COLLECTIVE EFFICACY IN NEW TEAMS	
Defining success in mastery terms	Mastery
Mastery climate	Mastery
Team goal setting	Mastery
Modifying the task	Mastery
Simulations	Mastery
Manipulating schedules	Mastery
COLLECTIVE EFFICACY IN ESTABLISHED TEAMS	
Verbal persuasion	Coach persuasion
Positive team talk	Coach persuasion
Building team cohesion	Social persuasion
Team attributions	Coach persuasion
Videotaping success	Vicarious
Coach modeling confidence	Vicarious
Controlling group size	Multiple sources
Shifting the focus off the score	Mastery

Enhancing Efficacy Beliefs of Coaches

> Leadership is a matter of having people look at you and gain confidence, seeing how you react. If you're in control, they're in control.
>
> *Tom Landry, head coach, Dallas Cowboys (National Football League), 1960-1989*

As we described in chapter 5, coaching efficacy is a central construct in the behavioral repertoire of a coach. Consistent with one of the main themes of this text, it is important to know why and how to enhance these perceptions. To very briefly review chapter 5, coaching efficacy is defined as "the extent to which coaches believe they have the capacity to affect the learning and performance of their athletes" (Feltz, Chase, Moritz, & Sullivan, 1999, p. 765). This is a multifactorial construct, consisting of confidence with respect to game strategy, motivation, teaching technique, and character building. Recognized sources of coaching efficacy include previous experiences, past success or perceived improvement of one's athletes, social support, and educational experiences. Known consequences include the behavior, satisfaction, and commitment of the coach, as well as athletes' performance and efficacy beliefs.

At any level, the role of coach is a central and profoundly influential one. From introductory sports to elite athletics, a coach is responsible for the sport education, motivation, and personal development of the athlete. Young children involved in organized sport for the first time will mimic their coach's enthusiasm. Olympic medalists regularly attribute their success to their coach or coaches. Coaching, whether it is good or bad, can have immediate and long-lasting effects on the attitudes and behavior of players.

Given the impact that the central role of coaching has, we must also acknowledge the central role of the construct of efficacy within the psychological profile of the coach. Because coaching has far-reaching implications in athletes and teams, coaching efficacy may be the most influential psychological construct in sport psychology. Thus, it is certainly worthwhile to investigate how to increase a coach's sense of efficacy.

In our original paper on this topic (Feltz et al., 1999), we noted four primary sources of coaching efficacy. These were the extent of coaching experience and preparation; prior success (i.e., win/loss record); perceived skill of athletes; and school, community, and parental support. We found support for several of these sources, noting that past win/loss records, years in coaching, perceived team ability, community support, and parental support correlated significantly with at least one dimension of coaching efficacy. This original list was expanded by Chase and colleagues (2005) to include player improvement, social support from the coach's athletes, and coach's development. Knowledge and preparation (e.g., knowledge of the game and rules), leadership skills (e.g., developing a coaching philosophy), and past experience (e.g., positive

The Efficacy of a Novice Coach

Today, Ken Hitchcock is an elite hockey coach. He has coached in Olympic and world championships. His teams have won championships at every level he has coached, including a Stanley Cup championship with the Dallas Stars of the NHL in 1999. Since becoming a professional coach in 1984, he has never coached a team with a losing record.

We would expect such a coach to have a vast repertoire of impressive coaching attributes, including high coaching efficacy. However, his current level of coaching efficacy is not the point of this example. Rather, if we look at the coach prior to this success, we see a different story. The Ken Hitchcock who took his first professional coaching post with the Kamloops Blazers in 1984 was a very different coach than the one who helped to coach Canada to the Olympic gold medal in 2002. Hitchcock himself acknowledges that his confidence was quite low at that point, and understanding how he built this confidence is essential to understanding what makes him an elite coach today.

In his own words, Hitchcock had no ambitions to be a coach, let alone reach the NHL (Robertson, 2005). He became a coach after being asked by a group of friends to help them organize their team for half a season. This experience led to his being a volunteer youth coach for 11 years and ultimately the opportunity to coach a major junior team in the Western Hockey League (roughly the hockey equivalent to AAA Minor League Baseball). At this point, Hitchcock was a certified coach, with many years of experience and a certain amount of success. If he felt confident in this new endeavor, this confidence quickly vanished. His first season with the Kamloops Blazers in the WHL was a rude awakening:

> As much as I thought I knew what I was doing, if I hadn't had a good veteran team in 1984, and really good players who carried me, I don't think I would have survived; I think I would have fallen apart. . . . I was just a guy who coached minor hockey. I had no clue about what was going on in the WHL, I didn't know where the cities were, or even who was in the conferences. I didn't know anything about the business of hockey or about scheduling, travel, budgets, or draft lists. (Robertson, 2005, p. 7)

How did the future Olympic coach deal with this lack of confidence? In addition to the social support of his veteran players, Hitchcock took his coaching education seriously—he attended multiple coaching clinics, and he sought out trustworthy and knowledgeable people with knowledge of the game that he did not have. In his own words, "I surrounded myself with as many good people as I could get and I really listened to them" (Robertson, 2005, p. 7).

relationships with players) were also articulated by these coaches as important sources of their confidence. The coaching confidence questionnaire in chapter 5 summarizes the development of sources of coaching efficacy from our original paper to Chase and colleagues' (2005) study.

Our discussion of ways to enhance coaching efficacy is structured around two coaching examples that typify a coach's most basic competency needs: building coaching efficacy in the case of a novice coach, and maintaining the efficacy of a more proven and experienced coach. The sources noted in the questionnaire are referred to as they are relevant to building or maintaining confidence.

Techniques for Enhancing the Efficacy of Novice Coaches

The Hitchcock case study provides an excellent example for the first major section of this chapter—how to build the confidence of a coach. Despite his previous success in coaching youth hockey, Hitchcock could be considered to have been a novice coach in the ranks of major junior hockey when he began coaching the Kamloops Blazers. As such, one thing that characterized him was his self-admitted lack of confidence. A variety of sources would be appropriate for building the coaching efficacy of a novice coach. Such coaches may lack in not just experience, but also credentials, knowledge, and coaching skills; and the need to build coaching efficacy is an imperative one. The Hitchcock example is used in the following discussion of techniques of coaching efficacy that are conceptually or empirically supported (or both) as significant sources of building coaching efficacy. In particular, these include coaching education, goal setting and coaching success, and social support.

TECHNIQUE 1: Coaching Education

Coaching education is the key to improvement in competent coaching (Woodman, 1993). This sentiment has resulted in what Campbell (1993) has noted as a worldwide investment in coaching education. Probably the most obvious way for a coach to build some confidence is to gain knowledge of how to coach by participating in an organized coaching education activity. For a minimal investment of time and money, coaches can be exposed to a variety of content on skills, techniques, and knowledge about their sport. By design, these activities exist to make their participants more competent.

Structured coaching education comprises two main activities—coaching education courses and formal apprenticeship programs. Coaching education courses are typically hierarchical; levels range from those appropriate for novice coaches to courses for international coaches. There is typically a balance of theoretical, technical, and practical curricula at each level (Campbell,

1993). Formal apprenticeship programs (as opposed to the informal mentoring that many coaches may experience) are relatively common and are designed with the same educational outcomes in mind as the courses.

Coaching Education Courses   Most sport governing bodies in most countries offer classroom-based courses for coaches. These courses are designed to present coaches with knowledge and skills relevant to their sport and context so as to improve their coaching and subsequent athlete outcomes. A typical course for the introductory coach is the one offered by the California Youth Soccer Association—South. On their Web site (www.calsouth.com/coachyouthsoccer_overview.htm), in their description of their local coaching education certification programs, they note that they aim to provide "a system which improves a coach's knowledge of the game, methodology, and teaching methods." This local program would be one designed for novice coaches, grassroots participation, or both. Worth noting is that the outcomes stated in the description echo the factors of coaching efficacy (e.g., strategy and teaching technique).

In youth sports in the United States, very few coaches have any formal training in how to coach. Some may have knowledge of the game through their own playing experience, but they rarely receive formal training in creating a healthy psychological environment (Smoll & Smith, 2001). One of the earliest education programs aimed specifically at increasing youth sport coaches' motivational and positive communication skills was Smith, Smoll, and Curtis' (1979) effectiveness training program for Little League baseball coaches. The authors randomly assigned one half of the coaches in a local youth baseball program to their training program, while the other half coached as they had previously. The coaches in the training program were taught to use a positive approach to coaching (frequent encouragement, positive reinforcement, corrective feedback). Although Smith and colleagues did not assess the coaches' efficacy beliefs, they found that the young baseball players whose coaches were receiving training had significantly higher self-esteem ratings over the course of a season than players whose coaches received no additional training.

In the decade that followed Smith and colleagues' (1979) training program, a number of other U.S. organizations developed generic coaching education programs that were designed to prepare coaches for success in youth or high school sports and were based on the positive approach to coaching. These included such programs as American Sport Education Program (ASEP: www.asep.com), PACE (a high school certification program designed by the Institute for the Study of Youth Sports at Michigan State University and in cooperation with the Michigan High School Athletic Association, described in chapter 5; Seefeldt & Brown, 1990), and the National Youth Sports Coaches Association (NYSCA). A listing of the Web sites of the various coaching education programs is presented in table 8.1.

TABLE 8.1   Some Examples of Coaching Web Sites

Source	Provider	Web site
International	International Council for Coach Education	www.icce.ws
National	Canada	www.coach.ca
	United Kingdom	www.sportscoachuk.org
	Ireland	www.nctc.ul.ie
	Hong Kong	www.hkcoaching.com/hk/programmes.asp
	Hungary	www.icse.hu
	United States	www.aahperd.org/naspe/template.cfm?template=programs-ncace.html
Sports	Baseball	nccp.baseball.ca
	Rugby	www.barla.org.uk
	Tennis	www.playerdevelopment.usta.com/content/home.sps?itype=7498&ihomepagecustomid=409
Educational	University of Bath (UK)	www.bath.ac.uk/education/coached
Institutions	University of Essex (UK)	www.essex.ac.uk/sport/coach/index.shtm
	University of Victoria (CAN)	www.educ.uvic.ca/phed/med_coaching.html
	University of Sydney (AUS)	www.edsw.usyd.edu.au/future_students/postgraduate/deg_med_coached.shtml

The programs are generally similar and cover topics on legal responsibilities, prevention and care of athletic injuries, organizing practices, motivating athletes, and sport-specific technical and tactical skills. The program lengths vary from 7 to 12 hr. A more detailed outline of the topics is presented in table 8.2. These programs are based on efforts to increase coaches' knowledge in these areas, and in turn their competence and confidence. The main criticisms regarding these programs are (a) length insufficient to cover the topics in depth (Malete & Feltz, 2000) and (b) their voluntary nature, which is more of a criticism of the U.S. coaching system (Houseworth, Davis, & Dobbs, 1990).

A more comprehensive, national example of coaching education can be seen in Australia's National Coaching Accreditation Scheme (NCAS: www.ausport.gov.au/coach/ncas.asp). The NCAS is a progressive system of coaching education courses designed to serve coaches of all sports at all levels. It is a prototypical example of the hierarchical system described by Campbell (1993). The training programs of the NCAS include coaching principles (e.g., fundamentals of coaching and athletic performance), sport-specific knowledge (e.g., skills, techniques, strategies, and scientific approaches to the par-

TABLE 8.2   *Typical Topics Covered in Youth*
and High School Coaching Education Programs

Area	Topics
Risk management	Legal responsibilities of the coach
	Insurance coverage for coaches and athletes
	Emergency procedures for accidents and injuries
Training and conditioning	Prevention and care of athletic injuries
	Principles of training and conditioning
	Contraindicated techniques
Effective planning and organization	Role and responsibilities of the coach
	Planning for the season and practices
	Evaluating one's effectiveness
Motivation	Motivating young athletes
	Effective communication and providing feedback
	Maintaining discipline
Technical and tactical skills	Principles and stages of motor skill learning
	Skill progressions of the sport
	Common skill errors of the sport
	Tactical skills of the sport

ticular sport), and coaching practice (e.g., practical coaching and application of coaching principles). The following are the outcomes of the NCAS:

- Increase confidence and competence in coaching ability
- Promote an ongoing progressive improvement of knowledge and expertise
- Incorporate the basics of sports science, enabling a more in-depth approach to coaching
- Promote the use of safe and correct techniques
- Provide a structure to improve communication skills
- Encourage the development of innovative coaching techniques
- Provide quality-controlled learning in all training programs
- Increase the enjoyment of sport for coaches and athletes

It is interesting to note that the first outcome listed is the enhancement of coaching confidence. This, and the reflection of the Coaching Efficacy Scale (CES) factor structure in the grassroots soccer course, show that there is a certain amount of ecological validity to the construct of coaching efficacy and the notion that coaching education is a source of confidence. Further conceptual models of both coaching efficacy (Feltz et al., 1999) and coaching education (Sullivan, Paiement, Brachlow, & Bagnell, 2005) note that coaching educational experiences are a significant source of coaching efficacy.

Although such courses are offered for coaches at all levels and types of experience, they may be especially useful for inexperienced coaches, and taking a course was one of first things Hitchcock did as a novice coach to increase his competence. According to Robertson (2005), he attended "every clinic he could" (p. 7) and is such a believer in the coaching education process that he actively plans on continuing his role as a coach educator, saying, "I want to emphasize that mentorship from professional coaches is vital to the linkage for all coaches" (Robertson, 2005, p. 8).

So in terms of both theory and the pedagogical content of these programs, coaching education *should* increase coaching confidence. In fact, Fung (2003) went so far as to propose that our four-factor model of coaching efficacy (Feltz et al., 1999) should be used as an assessment of these courses. Her rationale was that because the courses should increase coaching efficacy, they should be designed toward this outcome and evaluated on this basis.

The empirical literature on coaching education as a source of coaching efficacy is relatively small, but quite consistent. Coaches who have participated in a coaching education program have been repeatedly shown to be significantly more confident in all aspects of coaching efficacy compared to either a control group of coaches who did not take a course, themselves before they took part in a program, or both (Campbell & Sullivan, 2005; Lee, Malete, & Feltz, 2002; Malete & Feltz, 2000).

The first study, by Malete and Feltz (2000), was discussed in detail in chapter 5. Briefly, the results showed that participation in PACE (Seefeldt & Brown, 1990) significantly increased the efficacy of coaches relative to both a control group and their precourse coaching efficacy scores. This finding has been replicated with different samples, in different nations, and based on different contents of coaching education.

For instance, the Campbell and Sullivan (2005) study used a large sample of novice coaches in Canada. In contrast to the PACE program, the National Coaching Certification Program (NCCP) in Canada is mandatory; all coaches are expected to be certified. The particular course from which participants were drawn was a Level One Theory course. This course presents broad-based content for introductory coaches across different sports. As opposed to focusing on technical or strategic content for any particular sport, the Level One Theory course covers such issues as the theory of practice planning, skill development, coach–athlete communication, organizational techniques, and emergency planning. Despite this broad content, Campbell and Sullivan found that the sample of coaches in the study showed a significant increase in all factors of coaching confidence after completing the course, and that females showed higher scores on motivation and character-building confidence than did male coaches. Unfortunately, because the NCCP is essentially mandatory, it was not feasible to have a control group of noncertified coaches in this study.

The effect of education on coaching efficacy is a robust one. Consistent with the mandate of these courses and conceptual literature, coaching education courses are a valid and consistent source of enhancing collective efficacy. Furthermore, the largest group of consumers for these courses is consistently novice coaches (Campbell, 1993)—who are the coaches most in need of the enhanced self-efficacy that these courses can instill.

This last point is reflected in the example of Ken Hitchcock. As a novice coach at the junior hockey level, he recognized a lack of confidence in his own abilities that would obviously have dire consequences. One of his most immediate responses was to invest in multiple coaching courses and clinics. We can assume that as a result of these clinics, his confidence in his ability as a coach would have increased. Furthermore, based on the research in the field, the increase would most likely have been a global increase in his coaching efficacy. His confidence in his ability to strategize, teach, motivate, and instill character in his athletes most likely increased.

However, not all coaching courses (or coach participants) are equal. As Campbell (1993) noted in her review of coaching education, most programs are hierarchical and incorporate a balanced curriculum. At each level, from novice to expert coaches, there are general, theoretical courses for coaches of all sports, sport-specific technical courses, and practical coaching educational components. These different contents may not have equivalent effects on one's coaching efficacy. For example, considering the broad, theoretical focus of the Level One Theory course studied by Campbell and Sullivan (2005), the NCCP also offers Level One Technical courses, which focus on sport-specific techniques and strategies for novice coaches. This balance of theoretical and technical courses continues up the levels of the hierarchy.

Gee and Sullivan (2005) examined the differential effects of course content and level in the hierarchical program typified by Australia's NCAS or Canada's NCCP and found that theoretically and technically based courses both act as important sources of coaching efficacy. However, the sport-specific technical courses tend to have a greater impact on the more *technical* efficacies—game strategy and teaching technique. This has been seen in a variety of technical courses, including those on soccer, rugby, baseball, and curling (Brachlow & Sullivan, 2006).

Even though there are differences in content and duration of coaching education programs, many may not be long enough or provide enough mastery experiences to lead to large improvements in coaching efficacy. For instance, the PACE program that Malete and Feltz (2000) studied was only 12 hr in length extending over two weekends. PACE significantly enhanced coaching efficacy, but the effect size was only moderate. Shorter programs tend to emphasize sport-specific skills and game strategy. As Malete and Feltz noted, longer programs could have components that place more emphasis on topics focused on building motivational and character-building efficacies, such as personality development, motivational techniques, and coaching ethics. Programs that also included more time for mastery experiences for coaches, with opportunities to role play giving positive feedback, instructing a skill, or maintaining control during a simulated practice, would help build coaches' sense of efficacy. These simulation experiences would help address the concern expressed by Dils and Ziatz (2000) that coaches' beliefs, developed through coaching education, may not transfer to coaches' actions with their athletes.

Considering the elaborate curriculum of coaching courses as mentioned by Campbell (1993), one could argue that this sole source of coaching efficacy may actually comprise several of the sources noted by Chase and colleagues (2005). These authors list coach development, knowledge/preparation, and leadership skills as different sources of efficacy. Although these sources could all be distinct, they are also all outcomes of coaching education. Coaching education courses aid in developing the knowledge base of the coach and may result in more effective leadership styles. Thus, it appears that coaching education may be an extremely influential way to increase the efficacy of coaches. Further, considering that novice coaches would have relatively inadequate knowledge and leadership skills, these courses should have their most profound impact on inexperienced coaches.

Apprenticeship Programs   Although coaching education is one of the primary sources of coaching efficacy, course-based certification programs are not the only form of coach pedagogy. Formal mentor–apprentice relations are a potent form of coach education and have been cited as one of the best ways to develop coaches (Salmela, 1996).

Weaver and Chelladurai (1999) proposed a model of mentorship in athletics whereby the compatibility of mentor and protégé serves to overcome certain psychological barriers (e.g., fear) to produce certain outcomes (e.g., satisfaction, salary, power). This relationship is conceptualized as occurring in four different phases (i.e., initiation, cultivation, separation, and redefinition). The mentor fulfills a variety of roles, such as protecting, promoting, and coaching the protégé. Specifically with respect to the apprenticeship process for coaches, Sullivan and colleagues (2005) noted that such mentoring programs have immediate impacts on two main psychological outcomes. One of these is coaching knowledge, and the other is coaching efficacy.

The importance of a mentoring program for coaches can be seen in a survey of over 300 coaches conducted by Gould, Gianinni, Krane, and Hodge (1990). With respect to "experience [as] most important to prepare an elite coach" (p. 339), the third most recognized source of coaching competence was "mentor program apprenticeship/experience working with top coaches"

(p. 339). This notion was endorsed by Piltz (1999), who noted that "the apprenticeship component was deemed to be paramount in the education of novice coaches, due to the fact that anecdotal evidence suggests that 'good coaches produce good coaches who follow them' . . . [and] no matter how effective a coach education course may be in terms of its structure it is impossible to give novices a real understanding of the nature of coaching unless they actually see coaches at work" (paragraph 1). This, in turn, should result in much more realistic (although perhaps lower) perceptions of coaching efficacy than structured coaching courses.

In one such program, Canada's Women in Coaching Apprenticeship Program, one of the primary duties of the mentor coach is to "develop the self confidence and self esteem" of the apprentice (Mercier, 2003). A graduate of this program, a successful field hockey coach, endorsed the program as providing "an invaluable opportunity to work at and really come to understand the high performance environment in women's field hockey . . . I feel that as a result of this program and what I have learned in the three years, I am now capable of coaching the senior national program. I feel *confident* in my abilities and I know what is required to work successfully at this level" (Werthner, 2003, paragraph 4, italics added).

Weiss, Barber, Sisley, and Ebbeck (1991) followed a sample of 28 novice (e.g., $M = 1.6$ years experience) female coaches through a season-long internship in which they were placed with a senior mentor coach. The results indicated that the experience was a successful one and that coaches perceived definite and specific improvements in various aspects of their coaching skills. Interestingly, the comments made by coaches were quite consistent with the framework of coaching efficacy—reflecting confidence in such factors as teaching technique, motivation, strategy, and character building, as well as a global sense of coaching confidence.

Specific examples included such statements as "I learned that I could coach . . . I didn't have doubts afterwards" (p. 345), "he's done a lot to build me and my confidence," and "I became more at ease as time went on . . . I was more confident" (p. 345). The effect of the apprenticeship program on technique and strategy efficacy can be seen in quotes such as "I learned a lot about how to set up practice" (p. 345) and "I've learned a little bit and am still learning I'm sure, how to structure a season, how to go about accomplishing things, how to set up practices" (p. 345).

Further comments exemplified a positive effect on motivation efficacy ("just knowing that I can communicate my skills in a way the girls could understand" [p. 344]) and character-building efficacy ("having that responsibility of being a role model and everything was very hard, but it was one of the most rewarding things" [p. 344]).

Interestingly, there were negative aspects of the internship process, and these too can be interpreted with reference to Feltz and colleagues' (1999) conceptual model. As one apprentice coach stated, "my biggest problem still . . . is coaching a game, the situation of coaching. This is what's happening on the floor. What do I do about it? How do I direct kids" (p. 348). This quotation reflects a lack of confidence with respect to game strategy. Perhaps more coaching experience would be necessary to increase the efficacy in game strategy for this coach.

Thus, despite the lack of any literature explicitly linking coaching efficacy (i.e., the CES) to apprenticeship, the apprentice–mentor relationship appears to be another significant source of coaching efficacy for novice coaches. This was apparent in the case of Ken Hitchcock, who talked about surrounding himself with as many good coaches as he could and really listening to them. More specifically, Hitchcock mentions three individuals, each of whom he considers a mentor to himself and other coaches in his position.

> They guided us through so much, gave up so much of their time and money, and shared their expertise so that all of us could have success. They taught us how to instruct the game of hockey. They taught us how to teach skill development and team development, how to build teams, and how to organize practices and schedules. They went over every aspect of how to become an organized coach, an intellectual coach in the game of hockey. They raised us to a whole other level. (Robertson, 2005, p. 8)

Clearly, this novice coach considered apprentice relationships extremely valuable in terms of his development as a coach. The preciseness of his comments reflects the recognized factors of coaching efficacy (e.g., strategy, teaching technique), as well as other situation-specific dynamics (e.g., funding) that point to the specificity of coaching efficacy.

Although apprenticeship programs are a form of coaching education, conceptually they differ from certification programs in terms of the sources of efficacy they represent. Coaching education courses provide a mastery experience for coaches; however, a relationship with a mentor coach provides a vicarious experience through which a coach can enhance his or her coaching efficacy. As an apprentice coach, an individual has a long-term opportunity to witness and interact with a more proven coach. These experiences allow the apprentice coach to see how the mentor experiences various aspects of coaching success, such as on-field performance, organized practices, and effective interactions with athletes.

Conceptual work on the mentorship process has suggested that this vicarious effect can benefit apprentices. Weaver and Chelladurai (2002) noted that one of the primary functions of a mentor is role modeling. This involves displaying efficient performance and effective interactions with athletes, colleagues, and supervisors. Further, in the design of coaching apprenticeship programs, mentors must be capable of providing advice and counsel, giving support and encouragement, and sharing insights on the politics of sport and organizational culture (Mercier, 2003). Thus, mentor coaches also act as a source of social persuasion for coaching efficacy beliefs.

These apprenticeship programs typically invest a great deal of effort in establishing a mutually beneficial apprentice–mentor relationship. This reflects some of the issues relevant to modeling-based sources and persuasion sources of efficacy, but not mastery experiences. As is noted in chapter 3, status and similarity are essential characteristics of an effective model. Mentor coaches in apprenticeship programs are typically very high-status coaches, individuals who have coached successfully at national and international levels. With respect to similarity of the model, Bandura (1997) noted that gender can be a very significant factor in the effectiveness of a model on an observer. As we have seen, coaching apprenticeship programs have been established specifically for female coaches. Other attributes such as playing experiences and geographic region are typically considered in determination of an apprentice–mentor relationship that will be successful. Further, in terms of social persuasion, as noted in chapter 3, the trustworthiness and credibility of the persuader (in this case the mentor) is also important to enhancing efficacy beliefs.

TECHNIQUE 2: Coaching Success

At this point in the book, it should come as no surprise that a primary way to build coaching efficacy is to have the coach experience success. We can intuit that one of the main reasons Hitchcock lacked confidence as a new coach in the WHL was that he had had no previous success at that level. Given how specific efficacy is as a construct, any confidence derived from previous success would be diminished in the significant leap from community coaching to major junior hockey.

However, considering the profound effect of mastery on efficacy, we could expect that once Hitchcock was successful as a coach, he would feel more confident. There is a problem with this, though: What if he had experienced only failure? It would not be unusual for such a coach to be overwhelmed by the demands of coaching at this level; he or she might never get the chance to experience success. Poor organization, substandard team play, and self-doubts could easily result in repeated unsuccessful performance. A coach could be fired before success ever occurred—becoming just another "failed" coach who returns to the ranks of lower competition or leaves coaching entirely. Such a situation seems more than possible, if dire. The point remains—if the primary source of efficacy is mastery, and mastering coaching is often easier said than done, how can one apply this source to increase the efficacy of a novice coach? The answer lies in examining what it means to "coach successfully."

As discussed in chapter 7, sport psychology has long recognized that all success is not equal, and it can be limiting to consider winning and success as synonymous. A team may fail to win a league championship while the coach may still have been quite successful. Herein lies the distinction between ego and task orientations (Nicholls, 1984b, 1989). We also refer to these as norm-referenced and self-referenced orientations in chapter 3. Ego- or norm-referenced orientations are based on social comparison or external standards. Success is defined only in terms of the outcome (not to be confused with outcome expectancies as defined by social cognitive theory in chapter 1) relative to how the competition did; success is only beating others or winning. This is a limited, and limiting, way to define success. Alternatively, task orientation is based on self-comparison. Success is defined by how one does relative to one's own capabilities and goals. A coach may coach as well as he or she is able to and, regardless of whether the team wins or loses, this could be considered successful.

So, one way to use mastery as a source of coaching efficacy would be to endorse a task-defined perspective of success. If we apply this to our case, Hitchcock might have built some confidence by focusing less on the team's wins and losses and more on how well the team played. If he, as coach, focused practice on such elements as winning face-offs or reducing turnovers, and he saw improvement in these processes during games, then he could experience success and become more confident.

There are other ways of defining success, even task-oriented success, besides team performance. A coach's perception of athlete improvement can be an important source of coaching efficacy (Chase et al., 2005). In Chase and colleagues' study building on the original sources of coaching efficacy, player development was the most often cited source of confidence. Specifically, coaches noted that getting players to play hard, developing players' skills, teaching team roles, player improvement in performance, and the personal development of players were ways in which they assessed their confidence in themselves as coaches. As one coach stated,

> you need to develop what you feel are the skills necessary to be successful in the game. What skills do you feel the kids need to have. Develop those skills to the fullest and then mold them together as a team. Individual skills are the absolute bottom building block. (Chase et al., 2005, p. 32)

For a novice coach like Hitchcock, these results suggest that he could have developed an enhanced sense of self-efficacy through developing the abilities and skills of his individual players. Likewise, he could have felt a sense of mastery through development of the team as a whole or the personal development of his athletes.

Another way to expand on the notion of successful coaching has to do with the fact that coaching efficacy, and coaching itself, are multifactorial. We have already discussed confidence with respect to strategy, motivation, teaching technique, and character building. Each of these elements of coaching presents its own opportunities for success. Instead of focusing on the global nature of coaching efficacy, we suggest that confidence, particularly for the novice, could be enhanced by stressing the specific components of coaching. Teaching and implementing one successful strategy should enhance game strategy efficacy. Motivating one athlete or the team for one tough game could prove mastery enough to build motivation efficacy. Returning again to Hitchcock, although he had severe doubts about many of the roles of coaching in the WHL, teaching technique did not appear to be among them. Thus, he might more easily have experienced mastery in this role in his new position and subsequently felt more potent in that aspect of coaching efficacy.

In summary, the most powerful way to increase or build coaching efficacy is through experience of coaching success, but this does not mean that winning has to occur. Coaching success can be defined in terms of team or player improvement, coaching improvement, or self-relevant performance. Further, considering the specificity of efficacy beliefs as a construct, a successful experience might not have anything to do with on-field performance per se, but be defined more by a successful experience motivating an athlete or teaching a skill.

TECHNIQUE 3: Goal Setting

In order to achieve success in the ways discussed so far, coaches must set goals. Just as we suggested in chapter 6 regarding goal setting for athletes (Technique 5), coaches have a better yardstick with which to measure their success if they set goals for each of the coaching efficacy dimensions. Such goals would be considered task or process goals because they are not based on wins and losses but rather on coaching skills themselves. For instance, the goal of teaching and implementing a particular game strategy that the team is able to execute effectively would be considered a task goal. The principles of goal setting provided in table 6.1 are also applicable to coaches; goals should be specific, measurable, action oriented, realistic, and time bound. Just as athletes should set daily practice goals, so too should coaches set specific goals for each practice that build toward reaching their overall seasonal goals. Similar to our suggestion in chapter 6, a good question for coaches to ask themselves is, "Why am I having practice today?"

TECHNIQUE 4: Obtaining Feedback

As also noted in chapter 6, goals and feedback are related. In order for feedback to be effective, it must be provided in relation to a defined goal or standard (Bandura, 1997). Coaches rarely receive constructive feedback from others in relation to the goals they have set for themselves. However, they can evaluate their own progress toward their goals, thus providing their own feedback. For beginning-level coaches, however, having an outside consultant or a well-meaning athletics director perform an evaluation on key areas of coaching competence could be very helpful. As described in chapter 5, Myers, Feltz, Maier, Wolfe, and Reckase (2006) developed the Coaching Competence Scale (CCS) to match the dimensions of the CES. Their tests of the instrument were conducted via athletes' perceptions of their coaches' competencies; however, this measure could also be used by an outside evaluator to help coaches determine their strengths and weaknesses in terms of teaching technique, game strategy, motivation, and character building.

TECHNIQUE 5: Social Support

Although most coaching positions have similarities in terms of duties, responsibilities, attributes, and behaviors, coaching is a highly contextualized social process. Lyle (1999) noted that any coach is influenced by larger social contexts and processes, including the abilities and attributes of the athletes, the nature and subculture of the particular sport, and the social network within which the team operates. This last point is quite important, and it has supported theoretical and empirical links with coaching efficacy.

As head coach on a major junior hockey team, Hitchcock would have had a coaching staff of several assistant coaches, as well as trainers, medical staff, therapists, and a variety of other officials. The team itself would have consisted of a given number of athletes, including those in roles such as captain and assistant captain. Within this structure is a dynamic balance of roles (e.g., leader), attributes (e.g., motivation), and social dynamics (e.g., cohesion) that would have influenced such factors as participation and performance. However, no team is an island. If the focus is widened, one can appreciate the social context that a coach must exist within.

Hitchcock would have had to interact not just with his coaching staff and athletes, but with the general manager, team owner, and board of directors. And considering the context of the team in the community, parents, alumni, city spokespeople, community sponsors, and numerous other invested parties would also have been influential. We noted in our conceptual model of coaching efficacy (Feltz et al., 1999) that social support is related to all aspects of coaching efficacy. For instance, a coach who has the full support of the general manager, owner, and community should be a very confident coach (all other things being equal). If, however, these stakeholders display a lack of support for the coach, then the coach could experience a relative lapse in confidence, even if he or she is highly qualified and the team is performing quite well.

While developing the CES, we analyzed the relationships between coaching efficacy and the coaches' perception of community support (Feltz et al., 1999). A sample of 69 high school basketball coaches (all were male) were asked to rate their perceived social support from five different sources: athletic director, faculty, students, parents, and community. Of these, parental support correlated significantly with a score of total coaching efficacy, and community support was significantly correlated with every factor except character-building efficacy. A second study, by Myers, Vargas-Tonsing, and Feltz (2005) yielded similar results. Using a similar sample and the same five-factored view of social support (i.e., athletic director, faculty, students, parents, and community), the authors found that the perceived support offered by athletes' parents and the greater community were significant sources of coaching efficacy. Specifically, parents' support was related to all efficacy dimensions except game strategy, whereas the support of the community was related to motivation and character-building efficacy. One reason Myers and colleagues may have found slightly different patterns with social support was that they used a much more heterogeneous sample of sports (e.g., softball, baseball, soccer, and basketball) and a different organizational context (small, primarily religiously based colleges) than Feltz and colleagues did. Overall, though, these two studies show a consistent pattern in which perceived social support is an important and influential source of coaching confidence.

Our 1999 operationalization of social support fits within what Lyle (1999) considers the contextualization of the coaching process. This recognition is consistent with the model of coaching effectiveness proposed by Horn (2002) that we described in chapter 5. Horn proposed that such contextualized factors as coaches' social support influence coaching behavior indirectly by affecting coaches' beliefs and expectancies. Thus, there is consistency in these models regarding how important the larger social system is for coaches and how specifically coaching confidence is affected by social support.

Coaches who are not yet fully confident in their abilities could benefit from concrete and contingent statements of support. Further, although we may suppose that the support of those within the sporting structure (i.e., athletic director) may be most influential, it has been repeatedly found that coaches perceive the support of the outside community, including parents, to be the most important. Although the support of parents, community members, and higher-ups in the organization would have most likely increased Hitchcock's confidence, the one source of social support that he explicitly noted came from his players, notably his most experienced players. This relates to the building of mutual respect between coaches and players, noted by Chase and colleagues (2005) as a significant source of coaching efficacy.

Although this would depend on the level of competition, it may be a useful thing for a coach to be proactive in eliciting social support. For example, the coach of a high school or youth team may encourage interaction with players' parents by such means as a parents' orientation meeting, informal social events, and fund-raising activities. If coaches endorse the use of open and honest communication, they could optimize a source of coaching confidence that may be largely overlooked. Parent orientation meetings provide coaches with the opportunity to inform parents about the league's and their objectives, about the coach's expectations of the athletes and the parents, about the process for communicating concerns, and about how parents can help the team reach its goals. Ewing, Feltz, and Brown (1992) and Martens (2005) provide sample parent orientation agendas for coaches to follow. We have included a selection of topics in table 8.3. It is easier to gain the support of parents when they have been informed.

TABLE 8.3 *Typical Topics Covered in a Parent Orientation Meeting*

Area	Topics
Program structure	Administrators and sponsors
	Program philosophy and league structure
	Costs
	Medical requirements and accident insurance
Coaching philosophy	Approach to coaching
	Goals
	Playing time for athletes
Understanding the sport	Basic rules and strategies
	Potential for injury and safety guidelines
Equipment needs	Sources
	Quality, cost, and recommendations
Policies for players	Practices
	Game behavior
	Off-field or off-court behavior
Policies and expectations for parents	How and when to communicate with the coach
	How to communicate with child-athlete
	Conduct at games
	Emergency procedures
Distribution and review	Game schedule
	Practice schedule

Garnering the support of the larger community would also be an asset for the burgeoning confidence of a novice coach. By involving community members in team (e.g., pep rallies, tailgate parties) and community (e.g., fundraising, community services) issues and activities, the coach could establish a wider web of social contacts to call on for social support.

Case Study

The Efficacy of an Experienced Coach

Examples of such novice coaches as Ken Hitchcock are one thing, but we cannot assume that lacking confidence is an issue only for coaches at lower levels of competition. It would be naive to think that coaches at more elite levels of competition are free from such self-doubts. Although such coaches are likely more confident than coaches at lower levels, efficacy is still a dynamic construct. Confidence is largely influenced by the situation the coach is in, and elite and professional coaches can find themselves in very trying circumstances. An example is Phil Jackson, coach of the Los Angeles Lakers of the NBA. During the 2004-2005 season with the Lakers, Jackson had to deal with coaching his defending championship team, managing two conflicting superstar egos (Shaquille O'Neil and Kobe Bryant), and Bryant's highly publicized criminal trial for rape. Jackson discussed the challenges of coaching a team in these circumstances in his book, *Season on the Brink*. Jackson admits that this season promised to be so challenging that he "decided to enlist a therapist to help me cope with what will surely be the most turbulent season of my coaching career" (http://sportsillustrated.cnn.com/2004/basketball/nba/10/12/jackson). Jackson repeatedly commented on such factors as "acrimonious" relationships with certain players, "narcissistic behavior," and the team as "the longest-running soap opera in professional sports," not to mention the pressures of repeating as league champions in one of the largest media markets on the continent.

Obviously, such conditions were somewhat overwhelming to Jackson, and he admitted as much in his decision to recruit a therapist to help him deal with these pressures.

Techniques for Enhancing the Efficacy of Experienced Coaches

Knowing what we know about coaching efficacy, what could we have suggested to help Jackson maintain his confidence under these circumstances? To answer this question, we can revisit some of the sources we have already discussed for building confidence, as well as some that should be more applicable to maintaining coaching efficacy.

TECHNIQUE 6: Continued Coaching Education and Mentoring

As mentioned earlier in connection with novice coaches, coaching education is a primary source for increasing one's confidence. However, the efficacy-enhancing effect of these courses is not limited to novices. As noted by

Campbell (1993) and exemplified in Canada's NCCP and Australia's NCAS programs, these courses comprise a hierarchy of five different levels. Although the most subscribed courses are introductory ones aimed at coaches with limited experiences, the intermediate and higher levels are designed for coaches with increasing amounts of certification and experience. Thus, by design, Courses 3 through 5 out of a five-level structure should serve the same efficacy-enhancing function for intermediate and expert coaches that Levels One and Two do for novice coaches. In addition, every sport governing body has its own coaches association licensing levels.

At the time of writing this chapter, there was no research that we were aware of on the effect of these courses on the efficacy of experienced coaches. However, given the robust finding for this effect at lower levels of certification or experience, and the clear mandate of these courses to affect the confidence of coaches, it is reasonable to expect that higher levels of coaching education should be a source of efficacy for more experienced coaches.

These courses can differ substantially from those offered for novice coaches, both in content and in design. For instance, whereas introductory theory courses, such as the NCCP Level One or the PACE program studied by Malete and Feltz (2000), take about 12 hr and are usually delivered in one weekend, higher-end courses typically are more like a course of study leading to a college diploma and can take from one to two years to complete. As such, they could be a constant source for maintenance of coaches' confidence throughout the season as well as the off-season.

As mentioned in connection with building efficacy for the novice coach, the formal mentor–apprentice relationship is a separate type of educational experience, and these relationships also may be designed for more experienced coaches. Such relationships could provide a steady source of coaching knowledge, social support, and coaching development, directly affecting multiple sources of coaching efficacy toward the maintenance of the experienced coach's confidence.

TECHNIQUE 7: Focus on Success and Self-Improvement

We have already discussed defining success in order to utilize it as a source of confidence. With respect to *maintaining* the confidence of an established coach, our primary suggestion would be to focus on the multidimensional nature of coaching efficacy. As noted by Feltz and colleagues (1999), coaching efficacy comprises confidence in teaching technique, game strategy, character building, and motivation. To maintain one's confidence, it may be beneficial to reflect on specific aspects of coaching.

The coaching process is dynamic and unpredictable. On any given day, a coach can experience differing degrees of success in different aspects of coaching. If a coach is proactive in monitoring the various aspects of coaching confidence, she should be able to regularly experience some success that would help in maintaining her confidence. For example, a particular game might have been lost, but the coach might have displayed some competence with her strategy. Or a practice might have been disorganized and not have accomplished much, but the coach might have had a positive one-on-one connection with an athlete. In these two examples, the coach experienced success in terms of game strategy and character building, respectively. By incorporating these specific subfactors of coaching efficacy into a daily check of coaching success, an experienced coach can continuously use success as a source of coaching efficacy. With respect to the case of Phil Jackson, although his motivational coaching efficacy might have been diminished, he might still have been able to maintain his global coaching confidence by analyzing his success as a strategist.

Focusing on success does not mean that coaches should ignore their mistakes. On the contrary, they should acknowledge and evaluate decisions that led to inadequate results in a task-diagnostic, rather than a self-diagnostic, manner (Bandura, 1997). Instead of questioning their coaching ability, coaches should diagnose what they did incorrectly, analyze what other options they could employ next time, and focus on those systematically.

Fans and sports writers probably compare coaches' records more at the experienced stages than at the novice levels. It is easier to fly under the radar of scrutiny at the preparatory sport levels. Coaches are continually confronted with comparative appraisals, and it is difficult, when one is compared unfavorably not to view the appraisal as an indicator of personal deficiency or failure. If coaches focus on their own self-improvement against personal standards or goals instead of comparison to other coaches, they can avoid the demoralizing effects of social comparisons made by the media and fans. However, as Bandura (1997) notes, "self-improvement never follows a uniform, ever-rising course. Rather, it is characterized by spurts of improvement, setbacks, plateaus, and variations in the rate of progress. Hence, self-comparison can be self-demoralizing or self-enhancing depending on whether individuals mainly dwell on their shortfalls in the mixed constellation of changes or accent their gains" (p. 457). Thus, focusing on the gains, while diagnosing the failures and moving beyond them, is the most effective way to maintain one's efficacy in the face of coaching pressures.

TECHNIQUE 8: Imagery

One source of coaching efficacy that is best discussed within the context of maintaining confidence for the experienced coach is imagery. Although imagery is best described as a vicarious, not true, mastery experience, it has been shown to be related to an individual's confidence. See chapters 3 and 6 for a more complete discussion of imagery as a source of self-efficacy. Recent research has broached the issue of imagery as source of the confidence of the coach in addition to that of the athlete.

Short (2006a) examined the cognitive and motivational functions of imagery use in a sample of over 200 coaches from 23 different sports. Her results showed that coaches frequently used imagery; cognitive-specific imagery (e.g., imaging specific skills of their performance) was the most popular technique. Imagery use did not differ according to several personal characteristics of the coaches (i.e., age, gender, level of education). Analyses based on prior athletic experiences (i.e., whether coaches were former athletes, their highest competitive level, and whether they coached a sport in which they had formerly participated) showed that coaches who had competed at the college and professional levels used imagery more for motivational purposes than those who had played only in high school. Furthermore, the more the coaches had used imagery when they had been athletes, the more they tended to use it as coaches. Finally, coaches of individual sports used imagery more than coaches who coached team sports.

As described in chapter 5, Short, Smiley, and Ross-Stewart (2005) examined how this use of imagery by coaches related to their confidence. They found that imagery was a significant predictor of total CES efficacy scores even after statistically controlling for experience (i.e., total years coaching) and success (i.e., career win/loss record). With respect to the specific factors of coaching efficacy, cognitive imagery (e.g., imagery for the purposes of optimizing skills and strategies) was significantly related to strategy and teaching technique, whereas motivation imagery (e.g., imagery focused on psychological states and goal achievement) was significantly related to motivation and character-building efficacy. Thus, it appears that one way for coaches to become more confident is to practice the skill of imagery, a skill often learned as an athlete. For instance, practicing images of appearing confident in front of opponents, being in control in difficult situations, and being focused should help coaches enhance their efficacy in these areas. And, although there appear to be some very specific relationships, imagery is capable of boosting all aspects of coaching efficacy.

Having discussed a variety of sources for enhancing and maintaining coaching efficacy, we will conclude this chapter with two sections. First we discuss the importance of reflection on the part of coaches; then we consider the gender difference in coaching efficacy and how this might influence the use of various sources of coaches' self-efficacy.

Reflection and Enhancing Coaching Efficacy

According to Schön (1983), professionals such as coaches are constantly involved in conscious reflection on their own competencies. These reflections are the basis of a series of tacit theories of action according to which professionals act, even if they cannot articulate these theories. Schön stated that reflection is a process most applicable to an environment characterized by "a high priority on flexible procedures, differentiated responses, qualitative appreciation of complex processes, and decentralized responsibilities for judgment and action" (Schön, 1983, p. 338), which are all characteristics of the coaching context (Gilbert & Trudel, 2001). Further noting that Schön's (1983) framework had been repeatedly applied to the process of how teachers learn through experience, Gilbert and Trudel (2001) examined how applicable the framework would be to coaching. They used a multiple case study design with six youth team sport coaches. Data collection included multiple interviews, documents, observation, and video- and audiotaping. The guiding principles of data analysis, in line with Schön's framework, were that coaches engage in reflection to learn through experience and that issues in coaching can trigger this reflection.

There were several common components to this self-directed reflective process. The authors noted six significant stages, the first of which is (1) a coaching issue. This issue is defined through the process of (2) issue setting. In issue setting, the coach frames the issue that he or she is dealing with within a framework that will allow for a more complete and constructive understanding of the issue. Personal observations and comments from others (both solicited and unsolicited) are used to determine the setting for the issue. Once the issue has been clearly defined, the process of (3) strategy generation begins. This refers to consulting various interacting sources to develop a coaching strategy, including advice from others, coaching materials, existing coaching behaviors, creative thought, and reflective transformation. Whatever solutions may be generated from these processes are then entered into the cyclical pattern of (4) experimentation and (5) evaluation. That is, a coach experiments with a probable solution to the issue and evaluates how effective it was. If the solution seems ineffective, an alternative solution will be tried. If the solution seems effective, experimentation ends. Finally, all of these processes are bound by the (6) role frame of the coach. It is important to note that the specifics of the coach's role will affect this reflective process. Coaches are not all equal, and idiosyncrasies in the individual's role (e.g., amount of playing experience, level of sport, professional status, gender of the athlete or athletes) influence the entire process, from how the issue is perceived to what experimental strategies are devised and evaluated as solutions.

The reflective conversation that coaches engage in is implicit in all coaching decisions and actions. However, according to Gilbert and Trudel (2001), it must be initiated by a particular issue facing the coach. As such, it is much more relevant to the case of a coach whose confidence is shaken, as after Hitchcock started his WHL job. This case involves two distinct reflective processes for our present purposes: (1) the issue of recognizing a lack of confidence and (2) the issue of deciding if the source enlisted was effective.

For instance, in his own words, shortly after Hitchcock began coaching in the WHL, he felt a tremendous lack of confidence in his ability. This decision in itself would have been the result of an intensive reflective conversation that would have included issue setting through his observations and the comments of others. A strategy would have been generated concerning a source that would be most appropriate; in discussion with others, and through reflective thinking, Hitchcock chose to take multiple coaching clinics. These strategies resulted in the dual processes of experimentation and evaluation. Although Hitchcock stated that he "attended every clinic he could" (Robertson, 2005, p. 7), this had to start with one clinic. That was an experiment—a trial in the real world that was the result of critical reflection. After evaluating its outcome, through introspective review of personal observations and discussions with important others, Hitchcock concluded that the clinic was a good source of coaching efficacy and attended more.

Theoretically, then, a coach could receive the benefits of these sources of confidence only if this reflective conversation concluded that they were effective. If Gilbert and Trudel (2001) were correct in applying Schön's (1983) concepts to coaching, then the reflective conversation is a significant part of coaches' daily lives. Therefore, any source of coaching efficacy that has been discussed in this chapter (e.g., education, social support, mastery) can be effective only if the individual, through reflective conversation, concludes that it is successful.

As we discussed in chapter 5 on coaching efficacy, the confidence that a coach has in him- or herself is a significant, influential, and dynamic thing. It is important to recognize the self-perceptions that coaches have regarding their competence. As the theme of this current chapter suggests, it is also important to recognize and potentially manage the sources of this confidence in order to optimize the psychological attributes of coaches, as well as the subsequent effects on the behaviors and attitudes of their athletes.

The primary ways to increase coaching efficacy are to experience success (which may be defined in various ways), to participate in coaching education sessions, to modify the social support that one receives from the general community, and to utilize imagery. It is important to recognize that these sources, although consistently influential, ultimately depend on the reflective process of coaches. A summary of the techniques we presented are listed in table 8.4.

Revisiting the case studies we included in this chapter, the first involved Ken Hitchcock, a novice coach who was in the process of building his coaching efficacy. Although Hitchcock utilized a variety of sources to enhance his confidence, the one he used first and most frequently was coaching education sessions. Many courses are designed and structured for inexperienced coaches, and research has routinely shown that participants tend to experience enhanced confidence with respect to strategy, teaching technique,

TABLE 8.4 *Summary of Techniques for Enhancing and Maintaining Coaching Efficacy*

Technique	Source
ENHANCING COACHING EFFICACY OF NOVICE COACHES	
1. Coaching education 　a. Formal courses, certifications 　b. Apprenticeships	Mastery and preparation
2. Coaching success	Mastery
3. Goal setting	Mastery
4. Obtaining feedback	Self- and other persuasion
5. Seeking social support	Social support
ENHANCING COACHING EFFICACY OF EXPERIENCED COACHES	
6. Continued education	Mastery and preparation
7. Focus on success and self-improvement	Mastery and self-persuasion
8. Imagery	Multiple sources

motivating their athletes, and character-building abilities. Coaches must use their new information immediately in order for it to transfer to their interactions with athletes. Keeping a journal in which they can self-monitor the coaching behaviors that produce successful and unsuccessful outcomes can help with this transfer. Further, it is obvious from Hitchcock's comments (Robertson, 2005) that he was involved in a very thoughtful process, both in his decision to attend these courses and in his response to having taken them. Such critical reflection is consistent with the comments of Trudel and Gilbert (2001).

Secondly, we considered the case of Phil Jackson as he coached the Los Angeles Lakers. Here was a very experienced and successful coach who nonetheless was experiencing self-doubts. This lack of confidence mostly centered on his ability to manage some very different personalities on the team. Here we recognize that such proven sources of efficacy as coaching education would not have been applicable. However, we suggested that Coach Jackson might have made efforts to define his success as a coach in terms of the specific facets of motivation and character building. Experiencing some success in these aspects of coaching efficacy would have resulted in increasing his confidence as a coach, hopefully easing the self-doubts he reported experiencing. In addition, we mentioned focusing on self-improvements rather than social comparisons with other coaches.

Future Directions
for Research
on Efficacy Beliefs

> To succeed . . . You need to find something to hold on to, something to motivate you, something to inspire you.
>
> *Tony Dorsett, member of the Pro Football Hall of Fame*

Throughout the first eight chapters, we have shown that there is a strong relationship between efficacy beliefs and goal-striving behavior in sport. Counter to Roberts' (2001) declaration, efficacy research in sport has not come to a standstill. Rather, it has expanded to include investigations of teams, coaches, unique sources of self-efficacy within sport, relationships to other social cognitive variables, and the self-regulation of other processes beyond physical performance in sport. In this last chapter, however, our purpose is not to look backward and summarize the information already presented, but rather to direct attention forward to areas for future research.

This chapter is divided into five main sections. The first four sections contain ideas for future directions for research projects corresponding to the material covered in the previous chapters. We organized these ideas by measurement, athletes, teams, and coaches. In most cases, each idea actually contains several research questions, and although some of the ideas are presented under a particular heading (e.g., self-efficacy beliefs), they are certainly applicable to the other types of efficacy beliefs as well (e.g., collective efficacy and coaching efficacy). In general, we believe that future research on efficacy beliefs in sport should avoid simply addressing whether relationships exist between certain variables unless these ideas are truly unique. Instead, we recommend thinking of research questions that tackle such topics as "Under what conditions should we find a relationship between X and Y?" or "Under what conditions does the relationship between X and Y differ?" In the fifth section, we describe two different approaches recently proposed for studying efficacy beliefs that are relational and cut across athletes, teams, and coaches.

Future Directions for Research on Efficacy Measurement

These first four suggestions focus on efficacy measurement. Idea 1 is related to the concept of generality (or transferability) of efficacy beliefs across different domains of functioning. The second idea introduces efficacy beliefs as a multidimensional construct. The third idea focuses on elite athletes and the need to develop efficacy measures capable of capturing the slightest differences in efficacy beliefs among these top-level performers. The fourth idea points to the need to develop efficacy measures that can be used to assess efficacy beliefs during competition.

IDEA 1: Explore the Processes Through Which Generality (and Transferability) of Efficacy Beliefs Occur

Few studies have examined the generality of efficacy beliefs in the sport domain (exceptions are Brody, Hatfield, & Spaulding, 1988; Holloway, Beuter, & Duda, 1988). As we noted in chapters 1 and 2, "generality" indicates the number of domains of functioning in which people judge themselves to be efficacious and includes the notion of the transferability of one's efficacy judgments across different tasks or activities, such as across different sports. Simply documenting that efficacy beliefs are generalizable does not add much to the understanding of how and what aspects of self-efficacy are transferred to different contexts and domains of functioning; these are the areas that we believe are important to study.

There are plenty of examples of athletes making successful transfers to other sports or achievement domains. For instance, soccer players have become successful kickers in professional football (e.g., Matt Bahr); basketball players have become successful track athletes and professional football players (e.g., Marion Jones and Antonio Gates), and numerous athletes have become successful business executives (e.g., Earvin "Magic" Johnson, chairman and CEO, Johnson Development Corporation). There are also examples of those who were not as successful in transferring their athletic success from one sport to another (e.g., Michael Jordan's unsuccessful transition from professional basketball to baseball).

Another kind of transformation within sport is that of athlete to coach. Although most coaches have some playing experience, playing excellence does not appear to translate to coaching excellence. Many of the superstar athletes who attempted coaching met with mixed success at best (e.g., Isiah Thomas, Bryan Trottier). And many of the best coaches in a given sport (e.g., Joe Torre, Phil Jackson) were talented, but not superstar, athletes. The few individuals who achieved excellence as both a player and coach (e.g., Mike Ditka, Larry Bird, Lenny Wilkins) appear to be the exception, not the rule. One of the most publicized instances of a superstar athlete making the transition to coaching has recently unfolded in the NHL. Wayne Gretzky, considered the best hockey player of all time, took on the role of head coach for the Phoenix Coyotes (a team for which he is also the managing partner). Considering that the roles of athlete and coach are two of the most widely researched with respect to efficacy, studying these transitions also holds much potential for research.

We contend that transformational actions are most likely based on athletes' confidence in their ability to transfer their successful capabilities from one context to another. However, as Bandura (1997) has stated, "the point at issue is not whether efficacy beliefs can be generalized to some extent, but the processes through which generality occurs and how it should be measured" (p. 53). Bandura identified a number of processes by which efficacy beliefs might generalize across different domains. We highlight the following five: similar subskills, self-regulatory skills, effort, coping, and emphasized commonalities. Thus, some athletes might successfully switch from one sport to another because the two sports have similar subskills (e.g., speed). However, the generalized self-efficacy also could be due to the successful self-regulatory skills (or "metastrategies") or coping skills learned in one sport that are transferred to another (e.g., goal setting, managing distractions, imagery, positive self-talk), or the sense of effort efficacy to master challenges. Lastly, the underlying process for successful generalized efficacy beliefs could be due to one's focus on the familiar or common aspects of performance in the two domains, rather than on the novel features.

Research on the processes people use to transfer their efficacy beliefs to different domains (within sport and outside of sport) can provide helpful guidelines on how to enhance successful performance transitions across domains of functioning. One suggestion regarding how to conduct this type of research would be to use a qualitative approach, such as a retrospective interview. People who have experience in two different domains could be asked to explain why they perceived they were successful in both areas, or perhaps why they were successful in one area but not the other. An efficacy belief questionnaire that tapped the similar subskills, self-regulatory skills, effort, coping, and commonalities could also be used to assess confidence in the similar contexts to examine which processes are most related to each other and to performance. Such an instrument would assess the multidimensionality of efficacy beliefs that we discuss next.

IDEA 2: Assess the Multidimensionality of Efficacy Beliefs in Sport

Bandura (1997) stated that a common mistake is to judge ability by physical skills alone. Self-efficacy measures have been typically task specific and unidimensional, focusing mostly on efficacy to perform specific motor skills. As we have presented, there is more to success in sport than the execution of physical skills. We recommend assessing self-efficacy for strategy, for decision making, for self-regulation, for managing pressure, and so on. The measures that we have developed to assess collective efficacy (Short, Sullivan, & Feltz, 2005) and coaching efficacy (Feltz, Chase, Moritz, & Sullivan, 1999) are multidimensional questionnaires based on Bandura's (1997) contention that people judge their efficacy across the full range of task demands within a given domain. Vealey and Knight (2003) also have developed the multidimensional Sport Confidence Inventory (SCI), which taps three types of sport confidence (SC-Physical Skills and Training, SC-Cognitive Efficiency, SC-Resilience) in athletic functioning based on the types of efficacy beliefs needed to meet the demands of competitive sport. Physical Skills and Training represents skill execution confidence and confidence in physical conditioning and training. Cognitive Efficiency represents confidence about decision making, managing thoughts, and maintaining focus. Resilience includes confidence about overcoming obstacles, setbacks, and doubt. A number of questions need further investigation: How well do the subdomain efficacy beliefs correlate with each other under different circumstances? If interventions are designed to enhance efficacy beliefs in one subcategory, do those beliefs generalize to other subcategories? Do athletes, teams, and coaches who have moderate confidence in all areas perform better than those with high confidence on only one or two?

IDEA 3: Develop Measures to Capture the Fine Differences in Efficacy Beliefs at the Elite Levels of Competition

Athletes and coaches indicate, anecdotally, that performance differences at the elite level are due to psychological factors; but, as we covered elsewhere in this book, this may actually be a form of attributional reasoning. However, it is possible that elite athletes do differ in the strength of their efficacy beliefs. Just as fractions of seconds and inches make the difference between who medals and who does not at the Olympic Games and other major sport events, it is possible that the slightest differences in efficacy beliefs could be a differentiating factor. To test this hypothesis, measures are needed that would capture these differences. The visual analog scale (VAS) as a type of efficacy scale and the creation of more difficult efficacy items were presented in chapter 2 as possible solutions to assessing elite-level differences in efficacy beliefs, but these ideas need to be field tested.

IDEA 4: Develop Measures That Capture Changes in Efficacy Beliefs as They Take Place During Competition

As we have noted throughout this book, efficacy beliefs are modifiable. They can change as circumstances within the environment change. They can change over the course of a single competition. Thus, measures are needed to capture these changes in a way that does not disrupt performance but still provides valid assessments of efficacy beliefs. To capture these changes in efficacy beliefs, one possibility is to use small microphones with tape-recording devices to record the dialogue that takes place throughout a competition. Another possibility is the use of a one-item efficacy measure. Although in chapter 2 we recommended against using one-item efficacy scales, a verbally recorded numeral response at specifically prompted time points in a competition might provide an indication of intraindividual changes in efficacy beliefs across a competition. This technique would be similar to the Borg scale (1998) that measures people's ratings of perceived exertion (RPE). We understand that the practicality of using such measures may be dependent on the specific sport or situation. Sports that have regular breaks in play (e.g., football, volleyball) would be more amenable to this type of research than others. The same notion would hold true for certain positions. For example, the breaks between pitches for a pitcher in a baseball game may allow for a quick, Borg-type response, but the same could not be said for a hockey goalie, who may make two or more saves in a span of seconds.

One study relevant to this of line of inquiry was conducted by Thomas, Hanton, and Jones (2002). They investigated the utility of using a short-form self-report assessment of competitive anxiety. Their measure was based on the subscales in the Competitive State Anxiety Inventory-2 (CSAI-2) and therefore contained a self-confidence measure as well. The study was designed to be a concurrent validity-based study (against the CSAI-2 with additional direction and frequency scales), and the authors adopted a temporal design in which participants completed the measures one week, two days, one day, 2 hr, and 30 min prior to competing. Thus, they were not interested in assessing psychological states *during* a competition, but rather *leading up to* the competition. Nevertheless, the results showed that their scale (called the IAMS, Immediate Anxiety Measurement Scale) had higher (and over time, consistently better) correlations with the CSAI-2 than previous single-item scales on anxiety such as the Mental Readiness Form (Krane, 1994). What was different was that Thomas and colleagues did not use items reflective of cognitive anxiety, somatic anxiety, and self-confidence (e.g., by asking about symptoms such as concern) but actually used the terms "cognitive anxiety," "somatic anxiety," and "self-confidence." However, the only way they could use those terms was by introducing a structured education program in which participants were taught what cognitive anxiety, somatic anxiety, and self-confidence actually were; how they were manifested; what the associated symptoms were; and how they could be recognized. Then the authors taught the participants how to rate the level or intensity of the associated symptoms, how to interpret the direction of the intensity of the symptoms, and how to rate the frequency of the cognitive intrusions (i.e., the amount of time competition thoughts entered the mind).

Thomas and colleagues (2002) showed that using single-item measures may require a lot of preparation in terms of teaching the participants how to use and adopt them. To this end, researchers interested in pursuing this idea should be prepared to spend substantial time teaching athletes how to use these measures so that the athletes can rate their efficacy beliefs at key moments during their performance with a great deal of accuracy and, importantly, speed. Such studies will be challenging for researchers because it will likely complicate the data collection to institute a training program (often with large numbers of participants) before the "real" data collection can start. However, the information gained from such studies would be enlightening, especially if efficacy judgments could be interpreted along with "game action" such as changes in scoring, time-outs, and the like.

Future Directions for Research
With Athletes (Self-Efficacy Beliefs)

Here we suggest five ideas for future research that focus specifically on the self-efficacy beliefs of athletes. The last two ideas have strong practical applications for coaches and can also be tied in with self-efficacy and goal-setting research.

IDEA 5: Study the Efficacy–Performance Relationship as a Function of Skill Expertise

Although a number of studies have examined the relationship between self-efficacy and sport performance, far less work has explored this relationship as a function of skill expertise (Beilock & Feltz, 2006). Experts are not only more efficacious in their physical proficiency than less skilled individuals; they are also more efficacious in their cognitive self-regulation skills. For instance, experts have been found to be highly confident in their ability to read shifting game situations, to select effective performance strategies, to predict opponents' likely actions, to make "in the moment" decisions, to utilize imagery, to manage pressure and setback situations, and to manage distractions (Bandura, 1997; Bull, 1991; Highlen & Bennett, 1983; Tenenbaum, Levy-Kolker, Sade, Lieberman, & Lidor, 1996). More research is needed to clarify how self-efficacy relates to expert performance in sport. Specifically, what aspects of self-efficacy (e.g., task, self-regulatory, coping) differentiate expert performers from novices? Is self-efficacy a better predictor of performance as skill level increases? To conduct this research, measures will be needed that can capture fine differences in efficacy beliefs at these elite levels (see Idea 3), but perhaps in-depth qualitative studies could be used that include approaches such as diaries or multiple interviews.

IDEA 6: Assess Efficacy Beliefs and the Sources of Efficacy Over Time and Across Seasons

The majority of research on self-efficacy beliefs in sport has been approached in a static, cross-sectional type of way. That is, in most cases the self-efficacy–performance relationship has been measured at one point in time. Athletes, however, perform for an entire season and for multiple seasons. For these reasons, longitudinal-type research designs should be used to track efficacy levels. There is little doubt that efficacy beliefs fluctuate over time (see also Idea 4). What is important to understand is the *causes* of those fluctuations. As we described in chapter 1, the discrepancies between past performance accomplishments and goals influence efficacy beliefs and future efficacy beliefs in complex ways that involve self-reactive influences to success or failure sequences, attributions, and the resiliency of one's efficacy beliefs. Sometimes complacency sets in after easy successes or in the face of unchallenging goals (Bandura, 1997). Sometimes athletes find themselves in downward efficacy–performance spirals that they have difficulty breaking out of. Intraindividual designs are necessary to follow these sequences of efficacy beliefs, goals, performance, and self-reactions over time.

We also recommend that future research examine the sources of efficacy information and the heuristics involved in weighting and integrating these sources over time. For example, are the performance accomplishments obtained during a competitive season in college still a salient source of efficacy information for an athlete competing in a higher level of sport? How do these prior standout seasons compare to the potency of a poor game at a higher level of sport (i.e., "You're only as good as your last performance")? How are athletes' efficacy levels affected when they go from being the "best" on their team one year to a rookie who rarely plays the next?

IDEA 7: Empirically Test the Differentiated Relationships That Preparatory and Performance Efficacy Are Hypothesized to Have With Performance

Recall that Bandura (1986b, 1997) differentiates between preparatory efficacy and performance efficacy. As we described in chapters 1 and 6, the distinction is made based on the two phases and their effects. Bandura's assertions imply a curvilinear, or inverted-U, relationship in the skill acquisition phase between self-efficacy beliefs and effort and persistence as the dependent variable. Similarly, preparatory efficacy should also influence performance in a curvilinear fashion because of the effort and persistence effects (Bandura, 1997). When performance efficacy is considered, the relationship changes. Bandura (1997) predicts a more linear relationship between self-efficacy beliefs and performance as the dependent measure. To our knowledge this differentiation between preparatory and performance efficacy and their relationships with effort, persistence, and performance has not been empirically tested.

IDEA 8: Investigate How Feedback Can Influence Efficacy Beliefs in Training and Practice Settings

As noted in chapter 3, the feedback given to an athlete can either undermine self-efficacy or boost it (Bandura, 1997). Most researchers have examined the effect of feedback on self-efficacy beliefs by using success and failure manipulations (see chapter 3). However, there are other forms of feedback that deserve research attention. According to Bandura, "the point of reference from which successive attainments are socially evaluated can affect appraisal of personal capabilities. Social evaluations that focus on achieved progress underscore personal capabilities; whereas, evaluations that focus on shortfalls from the distant goal highlight existing deficiencies in capabilities" (p. 102). Bandura refers to this as framing, and notes that to systematically test framing effects, "the performance feedback is factually equivalent but simply varies whether the evaluative reference point is the performance level at which one began or the level to be fulfilled" (p. 102). Using his example, if an individual performs at a 75% level of a selected standard, feedback may emphasize the 75% progress already achieved (i.e., gain framing) or the 25% shortfall (i.e., deficit framing). He hypothesizes that gain framing will build self-efficacy whereas deficit framing will diminish it.

In sport, the study of how feedback can influence the development of self-efficacy beliefs seems especially suited for those events that have certain standards, such as making a time cut in swimming or a weight in strength training. This line of research is likely to be especially useful to practitioners. Often in sport psychology, we restrict ourselves to studying psychological behaviors and processes during competition. However, the fact is that athletes spend far more time training than they do competing.

IDEA 9: Research the Salient Aspects of Pregame and Other Verbal Persuasion Speeches on Athletes' Efficacy Expectations by Athlete Type, Level, and Sport

Speeches are a significant part of sport competitions, and as shown in chapter 3, both coaches and their athletes believe that coaches' verbal boosts help to enhance athletes' efficacy beliefs. However, several unknowns with respect to pregame speeches warrant our attention. A number of research questions are worth considering. How important is the delivery of the speech in comparison to the content of the speech? What types of content (i.e., informational, emotional) are the most important? Is the order in which information is presented in the speech important (i.e., primacy, recency effects)? Does the impact of the speech vary according to who delivers it (coaches vs. assistant coaches)? What are the effects of not saying anything at all? Can speeches interfere with an athlete's pregame preparation? Could the content of speeches actually be a source of pressure for athletes? Could speeches decrease an athlete's sense of efficacy? Should speeches be different from one game to the next, or should there be a common theme that runs throughout the various speeches? What types of speeches are more effective for athletes who compete in sports like softball, where doubleheaders are common?

A more specific question related to pregame speeches involves which types of pregame speeches are most effective in raising self- and team efficacy beliefs for athletes in different age-groups, of different playing abilities or levels, and of different genders. We described research on coaches' pregame speeches in chapter 5. Only one study has examined the effect of authentic pregame speeches on the efficacy beliefs of young male and female soccer players (Vargas-Tonsing, 2004). In this study, perceived instructionally focused speeches predicted athletes' self-efficacy beliefs more than perceived emotionally focused speeches. However, Vargas-Tonsing measured perceived content rather than actual content of the speeches. Knowing what types of speeches are most effective for different types of athletic teams would help coaches decide how best to prepare their teams.

In addition to these questions, another area that has not been addressed concerns the longevity of efficacy-boosting strategies conveyed through verbal persuasion methods. Bandura (1997) posits an interaction effect. He stated that "social appraisals that differ markedly from peoples' judgments of their current capabilities may be considered believable for the distant future, but not in the short run" (p. 105). He considers feedback the most believable when its content is only "moderately beyond" what the individual can do at the time. In his words, "inflated persuasory appraisals that mislead performers to repeated failures undermine the diagnostic credibility of the persuaders and further reinforce the performers' belief in their inherent limitations" (p. 105).

Related to pregame speeches are half-time talks and postgame speeches. What kinds of messages are most effective in raising athletes' efficacy beliefs in the face of poor performance in the first half? What should be included in postgame speeches? Should coaches provide an opportunity for athletes to positively reflect on their performances? Would doing so eliminate the negative carryover effects of failure? Would using attributions and other recovery strategies be effective for regaining efficacy beliefs after failure? To date, little is known about the efficacy-altering effects of half-time talks and postgame speeches.

Future Directions for Research With Teams (Collective Efficacy Beliefs)

Next we highlight research ideas related to collective efficacy beliefs, and therefore team research. As we mentioned in chapter 4, research on collective efficacy beliefs using teams is typically harder to conduct than self-efficacy research with individual athletes. Here we propose seven ideas for future research with teams on collective efficacy beliefs. While many techniques have been proposed and used to enhance self-efficacy beliefs in athletes, limited research has involved testing the effectiveness of collective efficacy techniques. An interesting offshoot of this idea would be to examine the impact of collective efficacy interventions on self-efficacy beliefs (and vice versa).

IDEA 10: Examine Issues Related to the Consensus of Efficacy Beliefs

As noted in chapter 2, the issue of consensus is especially important to collective efficacy research. Athletes who participate in team sports can differ in their efficacy beliefs about the team's collective capabilities. Some athletes (from the same team) may believe that their team is very capable while their teammates may perceive the team to be less capable. This variability of the athletes' responses within a specific team may have important implications related to the team's functioning. To this end, we suggest that future research use the degree of variability in collective efficacy beliefs as an independent variable on such constructs as collective efficacy scores, cohesion, team satisfaction, and performance (Moritz & Watson, 1998). As we suggested in chapter 2, multilevel statistical packages are also useful for these purposes. The degree of variability could also be used as a dependent variable to show whether or not there are differences between rookies and veterans, or starters and nonstarters, for example. We address the issue of team dispersion and its implications in greater detail later in this chapter.

IDEA 11: Extend Research on the Effects of Collective Efficacy Beliefs on Team Functioning to Include Measures Other Than Performance and Under Different Settings

Much of the research on collective efficacy in sport has focused on its relationship with team performance because successful performance is what teams and coaches strive for. However, on the path to performance achievement, teams have proximal goals regarding effort in practice and games, teamwork and task cohesion, team communication, and so on that have not been measured. According to Bandura (1997), collective efficacy is likely to influence how much effort players put forth together, their ability to remain perseverant and task oriented during periods when the team is struggling, and their capability to bounce back from wrenching defeats. Thus, measuring how well collective efficacy predicts achievement of these other dependent variables and under different settings (i.e., when the team is struggling) is also important.

IDEA 12: Examine Collective Efficacy Beliefs in Conjunction With the Stages of Group Development

The stages of group development proposed by Tuckman (1965; Tuckman & Jensen, 1977) is considered a classic in group dynamics. He proposed a sequence in the way groups develop that consists of several stages—forming, storming, norming, performing and, in some cases, adjourning (descriptions of these stages abound and are not repeated here; see also chapters 4 and 7). The basic tenet is that the degree to which a group's social structure has evolved will determine the group's ability to perform various tasks. From our perspective, it is likely that the level of collective efficacy beliefs varies according to these stages. Of course, Tuckman's is just one model of group development; others could be investigated as well. Doing so would require a measure that could be used to reflect the stages of group development, however.

IDEA 13: Study the Similarities and Differences Between Successful and Less Successful Teams

In addition to studying teams in various stages of development (Idea 12) and teams from novice to expert (an extension of Idea 5), it would be worthwhile for researchers to explicitly compare successful and less successful teams in terms of their regulatory and coping efficacy. Little or no research to date has involved this type of comparison. One could ask, for example, what are the collective efficacy correlates of successful and less successful teams? How do successful teams manage competitive pressure, performance slumps, and team strategy decisions in a manner that results in successful performance outcomes (Beilock & Feltz, 2006)? Bandura (1997) wrote about the potential differences between successful and less successful teams, and the following quote offers several suggestions for future research.

> Successful teams have a strong group sense of efficacy and resiliency. They believe firmly that they have whatever it takes to succeed, and they never concede anything. They do not collapse or panic when they fall behind. Rather, they typically stage successful comebacks by determined effort in pressure-packed closing periods of games. In contrast, mediocre teams and those plagued by inconsistencies, seem to perform much of the time in an inefficacious frame of mind. They do not expect much of themselves as a team, and, as a consequence, do not do all that well. (pp. 402-403)

Bandura also noted that mediocre teams may concede games before the players even step onto the field, may beat themselves by having uninspiring play, and may have weak staying power in the face of mounting pressure. Studying the similarities and differences between successful and less successful teams would be one way to examine Bandura's (1997) assertions. Tracking teams through their competitive seasons would likely illuminate the natural ups and downs relative to performance (and other performance indicators in addition to win/loss records). Teams with winning seasons could then be compared with losing-season teams.

IDEA 14: Examine the Theoretical Tenets of Collective Efficacy With Teams Characterized by Lower Interdependence

As we presented in chapter 4, much of the research on collective efficacy has been conducted with teams from sports that can be characterized by a high degree of interdependence. The relative predictive strength of self-efficacy and collective efficacy may vary according to the degree of interdependent performance (Bandura, 1997). That is, according to Bandura (1997), collective efficacy may be especially relevant to team performance where team attainments require high interactive effort because members' beliefs about the team encompass the coordinative and interactive dynamics that operate within a team. He suggests that self-efficacy, on the other hand, may be an adequate predictor of team performance in additive sports when team attainments represent largely the summed contributions of individual members (i.e., in sports such as archery, track, or swimming). However, one's confidence in one's teammates to contribute to an overall team success may influence one's individual efforts (e.g., social loafing) even for additive sports or individual tasks within interactive sports. Researchers can examine the impact of the degree of interdependence in a single sport—for example, in baseball and softball, where batting would be at the low end of the interdependence continuum whereas most fielding (e.g., making a double play) would be higher in interdependence. Sports such as these provide a natural setting for examination of the effect of the degree of interdependence on efficacy and dependent variables like performance. Furthermore, these settings offer the researcher the advantages of a within-subjects design. These relationships should be examined in both performance and training contexts.

IDEA 15: Examine the Effect That One Person Can Have on a Team's Functioning

Another logical extension of the research effort on collective efficacy is to study the effect that one person can have on a team's functioning. What are the effects of a slumping athlete on his or her team's efficacy? Do the effects differ if the slumping athlete is a starter or nonstarter, captain or not, leader or not? There are two possibilities. Display of "ineffectiveness" on the part of some players could *undermine* the teammates' sense of efficacy (Bandura, 1997, p. 403) and result in poorer performance. "Contagious ineffectiveness leads everyone to start pressing in ways that disrupt skills, breed mistakes, and leave players talking disparaging to themselves" (Bandura, 1997, p. 403). Alternatively, teams could come together under such situations, perhaps because of some perceived pressure they feel that they need to be the ones to pick up the slack. A similar research question concerns the effect that a slumping player has on his or her opponents. As noted by Bandura (1997), modeled ineffectiveness, especially on the part of superstars, could also depress team performance by inflating perceptions of how overpowering opponents are. Tracking such "contagious" influences would involve different research methods, such as the use of agent-based modeling techniques (Axtell, 2000; Axtell & Epstein, 1996; Gilbert & Bankes, 2000).

On a related note, are there athletes who may elevate their teammates' sense of efficacy? It is likely that in his later years, superstar basketball player Michael Jordan helped build efficacy in his teammates by passing them the ball in the most critical of situations. Thus, research on contagious efficacy could focus in either direction—the undermining or the boosting of efficacy beliefs—or both.

IDEA 16: Design and Evaluate Interventions that Enhance Collective Efficacy

According to Bandura (1997), "it is one thing to build athletes' sense of personal efficacy. It is another to forge a sturdy sense of group efficacy from a collection of individuals and to sustain it the face of setback and defeats" (p. 402). In chapter 7, we suggested a number of strategies, including team goal setting, structuring a mastery-oriented climate, using simulations, building team cohesion, and using appropriate team attributions, that could be used to build, maintain, or regain collective efficacy beliefs; but these strategies have not been field tested for their effectiveness. A number of authors have suggested using team-building exercises to enhance team cohesion (e.g., Burke, 2006; Hodge, Lonsdale, & McKenzie, 2006). As we noted in chapter 7, whether or not team-building strategies also have an effect on collective efficacy beliefs awaits future research.

Future Directions for Research With Coaches (Coaching Efficacy Beliefs)

The last six research ideas involve coaches and coaching efficacy beliefs. These ideas expand on the coaching efficacy model (Feltz et al., 1999) described in chapter 5.

IDEA 17: Examine Dimension- and Coaching-Level-Specific Sources of Coaching Efficacy

As we stated in our original paper (Feltz et al., 1999), the coaching efficacy model provided a starting point for refinement and expansion by further research. For instance, we suggested in our 1999 paper that specific support from the community, administration, and parents for the coach to undergo training in good sporting behavior might be a stronger source of character-building efficacy than general support from these constituencies. Other sources specific to character-building efficacy might be education in coaching ethics and past sporting behavior of players, and perhaps even the past playing behavior of the coach as a former athlete. In addition, some sources of efficacy information may be more important at different levels of coaching.

For example, Feltz, Hepler, Roman, and Paiement (2006) found that for youth sport coaches, player improvement was a stronger source of coaching efficacy on all dimensions except character building than was perceived player ability. Comparisons were not made with coaches of other levels, however. Finally, the potency of certain sources may change across a season of competition and across years of coaching experience. Longitudinal studies of coaching efficacy sources would provide useful information for understanding how coaching efficacy develops and is maintained.

IDEA 18: Expand the Dimensions of Coaching Efficacy

We mentioned in chapter 2 that the Coaching Efficacy Scale (CES) does not tap training and conditioning efficacy. Although we have research currently under way to evaluate a revised measure of the CES that includes training and conditioning, Bandura (1997) also suggests that recruitment efficacy and managerial efficacy with respect to "troublesome" players may be other facets of coaching efficacy, especially at the more elite levels of competition. Recruitment efficacy, according to Bandura, involves confidence not only in recognizing talent and potential in prospective players and the right mix for the team, but also in one's persuasive ability to recruit them. We have one item on the CES, "recognize talent in athletes," that loads on the technique and diagnostic dimension, but this could be a dimension in itself with more items.

Different measures with different dimensions of efficacy may be appropriate for various levels of coaching. For instance, youth and high school sport coaches are not involved in recruiting or managing highly paid athletes. A separate efficacy measure for college and professional coaches that better represents their key coaching competencies might show stronger relationships with coaching behaviors at those levels.

IDEA 19: Explore Specific Relationships Between Coaching Efficacy Dimensions and Coaching Behavior and Athlete Consequences

Each efficacy dimension should be linked to its corresponding coaching behavior and athlete behavior. For instance, coaches' character-building efficacy should predict their emphasis on good sporting behavior in their instructions to athletes and their role modeling with referees, which should in turn predict their athletes' sporting attitudes and behavior. In our original study (Feltz et al., 1999), we observed coaches using the Coaching Behavior Assessment System (CBAS). However, the CBAS tapped only coaches' instructional communication, positive feedback, and control behavior. More specific coaching behaviors that match the CES dimensions, such as the example just provided, would extend this research. Thus, technique efficacy should predict diagnostic knowledge and detection of skill errors; strategy efficacy should predict coaches' strategy adaptations in games; and motivation efficacy should predict coaches' motivational behaviors. These coaching behaviors should, in turn, predict corresponding behaviors, attitudes, and performance in one's athletes.

In addition, some coaching behaviors that are influenced by one's sense of coaching efficacy may transcend specific efficacy dimensions. Research has yet to determine whether coaching efficacy beliefs influence coaches' expectancy bias toward athletes, the types of goals they set for themselves as well as for their athletes, the motivational climate they set for practices and games, the types of pregame speeches they give, and their willingness to take risks. Furthermore, for coaching expectancy, in particular, examining its relationship to coaching efficacy as a source (in the CES model) and as a consequence (in the Horn, 2002 model) may help clarify its role in these two models.

IDEA 20: Explore the Relationship Between Coaching Efficacy and Coaching Development

As we mentioned in chapter 5, much of the research on coaching efficacy and coaching effectiveness has focused on coaches' behavior as it relates to athletes' psychosocial growth and development. Not much research has been devoted to the extent to which coaching efficacy beliefs influence coaches' commitment, coping abilities, satisfaction, burnout, and attrition. With the high turnover rate in coaches and the consequent lack of continuity among coaching staffs, especially at the youth and high school levels, it is difficult to build the skills of young athletes. Thus, determining the relationship between coaching efficacy and coaches' abilities to cope with the demands of coaching may also help determine how best to retain qualified coaches and develop stable athletic programs.

IDEA 21: Design and Evaluate Coaching Education Courses That Focus Directly on Enhancing Coaching Efficacy

In chapters 5 and 8, we described research that supports the value of coaching education programs on coaching efficacy. The two dimensions that seem to be most influenced by many of the traditional certification programs are technique and strategy efficacy. Longer programs need to be designed to allow participants time to learn the motivational and character-building skills involved in coaching. Wiersma and Sherman (2005) found that youth sport coaches saw pedagogical, psychological, and managerial aspects as the education content that they needed most. In addition, they wanted more "hands-on" workshops, mentoring, and roundtable discussions. As mentioned in chapter 8, these types of experiences would help build coaches' sense of efficacy, as would programs that included more time for mastery experiences in which coaches had opportunities to role play giving positive feedback, instructing a skill, or maintaining control during a simulated practice. These types of programs should then be evaluated for their efficacy-enhancing effectiveness. Apprentice–mentor types of programs are coaching education programs that can be designed with the specific purpose of raising coaching efficacy.

IDEA 22: Where Possible, Expand the Study of Coaching Efficacy to a "Team" Level So That the Entire Coaching Staff Can Be Considered

In many sports, several coaches are responsible for a specific team. For example, the coaching staff for a football team may consist of 10 or more positional coaches who are individually responsible for a specific group of athletes (i.e., offensive line, defensive line, kickers, quarterbacks, etc.). Another area of inquiry involves coaches' sense of efficacy regarding the coaching staff as well as regarding the team's ability to be successful and the degree of consensus around these ratings. Just as with collective efficacy among athletes, the variability of the coaches' responses may affect their coaching behavior. One or two coaches who believe that their team has limited potential for success may be a cancer in the organization, as their doubt may affect relationships with other coaches and the athletes.

New Lines of Inquiry

We next present two lines of inquiry that we believe can enhance understanding of the role of efficacy beliefs in the complex dynamics of sport performance and similar achievement-striving settings. The first has to do with efficacy beliefs in relation to another person (Lent & Lopez, 2002), and the second deals with the concept of dispersion of efficacy beliefs in teams (DeRue, Hollenbeck, Ilgen, & Feltz, 2005). These are broad areas that have the potential to generate entire programs of research, as they each include several specific research questions.

Relational Efficacy: A Tripartite View of Efficacy Beliefs

One new line of inquiry in the study of efficacy beliefs in sport involves the tripartite view of relational efficacy beliefs proposed by Lent and Lopez (2002). These authors view relational efficacy in three forms: self-efficacy, other-efficacy, and relation-inferred self-efficacy (RISE). To the best of our knowledge, only one unpublished study has fully addressed this conceptual extension of self-efficacy theory in the sport domain (Cilz & Short, 2006).

The impetus for the proposal of the tripartite view was Lent and Lopez's (2002) perception of the neglect of the interpersonal context in the study of efficacy beliefs. Lent and Lopez believe that there are many situations in which close relationships and social support serve as a context for building, maintaining, regaining, and even destroying one's sense of efficacy. In sport, we hear of this when athletes use phrases such as "I couldn't have done it without . . ." after winning competitive events and during award ceremonies. For example, in 2005, Marat Safin won the Australian Open, one of the major tournaments in professional tennis. His last major victory had been five years earlier at the U.S. Open (2000). Safin's professional career has been characterized by ups and downs. When interviewed about his 2005 win, Safin credited his resurgence to his new coach, Peter Lundgren. He is on record as saying, "I never believed in myself before at all, until I started to work with him."

The basic tenet of the tripartite view proposed by Lent and Lopez (2002) is that efficacy beliefs exist in dynamic interaction with the beliefs that people hold about the efficacy of others (other-efficacy), and about how others view them (RISE). The authors also propose multiple sources and effects of these beliefs. For example, sources may include perceptions of the other's accomplishments in past situations, experiences with similar others, information conveyed by third parties about the other, and social and cultural stereotypes. The efficacy beliefs are thought to affect the activities in which a person chooses to engage with another, the type and amount of effort expended in joint pursuits, one's attentiveness to and reliance on one's partner as a valid source of self-efficacy, and one's satisfaction with and intention to persist in the relationship despite conflict or other difficulties. Thus, the view is grounded in efficacy theory proposed by Bandura (1986b, 1997).

In our opinion, the tripartite view of efficacy beliefs is well described by Lent and Lopez (2002), so we will not cover the details. Rather, we focus on key definitions, some criticisms, and the potential application of the model for research purposes. Note that although the context in which Lent and Lopez introduced the tripartite view was counseling psychology, where therapists work with patients and clients, we think the view is applicable to all close relationships: athlete–athlete, athlete–coach, sport psychologist–athlete, sport psychologist–coach, and so on. It could even be applied to lesser-studied relationships, such as those between athletes and athletic trainers, for example.

The tripartite view includes three forms of belief: self-efficacy, other-efficacy, and relation-inferred self-efficacy (RISE). We focus on the latter two beliefs. Lent and Lopez (2002) defined *other*-efficacy as *"each partner's view of the other's efficacy"* (p. 262). In other words, other-efficacy is person A's beliefs about person B and vice versa. *RISE beliefs* encompass *each person's beliefs about how his or her efficacy is viewed by the other.* That is, RISE involves person A's appraisal of how the other (person B) views person A, as well as person B's appraisal of how he or she is viewed by person A.

In our opinion, there seems to be some confusion over how Lent and Lopez (2002) *conceptualized* other-efficacy and RISE beliefs and how they *operationalized* these in their research. Regarding other-efficacy, in 1991, they used the stem: "rate your confidence in your partner's abilities to . . ." to assess these beliefs. This stem is not the same as "rate your partner's confidence to . . . ," which would be more aligned with their definition. In fact, the operationalization appears to be more in line with Bandura's conceptualization of collective efficacy (i.e., rate your confidence in your team's capabilities) that we presented in chapters 2 and 4, whereas their stated definition is more in line with the collective efficacy definition used by Paskevich and colleagues (1999) (i.e., rate your team's confidence).

To illustrate how these different interpretations could lead to different ratings for *other*-efficacy, consider the following example. Dan and Mike are doubles partners in tennis. Dan may have confidence in Mike's ability, but Dan could still feel that Mike does not have confidence in himself. In this case, Dan's *other*-efficacy "ability-focused" ratings may be high, but his *other*-efficacy "confidence-focused" rating might be lower. Alternatively, Dan could feel that Mike has a lot of confidence in himself, but Dan might not have much confidence in Mike's actual ability. In this second example, Dan's *other*-efficacy "ability-focused" ratings would likely be lower than Dan's *other*-efficacy "confidence-focused" rating.

Similarly, using the Dan and Mike example for RISE beliefs, assessing Mike's RISE belief would involve having him rate how confident (or able) he thinks Dan thinks Mike is. Dan would similarly rate how confident (or able) he thinks Mike thinks Dan is. As a popular sport example from professional basketball, Michael Jordan would probably rate Phil Jackson's confidence in him as very high.

Our point is to show that athletes could respond differently when giving their *other*-efficacy and RISE belief ratings depending on whether they are instructed to rate their confidence in their partner's abilities or to rate their perceptions of their partner's efficacy or confidence. The two operational definitions also could lead to different relational behaviors. If Dan thinks that Mike is more confident than his abilities would suggest (by Dan's judgment), Dan might not wish to continue to partner with him. On the other hand, if Dan has high confidence in Mike as a tennis partner but doesn't think Mike is as confident in himself as he should be, Dan might try to bolster Mike's confidence. Thus, we believe that assessments of *other*-efficacy and RISE beliefs could take both forms, and we offer the following suggestions for stems:

- Ability-focused assessments of other-efficacy: "rate your partner's ability to . . ."
- Confidence-focused assessment of other-efficacy: "rate your partner's confidence in his/her ability to . . ."
- Ability-focused assessments of RISE beliefs: "how do you think your partner would rate your ability to . . ."
- Confidence-focused assessment of RISE beliefs: "how confident do you think your partner thinks you are?"

Researchers should examine the relationships between these forms of assessment. In their study of the coach–athlete relationship, Cilz and Short (2006) found that correlations between the "ability-focused" and "confidence-focused" measures were high, but were not perfect. That is, athletes and coaches responded differently when giving their ratings depending on whether they were instructed to rate their ability to do the task or to rate their efficacy. A review of related research in sport shows that other researchers have assessed coaches' efficacy beliefs about their team's abilities (Chase, Lirgg, & Feltz, 1997), athletes' beliefs about their coaches' efficacy (Short & Short, 2004), and athletes' beliefs about their coaches' abilities (Myers, Feltz, Maier, Wolfe, & Reckcase, 2006). Beauchamp and Whinton (2005) had equestrians assess their own self-efficacy and *their horses' abilities* (other-efficacy) prior to competition. We believe that attention must be paid to the stem that is used, and that the choice of stem should be aligned with the research question. An interesting area for future research would be to see if the sources for these beliefs differ according to the stem used.

There is considerable potential for the application of the tripartite view of efficacy beliefs in sport. We believe that studying these forms of efficacy beliefs in sport is likely to significantly advance our understanding of close relationships in the sport context. There is already evidence to show that the relationships between coaches and athletes can be extreme and powerful (Short & Short, 2005b). A couple of the more interesting relationships that often occur in sport contexts and could have important practical implications are seen when an athlete is married to his or her coach (e.g., Jackie Joyner-Kersee and Bob Kersee) or when a parent coaches or manages his or her child(ren) (e.g., Richard Williams and Serena and Venus Williams). Another appeal of the tripartite view is its direct application to the sport psychologist–athlete or sport psychologist–coach relationship.

Before ending this section on the tripartite view of relational efficacy beliefs, we would like to note a few points. First, this view is not at odds with Bandura's (1986b, 1997) efficacy theory. In fact, Lent and Lopez (2002) presented it as a complement to Bandura's theory. Although Bandura and Lent and Lopez appear to disagree in a couple of areas (i.e., Bandura views RISE as part of the verbal persuasion source, but Lent and Lopez see it as a separate but complementary mechanism), many of the sources and outcomes of the forms of efficacy for Lent and Lopez are consistent with Bandura's theory. Second, the introduction of self- and other-efficacy beliefs and RISE is not entirely new. Bandura (1986b) wrote about "interactive efficacy"—the judgments that people make of one another's capabilities and how these beliefs have facilitative or constraining effects on behavior. Bandura's research (Taylor, Bandura, Ewart, Miller, & DeBusk, 1985) was the first to show that patients' efficacy beliefs in their significant others' capabilities could have an effect on behavior (i.e., recovery from heart attacks could be facilitated by enhancing the patients' spouses' beliefs regarding the cardiac capabilities of the patient). A third point is related to the conceptual similarities between the *other*-efficacy construct and the "proxy efficacy" construct proposed by Bandura (1997).

Efficacy Dispersion and Trajectory in Teams

As we mentioned in connection with Idea 10, athletes who participate in team sports can differ in their efficacy beliefs about the team's collective capabilities. As discussed in chapters 2 and 4, researchers on collective efficacy to date have assumed that because collective efficacy is defined as a shared belief, an "adequate" level of consensus *must* be observed within teams before athlete-level beliefs can be considered a team concept (Myers & Feltz, 2007). Moritz and Watson (1998) argued, however, that to ignore the individual, within-team perceptions of collective efficacy may be misguided because this disregards interesting within-team variability that could be partitioned and explained. Consistent with this argument, DeRue and colleagues (2005) proposed that the dispersion of efficacy perceptions within the team, as well as how this dispersion changes over time, is fundamental to considering the relationship between collective efficacy and effectiveness. They argue that collective efficacy dispersion is especially important in the preparatory phase of performance, in which knowledge and skill development, learning, planning, and adaptation are essential (Bandura, 1997).

DeRue and colleagues (2005) define *dispersion* as the team-level variability in the magnitude of team efficacy perceptions within the team. Dispersion might be thought of as the inverse of consensus; and DeRue and colleagues contend that, in general, the greater the dispersion the greater the team's effort and capacity to perform in the preparatory stage because dispersion causes team members to reappraise the team's task strategies. They argue that this reappraisal process enhances cognitive (e.g., learning, adapting) and behavioral (e.g., planning, structuring, effort) processes in the team. How dispersion changes over time is conceptualized as *trajectory*. The authors present a taxonomy of various types of dispersion configurations and trajectory in collective efficacy, and then propose a model of efficacy dispersion and trajectory that articulates how variability in collective efficacy over time influences team viability and performance. Thus, keeping magnitude of collective efficacy constant, teams are classified as having no dispersion (shared), having a "lone dissenter" (minority dissent), having a bimodal distribution, or having dispersion across all members (fragmented) regarding their belief in the team's capabilities to meet their goals.

Shared consensus efficacy may be more evident in teams that have been together for some time. While DeRue and colleagues (2005) argue that shared consensus tends to hinder effort and performance in the preparatory phase because teams are not motivated to reappraise their skills, they suggest that it enhances team viability. The minority dissent profile could include a single member whose confidence in the team is lower or higher than that of the others. For instance, a team captain or the coach could represent the minority dissent and try to raise or lower the team's confidence if it is perceived as too high (complacency problem) or too low (discouragement problem).

DeRue and colleagues (2005) present the bimodal distribution as representing subgroups within the team and creating the greatest variability. Depending on why these subgroups formed, they could help team efforts or hinder them. For instance, on high school or collegiate teams, returning players might have a more realistic assessment of the team's capabilities than new players, which could help the team's efforts, planning, and adjustments. However, factions within the team can be very detrimental to a team's efforts. Sullivan and Feltz (2005) relay the story of the 1986 Oxford rowing team, whose newer rowers, from the United States, did not agree with the established training routines and tried to oust the club president. Half of the membership ended up leaving the team with just six weeks to prepare for the boat race against Cambridge. Although Oxford pulled off a historic upset victory against Cambridge in the end, the immediate effects of this faction were disastrous.

The fragmented efficacy pattern also represents the great variability among team members. This may be seen in newly formed teams or with teams that are learning a new system of play. As described previously, DeRue and colleagues (2005) posit that, in general, fragmented efficacy patterns enhance the team's efforts and capacity to perform.

In addition, the team's trajectory of dispersion can be classified as constant, emerging consensus, or growing discord. Although a team can be in a steady state of efficacy dispersion for a period of time, DeRue and colleagues suggest that its variability is likely to change at certain time points. They describe emerging consensus as a pattern of decreasing efficacy dispersion over time, whereas growing discord involves the opposite pattern. While we suggested in connection with Idea 12 that collective efficacy levels should change as a function of team development (e.g., forming, storming, norming, and performing), DeRue and colleagues suggest that collective efficacy dispersion should change also. Thus, in the forming and storming stages, one would expect greater dispersion but less trusting and bonding (we would add team cohesion), resulting in less team viability. In the norming and performing stages, as teams move toward consensus, one should see less dispersion, but greater team viability.

DeRue and colleagues (2005) developed 12 propositions based on their conceptual model of efficacy dispersion and trajectory: four main-effect propositions and eight interactions. Discussion of the interactions effects is beyond the scope of this book, but we have listed the main-effect propositions:

> Proposition 1: Dispersion in team efficacy, holding the magnitude of team efficacy constant at the team level, is positively related to team preparatory

performance as a result of more structuring, planning, learning, and adapting in the team.

Proposition 2: Dispersion in team efficacy, holding the magnitude of team efficacy constant at the team level, is negatively related to team viability as a result of less trusting and bonding in the team.

Proposition 3: Increasing the dispersion in team efficacy over time (growing discord) leads to higher team preparatory performance but lower team viability.

Proposition 4: Decreasing the dispersion in team efficacy over time (emerging consensus) leads to lower team preparatory performance but higher team viability.

These propositions offer a number of research possibilities that begin to move the study of collective efficacy beyond examination of just magnitude over time to examination of how dispersion and trajectory in collective efficacy can influence preparatory performance and team viability. Testing the propositions would require manipulations of efficacy dispersion in the lab because it would not be appropriate to create this variability with real teams in actual sport settings. If these propositions are supported in laboratory studies, then field research might start with documentation of teams and contexts that exhibit the various types of efficacy distributions. How do successful and less successful teams differ in terms of efficacy dispersion and trajectory? How do success and failure influence efficacy dispersion? In sport, what are the dependent variables in preparatory phases that are affected by efficacy dispersion? Effort is an obvious variable, but researchers might also examine coaches' ratings of team adjustments and learning during practices. To determine whether dispersion and trajectory affect task and social cohesion in the manner proposed in the four propositions for team viability could also broaden our understanding of the efficacy cohesion relationship. Finally, athletes, coaches, and sport psychologists will want to know how efficacy dispersion in the preparatory phase influences performance in the competition phase.

In summary, we have presented 22 ideas for future research and two new lines of inquiry that could be pursued in the area of interactive efficacy in terms of pairs or teams. We hope that these ideas pique the interest of our readers in launching further studies in these areas and expanding our knowledge of social cognitive theory as it relates to efficacy beliefs.

Appendix

TABLE A: *Research on the Self-Efficacy–Performance Relationship in Sport*

Statistical analyses	References
Meta-analysis	Craft et al., 2003
	Lirgg, 1991
	Moritz et al., 2000
	Woodman & Hardy, 2003
Path analysis	Escarti & Guzman, 1999
	Feltz, 1982
	Feltz, 1988a
	Feltz & Albrecht, 1986
	Feltz, Chow, & Hepler, 2006
	Feltz & Mugno, 1983
	Fitzsimmons et al., 1991
	George, 1994
	Haney & Long, 1995
	Kane et al., 1996
	Martin & Gill, 1995
	McAuley, 1985
	Theodorakis, 1995
	Theodorakis, 1996
	Zimmerman & Kitsantas, 1996
Correlation and regression	Barling & Abel, 1983
	Beauchamp, Bray, & Albinson, 2002
	Beauchamp & Whinton, 2005
	Bond, Biddle, & Ntoumanis, 2001
	Burke & Jin, 1996
	Chase, 2001
	Chase et al., 1994
	Chow & Feltz, 2006
	Cilz & Short, 2006
	Cleary & Zimmerman, 2001
	Cumming et al., 2006
	Feltz, Landers, & Raeder, 1979
	Feltz & Lirgg, 1998
	Feltz & Riessinger, 1990
	Gayton & Nickless, 1987
	Gernigon & Delloye, 2003
	Gould & Weiss, 1981
	Hardy et al., 2005
	Kavanagh & Hausfeld, 1986
	Kavussanu, Crews, & Gill, 1998
	Kitsantas & Zimmerman, 1998
	Kitsantas & Zimmerman, 2002
	LaGuardia & Labbe, 1993
	Lane, 2002

(continued)

TABLE A *(continued)*

Statistical analyses	References
Correlation and regression *(continued)*	Lee, 1982 Lee, 1988 Lerner & Locke, 1995 Martin, 2002 Martin & Gill, 1991 Martin & Gill, 1995 McAuley & Gill, 1983 McCullagh, 1987 Miller & McAuley, 1987 Moritz, 1998 Murphy & Woolfolk, 1987 Myers, Feltz, & Short, 2004 Okwumabua, 1986 Shaw, Dzewaltowski, & McElroy, 1992 Short, Apostal, et al., 2002 Slobounov, Yukelson, & O'Brien, 1997 Solomon, 2002 Starek & McCullagh, 1999 Sturm & Short, 2004 Treasure, Monson, & Lox, 1996 Vealey, 1986 Watkins, Garcia, & Turek, 1994 Weinberg, Gould, & Jackson, 1979 Weinberg, Yukelson, & Jackson, 1980 Weiss, Wiese, & Klint, 1989 Wells, Collins, & Hale, 1993 Wilkes & Summers, 1984 Woolfolk, Murphy, et al., 1985 Zimmerman & Kitsantas, 1997
Self-efficacy as an independent variable (i.e., the effect of self-efficacy on _____)	Boyce & Bingham, 1997 Eyal et al., 1995 Lohasz & Leith, 1997 Weinberg, 1985 Weinberg, Gould, & Jackson, 1979 Weinberg et al., 1981 Weinberg, Yukelson, & Jackson, 1980 Wilkes & Summers, 1984 Wise & Trunnell, 2001 Yan Lan & Gill, 1984

Self-efficacy as a dependent variable (i.e., the effect of _____ on self-efficacy beliefs as related to performance)	Manipulated efficacy beliefs using confederates
	    Eyal et al., 1995
	    Feltz & Riessinger, 1990
	    Shaw, Dzewaltowski, & McElroy, 1992
	    Weinberg, 1985
	    Weinberg, Gould, & Jackson, 1979
	    Weinberg et al., 1981
	    Weinberg, Yukelson, & Jackson, 1980

Statistical analyses	References

Self-efficacy as a dependent variable (i.e., the effect of _____ on self-efficacy beliefs as related to performance) *(continued)*	Manipulated efficacy beliefs using feedback
	    Escartí & Guzmán, 1999 (success or failure)
	    Fitzsimmons et al., 1991 (lifted more or less)
	    Gernigon & Delloye, 2003
	    Gernigon, Fleurance, & Reine, 2000
	    Grieve et al., 1994
	    Weinberg, 1985
	    Weinberg, Gould, & Jackson, 1979
	    Weinberg et al., 1981
	    Weinberg, Yukelson, & Jackson, 1980
	    Wells, Collins, & Hale, 1993
	    Yan Lan & Gill, 1984
	
	Skill level
	    Barling & Abel, 1983
	    Cleary & Zimmerman, 2001 (expertise)
	    Clifton & Gill, 1994 (cheerleaders/non)
	    Feltz & Albrecht, 1986 (divers/avoiders)
	    George, 1994 (high school/college)
	    Kitsantas & Zimmerman, 2002 (experts/non)
	    Miller, 1993
	
	Win/Loss
	    Feltz & Lirgg, 1998
	    Lane, Jones, & Stevens, 2002
	    Moritz et al., 1996
	    Treasure, Monson, & Lox, 1996
	    Vadocz, Hall, & Moritz, 1997
	
	Modeling
	    Brody, Hatfield, & Spalding, 1988
	    Carnahan, Shea, & Davis, 1990
	    Feltz, Landers, & Raeder, 1979
	    George, Feltz, & Chase, 1992
	    Gould & Weiss, 1981
	    Lirgg & Feltz, 1991
	    McAuley, 1985
	    McCullagh, 1987
	    Ram & McCullagh, 2003
	    Rushall, 1988
	    Singleton & Feltz, 1999
	    Soohoo, Takemoto, & McCullagh, 2004
	    Starek & McCullagh, 1999
	    Weiss et al., 1998
	    Winfrey & Weeks, 1993
	    Wise & Trunnell, 2001

(continued)

TABLE A *(continued)*

Statistical analyses	References

Self-efficacy as a dependent variable (i.e., the effect of _____ on self-efficacy beliefs as related to performance) *(continued)*	Attributions
	    Jourden, Bandura, & Banfield, 1991 (conception of ability)
	    Kitsantas & Zimmerman, 1998
	    Lirgg et al., 1996 (conception of ability)
	    Orbach, Singer, & Price, 1999
	    Rudisill, 1988
	    Shaw, Dzewaltowski, & McElroy, 1992
	    Solmon et al., 2003
	    Vealey, 1986
	    Zimmerman & Kitsantas, 1997
	
	Goal setting
	    Boyce & Bingham, 1997
	    Galloway, 2003
	    Hardy et al., 2005
	    Kane et al., 1996
	    Kitsantas & Zimmerman, 1998
	    Miller, 1993
	    Miller & McAuley, 1987
	    Theodorakis, 1995
	    Theodorakis, 1996
	    Zimmerman & Kitsantas, 1996
	    Zimmerman & Kitsantas, 1997
	
	Self-talk, positive thoughts, mood, momentum
	    Brown, Malouff, & Schutte, 2005
	    Cumming et al., 2006
	    Hardy et al., 2005
	    Kavanagh & Hausfeld, 1986
	    Lohasz & Leith, 1997
	    Mack & Stephens, 2000
	    Weinberg, 1985

Note: Some studies may appear more than once if they included multiple variables or statistical methodologies. All studies are described in the annotated bibliography.

TABLE B: Research on the Self-Efficacy–Imagery Relationship in Sport

Statistical analyses	References
Imagery *intervention* studies (effect of imagery on self-efficacy)	Callow, Hardy, & Hall, 2001 Cumming et al., 2006 Evans, Jones, & Mullen, 2004 Feltz & Riessinger, 1990 Garza & Feltz, 1998 Hanton & Jones, 1999 Jones et al., 2002 Kitsantas & Zimmerman, 1998 Mamassis & Doganis, 2004 Martin & Hall, 1995 McKenzie & Howe, 1997 Nordin & Cumming, 2005 Short, Bruggeman, et al., 2002 Soohoo, Takemoto, & McCullagh, 2004 Taylor & Shaw, 2002 Thelwell & Greenlees, 2003 Wilkes & Summers, 1984 Woolfolk, Murphy, et al., 1985
Self-efficacy scores used as independent variable on imagery scores	Abma et al., 2002 Mills, Munroe, & Hall, 2000 Moritz et al., 1996 Short & Short, 2005a
Correlation and regression	Beauchamp, Bray, & Albinson, 2002 Callow & Hardy, 2001 Cumming et al., 2006 Milne, Hall, & Forwell, 2005 Moritz et al., 1996 Short, Tenute, & Feltz, 2005 Vadocz, Hall, & Moritz, 1997

Note: Some studies may appear more than once if they included multiple variables or statistical methodologies. All studies are described in the annotated bibliography.

Annotated Bibliography

In this section we include descriptions of research studies in which the authors assessed or manipulated efficacy or confidence *and* used a sport sample or sport-related task. The studies involve self-efficacy, coaching efficacy, and collective efficacy, and all are cited in the text (see the brackets for chapter citations). Review articles and papers that were not empirically based have not been included. In many cases, researchers examined several variables in a single study; we focus mainly on those results related to the efficacy belief construct.

Abma, C., Fry, M., Li, Y., & Relyea, G. (2002). Differences in imagery content and imagery ability between high and low confident track and field athletes. *Journal of Applied Sport Psychology, 14,* 67-75.

The authors looked at the relationship between confidence (as assessed by the Trait Sport Confidence Inventory) and imagery. Participants were 111 track and field athletes. Using a tertile split of scores, the authors examined the differences between high- and low-sport-confident track and field athletes on imagery content and imagery ability. Profile analyses showed that the high-sport-confident athletes used all types of imagery more than the low-sport-confident athletes, and there were no differences between the groups on imagery ability. [3, appendix]

Barber, H. (1998). Examining gender differences in sources and levels of perceived competence in interscholastic coaches. *The Sport Psychologist, 12,* 237-252.

This study examined gender differences in perceptions of competence as a coach and sources of that competence. Participants included 102 female and 138 male coaches, all of whom were head coaches of high school team sports. Several significant gender differences were found. Females placed greater emphasis than males on improvement of athletes and improvement of coaching skills. Females had a greater sense of their competence in teaching sport skills than males. For females, feedback from parents, feedback from administrators, and improvement of coaching skills were highly influential sources of perceived competence. Males showed a wider variety of influential sources, including those noted by females as well as others (e.g., competitive outcome, comparison to peers). [2, 5]

Barling, J., & Abel, M. (1983). Self-efficacy beliefs and tennis performance. *Cognitive Therapy and Research, 7,* 265-272.

The authors examined the relationship between self-efficacy beliefs and tennis performance. Participants were 40 tennis players. Results showed significant correlations between a task-specific measure of self-efficacy and tennis performance (as assessed by self-report and external judges' ratings). More skillful players had higher efficacy ratings. This was one of the first studies to show the generalizability of the self-efficacy–performance relationship to a nonpathological setting. [3, appendix]

Beauchamp, M.R., Bray, S.R., & Albinson, J.G. (2002). Pre-competition imagery, self-efficacy and performance in collegiate golfers. *Journal of Sports Sciences, 20,* 697-705.

The authors administered an eight-item golf self-efficacy questionnaire and a "state" measure of imagery use (based on the Sport Imagery Questionnaire) to 36 championship varsity golfers. The performance measure was participants' scores from one round of golf. The results showed positive correlations between self-efficacy and all types of imagery except motivational general-arousal imagery (MG-A). Motivational general-mastery imagery (MG-M) predicted self-efficacy, and self-efficacy predicted performance in separate regression analyses. Results also showed that MG-M imagery use mediated the relationship between self-efficacy and performance (although the mediation analysis was reported incorrectly). [3, appendix]

Beauchamp, M.R., Bray, S.R., Eys, M.A., & Carron, A.V. (2002). Role ambiguity, role efficacy, and role performance: Multidimensional and mediational relationships within interdependent sport teams. *Group Dynamics: Theory, Research, and Practice, 6,* 229-242.

The authors investigated the correlates of role states in a highly interdependent team sport. A total of 271 rugby players reported their perceived ambiguity, efficacy, and effectiveness of identified primary offensive and defensive roles. Results showed that role ambiguity was negatively correlated with role performance and that role efficacy was a significant predictor of role effectiveness. Further, negative relationships between role ambiguity and performance were mediated by role efficacy. [7]

Beauchamp, M.R., & Whinton, L.C. (2005). Self-efficacy and other-efficacy in dyadic performance: Riding as one in equestrian eventing. *Journal of Sport and Exercise Psychology, 27,* 245-252.

The authors assessed perceptions of equestrian riders' self-efficacy (their abilities) and other-efficacy (horses' abilities) in relation to riding performance. Participants were 187 riders competing in dressage, show jumping, and cross-country events. Participants completed task-specific efficacy measures 30 min prior to their event. Performance was assessed using the standard scoring procedures. Regression analyses showed that other-efficacy was able to explain unique variation in riding performance beyond that explained by self-efficacy alone. [3, 9, appendix]

Bond, K.A., Biddle, S.J.H., & Ntoumanis, N. (2001). Self-efficacy and causal attributions in female golfers. *International Journal of Sport Psychology, 31,* 243-256.

The authors assessed level and strength of self-efficacy using a task-specific measure and performance by actual scores and feelings of satisfaction in a sample of female golfers ($n = 81$). Self-efficacy was assessed before and after a competition. The sample was divided into "success" and "failure" groups based on satisfaction scores; results showed that the self-efficacy and attribution scores were positive for the success group and negative for the failure group. Regression analysis showed that precompetition self-efficacy predicted postcompetition self-efficacy for both groups. Using self-efficacy change scores to make two groups (self-efficacy increase and self-efficacy decrease), the authors showed that the self-efficacy increase group made more stable and internal attributions, which may mean that success and failure moderate this relationship. [3, appendix]

Boyce, B.A., & Bingham, S.M. (1997). The effects of self-efficacy and goal-setting on bowling performance. *Journal of Teaching in Physical Education, 16,* 312-323.

This study was field research in which college students enrolled in bowling classes were assigned to one of three groups (assigned goals, self-set goals, and control). Based on scores from a task-specific self-efficacy measure, students were also divided into three self-efficacy groups (high, medium, and low). A $3 \times 3 \times 10$ (Goal group $\times$ Self-efficacy level $\times$ Trial) ANCOVA with repeated measures and baseline scores as the covariate showed a main effect for self-efficacy and performance. Those in the high-self-efficacy group were also more likely to achieve their goals, with the assigned goals group outdoing the self-set goals group. Self-efficacy also affected spontaneous goal setting; participants with high and medium self-efficacy levels were more likely to spontaneously set goals for themselves. [3, appendix]

Bray, S.R. (2004). Collective efficacy, group goals, and group performance of a muscular endurance task. *Small Group Research, 35,* 230-238.

The author examined the relationships among collective efficacy, group goals, and performance. Participants ($n = 111$ undergraduate students) were randomly assigned to a same-sex triad that completed a medicine ball task. Collective efficacy was measured in a task-specific manner with groups completing the questionnaire together. Between the first and second trial, all groups set a performance goal. Results showed that collective efficacy was positively correlated with performance for Trial 2 (after Trial 1 performance was controlled for) and that goals mediated this relationship (for Trial 2). [2, 4]

Bray, S.R., Brawley, L.R., & Carron, A.V. (2002). Efficacy for interdependent role functions: Evidence from the sport domain. *Small Group Research, 33,* 644-666.

The authors present the development of and support for the validation of an instrument designed to measure role efficacy within interdependent teams. Participants, 109 male and female basketball players, completed a role efficacy questionnaire that focused on their four primary offensive and defensive roles in the team. They also completed measures on self-efficacy and collective efficacy. Role efficacy and self-efficacy were positively and moderately correlated. Further, intraclass correlations supported that whereas collective efficacy perceptions were shared within the team, role efficacy perceptions were not. [4]

Bray, S.R., & Widmeyer, W.N. (2000). Athletes' perceptions of the home advantage: An investigation of perceived causal factors. *Journal of Sport Behavior, 23,* 1-10.

The authors assessed athletes' perceptions of the home advantage and examined athletes' beliefs as to what game location factors contribute to the home advantage (including athletes' perceptions of their team's collective efficacy). Female basketball players ($n = 40$) completed a questionnaire. Results showed that athletes perceived there was a home advantage and reported being more efficacious in their overall play and specific team skills when playing at home versus away. [4]

Brody, E.B., Hatfield, B.D., & Spalding, T.W. (1988). Generalization of self-efficacy to a continuum of stressors upon mastery of a high-risk sport skill. *Journal of Sport and Exercise Psychology, 10,* 32-44.

A sample of 34 participants, high in sensation-seeking behavior, was randomly assigned to either a participant-based modeling with self-directed mastery group or a control. Results showed that the modeling group increased their self-efficacy scores toward the rappel situation and that the increase was generalized to other high-risk activities but not to nonsimilar tasks (pursuit rotor or subtraction). Self-efficacy was assessed using a task-specific measure. [3, 9, appendix]

Brown, L.J., Malouff, M.J., & Schutte, N.S. (2005). The effectiveness of a self-efficacy intervention for helping adolescents cope with sport-competition loss. *Journal of Sport Behavior, 28,* 136-151.

By randomly assigning adolescent athletes who lost a competition (n = 75) to either an experimental or control group, the authors showed that a significant decline in positive affect could be prevented by having the participants focus on or image certain thoughts or images related to three sources of self-efficacy. The thoughts or images related to personal mastery, verbal encouragement, or vicarious mastery; the items "think of something you did really well during the game" and "think of winning your next game and how you felt" were the two most often selected. [3, appendix]

Burke, S.T., & Jin, P. (1996). Predicting performance from a triathlon event. *Journal of Sport Behavior, 19,* 272-287.

The authors examined the comparative strength of self-efficacy (as measured by estimations of finishing times) with other physiological and psychological variables in predicting the performance of 40 triathletes. Variables included age, body composition (skinfold), $\dot{V}O_2$max, weight, anxiety (cognitive and somatic, state and trait), self-confidence (CSAI-2), attributions, sport confidence (SSCI and TSCI), and self-efficacy (as assessed by estimations of finishing times). The dependent variable was total performance time in an Ironman triathlon event. Results showed that performance was predicted most accurately by self-efficacy, performance history, and weight. [3, appendix]

Callow, N., & Hardy, L. (2001). Types of imagery associated with sport confidence in netball players of varying skill levels. *Journal of Applied Sport Psychology, 13,* 1-17.

Data provided by 110 netballers from two skill levels (high and low) were analyzed to examine the relationship between imagery type and confidence (as measured by the State Sport Confidence Inventory). Hierarchical regression analyses showed that motivational general-mastery imagery (MG-M) and cognitive general imagery (CG) predicted confidence for the lower-skilled group, while MG-M was a negative predictor of confidence. For the highly skilled group, only motivational specific imagery (MS) predicted confidence. The authors suggested that MG-M-type images may be particularly pertinent for lower-skilled athletes because these images allow them to see themselves mastering challenging situations. The authors raised the point that different images could serve different *functions* for different athletes. [3, appendix]

Callow, N., Hardy, L., & Hall, C. (2001). The effects of a motivational general-mastery imagery intervention on the sport confidence of high-level badminton players. *Research Quarterly for Exercise and Sport, 72,* 389-400.

The authors examined the effects of a motivational general-mastery imagery (MG-M) intervention on the sport confidence of high-level junior badminton athletes (n = 4). Sport confidence data were collected weekly across 21 weeks using the State Sport Confidence Inventory (SSCI). The imagery intervention consisted of six sessions and was staggered across the participants. Participant 1 and Participant 2 reported a significant increase in sport confidence. Participant 3 experienced a significant decrease in sport confidence. Participant 4 reported a delayed increase in sport confidence. [1, 3, appendix]

Campbell, T., & Sullivan, P.J. (2005). The effect of a standardized coaching education program on the efficacy of novice coaches. *Avante, 11,* 56-68.

In many ways, this study was a replication of Malete and Feltz's (2000) study on coaching education and coaching efficacy. However, the coaching education program in question (the National Coaching Certification Program) was a larger-scale and more mandatory program than had been previously investigated. Participants, 213 novice coaches, completed the Coaching Efficacy Scale prior to and after an introductory coaching education program. There was a significant effect for having completed the course; significant increases were observed in each of the factors of coaching efficacy. There was also a significant main effect for gender; females scored higher than males on motivation and character-building efficacies. [5, 8]

Carnahan, B.J., Shea, J.B., & Davis, G.S. (1990). Motivational cue effects on bench-press performance and self-efficacy. *Journal of Sport Behavior, 13,* 240-254.

The authors examined the effects of motivational cues (i.e., verbal, visual, verbal-visual, and no cue) on bench press performance and self-efficacy using a sample of 11 male undergraduate student weightlifters. The visual cue was considered a type of participant modeling. All participants completed four performance sets in each of the four motivational cue conditions (spaced 48 hr apart). Self-efficacy was measured by having the participants rate their confidence that on the next set they would be able to do the same number of reps, or more, than they had just completed. A 4 × 3 (Motivational cue × Set) ANOVA with repeated measures on both factors was used for the self-efficacy analysis. There was a main effect only for set. The mean self-efficacy ratings collapsed over the cue conditions increased across sets. Interestingly, as the number of lifts across sets decreased, self-efficacy ratings increased. [3, appendix]

Cartoni, A.C., Minganti, C., & Zelli, A. (2005). Gender, age, and professional-level differences in the psychological correlates of fear of injury in Italian gymnasts. *Journal of Sport Behavior, 28,* 3-17.

The authors looked at the relationship among self-efficacy, anxiety, and fear of injury as a function of age, gender, and level of competition. Participants, 186 gymnasts attending summer camps, were divided into three age groups and two competition level groups. Self-efficacy was assessed using a "self-efficacy for physical abilities" questionnaire. ANOVAs (with gender, age, and competition level as fixed factors) showed that males were more efficacious than females. The negative correlations between self-efficacy and fear were stronger for females than males, older gymnasts than younger gymnasts, and regional- compared to national-level competitors. Gymnasts who were more confident had less fear. [3]

Chase, M.A. (1998). Sources of self-efficacy in physical education and sport. *Journal of Teaching in Physical Education, 18,* 76-89.

The author interviewed 24 children, divided into three age groups (8-9, 10-12, and 13-14 years) about the meaning of self-confidence and their sources of self-confidence. Results from an inductive content analysis showed that the primary sources of efficacy information for the 8- to 9-year-olds were subjective successful performances and significant others' praise and encouragement. The 10- to 12-year-olds stressed the importance of praise and encouragement from significant others such as family, coaches, and peers, in addition to practicing hard to improve on a skill. The 13- to 14-year-olds described significant others' praise and encouragement, emphasizing how the coach's evaluation was central to their confidence, followed by their self-appraisal of successful personal performances. [3]

Chase, M.A. (2001). Children's self-efficacy, motivational intentions, and attributions in physical education and sport. *Research Quarterly for Exercise and Sport, 72,* 47-54.

Children (n = 289) from grades 3, 5, and 8 were assigned to either a high- or low-efficacy group, exposed to a failure scenario, and then asked to complete questionnaires for intended effort, persistence, choice, future self-efficacy, and attributions. Results showed that the low-self-efficacy group attributed their failure to a lack of ability more than the high-self-efficacy group did. Also, children with higher self-efficacy *chose* to participate more and had higher future self-efficacy scores than those with lower self-efficacy. Correlations among persistence, effort, and self-efficacy were positive and moderate in size. [3, appendix]

Chase, M.A., Ewing, M.E., Lirgg, C.D., & George, T.R. (1994). The effects of equipment modifications on children's self-efficacy and basketball shooting performance. *Research Quarterly for Exercise and Sport, 65,* 159-168.

The authors examined the effects of basket height and ball size on self-efficacy and performance (also using age and gender as independent variables). Participants were 74 children from a recreational basketball program. A task-specific measure of self-efficacy was used. Performance (basketball shooting task) was measured using a 4-point system. Results showed that children had higher self-efficacy ratings before shooting compared to after shooting; boys had higher ratings than girls; and self-efficacy ratings were higher when participants shot at the 8 ft compared to the 10 ft basket (for both ball sizes), as well as higher with use of the smaller ball compared to the larger ball at the 10 ft basket. Correlations between self-efficacy and performance were also reported. [2, 3, 6, appendix]

Chase, M.A., Feltz, D.L., Hayashi, S.W., & Hepler, T.J. (2005). Sources of coaching efficacy: The coaches' perspective. *International Journal of Exercise and Sport Psychology, 1,* 7-25.

The authors examined sources of coaching efficacy information using structured interviews. Coaches of high school boys' basketball participated ($n = 12$). From highest to lowest frequency, coaches identified athlete development, coach's development, knowledge/preparation, leadership skills, support from athletes, and past experience as sources of efficacy information. These sources were interpreted as consistent with both the coaching efficacy model and self-efficacy theory. [5, 8]

Chase, M.A., Feltz, D.L., & Lirgg, C.D. (2003). Sources of collective and individual efficacy of collegiate athletes. *International Journal of Exercise and Sport Psychology, 1,* 180-191.

The authors examined the sources of efficacy information and patterns among sources for athletes and teams. Data were collected from women's collegiate basketball athletes ($n = 34$) prior to 12 games. Sources were coded as either past performance, persuasion, social comparison, physiological/emotional states, or "outside sources" using a deductive method of analysis. Results showed that athletes did not identify the same sources for collective efficacy as they did for self-efficacy. Social comparison was a more pertinent source of information for self-efficacy than for collective efficacy. Past performance, particularly in practice, was a pertinent source of information for both efficacies. The authors also showed that athletes often perceive a "bouncing back" or "we're due" effect after previous poor performances. [1-4]

Chase, M.A., Lirgg, C.D., & Feltz, D.L. (1997). Do coaches' efficacy expectations for their teams predict team performance? *The Sport Psychologist, 11,* 8-23.

The authors examined the relationship between coaches' efficacy expectations for their teams and ratings of opponent's ability, perceived control over outcome, perceived importance of success, and basketball performance. Four collegiate women's basketball coaches participated prior to 10 games each. Opponent ability was a statistically significant predictor of coaches' efficacy expectations. Qualitative methods identified previous game performance, practice performance, and comparison with opponent as additional sources of coaches' efficacy expectations. Coaches' efficacy expectations were a statistically significant predictor of free throw percentage and turnovers. [5, 9]

Chow, G.M., & Feltz, D.L. (2006). Exploring relationships between efficacy beliefs, perceptions of performance, and team attributions. Manuscript submitted for publication.

The authors examined the effects of self-efficacy, collective efficacy, and perceptions of team performance on team attributions. Participants were track relay athletes ($n = 71$) from 20 teams. Efficacy measures were administered prior to the competition, and causal attributions for team performance were completed following the race. A multilevel framework was employed to analyze both individual and group-level predictors of team causal ascriptions. Perceptions of team performance emerged as a significant predictor of the team locus of causality and stability dimensions. Collective efficacy was positively related to individual perceptions of team controllability. [4, appendix]

Cilz, J., & Short, S.E. (2006). The relationship between self-efficacy, other-efficacy, and relation-inferred self-efficacy with performance in soccer. Unpublished manuscript, University of North Dakota, Grand Forks.

This is the first known study to assess the relationships between self-efficacy, other-efficacy, relation-inferred self-efficacy, and performance in a sport setting. The participants were 3 head coaches and 40 athletes from three soccer teams. Efficacy measures were task specific and concordant with the performance task. Results showed high correlations between ability-focused and confidence-focused measures. There was also a significant correlation between relation-inferred self-efficacy and self-efficacy, showing that coaches' and athletes' perceptions were similar. However, efficacy beliefs did not predict performance, likely because of the difficulty of the performance task. [3, 9, appendix]

Cleary, T.J., & Zimmerman, B.J. (2001). Self-regulation differences during athletic practice by experts, nonexperts and novices. *Journal of Applied Sport Psychology, 13,* 185-206.

The researchers studied self-efficacy beliefs and performance for three groups of male high school basketball players (expert, nonexpert, and novices). Self-efficacy beliefs were assessed using an oral strategy before shooting, following success, and following misses. Other variables included age, time spent practicing, prior playing experience, free throw knowledge, satisfaction, goal setting, strategy choice, and attributions. Experts performed better than the nonexperts and novices and had higher self-efficacy scores. Results also showed that self-efficacy was related to goals, strategies, and attributions. [3, appendix]

Clifton, R.T., & Gill, D.L. (1994). Gender differences in self-confidence on a feminine-typed task. *Journal of Sport and Exercise Psychology, 16,* 150-162.

The authors administered a self-confidence and gender appropriateness questionnaire to a sample of 401 college cheerleaders and 117 noncheerleaders. Self-confidence was assessed as an overall estimate and specifically for five different cheerleading tasks. Results showed that females were more confident than males. With respect to gender appropriateness, male and female cheerleaders were aware of the stereotypes of their sport, but viewed it as more gender neutral than noncheerleaders. [3, appendix]

Corbin, C.B., Landers, D.M., Feltz, D.L., & Senior, K. (1983). Sex differences in performance estimates: Female lack of confidence vs. male boastfulness. *Research Quarterly for Exercise and Sport, 54,* 407-410.

The purpose was to determine the extent to which male boastfulness versus female lack of confidence accounted for differences in performance estimates. In this study, 30 male and 30 females were randomly assigned to either a polygraph group or no-polygraph group. Although the polygraph was operational, it was used only so that the participants would make "truthful" estimates of their expected performance on a muscular endurance task using an 11-point continuum. Results showed that males made higher performance estimates than females. The authors concluded that sex differences existed for performance estimates on a task perceived as "male" in orientation. However, the lack of a sex-by-treatment interaction showed that these were not caused by male boastfulness but could have been caused by female modesty. [3]

Corcoran, J.P., & Feltz, D.L. (1993). Evaluation of chemical health education for high school athletic coaches. *The Sport Psychologist, 1,* 298-308.

The authors examined the effectiveness of a chemical health education and coaching program. A sample of high school athletic coaches (n = 218) was divided into an experimental group (n = 113) and a control group (n = 105). Coaches who were exposed to the program were more knowledgeable about chemical health and were more confident in their ability to apply that knowledge than were coaches who did not participate in the program. [5]

Craft, L.T., Magyar, M., Becker, B.J., & Feltz, D.L. (2003). The relationship between the Competitive State Anxiety Inventory-2 and sport performance: A meta-analysis. *Journal of Sport and Exercise Psychology, 25,* 44-65.

The authors completed a meta-analysis on studies that used the CSAI-2 and athletic performance. Results from 29 studies (246 correlations) for the self-confidence and sport performance relationship produced an effect size of .25 and Beta of .36. [1-3, appendix]

Cumming, J., Nordin, S.M., Horton, R., & Reynolds, S. (2006). Examining the direction of imagery and self-talk on dart-throwing performance and self-efficacy. *The Sport Psychologist, 20,* 257-274.

The authors investigated whether a combination of facilitative imagery and self-talk would enhance the self-efficacy and performance of a dart-throwing task and whether a combination of debilitative imagery and self-talk would worsen self-efficacy and performance. Participants (n = 95) were randomly assigned to one of five experimental groups. There were no differences in baseline self-efficacy among the groups. A 5×3 (Group $\times$ Trials) ANOVA showed a main effect only for Trial (a decrease in self-efficacy from baseline to Trial 1). Additional analyses showed that imagery had no effect on self-efficacy beliefs, nor did the addition of self-talk. Significant correlations were reported for self-efficacy and performance, but not when past performance was partialled out (the authors suggested that these results showed that the participants rated their self-efficacy based on previous performance). [3, appendix]

Cunningham, G.B., Sagas, M., & Ashley, F.B. (2003). Coaching self-efficacy, desire to become a head coach, and occupational turnover intent: Gender differences between NCAA coaches of women's teams. *International Journal of Sport Psychology, 34,* 125-137.

This study focused on the construct of self-efficacy as a determining factor in the decision of male and female assistant coaches to become head coaches. Participants were 173 assistant coaches of female university teams. Variables included coaching self-efficacy, desire to be a head coach, and intended turnover, as well as several demographic factors. Male assistant coaches had significantly higher coaching efficacy and desire to become a head coach than females. Females had significantly higher occupational turnover intentions than males. [5]

Dils, A.K., & Ziatz, D.H. (2000). The application of teacher education curriculum theory to interscholastic coaching education: Learning outcomes associated with a quality interscholastic athletic program. *Physical Educator, 57,* 88-98.

The National Association for Sport and Physical Education has noted that interscholastic coaches should be familiar with the benefits and objectives of interscholastic sport. However, these benefits and objectives had not been articulated at the time of this study. Dils and Ziatz surveyed 25 experts in the field to determine their perspective on these outcomes. They found that the most highly rated learning outcomes included self-confidence, self-respect, and fitness standards. They proposed that these identified outcomes and benefits be incorporated into future coaching education research and policy. [8]

Edmonds, W.A. (2003). The role of collective efficacy in adventure racing teams. Unpublished doctoral dissertation, Florida State University, Tallahassee.

The author investigated the relationships between self-efficacy, collective efficacy, and performance in a team adventure racing task with a sample of 17 teams ranging in size from two to four members. A collective efficacy scale was designed in accordance with the suggestions of Bandura (1997) that assessed each individual's confidence in the team's ability with respect to the five performance areas of adventure racing: marathon/trekking, canoeing, mountain biking, climbing (e.g., rope skills), and orienteering/navigating. Self-efficacy was measured through individual athletes' confidence in their ability to execute the course to secure a top-place finish. Measures were taken at three separate checkpoints during the race. Team was used as the unit of analysis. Results showed a consistent and moderate relationship between collective efficacy and subsequent performance at each stage of the race. [2, 4]

Escarti, A., & Guzman, J.F. (1999). Effects of feedback on self-efficacy, performance, and choice on an athletic task. *Journal of Applied Sport Psychology, 11,* 83-96.

The authors examined the relationships among self-efficacy, performance, and task choice, as well as the mediating effect of self-efficacy in the feedback–performance and feedback–task choice relationships. The experimental paradigm consisted of three sessions, involving a hurdling task, that included giving the participants (n = 69) manipulated success or failure feedback.

Self-efficacy was assessed in a task-specific manner. Results showed that self-efficacy was modified and future performance influenced by the manipulation. Structural equation modeling confirmed a model in which feedback had direct positive effects on self-efficacy, performance, and task choice. Participants who received positive feedback had higher self-efficacy, performed the task better, and chose more difficult tasks. [3, appendix]

Evans, L., Jones, L., & Mullen, R. (2004). An imagery intervention during the competitive season with an elite rugby union player. *The Sport Psychologist, 18,* 252-271.

The authors explored the use of imagery by an elite rugby union player and examined the effects of an imagery intervention in a practical performance environment. This was a case study. The data were collected by means of interview, diaries, and questionnaire. The study was conducted over 14 weeks. As a result of the intervention, the participant reported an improvement in his ability to generate confidence prior to games. Cognitive functions of images were more related to gaining and maintaining confidence than were the motivational images. [3, appendix]

Everhart, C.B., & Chelladurai, P. (1998). Gender differences in preferences for coaching as an occupation. The role of self-efficacy, valence, and perceived barriers. *Research Quarterly for Exercise and Sport, 69,* 188-200.

This study was undertaken to add to information about the under-representation of women in coaching. A sample of male and female collegiate players completed surveys that assessed their confidence to be a coach, their perceived value of coaching, and perceptions of barriers to coaching as a profession. There were no gender differences on any of the variables. For both genders, working hours as a barrier was a significant predictor of desire to be a head coach at various levels (e.g., high school, Division 1 university, Division 2 university). Neither gender of coaches nor gender of players had any significant effects on coaching self-efficacy. Correlations showed that the higher the perceived coaching self-efficacy, the higher the desire to coach. [5]

Eyal, N., Bar-Eli, M., Tenenbaum, G., & Pie, J.S. (1995). Manipulated outcome expectations and competitive performance in motor tasks with gradually increasing difficulty. *The Sport Psychologist, 9,* 188-200.

The authors investigated the effect of generalization of self-efficacy beliefs on a continuum of motor tasks that followed the mastery of one motor task. In all, five similar tasks requiring movement precision and eye–hand (or eye–leg) coordination were used. Participants (90 males) were randomly assigned to a low-, medium-, or high-self-efficacy group (self-efficacy was manipulated using a confederate). Measures included two task-specific self-efficacy measures (before and after the manipulation and performance of the first task) and the performance scores. Results showed that the self-efficacy ratings for tasks B through E gradually differed from the rating made for task A. The generalization gradient of the medium group was higher than that for the high group; and the highest performance scores, across tasks, were achieved by participants in this medium group, with the greatest difference for the intermediate-difficulty tasks. [1, 3, appendix]

Eys, M.A., & Carron, A.V. (2001). Role ambiguity, task cohesion, and task self-efficacy. *Small Group Research, 32,* 356-373.

The authors were interested in the relationships between role ambiguity, cohesion, and task efficacy within sport teams. A sample of 79 basketball players participated in the study by completing instruments on task cohesion, task efficacy, and role ambiguity during the later part of their season. The role ambiguity measure comprised four recognized aspects of the construct (i.e., scope of responsibilities, behavior to fulfill responsibilities, evaluation of role-related performance, and consequences of not fulfilling responsibilities). Role ambiguity was found to be a significant predictor of both factors of task cohesion and both offensive and defensive task efficacy. [7]

Feltz, D.L. (1980). Teaching a high-avoidance motor task to a retarded child through participant modeling. *Education and Training of the Mentally Retarded, 15,* 152-155.

A case study design was used to investigate the effectiveness of participant modeling as a technique for teaching a mentally impaired (IQ = 54 on Slosson Test) 12-year-old male to perform a modified forward dive from a diving board. A peer with slightly higher IQ was the peer model. Thirteen intermediary steps were used over the four 30 min teaching sessions to reach the target behavior. An instructor provided physical guidance if the participant could not perform the step alone. The student retained skill proficiency at 3-week follow-up. Although self-efficacy beliefs were not possible to assess with this student, participant modeling is one of the strongest methods of enhancing self-efficacy beliefs because it operates through mastery experiences. [6]

Feltz, D.L. (1982). A path analysis of the causal elements in Bandura's theory of self-efficacy and an anxiety-based model of avoidance behavior. *Journal of Personality and Social Psychology, 42,* 764-781.

The author examined the utility of both self-efficacy theory and an anxiety-based model to predict the approach–avoidance behavior of 80 female college students on a motor performance (diving) task. Using path analysis, results provided limited support for either of the conceptual frameworks that had been posed a priori. A respecified model, in which both previous performance and self-efficacy were predictors of performance, explained more variance than did either of the two a priori models. Results supported a reciprocal or temporally recursive cause-and-effect relationship between self-efficacy and performance in which past performance had a greater influence on self-efficacy than self-efficacy had on performance. [1-3, appendix]

Feltz, D.L. (1988a). Gender differences in the causal elements of self-efficacy on a high-avoidance motor task. *Journal of Sport and Exercise Psychology, 10,* 151-166.

This study replicated Feltz's (1982) examination of the causal elements of self-efficacy theory, except that participants were 40 males and 40 females and only two dives were used. Results showed no gender differences for efficacy expectations, heart rates, past performance accomplishments, and performance behavior. Males reported lower perceptions of arousal and anxiety than females; males underestimated their changes in heart rate and females overestimated their changes. The model (tested by path analysis) fit the data better for females than for males. The reciprocal relationship between self-efficacy and performance was supported for females, but not for males. Past performance and self-efficacy were strong predictors of subsequent performance for both males and females. [1, 3, appendix]

Feltz, D.L., & Albrecht, R.R. (1986). The influence of self-efficacy on the approach/avoidance of a high-avoidance motor task. In J.H. Humphrey & L. Vander Velden (Eds.), *Psychology and sociology of sport* (pp. 3-25). New York: AMS Press.

The authors reported on two studies (Feltz, 1982: Feltz & Mugno, 1983) on the role of self-efficacy as a mediating variable in the performance of a high-avoidance diving task and followed up with additional analyses from those studies to compare "divers versus avoiders." The variables measured were heart rate, state anxiety, autonomic perception, self-efficacy, performance, and past performance accomplishments. Participants' data, categorized as either divers or avoiders, were subjected to Group-by-Trials ANOVAs with repeated measures on anxiety, self-efficacy, and heart rate. Results showed significant group main effects, trial effects, and interactions. Divers reported less anxiety, higher self-efficacy, higher increases in heart rate, and lower autonomic perceptions scores than avoiders. Anxiety decreased over trials for divers, but increased for avoiders. Self-efficacy increased over trials for divers, but decreased or stayed the same for avoiders. Heart rate decreased over trials for divers, but there were no changes for avoiders. For autonomic perceptions, divers' scores decreased while avoiders' scores increased. Using standardized efficacy and performance scores, divers were also shown to be more accurate in their efficacy judgment than avoiders. [1, 3, appendix]

Feltz, D.L., Bandura, A., Albrecht, R.R., & Corcoran, J.P. (1988, June). Perceived team efficacy in ice hockey. Paper presented at the annual meeting of the North American Society for the Psychology of Sport and Physical Activity, Knoxville, TN.

The relationships among team efficacy, player efficacy, and team performance were examined in Game 1 of a 32-game season. This study was the pilot for the Feltz and Lirgg (1998) study. Team and self-efficacy beliefs for six teams were assessed within 24 hr prior to the game. Official team performance statistics included scoring percentage, margin of win, power play percentage, and short-handed goals. Using team as the unit of analysis, results showed that team efficacy correlated with power play percentage ($r = .54$) and that player efficacy correlated with power play goals ($r = .59$) and scoring percentage ($r = .73$). The results suggest that at the beginning of the season, aggregated team efficacy is not more closely related to team performance than aggregated player efficacy. Teams' player efficacy scores were also slightly higher than their team efficacy scores. [4]

Feltz, D.L., Chase, M.A., Moritz, S.A., & Sullivan, P.J. (1999). A conceptual model of coaching efficacy: Preliminary investigation and instrument development. *Journal of Educational Psychology, 91,* 765-776.

The authors presented a conceptual model of coaching efficacy intended for high school and youth coaches. Using two independent samples of high school coaches of various sports, the authors provided evidence for the measurement of the Coaching Efficacy Scale (CES). They also provided initial support for the sources and outcomes of coaching efficacy within the model using high school male basketball coaches. Confirmatory factor analysis supported four dimensions of the CES: game strategy, motivation, teaching technique, and character building. Significant sources of coaching efficacy included a coach's past success, coaching experience, perceived player talent, and social support. Significant outcomes of coaching efficacy were coaching behavior, player satisfaction, and current success. [2, 5, 8, 9]

Feltz, D.L., Chow, G., & Hepler, T. (2006). Revisiting the Feltz (1982) dive study. *Journal of Sport and Exercise Psychology, 28,* S66.

This study reanalyzed the Feltz (1982) data set in order to compare the predictive validity of self-efficacy on performance in three different statistical models. Path analyses were conducted using (a) raw past performance, (b) residual past performance, and (c) residual past performance and residual self-efficacy. Residual past performance scores were obtained by regressing past performance on self-efficacy and entering the residual scores into the model as a statistical control. Bandura argues that residualizing past performance removes the prior contribution of self-efficacy that is embedded in past performance scores. In addition, the data were analyzed according to a new method proposed by the researchers that residualizes both past performance and self-efficacy. The researchers argued that residualizing past performance and self-efficacy is a way to avoid unfair statistical over-correction for either variable. Results from the path analyses revealed that self-efficacy was a stronger predictor of performance in the residualized past performance model and the proposed model than in the raw, unadjusted past performance model. Furthermore, the influence of past performance on future performance was weaker when the residualized and proposed methods were used. [2, 3, appendix]

Feltz, D.L., Hepler, T.J., Roman, N., & Paiement, C.A. (2006). Coaching efficacy of youth sport coaches: Extending validity evidence for the Coaching Efficacy Scale. Manuscript submitted for publication.

The sources of coaching efficacy proposed by Feltz, Chase, Moritz, and Sullivan (1999) and Chase, Feltz, Hayashi, and Hepler (2005), namely, years of coaching experience, extent of coaching education, support (parent, organizational, and player), and previous playing experience, were examined as predictors of the four dimensions of coaching efficacy with a sample ($N = 492$) of volunteer youth sport coaches. Confirmatory factor analysis of the Coaching Efficacy Scale (CES) supported the four-dimensional model of the CES with youth sport coaches. Multivariate multiple regression and canonical correlation analyses revealed that youth sport coaches who perceived greater improvement in their athletes, who perceived greater social support, and who had more experience in playing and coaching were more confident in their coaching in terms of technique and strategy. [5, 9]

Feltz, D.L., Landers, D.M., & Raeder, U. (1979). Enhancing self-efficacy in high-avoidance motor tasks: A comparison of modeling techniques. *Journal of Sport Psychology, 1,* 112-122.

The authors examined the effectiveness of participant, live, and videotaped modeling on the learning and performance of a high-avoidance motor performance task (back dive). Participants were female college students ($n = 60$). The participant-modeling treatment group performed more successful dives and had greater self-efficacy than did either the live modeling group or the taped modeling group. The live modeling group did not perform better than the taped modeling group, nor did they have greater self-efficacy. Correlations between self-efficacy and performance were significant and positive. [1, 3, 6, appendix]

Feltz, D.L., & Lirgg, C.D. (1998). Perceived team and player efficacy in hockey. *Journal of Applied Psychology, 83,* 557-564.

The relationships among team efficacy, player efficacy, and team performance were examined across a season of competition in collegiate ice hockey. The team and player efficacy beliefs of hockey players from six teams in a midwestern collegiate hockey league were assessed within 24 hr prior to 32 games and aggregated to the team level for analysis. A performance measure was obtained from a factor analysis of official game statistics to produce one usable performance measure. Consensus analyses, conducted for team and player efficacy for each game, supported the homogeneity of beliefs for both. Because of the small number of teams, the authors conducted a meta-analysis of the regression equations for each team using team and player efficacy beliefs as predictors. Results revealed the superiority of team efficacy in predicting team performance. Additionally, when team wins and losses were examined across the season, team efficacy significantly increased after a win and significantly decreased after a loss, but player efficacy was not affected. [1-4, appendix]

Feltz, D.L., & Mugno, D.A. (1983). A replication of the path analysis of the causal elements in Bandura's theory of self-efficacy and the influence of autonomic perception. *Journal of Sport Psychology, 5,* 263-277.

This study replicated and extended Feltz's 1982 path-analysis study. The authors examined the relationships between self-efficacy, performance, and perceived physiological arousal. Participants were female college students ($n = 80$). Self-efficacy and perceived physiological arousal predicted diving performance for Trial 1. After Trial 1, previous performance was the major predictor of subsequent performance. The results showed that the role of self-efficacy as a mediating variable between previous performance and subsequent performance was not as strong as the direct influence of one performance on another performance, but there was a reciprocal relationship between self-efficacy and performance. Perceived physiological arousal was a stronger predictor of self-efficacy than heart rate. When participants were attempting the dive for the first time, perceived physiological arousal was the most potent source of efficacy information, although it did not predict diving performance; instead it influenced performance through its mediating effect on self-efficacy. [1-3, appendix]

Feltz, D.L., & Riessinger, C.A. (1990). Effects on in vivo emotive imagery and performance feedback on self-efficacy and muscular endurance. *Journal of Sport and Exercise Psychology, 12,* 132-143.

The authors examined the effectiveness of in vivo emotive imagery and performance feedback on self-efficacy and competitive muscular endurance performance in a laboratory setting. Participants (n = 120) were randomly assigned to one of three conditions: mastery imagery plus feedback, feedback alone, or control. Performance was against a confederate, who always won by 10 sec. The manipulation for comparative self-efficacy was successful. For self-efficacy, a 3 × 4 (Group × Trials) MANOVA revealed a significant interaction. There was a significant increase in self-efficacy for the imagery group only, and this group gained self-efficacy after each trial. The MANOVA for performance showed a group-by-trial interaction as well. All groups decreased in performance from the first to the second trial, and the imagery group had the longest performance times. Analyses regarding the sources of efficacy showed that most participants used a form of past performance accomplishments as the basis for their beliefs. [1-3, 6, appendix]

Fitzsimmons, P.A., Landers, D.M., Thomas, J.R., & Van der Mars, H. (1991). Does self-efficacy predict performance in experienced weightlifters? *Research Quarterly for Exercise and Sport, 62,* 424-431.

In this study, 36 male weight trainers were randomly assigned to one of three treatment groups (manipulated feedback: lifted more, lifted less, and accurate feedback). One-repetition maximums and self-efficacy were assessed over six sessions. Results showed that those receiving false positive feedback increased performance more than the other groups. Correlations between self-efficacy and performance were positive and statistically significant. Path-analysis results showed that, over time, past performance was a stronger predictor of performance than was self-efficacy. [3, 6, appendix]

Fung, L. (2003). Coaching efficacy as indicators of coach education program needs. *Athletic Insight,* 5.

The author examined coaching efficacy, as measured by the Coaching Efficacy Scale, of high school coaches. Participants (n = 74) were a sample of coaches who participated in an accreditation system in Hong Kong (49 males, 25 females). Coaches reported the highest efficacy for character building and the lowest efficacy for game strategy. [5, 8]

Galloway, S. (2003). Motivation theory for elite karate athletes: A psycho-physiological approach. *Physical Training Fitness for Combatives,* 1-17. Retrieved August 20, 2005, from www.ejmas.com/pt/ptart_galloway_0703.html.

The author conducted a field study in which participants, 19 elite karate athletes, were taught to use Borg's (1988) Ratings of Perceived Exertion (RPE) Scale for their training sessions and to set goals for each training session as to which level of exertion they wished to achieve. Participants

318 Annotated Bibliography

were then classified as overachievers, underachievers, and those who met their RPE goals. Sport confidence was assessed three times (pre-, mid- and posttreatment) in a 6-week time period. A 3×3 (Group $\times$ Time) repeated-measures ANOVA showed that the athletes who consistently met their goals over a 6-week period had progressive increases in sport confidence compared to the overachievers and underachievers who started high but then decreased in their sport confidence ratings over time. [3, appendix]

Garza, D.L., & Feltz, D.L. (1998). Effects of selected mental practice techniques on performance ratings, self-efficacy, and competition confidence of competitive figure skaters. *Sport Psychologist, 12,* 1-15.

The authors examined the effectiveness of mental practice techniques (including imagery) for improving figure skating performance, self-efficacy, and self-confidence for competition. Paper freestyle drawing and walk-through on the floor and a control condition were compared. Participants were youth skaters ($n = 27$). The two mental practice groups experienced significant improvement in jumps and spins and in their self-confidence as compared to the control group. The walk-though on the floor group had greater self-efficacy than did the paper freestyle drawing group. [1-3, appendix]

Gayton, W.F., & Nickless, C.J. (1987). An investigation of the validity of the trait and state sport-confidence inventories in predicting marathon performance. *Perceptual and Motor Skills, 65,* 481-482.

The authors examined the construct validity of the State Sport Confidence Inventory and Trait-SCI by checking the ability of the scores to predict marathon performance. Participants were 42 runners (35 of whom completed the marathon). Both measures were significantly correlated with predicted and actual finishing times. [1, 3, appendix]

Gee, C., & Sullivan, P.J. (2005). The effect of different coaching education content on the efficacy of coaches. Manuscript submitted for publication.

This paper examined the effect of different coaching education courses on coaching efficacy. Although the finding that such courses increase coaching efficacy appears to be robust, it is worth noting that most coach education programs offer different courses for theoretical (i.e., pan-sports) and technical (i.e., sport specific) content. The authors found that a sample of 77 coaches who took an introductory theory course and 99 who took an introductory technical course showed a significant increase in all aspects of coaching efficacy. However, the coaches in the technical course showed a significantly higher increase in teaching technique efficacy than coaches in the theory course. [8]

George, T.R. (1994). Self-confidence and baseball performance: A causal examination of self-efficacy theory. *Journal of Sport and Exercise Psychology, 16,* 381-399.

The author examined the causal relationships of self-efficacy theory in a field setting. Participants were 53 collegiate and high school baseball players. They completed hitting self-efficacy, anxiety (CSAI-2), and effort questionnaires on 9 successive game days (waves) over 3 weeks. Hitting performance (contact percentage) was also measured. Path-analysis results showed that past performance experiences and anxiety were significant predictors of self-efficacy. Past hitting performance was positively related to self-efficacy, and anxiety was negatively related to self-efficacy. Lower levels of anxiety were associated with higher self-efficacy ratings. Results also showed self-efficacy to be the strongest and most consistent predictor of effort and a significant predictor of hitting performance. George also highlighted the point of studying contextual factors in the self-efficacy–performance relationship. [1-3, appendix]

George, T.R., Feltz, D.L., & Chase, M.A. (1992). Effects of model similarity on self-efficacy and muscular endurance: A second look. *Journal of Sport and Exercise Psychology, 14,* 237-248.

The authors examined the effect of model similarity on both motor performance and self-efficacy to determine which characteristic of a model (gender or ability) was more salient. Female college students ($n = 100$) with limited athletic experience were assigned to one of four conditions (athletic male model, athletic female model, nonathletic male model, nonathletic female model) or to a control group. Results showed that the model's ability level mattered more than the model's gender for enhancing self-efficacy and performance. Participants in the nonathletic model groups displayed more muscular endurance than those in the athletic model groups. Additionally, participants in the nonathletic model groups reported greater self-efficacy than those in the athletic model groups. [1, 3, 6, appendix]

Gernigon, C., & Delloye, J.B. (2003). Self-efficacy, casual attribution, and track athletic performance following unexpected success or failure among elite sprinters. *The Sport Psychologist, 17,* 55-76.

Using a sample of 62 national-level French sprinters, the procedure involved having the participants do a physical warm-up; complete a self-efficacy measure; run 60 m (after which they received falsified performance times according to success or failure manipulation); recover; complete an attributions questionnaire and another self-efficacy measure; and perform a second time (they then received true feedback). Results showed that in the success conditions, male and female levels of self-efficacy increased across trials; those in the success condition had higher levels of self-efficacy than those in the failure condition (whose self-efficacy decreased across trials). Results from the regression analyses showed that only stability significantly predicted feedback for both males and females, and this attribution mediated the relationship between unexpected success or failure feedback and self-efficacy for males. Personal control predicted self-efficacy beliefs for females. [3, appendix]

Gernigon, C., Fleurance, P., & Reine, B. (2000). Effects of uncontrollability and failure on the development of learned helplessness in perceptual-motor tasks. *Research Quarterly for Exercise and Sport, 71,* 44-54.

In this study, 60 high school students were randomly assigned to one of five experimental groups (contingent vs. noncontingent feedback; success vs. failure; or control). The experimental procedure consisted of four phases. In the familiarization phase, students were shown how to complete a gun-shooting task (video game). Then, in the pretreatment phase, they performed 40 shots. Compared to the failure group, the success group aimed at a larger target that moved slower. Next, a causal attributions questionnaire was completed. In the test phase, participants completed a self-efficacy measure and performed a modified shooting task (persistence measure). Participants were then debriefed. Results showed that participants in the success group performed better and had higher self-efficacy ratings than those in the failure group. Failure was associated with less persistence, and perceptions of failure provoked perceptions of learned helplessness. [3, appendix]

Gould, D., Hodge, K., Peterson, K., & Giannini, J. (1989). An exploratory examination of strategies used by elite coaches to enhance self-efficacy in athletes. *Journal of Sport and Exercise Psychology, 11,* 128-140.

The authors assessed the strategies that elite coaches use to enhance the self-efficacy of the athletes they instruct. Intercollegiate wrestling coaches ($n = 101$) indicated that they most frequently employed instruction-drilling, modeling confidence, rewarding statements, and positive talk. Most of these same strategies were also identified as the most effective. National team coaches ($n = 124$) indicated that they most frequently employed instruction-drilling, modeling confidence, positive talk, and emphasizing technique improvement while downplaying outcome. Strategies judged most effective were instruction-drilling, positive talk, modeling confidence, and rewarding statements. Few between-coach differences were observed. [1, 5]

Gould, D., & Weiss, M.R. (1981). The effects of model similarity and model talk on self-efficacy and muscular endurance. *Journal of Sport Psychology, 3,* 17-29.

The authors examined the degree to which observing a model (similar or dissimilar) who made self-verbalizations (positive, negative, and irrelevant self-talk) influenced an observer's efficacy and performance on a muscular endurance task (leg extensions). A sample of collegiate females were randomly assigned within a $2 \times 4 \times 3$ (Model Similarity $\times$ Model Talk $\times$ Trials) design. Participants who were exposed to a similar model demonstrated more muscular endurance than either those exposed to a dissimilar model or those in the control group. Results from a 2×4 (Model Similarity $\times$ Model Talk) ANOVA on self-efficacy level and strength scores showed that the similar-model group had higher levels of self-efficacy than the dissimilar-model group. Significant correlations were also reported for the self-efficacy and performance relationship. [1-3, 6, appendix]

Greenlees, I.A., Bradley, A., Holder, T., & Thelwell, R.C. (2005). The impact of opponents' non-verbal behaviour on the first impressions and outcome expectations of table tennis players. *Psychology of Sport and Exercise, 6,* 103-115.

The authors examined athletes' perceptions of a hypothetical opponent who varied on clothing (sport-specific vs. general sportswear) and body language (positive vs. negative posture and eye contact). Participants (18 male table tennis players) watched video clips of four table tennis players and then rated their perceptions of the likely outcome of a table tennis match with each of the targets they viewed (self-efficacy). They also rated the models on 10 dimensions including unconfident–confident. Results showed that participants felt less confident in their chances of defeating the models displaying positive body language. They also reported lower levels of self-efficacy when the opponents wore sport-specific clothing. [6]

Greenlees, I.A., Buscombe, R., Thelwell, R.C., Holder, T., & Rimmer, M. (2005). Perception of opponents in tennis: The impact of opponents' clothing and body language on impression formation and outcome expectations. *Journal of Sport and Exercise Psychology, 27,* 39-52.

The authors examined the impact of a tennis player's body language and clothing on the impressions made on others. Participants were 40 male, competitive, club tennis players competing at a championship. Four videos were created that varied as to positive or negative body language and general or sport-specific sportswear (a 2×2 design). Participants rated their hypothetical opponent on five dimensions, including not confident to confident, and their perceptions of the number of times they would defeat the opponent (i.e., self-efficacy). Results showed that positive body language led to favorable impressions of the opponent and lower outcome expectations. [6]

Greenlees, I.A., Graydon, J.K., & Maynard, I.A. (1999). The impact of collective efficacy beliefs on effort and persistence in a group task. *Journal of Sports Sciences, 17,* 151-158.

The researchers examined the causal relationship between collective efficacy and the effort and persistence exhibited in a group task. Collective efficacy was measured at the individual level. Twenty-two individuals were each assigned to a group of three (themselves along with two confederates) and were asked to perform on a cycle ergometer. Participants answered questions regarding their chances of winning the first prize (collective efficacy), their incentive to compete, and their perception of their teammates (confederates). Effort was measured by the individual's performance time and heart rate. Individuals high in collective efficacy exerted more effort in the pursuit of a goal whereas those in the low-efficacy condition showed a decrease in effort. [1, 2, 4]

Greenlees, I.A., Graydon, J.K., & Maynard, I.A. (2000). The impact of individual efficacy beliefs on group goal commitment. *Journal of Sports Sciences, 18,* 451-459.

The objectives were to examine the impact of collective efficacy beliefs on group goal selection and goal commitment of the members of the group. Twenty-six young males each participated and completed two time trials on a cycle ergometer in a group of three in which the two other group members were confederates. Before each trial, each participant was asked to individually set a time and finishing rank (compared to other competing teams) goal. Each participant also assessed his goal commitment with regard to his time and finishing goal. Between trials, participants were given bogus feedback about how their time in trial 1 compared to the times of the other groups in the competition and thus were assigned to either a low- or high-efficacy condition. Participants in the low collective efficacy condition significantly reduced their finishing time goals and group position goals from the first to the second trial. Participants in the high collective efficacy condition maintained their goals. [2, 4]

Greenlees, I.A., Nunn, R.L., Graydon, J.K., & Maynard, I.W. (1999). The relationship between collective efficacy and precompetitive affect in rugby players: Testing Bandura's model of collective efficacy. *Perceptual and Motor Skills, 89,* 431-440.

The authors investigated how collective efficacy beliefs influenced precompetitive anxiety. Prior to a competitive match, 66 male rugby players were asked to measure their confidence in their team's playing well in the upcoming match and to complete a measure of anxiety and a measure of affect. The results of stepwise multiple regressions did not provide great support for the relationship between collective efficacy and affective reactions. Results did show that collective efficacy predicted the intensity of cognitive anxiety and positive affect; however, collective efficacy did not predict somatic anxiety or negative affect. [2, 4]

Grieve, F.G., Whelan, J.P., Kottke, R., & Meyers, A.W. (1994). Manipulating adults' achievement goals in a sport task: Effects on cognitive, affective, and behavioral variables. *Journal of Sport Behavior, 17,* 227-245.

In this study, participants (113 psychology undergraduate students) completed measures related to sport achievement orientation, perceived ability (SSCI and other task-specific self-efficacy items), mood, attributions, and task difficulty and persistence. Participants were also randomly assigned to either mastery versus outcome goal and success and failure manipulations. Performance was assessed using a basketball shooting task. Analyses were a $2 \times 2 \times 2$ (Goal orientation $\times$ Success/Failure $\times$ Gender) ANCOVA with dispositional goal orientation and precompetition perception of ability as covariates. The results for perceived ability showed that participants who were given success feedback had higher levels of perceived ability than those who received failure feedback. [3, appendix]

Grove, J.R., & Heard, N.P. (1997). Optimism and sport confidence as correlates of slump-related coping among athletes. *The Sport Psychologist, 11,* 400-410.

This study provides some support for the relationship between self-efficacy and optimism in sport. The authors administered the Life Orientation Test, the Coping Inventory for Stressful Situations, and the Trait Sport Confidence Inventory to 213 athletes from a variety of individual and team sports. Although no correlation was reported between optimism and confidence (because different participants completed different measures), results did show that both optimism and confidence were positively correlated with the use of problem-focused coping strategies and negatively correlated with the use of emotionally oriented and avoidance-oriented coping strategies. [3]

Hall, E.G., & Erffmeyer, E.S. (1983). The effect of visuomotor behavior rehearsal with videotaped modeling on free throw accuracy of intercollegiate basketball players. *Journal of Sport Psychology, 5,* 343-346.

The authors randomly assigned a sample of 10 highly skilled female members of a collegiate basketball team to either a VMBR (videotaped modeling) condition or a progressive relaxation and visual imagery (no modeling) condition. The study ran for 2 weeks. A 2 (treatment) × 2 (test) ANCOVA was used with pretraining scores as the covariate. Results demonstrated that the VMBR group showed significant improvements in foul shooting performance. [3]

Haney, C.J., & Long, B.C. (1995). Coping effectiveness: A path analysis of self-efficacy, control, coping, and performance in sport competitions. *Journal of Applied Social Psychology, 25,* 1726-1746.

In this study, 178 student-athletes were invited to participate in a contest related to their sport (free throw and shot on goal). Manipulation checks were completed to ensure that the contest was important and challenging for the participants. Data were collected on five occasions over two rounds of competition. Ratings were given for stakes, emotions, self-efficacy, control, somatic anxiety, performance satisfaction, and coping. Results showed that older and more experienced athletes were more efficacious than younger and less experienced athletes. Path-analysis results showed that athletes with more experience felt more in control and more efficacious and used less disengagement coping, and that they performed better in round 2. Self-efficacy was a stronger predictor of performance than experience in round 1. For round 2, previous performance was a significant predictor (self-efficacy was not significantly related to second-round performance). Self-efficacy was shown to be a partial mediator of the control–performance relationship (for round 1). For round 2, coping influenced the self-efficacy and performance relationship. Self-efficacy was not related to performance satisfaction. The authors also reported negative correlations for self-efficacy and anxiety. [3, appendix]

Hanton, S., & Jones, G. (1999). The effects of a multimodal intervention program on performers: II. Training the butterflies to fly in formation. *The Sport Psychologist, 13,* 22-41.

The authors examined the effects of a multimodal intervention program on performers who perceived their precompetition anxiety to be debilitating. Participants were four male elite swimmers. A single-subject multiple-baseline across-subjects design was used. The intervention included a precompetition routine and a prerace routine that used goal setting, imagery, and self-talk. Results showed that after the intervention, the participants reported more facilitative interpretations of anxiety and greater confidence and improved their performances. [3, appendix]

Hanton, S., Mellalieu, S.D., & Hall, R. (2004). Self-confidence and anxiety interpretation: A qualitative investigation. *Psychology of Sport and Exercise, 5,* 477-495.

The authors interviewed 10 male elite athletes to determine how self-confidence levels influenced the perceived effects of precompetitive anxiety intensity, and to identify confidence management strategies used to protect symptom interpretation. Analyses of interview transcripts resulted in two conceptual frameworks showing the effects of high and low self-confidence on interpretations of competitive anxiety symptoms. Results showed that under both low- and high-self-confidence conditions, competitive anxiety intensity increased within the last hour prior to a competition. When self-confidence was low, anxiety symptoms were appraised as outside of one's control and were interpreted as debilitative to performance, reducing self-confidence levels further. On the other hand, under conditions of high self-confidence, symptoms appraised by the participants were deemed to be under control, interpreted as facilitative, and perceived to increase self-confidence. Confidence management strategies used to protect symptom interpretation were mental rehearsal, self-talk, thought stopping, and restructuring. [3]

Hardy, J., Hall, C.R., Gibbs, C., & Greenslade, C. (2005). Self-talk and gross motor skill performance: An experimental approach? *Athletic Insight.* Retrieved September 1, 2005, from www.athleticinsight.com/Vol7Iss2/SelfTalkPerformance.htm.

The authors conducted a single-blind randomly controlled experiment to investigate the effect of self-talk on sit-up performance and self-efficacy. Participants were 44 female undergraduate students assigned to either instructional self-talk, motivational self-talk, self-determined self-talk, or a control group. The manipulation check showed that these groups did not exclusively use the type of self-talks prescribed, so no between-group analyses were conducted. Self-talk was moderately and positively associated with self-efficacy, and self-talk valence had a stronger relationship to self-efficacy than directional interpretation of self-talk. Self-efficacy significantly predicted performance. [3, appendix]

Haugen, C., & Short, S.E. (2006). The relationship between coaching efficacy and coaching burnout. Manuscript submitted for publication.

The authors examined the relationship between efficacy and burnout in coaches. Participants (n = 68 high school basketball coaches) completed a modified burnout questionnaire and the Coaching Efficacy Scale. Based on a tertile split of preseason coaching efficacy scores, results from a 2 (high/low coaching efficacy) $\times$ 2 (pre–postseason) MANOVA with repeated measures showed a significant interaction. As time passed, the low-efficacy coaches exhibited higher burnout (emotional/physical exhaustion, devaluation). They also had higher scores for reduced sense of accomplishment and total burnout at both time periods compared to the high-efficacy coaches. Correlations between coaching efficacy and burnout scores were negative. [5]

Hepler, T.J., & Feltz, D.L. (2006). Self-efficacy and decision-making performance in baseball. Manuscript submitted for publication.

The authors examined the relationship between decision-making self-efficacy and decision-making performance in sport. Undergraduates ($N = 78$) performed 10 trials of a simulated baseball decision-making task. Decision speed and accuracy were used to create a performance index, which served as the dependent measure. Results showed that self-efficacy was a significant and positive predictor of decision-making performance over time, both within and between individuals, after past performance was controlled for. [3]

Heuze, J.P., Raimbault, N., & Fontayne, P. (2006). Relationships between cohesion, collective efficacy and performance in professional basketball teams: Investigating mediating effects. *Journal of Sports Sciences, 24*, 59-68.

The researchers examined the mediating effects in the relationships between group cohesion, collective efficacy, and individual performance in professional basketball teams. Participants were 154 professional male basketball players who completed the Group Environment Questionnaire (GEQ) or the QAG, the French version of the GEQ, and a 27-item collective efficacy measurement developed by one of the authors and an expert coach. Performance was measured using individual statistics provided by the professional league. Two significant mediating effects were found. Collective efficacy mediated the relationship between Group Integration-Task (GI-T) cohesion and performance, and GI-T mediated the relationship between performance and collective efficacy. [2, 4]

Highlen, P.S., & Bennett, B.B. (1983). Elite divers and wrestlers: A comparison between open- and closed-skill athletes. *Journal of Sport Psychology, 5*, 390-409.

The authors examined the differences in psychological factors associated with training and competition by groups of elite athletes from open (wrestlers) and closed skill (divers) sports. Self-confidence was assessed by a single item. Results showed that qualifiers from both sports reported greater self-confidence than nonqualifiers. [9]

Hodges, L., & Carron, A. (1992). Collective efficacy and group performance. *International Journal of Sport Psychology, 23,* 48-59.

The authors investigated group performance in female and male triads with different levels of collective efficacy in a muscular endurance task. Groups were determined via random assignment of each participant to a high- or low-efficacy group through provision of bogus feedback after a pretest session. Results showed that the high-efficacy groups improved their performance following failure whereas low-efficacy groups showed a decrease in performance after failure. No gender differences were found. [2, 4]

Holloway, J.B., Beuter, A., & Duda, J.L. (1988). Self-efficacy and training for strength in adolescent girls. *Journal of Applied Social Psychology, 18,* 699-719.

The authors examined the effects of a weight training program on the self-efficacy levels of adolescent girls (n = 59), as well as more dispositional measures of confidence and body attitudes. The study used a quasi-experimental pretest–posttest control group design, in which the independent variable was a strength training program and was compared with a fitness class or no class. Results for self-efficacy showed that the participants experienced significant improvements in self-efficacy related to weight training and other tasks. [9]

Horn, T.S. (1985). Coaches' feedback and changes in children's perceptions of their physical competence. *Journal of Educational Psychology, 77,* 174-186.

The author examined the relation between coaches' feedback and changes in self-perceptions of female athletes over a season of competition. A sample of high school coaches (n = 5) and many of the athletes whom they instructed (n = 72) participated in the study. Athletes' perceived sport competence and coaches' behaviors were statistically significant predictors of athletes' psychosocial growth. [1, 5, 6]

Jones, M.V., Mace, R.D., Bray, S.R., MacRae, A.W., & Stockbride, C. (2002). The impact of motivational imagery on the emotional state and self-efficacy levels of novice climbers. *Journal of Sport Behavior, 25,* 57-73.

The authors examined the impact of an imagery script intervention on levels of perceived stress, self-efficacy, and climbing performance. Participants were 33 female volunteers who had no previous climbing experience. They were randomly assigned to either an imagery script intervention group or a control group. The experimental group reported higher scores on measures of self-efficacy for technical climbing and climbing to the "best of ability" than did the control group. [3, appendix]

Jourden, F.J., Bandura, A., & Banfield, J.T. (1991). The impact of conceptions of ability on self regulatory factors and motor skill acquisition. *Journal of Sport and Exercise Psychology, 8,* 213-226.

The authors investigated the impact of conception of ability on the acquisition of motor skills. They manipulated conception of ability by telling participants that a pursuit rotor task either was indicative of natural ability (inherent aptitude) or was a skill that could be learned (acquirable skill). Participants were 48 undergraduate psychology students. Self-efficacy, self-evaluative reactions (satisfaction), and interest were assessed. Results showed that individuals assigned to the acquirable-skill condition demonstrated self-efficacy gains, more positive self-reactions to performance and interest in the activity, and a higher level of skill acquisition than those in the inherent-aptitude condition. [3, 6, appendix]

Kane, T.D., Marks, M.A., Zaccaro, S.J., & Blair, V. (1996). Self-efficacy, personal goals, and wrestlers' self-regulation. *Journal of Sport and Exercise Psychology, 18,* 36-48.

The authors tested a self-regulation model in competitive wrestling. Participants were high school wrestlers who attended a week-long wrestling camp. Measures included win/loss records from previous-season performance and for performance at the camp (including performance in overtime matches), camp goals, next-season goals, self-efficacy, and satisfaction with camp performance. Results from a path analysis showed that all hypothesized paths of the self-regulation model were statistically significant and in the hypothesized directions except for the direct influence of self-efficacy on performance (this relationship was mediated by personal goals). Hierarchical regression analyses showed that when only overtime performances were considered, the only significant predictor was self-efficacy. [2, 3, appendix]

Kavanagh, D.J., & Bower, G.H. (1985). Mood and self-efficacy: Impact of joy and sadness on perceived capabilities. *Cognitive Therapy and Research, 9,* 507-525.

In this study, 16 students, preselected for their hypnotic susceptibility, were hypnotized using a standard eye-closure induction. After the induction, participants entered specific mood states by imagining three situations that would put them in a happy, sad, or neutral mood (manipulation checked via assessment of mood states). While in each mood state, participants completed a questionnaire that assessed self-efficacy on a range of activities. Results showed that self-efficacy ratings were lowest when they were sad and highest when they were happy. [3]

***

Kavanagh, D., & Hausfeld, S. (1986). Physical performance and self-efficacy under happy and sad moods. *Journal of Sport Psychology, 8,* 112-123.

The authors tested the effect of mood on self-efficacy using sport-specific tasks (i.e., handgrip strength and push-ups). Results from study 1 showed that mood had no effect on self-efficacy for a handgrip strength task (n = 48 undergraduate students), but males had higher levels of self-efficacy and performed better than females. Correlations between self-efficacy and performance were high. In study 2, both a handgrip and a push-up task were used (n = 36). Again, for handgrip, there were no differences under happy and sad conditions on self-efficacy, but self-efficacy was correlated with performance in all three mood states. For push-ups, the results for self-efficacy were significant (the happy group thought they could perform more push-ups than the sad and control groups). The authors reasoned that the differences in findings could be attributed to the persistence required in the push-up task. [3, appendix]

***

Kavussanu, M., Crews, D., & Gill, D. (1998). The effects of single versus multiple measures of biofeedback on basketball free throw shooting performance. *International Journal of Sport Psychology, 29,* 132-144.

In this study 36 students (screened for basketball ability) were randomly assigned to one of three groups (multiple bidirectional biofeedback, single bidirectional biofeedback, or a control). At the pretest session, participants completed questionnaires assessing perceived control and self-efficacy and then shot free throws, generating a free throw shooting percentage score. All participants then had six 30 min biofeedback training sessions that included free throw shooting practice time. After the intervention, participants completed the shooting task and perceived control and self-efficacy measures. Results showed that all groups improved performance from pre- to posttest. Biofeedback did not influence perceived control or self-efficacy. Self-efficacy was significantly correlated with performance at pre- and posttest and was the only variable to predict performance in regression analyses. [3, appendix]

***

Kent, A., & Sullivan, P.J. (2003). Coaching efficacy as a predictor of university coaches' commitment. *International Sports Journal, 7,* 78-88.

The authors examined the relationship between coaching efficacy, as measured by the Coaching Efficacy Scale, and commitment to coaching. An international sample of 224 intercollegiate coaches (165 male, 58 female) participated. Coaching efficacy was a statistically significant predictor of both affective commitment and normative commitment. [5]

Kitsantas, A., & Zimmerman, B.J. (1998). Self-regulation of motoric learning: A strategic cycle view. *Journal of Applied Sport Psychology, 10,* 220-239.

This was the third study in a research program conducted by the same authors that examined how goal setting affects self-efficacy beliefs. The effects of performance strategies, goal setting, and self-evaluative recording on motor skill acquisition were studied using a sample of 90 high school girls. The treatment conditions were strategy (analytic or imaginal), goal (fixed or dynamic cue), or self-evaluation (present or absent). The dependent variables included self-efficacy, satisfaction, intrinsic interest, attributions, and dart throwing skill. The data for each dependent measure were analyzed with a 2 (goal setting) × 2 (self-evaluation) × 2 (strategy) ANOVA. Results for self-efficacy showed higher scores for dynamic cues versus fixed and for analytic strategy versus imaginal. In all cases, self-efficacy scores were higher when matched with self-evaluation. Correlations showed that self-efficacy predicted dart skill performance, self-satisfaction, and intrinsic interest. For the attribution data, attributions to strategy insufficiency were positively correlated with self-efficacy, and attributions to lack of ability or lack of effort were negatively correlated with self-efficacy (attributions were reverse coded). [3, 6, appendix]

Kitsantas, A., & Zimmerman, B.J. (2002). Comparing self-regulatory processes among novice, non-expert, and expert volleyball players: A microanalytic study. *Journal of Applied Sport Psychology, 14,* 91-105.

Participants were 30 women composing three groups (experts, non-experts, and novices). The procedure involved watching a videotaped demonstration of the serve; completing self-efficacy, perceived instrumentality (importance), intrinsic interest, goal-setting, and planning measures; practicing the skill for 10 min; and then being posttested on skill, strategy use, self-monitoring, self-evaluation, and self-satisfaction. Then participants were instructed to serve to a specific location (and when they missed twice they were asked about their attributions, adaptation processes, and self-efficacy), and complete a posttest for serving skill, strategy use, self-monitoring, self-evaluation, and self-satisfaction. Results showed that experts had higher self-efficacy perceptions than nonexperts and novices. The combined 12 measures of self-regulation were shown to predict 90% of the variance in serving skill performance. [3, appendix]

Kozub, S.A., & McDonnell, J.F. (2000). Exploring the relationship between cohesion and collective efficacy in rugby teams. *Journal of Sport Behavior, 23,* 120-129.

This study examined collective efficacy and group cohesion in competitive rugby teams. The authors hypothesized a significant positive relationship between collective efficacy and group cohesion. Ninety-six male rugby players, ranging in age from 19 to 51, and members of seven different competitive Rugby Union clubs answered the Group Environment Questionnaire and a seven-item collective efficacy measure based on Bandura's (1997) suggestions. The authors found a significant positive relationship between group cohesion and collective efficacy, with Group Integration Task being the strongest predictor of all four dimensions of group cohesion. [2, 4]

LaGuardia, R., & Labbe, E.E. (1993). Self-efficacy and anxiety and their relationship to training and race performance. *Perceptual and Motor Skills, 77,* 27-34.

In this study, participants (*n* = 63) completed a physical activity profile, the Physical Self-Efficacy Scale, a task-specific self-efficacy scale, and the Spielberger State-Trait Anxiety Inventory. They competed in three running events of their choice ranging from 1 mile to 10K in distance. Faster pace times for all races were correlated negatively and significantly with task-specific self-efficacy scores; that is, runners with higher self-efficacy scores had faster pace times than runners with lower efficacy scores. State anxiety scores and task-specific self-efficacy scores were also negatively correlated. Of all the variables measured, task-specific self-efficacy was also a significant predictor of pace times. The authors concluded that task-specific measures of self-efficacy were better predictors of performance than general self-efficacy measures. [3, appendix]

Lane, A.M. (2002). Relationships between performance toward accomplishment and self efficacy in amateur boxing. *Perceptual and Motor Skills, 94,* 1056.

The author examined the relationships between performance toward accomplishment and self-efficacy. The participants were 59 male amateur boxers. The self-efficacy measure was composed of ratings for winning their next contest, winning their next three contests, and achieving their season goals. Self-efficacy scores were positively associated with perceived performance. Self-efficacy was not correlated with win/loss percentage. [3, appendix]

Lane, A.M., Jones, L., & Stevens, M.J. (2002). Coping with failure: The effects of self-esteem and coping on changes in self-efficacy. *Journal of Sport Behavior, 25,* 331-345.

In this field study, the authors investigated the relationships among self-esteem, coping strategies, and changes in self-efficacy following defeat in a tennis tie-break competition. Participants were 91 tennis players. They completed the self-esteem and coping strategies measures before warming up. Then they completed the self-efficacy measure and played a tie-break. Next they completed a second self-efficacy measure and completed another tie-break. Fifty-nine athletes lost at least one tie-break and moved on to the next stage of analysis, where participants were divided into low- and high-self-esteem groups. ANOVA was used to investigate differences in self-efficacy over time by group. Results showed a significantly greater decrease in self-efficacy scores following defeat in the low-self-esteem group (23.5%), although the high-self-esteem group also experienced a decline (11.4%). The authors concluded by suggesting that interventions to reduce the debilitating effects of failure on self-efficacy should utilize specific adaptive coping strategies. [3]

Lee, C. (1982). Self-efficacy as a predictor of performance in competitive gymnastics. *Journal of Sport Psychology, 4,* 405-409.

In this study, self-efficacy beliefs were examined as a predictor of performance. Participants were 14 novice gymnasts and their coaches. Measures were obtained for previous performance, self-efficacy (in the form of estimates of performance), coach's estimates, and competition performance. Results showed that the coach's ratings were lower than the gymnasts' ratings. The gymnasts' and coach's self-efficacy ratings were correlated with competition scores. Previous performance did not correlate significantly with competition scores or self-efficacy. With respect to predicting competition performance scores, the coach's ratings were significant. Additional analyses showed that the better and more experienced gymnasts made more accurate ratings. [3, appendix]

Lee, C. (1988). The relationship between goal setting, self-efficacy, and female field hockey team performance. *International Journal of Sport Psychology, 20,* 147-161.

The author collected data from 27 different college teams representing nine sports ($n = 257$). A goal-setting measure was created with subscales representing team goals; participation and planning; coaches' support; feedback and rewards; conflict and stress; and specific, difficult goals. A subsample of only the female field hockey players ($n = 96$) was used in the next analysis that looked at task-specific self-efficacy, goal setting, and performance (as measured by teams' won/lost records). Self-efficacy was shown to be positively related to team's winning percentage. Results from regression analyses suggested that goal setting had a stronger direct relationship with winning percentage than self-efficacy, which the author concluded was support for the mediating role of goal setting in the self-efficacy–performance relationship. [3, appendix]

Lee, K.S., Malete, L., & Feltz, D.L. (2002). The strength of coaching efficacy between certified and noncertified Singapore coaches. *International Journal of Applied Sport Science, 14,* 55-67.

The authors examined the coaching efficacy, as measured by the Coaching Efficacy Scale (CES), of certified and uncertified coaches of youth sports in Singapore (female coaches = 66, male coaches = 169). The proposed oblique four-factor measurement model exhibited reasonable fit to the data. Certified coaches reported higher game strategy efficacy and technique efficacy than did uncertified coaches. Male coaches reported higher game strategy efficacy than did female coaches. [2, 5, 8]

Lerner, B.S., & Locke, E.A. (1995). The effects of goal setting, self-efficacy, competition, and personal traits on the performance of an endurance task. *Journal of Sport and Exercise Psychology, 17,* 138-152.

A random sample of 75 undergraduate students (stratified on ability) was randomly assigned to one of four experimental conditions (competitive or noncompetitive, medium or hard goals) or a "do your best" control group. During the pretest, participants completed the Sport Orientation Questionnaire (subscales for competitiveness, win, goal). Goal commitment was measured before each of three performance trials, as well as personal goal and self-efficacy. A manipulation check showed that all participants knew and did what they were supposed to be doing. Results were reported for the three trials combined. Results for self-efficacy showed that it was significantly related to personal goals, goal commitment, and performance. Regression analyses showed that personal goals and self-efficacy mediated the effect of assigned goals on performance and the personality effect on performance. Competition did not affect self-efficacy. [3, appendix]

Lichacz, F.M., & Partington, J.T. (1996). Collective efficacy and true group performance. *International Journal of Sport Psychology, 27,* 146-158.

The researchers wanted to extend the research on the collective efficacy and group performance relationship using a meaningful task for the group. A rope-pulling task was completed by 25 male undergraduate students, and perceived collective efficacy was manipulated through providing bogus feedback. Perceived collective efficacy was also varied by the use of groups that had performance histories (rowing crews and members of the same basketball team) and groups that had no experience playing together or playing team sports at all. Results showed that the group's performance was significantly affected by both collective efficacy factors, although more so by the group history factor than by the manipulation through bogus feedback. [2, 4]

Lirgg, C.D. (1991). Gender differences in self-confidence in physical activity: A meta-analysis of recent studies. *Journal of Sport and Exercise Psychology, 8,* 294-310.

This was a meta-analysis of 35 studies (46 separate effect sizes) on gender differences in self-confidence in physical activity. Studies were coded into five categories: sex type of tasks (masculine, feminine, and neutral), confidence measure (task specific, Perceived Competence Scale, Perceived Physical Ability Scale, Sport Confidence, Physical Self-Perception Profile, and Physical Estimation and Attraction Scale), age of participant (elementary, junior or senior high, college, adults, or mixed), year of study, and competitive situation. Results showed that males were more confident than females (ES = .40), that females were less confident than males on masculine tasks, and that females were not less confident than males in competitive situations. Other findings were that studies using general confidence measures produced smaller effect size differences than those that used task-specific measures, and that self-confidence differences between males and females were increasing over time. [3, 4, appendix]

Lirgg, C.D., Dibrezzo, R., & Smith, A.N. (1994). Influence of gender of coach on perceptions of basketball and coaching self-efficacy and aspirations of high school female basketball players. *Women in Sport and Physical Activity Journal, 3,* 1-14.

The authors examined the effect of coach's gender on the future coaching self-efficacy of female high school basketball players. Differences concerning the values that athletes and coaches place on basketball were also investigated. Total athlete sample size was 280, with 135 athletes coached by males and 145 coached by females. Coaching self-efficacy was not moderated by coach's gender. Coach's gender did, however, have an effect on athletes' level of aspiration to coach. Specifically, concerning coaching aspirations at the high school level, those athletes with female coaches were more likely to report a desire to become a head coach, whereas those athletes coached by males were more evenly split between head and assistant coach desires. [5]

Lirgg, C.D., & Feltz, D.L. (1991). Teacher versus peer models revisited: Effects on motor performance and self-efficacy. *Research Quarterly for Exercise and Sport, 62,* 217-224.

In this study 100 females were randomly assigned to one of five groups (skilled teacher model, skilled peer model, unskilled teacher model, unskilled peer model, and no model). The Bachman ladder task was used. Dependent variables included outcome score, form score, and self-efficacy ratings. Results showed that all groups performed better than the control group (outcome and form) and improved performance over time (across six trials). Participants who viewed a skilled model performed better and had higher self-efficacy ratings than those who watched an unskilled model. There was no model type by model skill interaction. Overall the authors concluded that the skill rather than the status of the model is important. [1-3, 6, appendix]

Lirgg, C.D., George, T.R., Chase, M.A., & Ferguson, R.H. (1996). Impact of conception of ability and sex-type of task on male and female self-efficacy. *Journal of Sport and Exercise Psychology, 18,* 426-343.

The authors examined the impact of both conception of ability and sex type of task on self-efficacy in males and females. Participants were collegiate students (male = 81, female = 79). Subjects were assigned within a $2 \times 2 \times 2$ design (Conception of ability $\times$ Gender $\times$ Sex type of task). Males were less confident than females on the female-type task (baton twirling). Females were less confident than males on the male-type task (kung fu). For females, both sex type of task and conception of ability were related to self-efficacy. Neither sex type of task nor conception of ability was related to self-efficacy for males. [3, appendix]

Lohasz, P.G., & Leith, L.M. (1997). The effect of three mental preparation strategies on the performance of a complex response time task. *International Journal of Sport Psychology, 28,* 25-34.

The authors examined the effectiveness of attentional focus, self-efficacy (operationalized as positive self-talk), and a self-determined strategy on the performance of a response time task. Participants were 45 male university varsity athletes. They underwent a three-session learning period in which they completed ten 1 min trials and a measure of pretreatment performance. Then they were randomly assigned into one of the experimental groups. Immediately following the mental preparation period, they completed another 1 min trial (for a total of three times). The only significant result from the 3×2 (Treatment $\times$ Time) ANOVA was that the self-efficacy group performed better than the attentional focus group. [3, appendix]

Mack, M.G., & Stephens, D.E. (2000). An empirical test of Taylor and Demick's multi-dimensional model of momentum in sport. *Journal of Sport Behavior, 23,* 349-363.

In this study, 125 university students participated in a simulative competitive situation involving a basketball shooting task. Measures included momentum, persistence, self-efficacy, affect, and arousal. Groups were formed on the basis of momentum classifications: positive momentum (n = 32), neutral momentum (n = 64), and negative momentum (n = 5). A momentum-by-time repeated-measures ANOVA on self-efficacy showed that the negative momentum group had significantly lower self-efficacy scores than did the neutral or positive momentum group. They also had fewer positive thoughts. In addition, the self-efficacy levels of all three momentum groups dropped from the first to the third response, reflecting the increase in task difficulty for the positive momentum group but a loss of confidence for the negative momentum group, whose shot difficulty did not change. The authors concluded that there could be an interaction between momentum and self-efficacy that was not identified using their assessment procedure. [3]

Maddalozzo, G.F., Stuart, M.E., Rose, D.J., & Cardinal, B.J. (1999). Enhancing chip shot performance in golf: Evaluation of modeled and queuing plus modeled instructional. *International Sports Journal, 9,* 66-79.

The authors examined the interaction between skill level and type of instructional strategy on the performance and learning of a sport skill. Participants were 46 beginner and intermediate golf students. They were stratified by skill level and assigned to either a SyberVision-only group or a SyberVision with verbal cues group. The design was a 2 × 2 × 5 mixed factorial. Self-efficacy was measured in a task-specific manner and was concordant with the performance measure (chip shot). Although both groups improved their form, there were no differences in performance accuracy or self-efficacy (form or accuracy). Self-efficacy scores did increase between the first day of acquisition and the final retention day for those in the SyberVision with verbal cues group. [6]

Magyar, T.M., & Feltz, D.L. (2003). The influence of dispositional and situational tendencies on adolescent girls' sport confidence sources. *Psychology of Sport and Exercise, 4,* 175-190.

The authors examined the influence of goal orientations and perceptions of motivational climate on the sources of sport confidence. Specifically, they tested whether one's dispositional goal orientation, perception of motivational climate, or a combination of the two tendencies would predict either adaptive or maladaptive sources. Participants were 180 female volleyball players (ages 12-18 years) from 27 different teams. Descriptive results showed that athletes placed more emphasis on task orientation and perceived a stronger mastery climate. The most salient sources of confidence were mastery, physical/mental preparation, and social support. A task orientation was linked with mastery and physical/mental preparation sources, while an ego orientation was associated with demonstration of ability, physical self-presentation, and situational favorableness. Perceptions of a mastery climate were positively correlated with mastery, and perceptions of a performance climate were negatively associated with coaches' leadership. Regression analyses showed that a mastery climate was a significant mediator for motivational climate in predicting social support and coach's leadership. [3, 7]

Magyar, T.M., Feltz, D.L., & Simpson, I.P. (2004). Individual and crew level determinants of collective efficacy in rowing. *Journal of Sport and Exercise Psychology, 26,* 136-153.

This study examined individual and group/boat level predictors of collective efficacy in the sport of rowing. Task self-efficacy, rowing experience, and task and ego goal orientations were hypothesized as individual level predictors of collective efficacy, while perceptions of motivational climate and boat size (double, 4, 8) were hypothesized as boat level predictors. Participants were 154 male and female adolescent rowers ages 13-18 yr. Athletes completed questionnaires to measure the variables of interest approximately 24 hours prior to a regional championship regatta. Using multilevel modeling, the researchers found that task self-efficacy significantly predicted individual perceptions of collective efficacy, whereas perceptions of a mastery climate significantly predicted boat-level collective efficacy scores. [2, 4]

Malete, L., & Feltz, D.L. (2000). The effect of a coaching education program on coaching efficacy. *The Sport Psychologist, 14,* 410-417.

The authors examined the effect of participation in a coaching education program compared to a control on coaching efficacy as measured by the Coaching Efficacy Scale (CES). The program consisted of two 6 hr sessions. Forty-six high school coaches and 14 coaching preparation students participated (experimental group = 36; control group = 24). Responses to the CES measured motivation efficacy, game strategy efficacy, technique efficacy, and character-building efficacy at pre- and posttest. Statistically significant differences between trained coaches and control group coaches were observed. [5, 8]

Mamassis, G., & Doganis, G. (2004). The effects of a mental training program on juniors pre-competitive anxiety, self-confidence, and tennis performance. *Journal of Applied Sport Psychology, 16,* 118-137.

The authors examined whether a 25-week-long mental training program that included imagery influenced athletes' somatic anxiety, self-confidence, and performance. Participants were nine elite junior tennis players. The Competitive State Anxiety Inventory-2 was used to measure self-confidence. The imagery part of the intervention consisted of participants' visualizing themselves executing their techniques and tactics perfectly, hitting all their shots with confidence, and winning all points. Results indicated that self-confidence showed the greatest difference between the groups at pre- and posttest. [3, 7, appendix]

Marback, T.L., Short, S.E., Short, M.W., & Sullivan, P.J. (2005). Coaching confidence: An exploratory investigation of sources and gender differences. *Journal of Sport Behavior, 28*(1), 18-34.

The authors examined the relationship between coaching efficacy and coaching competence (Barber, 1998). Participants were 187 coaches. Results showed some gender differences whereby males were higher in coaching confidence than females. Correlation analyses showed statistical redundancy between the coaching efficacy and coaching competence measures. Results from regression analysis showed that certain sources predicted the Coaching Efficacy Scale subscales. [5]

Martin, J.J. (2002). Training and performance self-efficacy, affect, and performance in wheelchair road racers. *The Sport Psychologist, 16,* 384-395.

In this study, 51 male wheelchair long-distance racers completed three self-efficacy measures (hierarchical performance, self-regulatory performance, and self-regulatory training), an outcome confidence measure, and the Positive and Negative Affective Schedule (PANAS). Among the self-efficacy measures, athletes' self-regulatory training efficacy scores were the lowest, followed by hierarchical performance and self-regulatory performance efficacy, although all forms of self-efficacy (including outcome confidence) were moderately to strongly associated with each other. There were also positive correlations between the self-efficacy measures and positive affect. For performance, only the correlation between outcome confidence and place was statistically significant. [3, appendix]

Martin, J.J., & Gill, D.L. (1991). The relationship among competitive orientation, sport-confidence, self-efficacy, anxiety and performance. *Journal of Sport and Exercise Psychology, 13*, 149-159.

In this study 73 male middle- and long-distance runners from high school track teams completed measures assessing competitive orientation, sport orientation, confidence (Trait and State Sport Confidence Inventories), self-efficacy, and state anxiety. Performance was measured using finishing time and place. TSCI scores accounted for 41% of the variance in SSCI scores, and TSCI was the only significant predictor of self-efficacy (19%). Goal orientation, as assessed by the Sport Orientation Questionnaire, was a significant predictor of performance self-efficacy (65%). Related to performance, self-efficacy and SSCI scores were correlated with finishing time, but only self-efficacy was a significant predictor in a regression analysis (52%). Identical results were obtained for finishing place. [3, appendix]

Martin, J.J., & Gill, D.L. (1995). The relationships of competitive orientations and self-efficacy to goal importance, thoughts, and performance in high school distance runners. *Journal of Applied Sport Psychology, 7*, 50-62.

The authors tested two expectancy-value models hypothesizing that competitive orientations, goal importance, self-efficacy, and goal thoughts would predict performance. Participants were 86 male high school distance runners. They completed the Sport Orientation Questionnaire, self-efficacy measures for time and place, and measures for goal importance and goal thoughts. The performance measure was the athletes' finishing time and place. Results showed that females were more confident than males. For both the win orientation/place model and the goal orientation/time model, there were significant path coefficients from win/goal orientation to self-efficacy, from goal importance to self-efficacy, and from self-efficacy to goal thoughts and self-efficacy to race place/time. [3, appendix]

Martin, K.A., & Hall, C.R. (1995). Using mental imagery to enhance intrinsic motivation. *Journal of Sport and Exercise Psychology, 17*, 54-69.

The authors examined the motivating functions of imagery. It was expected that participants who used mental imagery would have higher self-efficacy and greater levels of intrinsic motivation compared to a control group. Participants ($n = 39$) were randomly assigned to one of three conditions (performance plus outcome imagery, performance imagery, or control). Results for self-efficacy, based on a 3 (groups) $\times$ 6 (performance blocks) repeated-measures ANOVA, showed only a main effect for trial. Follow-up analysis on the discrepancies between self-efficacy scores and actual performance showed that the control group overestimated their abilities to a greater extent than the imagery groups. [3, appendix]

McAuley, E. (1985). Modeling and self-efficacy: A test of Bandura's model. *Journal of Sport Psychology, 7,* 283-295.

The author investigated the role of modeling (aided participant, unaided participant) as a teaching modality for motor skill acquisition and evaluated the roles of anxiety and self-efficacy as determinants of skill acquisition using a sample of 39 participants. The procedure was similar to that used in the early Feltz studies. The modeling groups had increased efficacy scores, lower anxiety, and better performances than the control group. The aided participant modeling group had higher performance scores compared to the unaided, but both performed better than the control group. Path analysis showed that the intervention had a direct effect on efficacy and an indirect effect on performance (via efficacy beliefs) and that increases in self-efficacy were associated with decreases in anxiety. The study provided support for the superiority of the self-efficacy–performance relationship compared to the anxiety-reduction–performance relationship, and showed that both self-efficacy and previous performance were predictors of performance. [1, 3, appendix]

McAuley, E., & Gill, D. (1983). Reliability and validity of the physical self-efficacy scale in a competitive sport setting. *Journal of Sport Psychology, 5,* 410-418.

The authors examined the relationship between the Physical Self-Efficacy Scale, task-specific self-efficacy measures, and performance. Participants were 52 female collegiate gymnasts from seven universities. They completed the Physical Self-Efficacy Scale and four task-specific self-efficacy measures (one each for vault, bars, balance beam, and floor exercises). Performance was assessed using official statistics from a gymnastics competition. All correlations between the task-specific self-efficacy measures and matched performance results were statistically significant. Regression analyses indicated that task-specific self-efficacy and the gymnasts' predictions of how they would perform were significant predictors of performance. [3, appendix]

McCullagh, P. (1987). Model similarity effects on motor performance. *Journal of Sport Psychology, 9,* 249-260.

The author recruited undergraduate females ($n = 75$) to participate in a study on the effects of model similarity and cueing on Bachman ladder performance. Participants were randomly assigned to each treatment condition, and measures were taken for perceived similarity to the model and level and strength of self-efficacy. Results for self-efficacy showed no group differences. The correlations between self-efficacy and performance for each group ranged from –.15 to .35 for level and from –.09 to .36 for strength. These low correlations were attributed to the discrepancies between what the participants thought they could do and what they actually did. [3, appendix]

McKenzie, A.D., & Howe, B. (1997). The effect of imagery on self-efficacy for a motor skill. *International Journal of Sport Psychology, 28,* 196-210.

The authors assessed the effect of an imagery training program on self-efficacy and performance for an indoor archery task. A multiple-baseline across-subjects design was used. Six participants completed 15 sessions. Results showed that the imagery intervention enhanced self-efficacy for two of the participants, did not affect self-efficacy for two, and decreased self-efficacy for two (likely because of the auditory feedback of missing the target). The author concluded that an imagery intervention works best on those who have imagery abilities, have previous task and intervention experience, and believe in the performance-enhancing capabilities of imagery. [3, appendix]

Mellalieu, S.D., Neil, R., & Hanton, S. (2006). Self-confidence as a mediator of the relationship between competitive anxiety intensity and interpretation. *Research Quarterly for Exercise and Sport, 77,* 263-270.

In this study, the authors tested whether self-confidence would mediate the relationships between worry intensity and direction, as well as somatic anxiety intensity and direction. Participants were 102 elite and 144 nonelite athletes from various sports. They completed the self-confidence subscale of the Competitive State Anxiety Inventory-2 (revised to assess trait anxiety) and the worry and somatic subscales from the Sport Anxiety Scale with the added direction component. For elite athletes, self-confidence mediated the relationship between worry intensity and direction. For nonelite athletes, self-confidence was a partial mediator of the worry intensity and direction relationship and for the somatic anxiety intensity and direction relationship. The results corroborate other findings by showing that confidence management strategies can protect against debilitating interpretations of anxiety. [3]

Miller, J.T., & McAuley, E. (1987). Effects of a goal-setting training program on basketball free-throw self-efficacy and performance. *The Sport Psychologist, 1,* 103-113.

In this study, 18 undergraduate students from a beginning basketball class were instructed in free throw shooting, matched by ability, and then randomly assigned to either a goal training or no-goal-training treatment condition. Performance was assessed every week for 5 weeks. Results from an ANCOVA using initial self-efficacy differences as the covariate showed that the goal training group had higher self-efficacy at the end of the study than the no-goal-training group. The treatment did not affect performance scores. The correlation between self-efficacy and performance was greater for the goal training group. [3]

Miller, M. (1993). Efficacy strength and performance in competitive swimmers of different skill levels. *International Journal of Sport Psychology, 24*, 284-296.

The author examined the relationship between efficacy strength and swimming performance while controlling for the influence of motivation. Participants (n = 84) were assigned to a low-, moderate-, or high-skill group. Within these groups, participants were assigned to either a low-efficacy or a high-efficacy condition based on goal times (those in the low-efficacy condition were assigned goal times that were faster than their best performance time; those in the high-efficacy condition were assigned times that were slower). Results from a 3 × 2 (Skill × Efficacy) ANCOVA with motivation as the covariate showed that for all skill levels, participants with low efficacy had poorer performances than those with high efficacy. Overall, efficacy was correlated with motivation. However, for the low-skill group, for both levels, the correlation was positive whereas for the high-efficacy skill groups the correlation was negative. [1, 3, appendix]

Mills, K.D., Munroe, K.J., & Hall, C.R. (2000). The relationship between imagery and self-efficacy in competitive athletics. *Imagination, Cognition, and Personality, 20*, 33-39.

The authors examined the relationship between self-efficacy and imagery use in training and competitive settings. Participants were 50 collegiate athletes from various individual sports (rowing, wrestling, track and field). They were divided into two groups, high and low in self-efficacy, based on a median split. Self-efficacy was measured for training/practice and competition. Results showed that the high-self-efficacy group (for the competition measure) used more Motivation Specific, Motivation General-Mastery, and Motivation General-Arousal imagery than the low-self-efficacy group. There were no differences for practice self-efficacy. [3, appendix]

Milne, M., Hall, C., & Forwell, L. (2005). Self-efficacy, imagery use, and adherence to rehabilitation by injured athletes. *Journal of Sport Rehabilitation, 14*, 150-167.

In study 1, 237 participants with various athletic injuries completed the Athletic Injury Self-Efficacy Questionnaire (AISEQ: based on task, barrier, and scheduling/coping types of efficacy). A CFA confirmed a two-factor (task and coping) structure. In study 2, the relationships among the AISEQ, imagery, and adherence to rehab were explored. Participants were 270 athletes with various injuries. With respect to self-efficacy, injured athletes reported higher levels of task self-efficacy than of coping self-efficacy. Results from regression analyses showed that only cognitive imagery significantly predicted task self-efficacy (imagery did not predict coping self-efficacy). For the measures of adherence, task self-efficacy predicted quality; coping self-efficacy predicted frequency; and both predicted exercise duration. Other analyses showed that those who had had three or more injuries were more confident about performing their rehab exercises than those who had been injured for the first time. There were no differences on self-efficacy for gender, competitive level, or the length of time athletes had been in rehabilitation. [3, 6, appendix]

Moritz, S.E. (1998). The effect of task type on the relationship between efficacy beliefs and performance. Unpublished manuscript, Michigan State University, East Lansing.

The author examined the effect of task type (additive vs. interdependent) on the self-efficacy–performance and collective efficacy–performance relationships using a bowling task. Participants were 250 students enrolled in bowling classes. Task type moderated the relationship between collective efficacy and performance: Collective efficacy was a significant predictor of performance in the interdependent condition but not in the additive condition for both the individual and team levels of analyses. Task type did not moderate the relationship between self-efficacy and performance at either level of analysis. Results also showed that perceptions of efficacy were positively correlated with participants' responses to an item that assessed the amount of effort they perceived they put into a bowling tournament. [2-4, appendix]

Moritz, S.E., Feltz, D.L., Fahrbach, K., & Mack, D. (2000). The relation of self-efficacy measures to sport performance: A meta-analytic review. *Research Quarterly for Exercise and Sport, 71*, 280-294.

This meta-analysis of 45 studies (102 correlations) showed the average correlation between self-efficacy and individual performance in sport to be .38. Moderators considered were the type of self-efficacy measures, the type of performance measures, the concordance between the self-efficacy and performance measures, the nature of the task, and the time of assessments. [1-4, appendix]

Moritz, S.E., Hall, C.R., Martin, K.A., & Vadocz, E. (1996). What are confident athletes imaging? An examination of image content. *The Sport Psychologist, 10,* 171-179.

The authors compared the imagery content used by high- and low-self-confident athletes (based on a tertile split of State Sport Confidence Inventory scores). Results showed that high-sport-confident athletes used more motivational imagery than their low-sport-confident counterparts. Motivation General–Mastery imagery was shown to be the type most associated with sport confidence (via regression). The authors concluded that when it comes to building confidence, imaging sport-related mastery experiences and emotions is better than imaging specific sport skills. Results also showed that the more successful athletes were more confident. [3, appendix]

Murphy, S.M., & Woolfolk, R.L. (1987). The effect of cognitive interventions on competitive anxiety and performance on a fine motor skill accuracy task. *International Journal of Sport Psychology, 18,* 152-166.

The authors tested part of the Oxendine hypothesis that predicts degradation of fine muscle coordination by arousal. Participants were 61 undergraduate students, screened for anxiety levels (low, moderate, high). Participants were then randomly assigned to a treatment condition: cognitive behavioral stress reduction, psyching up, or control. Participants completed a putting task and measures for self-efficacy, tension, and anxiety. Related to self-efficacy, the results showed that the correlations for self-efficacy and performance varied (.17 and .29), but using the posttest measures with pretest performance partialled out, the correlation was not statistically significant (0.06). The authors also noted that previous performance was a better predictor of posttest performance than was self-efficacy. [3, appendix]

Myers, N.D., Feltz, D.L., & Short, S.E. (2004). Collective efficacy and team performance: A longitudinal study of collegiate football teams. *Group Dynamics: Theory, Research and Practice, 8,* 126-138.

The authors examined the collective efficacy and team performance relationship in collegiate football teams. Participants, 197 offensive football players from 10 different university teams, completed self- and collective efficacy measures within 24 hr prior to each Saturday afternoon game. Results suggested that aggregated collective efficacy prior to performance positively influences subsequent offensive performance, and that previous offensive performance negatively influences subsequent aggregated collective efficacy within teams and across games. Self-efficacy was not a similar predictor.

Within weeks and across teams, aggregated collective efficacy prior to performance also was a positive predictor of subsequent offensive performance, and previous offensive performance was a positive predictor of subsequent aggregated collective efficacy. Consistent with Feltz and Lirgg (1998) and as hypothesized, aggregated collective efficacy appeared to positively influence offensive performance within teams and across games whereas aggregated self-efficacy did not. [1-4, appendix]

Myers, N.D., Feltz, D.L., & Wolfe, E.W. (2006). A confirmatory study of rating scale category effectiveness for the Coaching Efficacy Scale. Manuscript submitted for publication.

This study tested the validity of a version of the Coaching Efficacy Scale (CES) that utilized a five-category response structure in place of the original 10-category structure. Previous research provided evidence, with post hoc analyses of data from high school and college coaches, for the effectiveness of a reduced number of rating scale categories (Myers, Wolfe, & Feltz, 2005). Data from youth sport coaches ($N = 492$) that had been collected as part of a previous study (Feltz, Hepler, Roman, & Paiement, 2006) were used to test the effectiveness of the five-category-structure questionnaire (i.e., 1, No confidence; 2, Low confidence; 3, Moderate confidence; 4, High confidence; 5, Complete confidence) and a four-category post hoc structure that merged categories 1 and 2. Using effectiveness guidelines for evaluating rating scale categories, results supported both the five-category and four-category structures. However, the authors suggested that the four-category structure is preferable when the CES is used to measure coaching efficacy for youth, high school, and collegiate coaches. [2]

Myers, N.D., Payment, C., & Feltz, D.L. (2004). Reciprocal relationships between collective efficacy and team performance in women's ice hockey. *Group Dynamics: Theory, Research, and Practice, 8,* 182-195.

The authors examined the reciprocal relationship between collective efficacy and team performance in women's ice hockey. Collective efficacy beliefs and performance measures were taken from teams in situations in which opponents were the same over two consecutive games (Friday and Saturday). The results supported the author's hypothesis that the level of collective efficacy would moderately and positively influence the team's performance for that same-day performance when the previous day's performance was controlled for. Results also supported the hypothesis that previous day's performance would have a small and positive influence on the next day's collective efficacy scores. [1, 4]

Myers, N.D., Paiement, C.A., & Feltz, D.L. (2007). Regressing team performance on collective efficacy: Considerations of temporal proximity and concordance. *Measurement in Physical Education and Exercise Science, 11*, 1-24.

This study used some of the same data collected in the Myers, Payment, and Feltz (2004) study to determine whether collective efficacy was a stronger predictor of performance after the first, second, or third periods of play across a season of women's collegiate ice hockey. Collective efficacy beliefs of players from 12 teams (Division III = 7; Division I = 5) were assessed within 24 hr prior to Friday's game and Saturday's game across 7 weekends. Performance measures were obtained from a college hockey statistics Web site and were cumulative across the three time periods. Because of dependency issues, data were split into Friday's and Saturday's measures and subjected to hierarchical linear modeling. Results showed that collective efficacy was a significant predictor of team performance at all three of the performance intervals for both Friday's and Saturday's analyses. Further, the magnitude of the relationship did not differ among the cumulative time periods. Thus, preperformance assessments of collective efficacy may remain resilient over the ups and downs of performance within a competition. [4]

Myers, N.D., Vargas-Tonsing, T.M., & Feltz, D.L. (2005). Coaching efficacy in intercollegiate coaches: Sources, coaching behavior, and team variables. *Psychology of Sport and Exercise, 6,* 129-143.

The authors examined the influence of (a) sources of efficacy on dimensions of coaching efficacy and (b) coaching efficacy on team variables. Data were collected at two time points: near the beginning (head coaches = 135) and at three-fourths of the way through a season of competition (head coaches = 101, athletes = 1618). Social support was a stronger source of efficacy information for female coaches than for male coaches. Total coaching efficacy predicted reported coaching behavior, team satisfaction, and winning percentage for men's teams. Total coaching efficacy predicted only reported coaching behavior across women's teams. Within women's teams, coach's gender moderated the relationship between character-building efficacy and team satisfaction. Character-building efficacy was negatively related to team satisfaction in women's teams with male coaches. Motivation efficacy was positively related to team satisfaction in women's teams with female coaches. [5]

Myers, N.D., Wolfe, E.W., & Feltz, D.L. (2005). An evaluation of the psychometric properties of the coaching efficacy scale for American coaches. *Measurement in Physical Education and Exercise Science, 9,* 135-160.

This study evaluated the psychometric properties of the Coaching Efficacy Scale (CES; Feltz, Chase, Moritz, & Sullivan, 1999) using previously collected data from high school and college coaches and fitting the data to a multidimensional item response model. Results offered supporting evidence for the validity of the CES based on (a) the fit of a multidimensional conceptualization of the four dimensions of coaching efficacy, (b) the fit of the majority of items to the measurement model, (c) the internal consistency of CES estimates, and (d) the precision of unidimensional CES estimates. The authors found some problems with the rating scale structure (too many categories), precision of multidimensional CES estimates, and differential item functioning for different coaching levels and genders. [2]

Nordin, S.M., & Cumming, J. (2005). More than meets the eye: Investigating imagery type, direction, and outcome. *The Sport Psychologist, 19,* 1-17.

The authors examined the influence of imagery direction on self-efficacy and performance of a motor task (dart throwing). Participants (n = 75) were randomly assigned to either a facilitative imagery, debilitative imagery, or control group. Results for self-efficacy showed that the debilitative group had lower ratings than the facilitative group (and performed worse). Self-efficacy ratings were constant across trials for the facilitative group but decreased for the debilitative and control groups. For imagery type, Cognitive Specific and Motivational General-Mastery imagery did not relate differently to efficacy ratings. [3, appendix]

Okwumabua, T.M. (1986). Psychological and physical contributions to marathon performance: An exploratory investigation. *Journal of Sport Behavior, 8,* 163-171.

In this study, 82 marathon runners completed pre- and postrace questionnaires that included a self-efficacy measure. Results showed that self-efficacy level and strength scores were positively correlated with the number of training runs per week, weekly training mileage, and longest training run (and weekly training runs for strength). Both level and strength of self-efficacy were negatively correlated with best time, marathon goal times, and marathon finishing time. Self-efficacy was also a significant predictor of marathon finishing time. [3, appendix]

Orbach, I., Singer, R.N., & Price, S. (1999). An attribution training program and achievement in sport. *The Sport Psychologist, 13,* 69-82.

The authors examined the influence of an attribution training program on assessment of perceptions regarding performance, expectations for future success, and affective reactions to performance. Tennis players (n = 35) were randomly assigned to one of the three causal dimension orientation groups (controllable and unstable, uncontrollable and stable, and nonattributional). The study was conducted over four sessions. Expectancies were analyzed using a 3 (groups) × 11 (times) MANOVA with repeated measures. Results showed that players who were instructed to attribute their failures to controllable and unstable causes expected to perform better (or had higher self-efficacy) than the other groups. [3, 6, appendix]

Paskevich, D.M., Brawley, L.R., Dorsch, K.D., & Widmeyer, W.N. (1999). Relationship between collective efficacy and team cohesion: Conceptual and measurement issues. *Group Dynamics: Theory, Research, and Practice, 3,* 210-222.

The authors developed a collective efficacy measure for volleyball and examined the relationships between cohesion and collective efficacy in a sample of 70 volleyball players. They developed items for the collective efficacy questionnaire by searching through past collective efficacy research and then consulting with expert volleyball coaches and former elite players. Items covered key collective skills that volleyball athletes would be aware of and would consider important. The task-related aspects of group cohesion were strongly correlated with team members' shared beliefs about collective efficacy. Athletes perceiving high cohesion tended to be individuals who also viewed their team as higher in collective efficacy for various group-related skills. These findings indicate that relationships between collective efficacy and cohesion are reflective of a correspondence between selective aspects of both measures. [2, 4, 9]

Pellett, T.L., & Lox, C.L. (1998). Tennis racket head-size comparisons and their effect on beginning college players' achievement and self-efficacy. *Journal of Teaching in Physical Education, 17,* 453-467.

The authors examined the effects of different-sized tennis racket heads on skills, playing achievement, self-efficacy, and emotional well-being. Participants (n = 35 students in beginning tennis classes) were randomly assigned to one of the two racket head-size groups. Pre- and posttests were conducted during the 13-day unit. Self-efficacy was measured in a task-specific format. Results from a 2 × 2 (Group × Time) repeated-measures ANOVA for forehand and backhand self-efficacy were not statistically significant (ps = .08, .14). Effect sizes demonstrated moderate to large improvements in self-efficacy for participants using the larger racket head and smaller improvements for those using the smaller head. [6]

Prapavessis, H., & Grove, J.R. (1994). Personality variables as antecedents of precompetitive mood state temporal patterning. *International Journal of Sport Psychology, 22,* 347-365.

The authors examined personality mediators of precompetitive mood state temporal patterning among competitive rifle shooters (n = 106). Participants completed measures for sport confidence, neuroticism-stability subscale, optimism, self-handicapping, and hardiness a week prior to a national championship. Mood was assessed 48 hr, 24 hr, 12 hr, and 15 min before competition. Results showed that the high trait sport confidence group demonstrated more vigor and esteem-related affect, as well as less tension and confusion, than the low trait sport confidence group prior to competition. For total mood disturbance scores, the high trait sport confidence group exhibited less precompetitive mood disturbance than their lower-scoring counterparts. Confidence was a significant predictor of confusion, vigor, esteem-related affect, and total mood disturbance. [3]

Quinn, A.M., & Fallon, B.J. (2000). Predictors of recovery time. *Journal of Sport Rehabilitation, 9*, 62-76.

The authors explored the predictors of recovery time in 136 elite injured athletes. Participants completed a comprehensive sports injury survey that included measures for confidence (State Sport Confidence Inventory) and self-efficacy four times during the recovery process. Regression analyses showed that more confidence aided a quicker recovery; confidence in reaching full recovery in the estimated time was an important predictor at partial recovery; and confidence was the most important predictor at recovery. [6]

Ram, N., & McCullagh, P. (2003). Self-modeling: Influence on psychological responses and physical performance. *The Sport Psychologist, 17*, 220-241.

The authors tested the effectiveness of a modeling intervention on performance and self-efficacy. A multiple-baseline single-subject experimental design was used. Participants were five volunteers from an intermediate volleyball class. On 12 test days, participants performed overhand volleyball serves and completed self-efficacy measures. The modeling intervention consisted of a self-modeling video plus a "think-aloud" protocol. Results from a visual analysis of the data showed no changes in self-efficacy when the intervention was introduced, due to variability in baseline measures. One participant showed a definite increase in self-efficacy, however. [3, appendix]

Reuter, J.M., & Short, S.E. (2005). The relationships among three components of perceived risk of injury, previous injuries and gender in non-contact/limited contact sport athletes. *Athletic Insight, 7*. Retrieved September 1, 2005, from www.athleticinsight.com/Vol7Iss1/PerceivedRiskofInjuryNoContact.htm.

The authors examined the relationship among male and female collegiate athletes' perceptions of risk of injury, confidence in avoiding injury, and fear of injury in noncontact and limited-contact sports. Participants were 154 athletes from swimming/diving, track and field, and baseball/fast pitch. Results pertaining to confidence in avoiding injury showed that it had a negative relationship with fear of injury and probability of injury. Participants who had had more than one injury in the past year reported less confidence in avoiding injury than those who had had only a single injury in the same 12-month time period. [3]

Rudisill, M.E. (1988). The influence of causal dimension orientations and perceived competence on adult's expectations, persistence, performance and the selection of causal dimensions. *International Journal of Sport Psychology, 19,* 184-198.

In this study, 90 students, screened for perceived competence (high, average, and low), were randomly assigned to one of three causal dimension groups (internal, controllable, and unstable; internal, uncontrollable, and stable; or a nondimensional orientation). Measures included expectancy ratings, performance, and persistence scores (on a balance task). Results showed that internal, uncontrollable, stable attributions negatively influenced expectations while internal, controllable, and unstable attributions increased expectations for success. The author concluded that attribution retraining programs are more effective in increasing expectancies for success for people with high perceived competence compared to low perceived competence. [3, 6, appendix]

Rushall, B.S. (1988). Covert modeling as a procedure for altering an elite athlete's psychological state. *The Sport Psychologist, 2,* 131-140.

The author employed covert modeling (a procedure where a participant first imagines a fictional model performing successfully and then imagines himself performing successfully) to alter an athlete's loss of confidence. Results showed that it was an effective strategy in raising the self-efficacy level of a wrestler using a case study design. [3, appendix]

Ryska, T.A. (2002). Predicting prosocial intentions among young athletes: The mediating role of negative mood and comparative efficacy. *International Sports Journal, 6,* 14-30.

The author conducted a field-based test of the interaction between self-focused negative affect and competitive self-efficacy on the prosocial intentions of adolescent athletes. He hypothesized that competitive self-efficacy would mediate the detrimental effect of negative mood on prosocial intentions within competition. Participants were 206 junior tennis players. Measures included a modified version of the State Sport Confidence Inventory for self-efficacy, the Positive and Negative Affective Schedule for mood, and the Multidimensional Sportspersonship Orientations scale (MSO-25) for intentions to engage in prosocial behaviors. Results showed that tennis players experiencing negative affect prior to competition reported significantly lower prosocial intentions when they felt less efficacious compared to their opponent. Precompetitive negative mood had less of an adverse effect on prosocial intentions for those participants who were relatively high in competitive self-efficacy. [3]

Sanguinetti, C., Lee, A.M., & Nelson, J. (1985). Reliability estimates and age and gender comparisons of expectations of success in sex-typed activities. *Journal of Sport Psychology, 7,* 379-388.

In this study, a random sample of 90 male and female participants from three age groups (6-8, 11-13, and 17-21 years) rated how they would expect to perform if they were instructed in three tasks (football, ballet, and swimming). Ratings were made three times over a 2-week period. Data were analyzed using a 2 (gender) $\times$ 3 (age) $\times$ 3 (task) $\times$ 3 (time) repeated-measures ANOVA. Results showed that age and sex typing of the tasks affected the performance ratings. Younger children had higher mean expectancy scores and the sex-type of the task. Males had a higher expectation for success on the masculine task while females had a higher expectation for success on the feminine task. There were no differences for the neutral task. [3]

Schultz, R.M., & Short, S.E. (2006). Who do athletes compare to?: How the standard of comparison affects confidence ratings. *AAASP Conference Proceedings,* 82-83.

The authors examined how the selection of the "standard of comparison" used when people complete the Trait Sport Confidence Inventory affects confidence ratings. Participants were 190 high school and college-age athletes. Results showed that male athletes had higher scores than female athletes and that college athletes had higher scores than high school athletes. All athletes compared themselves to someone who played at or above their level, except for college females, who sometimes compared themselves to high school athletes. In general, the higher the comparison athlete, the lower the confidence score. [6]

Shaw, J.M., Dzewaltowski, D.A., & McElroy, M. (1992). Self-efficacy and causal attributions as mediators of perceptions of psychological momentum. *Journal of Sport and Exercise Psychology, 14,* 134-147.

The authors examined whether the behavioral patterns of success followed by success and failure followed by failure elicited changes in perceptions of psychological momentum and the mediating role that self-efficacy and causal attributions had on this relationship. Participants were 60 undergraduate students, randomly assigned to either a repeated success or repeated failure condition. Measures of momentum, self-efficacy, causal dimensions, and performance were taken in association with a free throw shooting competition. Self-efficacy changed over time in response to success but not failure. There were no significant relationships between momentum and self-efficacy for the success group, but these variables were negatively correlated with each other for the failure group. Self-efficacy was not consistently related to attributions, although there were a few significant findings in this area. For example, failure did not lower self-efficacy beliefs when unstable attributions were made. [3, appendix]

Short, S.E. (2006b). The effect of team size, type of sport, time of season and gender on collective efficacy beliefs in sport. Manuscript submitted for publication.

The author examined the relationship between team size, type of sport, time of season, and gender on collective efficacy. Participants (n = 224 athletes from 30 different teams) completed a background information questionnaire and the Collective Efficacy Questionnaire for Sport (CEQS). Results showed differences on CEQS subscale ratings for team size, time of season, and gender. Athletes who played on larger teams had higher efficacy scores than those who played on smaller teams (except for unity efficacy). The pattern of efficacy scores increasing across the season was evident for the subscales of effort, unity, and the total CEQs scores. For ability efficacy, the highest scores were also reported at the end of the season (but the lowest scores were reported for middle of the season). For persistence and preparation efficacy the middle of the season values were highest. Females had higher ratings than males. [4]

Short, S.E., Apostal, K., Harris, C., Poltavski, D., Young, J., Zostautas, N., Sullivan, P., & Feltz, D.L. (2002). Assessing collective efficacy: A comparison of two approaches. *Journal of Sport and Exercise Psychology, 24,* S115-S116.

The authors investigated the relationship between alternative operational definitions of collective efficacy. College athletes (n = 166) completed two versions of the Collective Efficacy Questionnaire for Sport that differed in the stem used for the 20 items (i.e., "rate your team's confidence . . ."; "rate your confidence that your team . . ."). Data were collected over three time periods. Correlations between the different scales at different times ranged from .65 to .90. When version was used as an independent variable, none of the ANOVAs for the subscales was significant. The authors concluded that there were no differences between the two assessment methods and that either could adequately assess collective efficacy. [2, appendix]

Short, S.E., Bruggeman, J.M., Engel, S.G., Marback, T., Wang, L.J., Willadsen, A., & Short, M.W. (2002). The effect of imagery function and imagery direction on self-efficacy and performance on a golf-putting task. *The Sport Psychologist, 16,* 48-67.

The authors conducted an experiment to examine the interaction between imagery direction and imagery function on self-efficacy and performance. Eighty-three participants were randomly assigned to one of six imagery groups or a control. Results for performance showed that negative images (missing the putt) had a debilitative effect on subsequent performance. Results from a 3 (direction) × 3 (function) × 2 (gender) ANCOVA on self-efficacy showed a significant three-way interaction. The authors concluded that imagery direction and imagery function can affect self-efficacy and performance and that males and females may respond differently to imagery interventions. [1, 3, 6, appendix]

Short, S.E., Monsma, E.V., & Short, M.W. (2004). Is what you see really what you get? Athletes' perceptions of imagery functions. *The Sport Psychologist, 18,* 341-349.

The authors examined athletes' perceptions of the functions of images as found on the Sport Imagery Questionnaire. Participants were 275 collegiate athletes from various sports. Results showed that a single image could have multiple functions for a single athlete and that different athletes used the same image for different functions. Many of the images were shown to have confidence-enhancing functions. [3, 6]

Short, S.E., Reuter, J., Brandt, J., Short, M.W., & Kontos, A.P. (2004). The relationships among three components of perceived risk of injury, previous injuries, and gender in contact sport athletes. *Athletic Insight, 6.* Retrieved September 1, 2005, from www.athleticinsight.com/Vol6Iss3/PerceivedRiskofInjury.htm.

This study looked at the relationships among probability of injury, worry/concern about being injured, and confidence in avoiding injury. Participants were 434 athletes from hockey, soccer, and football. Confidence about avoiding injury had a negative relationship with worry/concern and with probability of injury. Results also showed that athletes who had been injured in the past had the least amount of confidence in their ability to avoid reinjury. Several sport-specific and gender-specific findings were also reported. [3]

Short, S.E., & Short, M.W. (2004). Coaching efficacy: Coaches' assessments compared to athletes' perceptions. *Perceptual and Motor Skills, 99,* 729-736.

The authors compared coaches' assessments of their coaching efficacy with athletes' perceptions of the coaches' efficacy. Participants were nine football coaches and 76 athletes from the same team. Scores from the Coaching Efficacy Scale showed that the coaches were highly confident in their abilities, and for most coaches (seven of nine), their ratings of themselves were higher than the athletes' ratings. All coaches' ratings fell within the 95% confidence interval formed by the athletes' ratings. [5, 9]

Short, S.E., & Short, M.W. (2005a). Differences between high- and low-confident football players on imagery functions: A consideration of the athletes' perceptions. *Journal of Applied Sport Psychology, 17,* 197-208.

This replication study looked at the differences in image content between high- and low-sport-confident athletes. However, image content was assessed in two ways—according to the factor structure of the Sport Imagery Questionnaire (SIQ) and according to athletes' perceptions. The subscales of the SIQ included Cognitive Specific (CS), Cognitive General (CG), Motivational General-Arousal (MG-A), Motivational General-Mastery (MG-M), and Motivation Specific (MS). Participants were 79 football players. Results showed that the imagery–confidence relationship differed according to how the SIQ subscale scores were computed. When the original SIQ was used, the high-confident group used all forms of imagery more than the low-confident group (significant for CS, CG, MG-A); but when the modified SIQ was used, the high-confident group used more CG, CS, and MG-M than the low-confident group (significant for CS and MG-M). [3, appendix]

Short, S.E., Smiley, M., & Ross-Stewart, L. (2005). Relationship between efficacy beliefs and imagery use in coaches. *The Sport Psychologist, 19,* 380-394.

The authors examined the relationship between coaching efficacy and imagery use. Participants were 89 NCAA coaches. They completed a modified version of the Sport Imagery Questionnaire and the Coaching Efficacy Scale (CES). Results showed that each subscale of the CES could be predicted by one or more of the imagery functions. CES scores were also related to career win percentage and total years coaching. There were no gender differences on CES scores. [5, 8]

Short, S.E., Sullivan, P., & Feltz, D.L. (2005). Development and preliminary validation of the Collective Efficacy Questionnaire for Sports. *Measurement in Physical Education and Exercise Science, 9,* 181-202.

Responding to the piecemeal use of individual measures of team confidence, the authors proposed a generic scale to study collective efficacy in sport—Collective Efficacy Questionnaire for Sport (CEQS). A data-driven analysis revealed five interrelated aspects of team functioning that are relevant to team confidence in sport—preparation, effort, ability, unity, and persistence. The authors provide support for the face validity, internal consistency, and factor structure of the scale. Construct validity was supported through relations between the factors of the CEQS and those of the Group Environment Questionnaire, which has been widely used to measure team cohesion. The result is a valid and reliable 20-item questionnaire that can be used to measure team confidence in different team sport settings. [2, 4, 9]

Short, S.E., Tenute, A., & Feltz, D.L. (2005). Imagery use in sport: Mediational effects for efficacy. *Journal of Sports Sciences, 23,* 951-960.

The authors examined whether efficacy in using imagery mediated the relationship between imagery ability and imagery use. Participants were female collegiate athletes ($n = 74$). With use of the Sport Imagery Questionnaire, the results showed that the more athletes were confident in their ability to use imagery, the more they used it. Athletes were most confident in their ability to use Motivation General–Mastery imagery and least confident in their ability to use Motivation Specific imagery. Efficacy in using imagery was a mediator of the relationship between imagery ability and cognitive imagery use. [1, 3, 6, appendix]

Short, S.E., & Vadocz, E.A. (2002). Testing the modifiability of the State Sport Confidence Inventory. *Perceptual and Motor Skills, 94,* 1025-1028.

The authors compared the original SSCI to a modified version that did not include the comparison component. Participants were 31 figure skaters competing at an event. Although both measures had adequate internal consistencies, ratings were higher on the modified version than the original. [6]

Singleton, D.A., & Feltz, D.L. (1999). The effects of self-modeling on shooting performance and self-efficacy among intercollegiate hockey players. Unpublished manuscript, Michigan State University, East Lansing.

The authors examined the effectiveness of video self-modeling over a 10-week training period on self-efficacy and performance. Participants ($n = 22$ Division 1 hockey players) were randomly assigned to either the experimental or control group. A pretest–posttest design with repeated measures was used. Self-efficacy and backhand shot performance were assessed at three time periods. Results showed that the experimental group reported higher self-efficacy scores and performed better than the control group as a result of the intervention. [3, 6, appendix]

Slobounov, S., Yukelson, D., & O'Brien, R. (1997). Self-efficacy and movement variability of Olympic-level springboard divers. *Journal of Applied Sport Psychology, 9,* 171-190.

The authors examined the relationships among movement variability, self-efficacy, satisfaction, and performance using a sample of national-level divers. Self-efficacy was assessed using a task-specific rating scale. Participants (n = 6) performed five trials for three dives that increased in level of difficulty. Results showed a progressive rise in self-efficacy over the series of dives performed, and also an inverse relationship between self-efficacy and the degree of difficulty of the dive. Self-efficacy was positively correlated with several of the kinematic performance measures, judges' evaluations, and athletes' satisfaction ratings. The authors concluded that self-efficacy is a task-dependent cognitive property that varies over the time course of a single practice session, and that athletes acquire self-efficacy faster when practicing less complex dives. [3, appendix]

Solmon, M.A., Lee, A.M., Belcher, D., Harrison, L., & Wells, L. (2003). Beliefs about gender appropriateness, ability, and competence in physical activity. *Journal of Teaching in Physical Education, 22*, 261-279.

The authors investigated the influence of perceptions of gender appropriateness and conceptions of ability on beliefs about competence and efficacy. Participants (n = 432) rated interest, importance, perceived level of difficulty, ability level, and efficacy for hockey in general. Then they rated their conceptions of ability for specific hockey skills shown on a videotape (natural ability to acquired). The model on the tape was either an expert male or female. For just the hockey wrist shot, they also rated their efficacy in their ability to learn the skill and indicated their sources for this belief. Most participants believed that hockey was primarily for males but that the wrist shot was gender neutral. There were gender differences on ability, efficacy, and difficulty. For women only, ratings were lower for women who indicated hockey was a male activity compared to those who thought it was gender neutral. There was no effect for sex of the model. Efficacy levels differed as a function of conception of ability. Identified sources consisted of motivation, prior experience, ability, task difficulty, and practice. [3, appendix]

Solomon, G.B. (2001). Performance and personality impression cues as predictors of athletic performance: An extension of athlete expectancy theory. *International Journal of Sport Psychology, 32*, 88-100.

The author examined the potential of a performance impression cue (ability) and a personality impression cue (confidence) in the prediction of athletic performance. Participants were 115 athletes and 8 head coaches from team, dual, and individual sports. The Trait Sport Confidence Inventory was used to assess confidence and was completed by each athlete, as well as by each coach for each athlete. Results showed that the coaches' evaluations of athletes' confidence was the only significant predictor of performance. Team sport athletes were also shown to have higher confidence scores than individual or dual sport athletes. [5]

Solomon, G.B. (2002). Confidence as a source of expectancy information: A follow-up investigation. *International Sports Journal, 6,* 119-127.

The author examined confidence as a source of expectancy information. Participants were coaches and athletes from various individual and team sports. Measures included a demographic questionnaire, an expectancy rating scale for physical ability (as completed by the coaches for each athlete on the team), the Trait Sport Confidence Inventory (completed by athletes and by the coaches for each athlete on the team), and individual athlete performance scores (based on actual performance statistics from an entire competitive season). Results from a regression analysis (predicting athlete performance) showed that coaches' TSCI ratings for athletes were the only significant predictor. Results also showed that coaches' ratings were significantly lower than athletes' ratings. [3, 5, appendix]

Soohoo, S., Takemoto, K.Y., & McCullagh, P. (2004). A comparison of modeling and imagery on the performance of a motor skill. *Journal of Sport Behavior, 27,* 349-366.

The authors compared a modeling intervention to an imagery intervention to determine the differences in performance and self-efficacy on a squat lift. Participants ($n = 22$ female students) were randomly assigned to one of the two treatment groups (there was no control group). Results showed that the modeling and imagery groups increased their form scores by 16% and 21%, respectively, from pre- to posttreatment. For the outcome scores, the modeling group had higher scores than the imagery group. When interventions were switched (Trial 4) there were no differences on form or outcome. There were no differences for self-efficacy. The participants indicated that they preferred the modeling intervention over imagery. [3, appendix]

Spink, K.S. (1990b). Group cohesion and collective efficacy of volleyball teams. *Journal of Sport and Exercise Psychology, 12,* 301-311.

The author investigated the relationship between group cohesion and collective efficacy in 92 volleyball players participating on elite and recreational teams. To measure collective efficacy, athletes were asked which place they expected their team would finish in and how confident they were that the team would attain this placement. Athletes answered these questions and completed the Group Environment Questionnaire prior to their first game of a volleyball tournament. Results showed a positive significant difference in both Individual Attraction to the Group-Task and Group Integration-Social between teams of low and high collective efficacy beliefs. [2, 4]

Starek, J., & McCullagh, P. (1999). The effect of self-modeling on the performance of beginning swimmers. *The Sport Psychologist, 13,* 269-287.

The authors examined the effectiveness of peer modeling and self-modeling on performance, self-efficacy, and anxiety. Participants ($n = 10$) completed five swimming sessions, with the intervention occurring in the third and fourth sessions. Performance differences occurred in the third to fourth trials, and in the fourth trial those in the self-modeling condition performed better than those in the other-modeling condition. Self-efficacy increased across sessions, and the self-modeling group showed higher scores at all sessions. Participants who watched themselves as opposed to watching peers also had more accurate estimations of their performance, which the authors suggested was evidence that it was the accuracy of self-efficacy beliefs that increase performance, not the presence of increased self-efficacy alone. Correlations between self-efficacy and performance were also reported. [3, 6, appendix]

Stidwell, H.F. (1994). Application of self-efficacy theory: A treatment approach for sport performance phobias. *Journal of Mental Health Counseling, 16,* 196-204.

The author describes a self-efficacy-based intervention that he used to manipulate the self-efficacy beliefs of a 21-year-old female college student who had a sport-related phobia. [6]

Sturm, R., & Short, S.E. (2004). The relationships among self-efficacy, team efficacy, and team performance in baseball. Manuscript in preparation.

In this study, participants ($n = 133$ baseball players from 10 teams) completed self-efficacy and team efficacy measures; the aim was to see which correlated better with offense and defense performance scores. For the offensive performance measure (runs scored, runs batted in, batting average, and on-base percentage), the only significant correlation was for self-confidence. There were no significant correlations between the confidence measures and performance for defense performance scores (team fielding percentage and team errors). [2, appendix]

Sullivan, P.J., Gee, C.J., & Feltz, D.L. (2006). Playing experience: The content knowledge source of coaching efficacy beliefs. In A.V. Mitel (Ed.), *Trends in Educational Psychology.* New York: Nova Publishers.

The authors examined the relative importance of previous playing experience as a source of coaching efficacy information. Participants were a sample of curling coaches ($n = 81$) who completed the Coaching Efficacy Scale. Playing experience was a significant predictor of game strategy efficacy after the effect of coaching experience was controlled for. Coaching experience was also a statistically significant predictor of the other efficacies—motivation, technique, and character building. [5]

Sullivan, P.J., & Kent, A. (2003). Coaching efficacy as a predictor of leadership style in intercollegiate athletics. *Journal of Applied Sport Psychology, 15,* 1-11.

The authors examined the relationship between coaching efficacy, as measured by the Coaching Efficacy Scale, and the leadership style, as measured by the Leadership Scale for Sports, for coaches. An international sample of 224 intercollegiate coaches (165 male, 58 female) participated. Motivation efficacy and character-building efficacy were statistically significant predictors of positive feedback. Game strategy efficacy was a statistically significant predictor of democratic behavior. Technique efficacy and game strategy efficacy were statistically significant predictors of training and instruction. [2, 5]

Taylor, A.H., & May, S. (1996). Threat and coping appraisal as determinants of compliance with sports injury rehabilitation: An application of Protection Motivation Theory. *Journal of Sports Sciences, 14,* 471-482.

The authors examined whether susceptibility and severity and self-efficacy and treatment efficacy were related to sports injury rehabilitation compliance. Participants were 62 student-athletes from one sports injury clinic. Although the self-efficacy measures were weak (some items used the stems "I am" and "I have"), results showed that the participants who had stronger beliefs in their ability to complete the prescribed modalities, and those with greater expectancy of the benefits of doing so, were more likely to be compliant to the rehabilitation program. Self-efficacy was a predictor of compliance. [6]

Taylor, J.A., & Shaw, D.F. (2002). The effects of outcome imagery on golf-putting performance. *Journal of Sports Sciences, 20,* 607-613.

The authors determined the effects of outcome imagery on golf putting performance and self-confidence of golfers from different standards in competition. Participants were unskilled ($n = 25$) and skilled ($n = 26$) students.

Imagery condition was a repeated-measures factor; participants performed in a positive imagery, negative imagery, and control condition. Results from a 3 (imagery condition) × 2 (skill) ANOVA showed a main effect for skill (skilled golfers were more confident) and imagery condition (putting confidence was lower in the negative condition compared to the positive imagery condition and control group). The authors concluded that outcome imagery influences performance though confidence. [3, appendix]

Tenenbaum, G., Levy-Kolker, N., Sade, S., Lieberman, D., & Lidor, R. (1996). Anticipation and confidence of decisions related to skilled performance. *International Journal of Sport Psychology, 27,* 293-307.

This study investigated differences between expert, intermediate, and novice tennis players with respect to how anticipatory decisions are made and the confidence in those decisions. Tennis players of different expertise participated by watching a videotaped series of tennis strokes. Each participant was asked to comment on the cues available prior to the stroke that may have been used in deciding upon subsequent stroke execution. Participants also rated the confidence of their decision. Each individual's eye focus direction was also measured. Results showed that experts and intermediates were superior to novices in anticipatory decisions, particularly under shorter time constraints. Experts also displayed significantly more confidence in their decisions than intermediate and novice participants. [7, 9]

Thelwell, R.C., & Greenlees, I.A. (2003). Developing competitive endurance performance using mental skills training. *The Sport Psychologist, 17,* 318-337.

The authors examined the effects of a mental skills training package (goal setting, relaxation, imagery, self-talk) on triathlon performance. Participants ($n = 4$) competed against each other 10 times in a single-subject, multiple-baseline design. Qualitative data showed that goal setting, imagery, and self-talk all had an impact on confidence. For all mental skills, what was used, when, why, and its impact were reported. [3, appendix]

Theodorakis, Y. (1995). Effects of self-efficacy, satisfaction, and personal goals on swimming performance. *The Sport Psychologist, 9,* 245-253.

The author examined the effects of past performance, personal goal setting, self-satisfaction, and self-efficacy on performance of a swimming task. Participants were 42 undergraduate students. Performance was assessed as distance swum in 20 sec. There were two pretest trials and two experimental trials during which personal goals were set and measures taken. Self-efficacy and performance were significantly correlated, although there were no differences in self-efficacy for the two performances. Path analyses showed that self-efficacy predicted performance but past performance was the main determinant of future performance. Self-efficacy also affected goal setting (the more confident the athlete, the higher the goals and performance). When past performance was eliminated from the model, goal setting mediated the self-efficacy–performance relationship. The author concluded that goals were stronger regulators of performance compared to self-efficacy and self-satisfaction. [2, 3, appendix]

Theodorakis, Y. (1996). The influence of goals, commitment, self-efficacy and self-satisfaction on motor performance. *Journal of Applied Sport Psychology, 8,* 171-182.

The author examined the effects of goals, commitment, self-efficacy, trait self-efficacy, ability, and self-satisfaction. Participants (48 physical education students with tennis experience) performed four trials of a tennis serving task. Between trials 2 and 3 and trials 3 and 4, they completed questionnaires and set personal goals. Correlations showed that self-efficacy was related to performance. Results of a path analysis showed that the effects of self-efficacy on performance were both direct and indirect through goal setting. [appendix]

Theodorakis, Y., Beneca, A., Malliou, P., & Goudas, M. (1997). Examining psychological factors during injury. *Journal of Sport Rehabilitation, 6,* 355-363.

The authors examined the effects of a goal-setting program on the injury rehabilitation process. Performance and self-efficacy were assessed in a sample of 40 student-athletes who had recently had knee surgery. Participants were randomly assigned to either an experimental (goals and feedback) or a control group. Results from a 2 × 4 (Group × Trial) analysis with repeated measures showed that the self-efficacy scores of both groups increased across trials (there was no group main effect or interaction). [6]

Treasure, D.C., Monson, J., & Lox, C.L. (1996). Relationship between self-efficacy, wrestling performance, and affect prior to competition. *The Sport Psychologist, 10,* 73-83.

The authors examined the relationship between self-efficacy, wrestling performance, and affect prior to competition. Participants were male high school wrestlers ($n = 70$). Self-efficacy was positively correlated with positive affect and negatively correlated with negative affect and cognitive and somatic anxiety. Regression analyses showed that it was a positive predictor of positive affect and a negative predictor of anxiety. Correlations between self-efficacy and win/loss and points earned were positive, and self-efficacy was a predictor of performance. Self-efficacy was also shown to be the only variable that differentiated winners from losers. Athletes with higher self-efficacy perceived competitive wrestling situations as less threatening than athletes with low levels of self-efficacy. [1-3, appendix]

Tuton, K., & Short, S.E. (2004). Sources of coaching efficacy among female women's softball coaches. Unpublished manuscript, University of North Dakota.

In this study, 20 female women's collegiate softball coaches completed the Coaching Efficacy Scale and an open-ended questionnaire asking them to indicate the sources for their efficacy beliefs at the beginning and end of thei competitive seasons. A deductive qualitative approach was taken. Results showed that all responses could be coded as player development, coaches' development, knowledge/preparation, leadership skills, past experience, player support, and prior success (see Chase et al., 2005). The sources changed over the course of the season; prior successes were relied on more at the end of the season than at the beginning. Results also showed changes in CES scores. [5]

Vadocz, E.A., Hall, C.R., & Moritz, S.E. (1997). The relationship between competitive anxiety and imagery use. *Journal of Applied Sport Psychology, 9,* 241-253.

The authors examined whether imagery use was related to competitive anxiety and confidence. Participants ($n = 57$) completed the Competitive State Anxiety Inventory-2, Sport Imagery Questionnaire, and the Movement Imagery Questionnaire–Revised. Confidence was negatively correlated with cognitive and somatic anxiety. Motivation General–Mastery imagery was the only significant predictor of confidence. A discriminant function analysis showed that confidence discriminated between medalists and nonmedalists, with medalists having higher levels of confidence. [3, appendix]

Vargas-Tonsing, T. (2004). An examination of pre-game speeches and their effective-ness in increasing athletes' levels of self-efficacy and emotion. Unpublished doctoral dissertation, Michigan State University, East Lansing.

The author examined coaches' pregame speeches and the relationship that these speeches had to their athletes' self-efficacy and emotions. Participants were youth soccer athletes ($n = 151$) nested within 10 head coaches (male teams = 5, female teams = 5). Each team was observed prior to competition against a difficult opponent. Measures were taken upon the athletes' arrival (Time 1) and again after the pregame speech (Time 2). Change in athletes' self-efficacy was not statistically significant from Time 1 to Time 2; however, athletes' per-ceptions of the informational content of the speech were related to the change that did occur in self-efficacy. Change in athletes' emotion was not statistically significant from Time 1 to Time 2. Males reported greater self-efficacy than did females. Females perceived less informational content in the speeches than did males. Overall, the amount of perceived informational content in the pregame speech predicted the athletes' efficacy beliefs about playing well, playing to the best of their ability, and contributing to the team's victory. [1, 3, 5, 9]

Vargas-Tonsing, T.M., & Bartholomew, J.B. (2006). An exploratory study of the effects of pregame speeches on team efficacy beliefs. *Journal of Applied Social Psychology, 36,* 918-933.

Male (n = 45) and female (n = 45) soccer players read descriptions of two soccer teams who were about to play in a hypothetical soccer match. Participants were asked to imagine themselves as a member of one of the teams and to listen to one of three randomly assigned pregame speeches: one that was strategy information based, one that was emotionally persuasive based, or one on instructions about uniforms and staying hydrated (control). Results showed that the emotionally persuasive pregame speech elicited significantly greater beliefs in the team's capability of winning the competition. Athletes also predicted larger margins of victory when they had listened to the speech with confidence-building phrases. [3-5]

Vargas-Tonsing, T.M., Myers, N.D., & Feltz, D.L. (2004). Coaches' and athletes' perceptions of efficacy-enhancing techniques. *The Sport Psychologist, 18,* 397-414.

The authors compared coaches' and athletes' perceptions of efficacy-enhancing techniques. Male (n = 29) and female (n = 49) teams from Division II and III collegiate programs participated. Coaches perceived that they used instruction-drilling, modeling confidence, and positive talk most frequently. Most of these same strategies were also identified as the most effective. Athletes had mostly similar perceptions in regard to the rank-order of both the frequency and effectiveness of the techniques. Many differences were observed, however, with regard to the magnitude of the coaches' and team's ratings. [1, 3, 5, 6]

Vargas-Tonsing, T.M., Warners, A.L., & Feltz, D.L. (2003). The predictability of coaching efficacy on team efficacy and player efficacy in volleyball. *Journal of Sport Behavior, 26,* 396-407.

This study examined whether coaching efficacy could predict team and player efficacy. Athletes and coaches from 12 volleyball teams participated; team was the unit of analysis. Separate regression equations were run for team and self-efficacy with the factors of the Coaching Efficacy Scale used as predictor variables in both. Coaching efficacy was capable of predicting team efficacy but not the self-efficacy of players. Motivation and character-building efficacy of the coach were the significant predictors. [2, 4, 5]

Vealey, R.S. (1986). Conceptualization of sport-confidence and competitive orientation: Preliminary investigation and instrument development. *Journal of Sport Psychology, 8,* 221-246.

The author developed a sport-specific model of self-confidence in which sport confidence was conceptualized as both a trait and a state. A competitive orientation construct was also included. Scales to measure the constructs were put forth: Trait Sport Confidence Inventory (TSCI), State Sport Confidence Inventory (SSCI), and Competitive Orientation Inventory (COI). Data were collected from high school, collegiate, and adult athletes (n = 666). The item discriminations, internal consistencies, test–retest reliabilities, content validity, and construct validity of the measures were described as adequate. The TSCI and SSCI were shown to have a negative correlation with anxiety measures. From the COI, results showed that focusing on performing well was associated with high confidence but focusing on winning and losing was associated with low confidence. From Phase 5, more confident athletes were shown to make more internal attributions. Performance was shown to be a stronger predictor of confidence than confidence was of performance. [1-3, 6, appendix]

Vealey, R.S., Hayashi, S.W., Garner-Holman, M., & Giacobbi, P. (1998). Sources of sport-confidence: Conceptualization and instrument development. *Journal of Sport and Exercise Psychology, 20,* 54-80.

The authors present the most comprehensive examination of the study of sources of efficacy unique to sport competition. A four-phase research project utilizing over 500 athletes from a variety of sports was conducted to identify relevant sources of confidence for athletes and to develop a reliable and valid measure of the sources—the Sources of Sport Confidence Questionnaire (SSCQ). The authors identified nine sources of sport confidence for high school and intercollegiate athletes: mastery, demonstration of ability, physical/mental preparation, physical self-presentation, social support, coaches' leadership, vicarious experience, environmental comfort, and situational favorableness. [1, 3]

Watkins, B., Garcia, A.W., & Turek, E. (1994). The relation between self-efficacy and sport performance: Evidence from a sample of youth baseball players. *Journal of Applied Sport Psychology, 6,* 21-31.

The authors tested the across-time patterns of relationships between self-efficacy and sport performance using a familiar sport task for a sample of youth athletes participating in a baseball camp. Participants (n = 205) completed four trials in a batting cage and estimated their abilities to hit successfully from one to six pitches using a visual analog scale. Results showed that self-efficacy increased linearly with experience. On the basis of a series of stepwise regression analyses, the authors concluded that self-efficacy did not predict baseline hitting performance, but that previous efficacy ratings were modestly related to future hitting performance. Previous performance predicted subsequent hitting, although the size of the correlations diminished over trials (because participants got better at hitting). Hitting performance also predicted self-efficacy for all trials, and self-efficacy was a stronger predictor of performance across trials. The authors concluded that self-efficacy was as strong a predictor of performance as performance was of self-efficacy. [2, 3, appendix]

Watson, C.B., Chemers, M.M., & Preiser, N. (2001). Collective efficacy: A multilevel analysis. *Personality and Social Psychology Bulletin, 27,* 1056-1068.

The authors investigated collective efficacy using a multilevel approach. Collective and self-efficacy, as well as perceptions of leadership and performance, were measured at the beginning and end of the season with 275 basketball players. Specific hypotheses were made at the individual and team level. Results showed that at the beginning of the season, optimism and self-efficacy shaped collective efficacy beliefs more than the group's composition and previous performance. Collective efficacy was quite stable from the season's beginning to its end, and collective efficacy measured at the beginning of the season predicted both collective efficacy and overall team performance at season's end. With regard to leadership, teams with more confident leadership had stronger collective efficacy beliefs at the beginning of the season. [4]

Weinberg, R. (1985). Relationship between self-efficacy and cognitive strategies in enhancing endurance performance. *International Journal of Sport Psychology, 17,* 280-292.

The author examined the interaction of self-efficacy and cognitive strategies on muscular endurance performance. Participants ($n = 120$) were randomly assigned to a high- or low-self-efficacy condition and to a cognitive strategy condition (i.e., dissociation or positive self-talk). The manipulation check showed that high- and low-self-efficacy groups differed in their expectancy of success and were confident in their predictions. Results from a 2 (gender) $\times$ 2 (cognitive strategy) $\times$ 2 (efficacy) $\times$ 2 (trials) ANOVA with repeated measures showed that the high-self-efficacy group held their legs out longer and tried harder than those in the low-self-efficacy condition. Males outperformed females. The type of cognitive strategy employed did not affect performance. [3, appendix]

Weinberg, R., Gould, D., & Jackson, A. (1979). Expectations and performance: An empirical test of Bandura's self-efficacy theory. *Journal of Sport Psychology, 1,* 320-331.

The authors tested components of Bandura's self-efficacy theory in a competitive motor performance situation. Subjects (30 male, 30 female) were assigned within a $2 \times 2 \times 2$ design (Gender $\times$ Self-efficacy $\times$ Trial). Self-efficacy was manipulated in that participants in the high-self-efficacy condition thought they were performing against a person with weak ligaments and a knee injury who (they thought, via bogus feedback) had performed poorly on a related leg strength task. Those in the low-self-efficacy condition performed against a track athlete who, compared to the participant, displayed higher performance on a related leg strength task. Regardless of the condition, the participants always lost to the confederate. Results showed that the high-self-efficacy group was more efficacious and persisted longer than the low-self-efficacy group. In addition, the high-self-efficacy group increased their performance on the second trial, whereas the low-self-efficacy group performed worse on the second trial. [1-3]

Weinberg, R.S., Gould, D., Yukelson, D., & Jackson, A. (1981). The effects of preexisting and manipulated self-efficacy on a competitive muscular endurance task. *Journal of Sport Psychology, 4,* 345-354.

The authors examined the effect of preexisting and manipulated self-efficacy judgments on muscular endurance performance. Participants ($n = 96$) were selected based on their preexisting levels of self-efficacy (high or low) and then randomly assigned to either a manipulated high- or low-self-efficacy condition. A 2 (gender) $\times$ 2 (preexisting self-efficacy) $\times$ 2 (manipulated self-efficacy) MANOVA with two performance trials as the dependent variable was used. Results showed that the high-self-efficacy group had higher self-efficacy ratings and performance scores than the low-self-efficacy group. The high-self-efficacy group also responded to failure with greater persistence compared to the low-self-efficacy group, who had the lowest performance times. Preexisting self-efficacy expectations influenced performance on the first trial, but the manipulated self-efficacy intervention had a greater influence on the second trial. [3]

Weinberg, R., Grove, R., & Jackson, A. (1992). Strategies for building self-efficacy in tennis players: A comparative analysis of Australian and American coaches. *The Sport Psychologist, 6,* 3-13.

The authors compared responses from Australian tennis coaches and American tennis coaches (Weinberg & Jackson, 1990) on items that assessed the coaches' frequency of using selected efficacy-enhancing techniques and the effectiveness of these techniques. In this study, only Australian coaches were sampled ($n = 60$). The most often used and most effective strategies to enhance self-efficacy were encouraging self-talk, modeling confidence oneself, using instruction drills, using rewarding statements liberally, and using verbal persuasion. Although few differences were observed, it was shown that American coaches more frequently used instruction-drilling, identifying other successful athletes, an interpretation of anxiety as a sign of readiness, and an interpretation of failure as a result of lack of effort. [3, 5]

Weinberg, R., & Jackson, A. (1990). Building self-efficacy in tennis players: A coach's perspective. *Journal of Applied Sport Psychology, 2,* 164-174.

The authors examined the degree to which high school and age-group tennis coaches ($n = 222$) used selected efficacy-enhancing techniques, as well as the degree to which these coaches perceived these techniques as effective. All of the strategies were rated as used with at least a moderate frequency and were rated as at least moderately effective. The strategies that were rated as most frequently employed or as the most effective (or both) included positive self-talk, modeling confidence, instruction-drilling, rewarding statements, and verbal persuasion. [1, 3, 5]

Weinberg, R.S., Yukelson, D., & Jackson, A. (1980). Effect of public and private efficacy expectations on competitive performance. *Journal of Sport Psychology, 2,* 340-349.

This study was an extension of the work by Weinberg, Gould, and Jackson (1979). This time participants ($n = 112$) competed against each other in a back-to-back setup and made self-efficacy ratings either out loud (so the person the participant was competing against could hear) or in private (i.e., writing on a questionnaire) in a 2 (sex) $\times$ 2 (self-efficacy) $\times$ 2 (public or private) design. Success was manipulated through use of a confederate and bogus feedback to create high- and low-efficacy groups. Results showed that the high-self-efficacy group persisted longer than the low-self-efficacy group. The high-self-efficacy males extended their legs longer than the low-self-efficacy males, but there were no differences for females. Correlations showed that the self-efficacy–performance relationship was stronger for males compared to females. There were no differences as a result of the public or private efficacy manipulation. The authors concluded that the face-to-face competitive situation from the first study produced better performance and higher self-efficacy–performance correlations than the back-to-back situation. [1, 3, appendix]

Weiss, M.R., Barber, H., Sisley, B.L., & Ebbeck, V. (1991). Developing competence and confidence in novice female coaches: II. Perceptions of ability and affective experiences following a season-long coaching internship. *Journal of Sport and Exercise Psychology, 13,* 336-363.

The authors presented the results of an in-depth investigation of a season-long internship in which 28 novice coaches were placed with expert mentors. At the conclusion of the apprenticeship, participants were interviewed regarding the strengths and weaknesses of the program. Respondents reported overwhelmingly positive outcomes, including satisfaction of working with children, development of their coaching skills, and the benefits of social interaction and fun. Negative experiences included poor relationships with their mentor coach, lack of organizational support, and an overemphasis on competitive outcome (i.e., winning). [8]

Weiss, M.R., McCullagh, P., Smith, A.L., & Berlant, A.R. (1998). Observational learning and the fearful child: Influence of peer models on swimming skill performance and psychological responses. *Research Quarterly for Exercise and Sport, 69,* 380-394.

The authors examined the effect of both peer mastery and coping models on children's swimming skills, fear, and self-efficacy. Participants who were identified as fearful of the water ($n = 24$) were matched to control, peer mastery, or peer coping models. Data were analyzed in a series of 3×3 (Model type $\times$ Assessment period) repeated-measures analyses. Differences between modeling groups and the control group were observed on skill, self-efficacy, and fear of swimming at postintervention and follow-up. Coping models had a stronger effect on self-efficacy than mastery models. [1, 3, 6]

Weiss, M.R., Wiese, D.M., & Klint, K.A. (1989). Head over heels with success: The relationship between self-efficacy and performance in competitive youth gymnastics. *Journal of Sport and Exercise Psychology, 11,* 444-451.

The authors investigated the relationships among self-efficacy, competitive anxiety, worry cognitions, years of experience, and performance in young male gymnasts ($n = 22$). Self-efficacy was assessed by having the gymnasts record the scores they thought they were capable of attaining about 2 hr before the start of a state championship competition. Performance scores were official tournament results. Results showed that self-efficacy and performance were moderately or highly correlated. Regression analyses showed that only self-efficacy was a significant predictor of performance (i.e., self-efficacy was a stronger predictor of performance than anxiety). [3, appendix]

Wells, C.M., Collins, D., & Hale, B.D. (1993). The self-efficacy-performance link in maximum strength performance. *Journal of Sports Sciences, 11,* 167-175.

The authors investigated whether specific manipulation of self-efficacy levels would affect strength performance. Participants ($n = 24$ undergraduate students) were randomly assigned to one of three groups (light, heavy, or control); participants lifted a weight that was actually 10 pounds lighter or heavier than they had requested and believed it to be. Results from a 3 × 4 (Groups × Trials) ANOVA with repeated measures on self-efficacy scores showed a significant interaction effect whereby the heavy group was significantly different from the light and control groups, and this difference was found between the second and third trials when the manipulation occurred. The self-efficacy ratings for the heavy group decreased. Stepwise regression analyses showed that initial self-efficacy ratings predicted baseline performance, while manipulated self-efficacy ratings were a significant predictor of performance change. [3,appendix]

Wilkes, R.L., & Summers, J.J. (1984). Cognitions, mediating variables, and strength performance. *Journal of Sport Psychology, 6*, 351-359.

The authors examined the relationship between cognitive strategies and strength performance by independently looking at the effect of arousal, attention, self-efficacy, and imagery instructions on changes in strength. These variables were also examined as potential mediators. Participants ($n = 60$ male undergraduates) were randomly assigned to one of four mental preparation groups (arousal, attention, imagery, positive self-efficacy) or a control. Participants performed three pretest and three posttest trials. Results from a 2 (pre–posttest) × 5 (conditions) ANCOVA showed a main effect for group. The arousal group produced greater strength performance than the control and imagery groups. The self-efficacy group also performed significantly better than the controls. All groups showed pre- to posttest improvement (self-efficacy group = 16.7%). Strength change was not significantly correlated with a "confidence in doing well" item ($r = .19$). [3, appendix]

Wilson, R.C., Sullivan, P.J., Myers, N.D., & Feltz, D.L. (2004). Sources of sport confidence of master athletes. *Journal of Sport and Exercise Psychology, 26*, 369-384.

The authors examined sources of sport confidence, using the Sources of Sport Confidence Questionnaire (SSCQ), for master athletes and the relationship of these sources to trait sport confidence. Participants were master athletes ($n = 216$). Confirmatory factor analysis failed to replicate the a priori internal model of the Sources of Sport Confidence Questionnaire. Physical/mental preparation and mastery were the highest-ranked sources; physical/mental preparation and demonstration of ability were statistically significant predictors of trait sport confidence. [1, 3]

Winfrey, M.L., & Weeks, D.L. (1993). Effects of self-modeling on self-efficacy and balance beam performance. *Perceptual and Motor Skills, 77,* 907-913.

The authors assessed whether self-modeling via videotape replay, edited to show successful performance, could be used in a gymnastics setting to increase participants' self-efficacy and enhance performance on the balance beam. Participants (n = 11) were randomly assigned to either the control group or the self-modeling group. The intervention was conducted over six weeks. The State Sport Confidence Inventory was used to measure self-efficacy. Results from a 2 × 4 (Group × Time) ANOVA with repeated measures were not statistically significant for confidence or performance. Both groups reported increases in sport confidence over time. Correlations between self-rated performance and actual performance were higher for the self-modeling group than the control group. [3, appendix]

Wise, J.B., & Trunnell, E.P. (2001). The influence of sources of self-efficacy upon efficacy strength. *Journal of Sport and Exercise Psychology, 23,* 268-280.

The authors examined the influence of different sources of efficacy information on self-efficacy beliefs. Participants were 48 women. Each experimental group received three sources of bench press efficacy information (performance accomplishment, model, verbal message) presented in a different sequence. Bench press efficacy was measured after each source of efficacy information was presented. Results indicated that a performance accomplishment led to significantly stronger bench press efficacy than did observation of a model, which in turn was more effective than hearing a verbal message. Performance accomplishment information also enhanced efficacy ratings even when it followed one or both of the other sources (i.e., showing an additive effect). The verbal persuasion message was the most effective in increasing efficacy scores when it followed a performance accomplishment. [3, appendix]

Woodman, T., & Hardy, L. (2003). The relative impact of cognitive anxiety and self-confidence upon sport performance: A meta-analysis. *Journal of Sports Sciences, 21,* 443-457.

The authors report the results of a meta-analysis on 48 studies that examined the relationships between state cognitive anxiety and performance and between self-confidence and performance (in a field setting). Self-confidence measures primarily included the Competitive State Anxiety Inventory-2 (CSAI-2). Results showed that mean effect size for self-confidence and performance was .24 (weight = .23), which was larger than the cognitive anxiety–performance effect size (–0.10). Moderator variables included intra- versus interindividual measurement, type of measurement (effect sizes calculated with the CSAI-2 were smaller than those using other measures of self-confidence), sport type, standard of competition (effect sizes for confidence were larger for high-standard athletes compared to low-standard athletes), and sex (the effect size for self-confidence was larger for men than women). [3]

Woolfolk, R.L., Murphy, S.M., Gottesfeld, D., & Aitken, D. (1985). Effects of mental rehearsal of task motor activity and mental depiction of task outcome on motor skill performance. *Journal of Sport Psychology, 7,* 191-197.

The authors examined the mechanisms whereby performance is affected by imagery and the relative influence of performance versus outcome components of imagery. Participants ($n = 50$), male college undergraduates, were randomly assigned to one of six groups (positive outcome with performance, negative outcome with performance, performance only, positive outcome only, negative outcome only, or a control). Results showed that self-efficacy was positively correlated with performance. A partial correlation between self-efficacy and subsequent performance with the effects of prior performance removed was not statistically significant. Self-efficacy was not affected by the intervention. [3, 6, appendix]

Yan Lan, L., & Gill, D.L. (1984). The relationships among self-efficacy, stress responses, and a cognitive feedback manipulation. *Journal of Sport Psychology, 6,* 227-238.

This study yielded findings on the influence of self-efficacy on stress responses (heart rate and self-reported anxiety). Participants ($n = 32$ female undergraduate students) were randomly assigned to two groups (easy to difficult task, and difficult to easy task). The task was an "echo game." Results showed that the easy task elicited higher perceptions of self-efficacy than the difficult task (manipulation check). Participants had lower heart rates when they were performing the high-efficacious task. From Competitive State Anxiety Inventory-2 data, participants reported lower cognitive worry and somatic anxiety and higher self-confidence when performing the high-efficacious task. The manipulation (providing participants with bogus feedback and the suggestion that their elevated arousal levels were indicative of good performance) did not affect self-efficacy. [3, appendix]

Zimmerman, B.J., & Kitsantas, A. (1996). Self-regulated learning of a motoric skill: The role of goal setting and self-monitoring. *Journal of Applied Sport Psychology, 8,* 60-75.

This was the first in a series of studies that examined how goal setting affects self-efficacy beliefs in a self-regulation learning framework. High school girls ($n = 50$) were randomly assigned to one of four experimental conditions (process or product goal and self-monitored or not) or a no-practice control group. The task was dart throwing. The group who received the process goal and who self-recorded were the most self-efficacious, had the best performances, were the most satisfied, and had the most intrinsic interest in the activity. The lowest scores on all dependent variables were obtained by the product goal group who did not self-record. [3, appendix]

Zimmerman, B.J., & Kitsantas, A. (1997). Developmental phases in self-regulation: Shifting from process goals to outcome goals. *Journal of Educational Psychology, 89*, 29-36.

This was the second study in a series that addressed the relationship between goal setting and self-efficacy. This study included eight experimental conditions: four types of goals (process, outcome, transformed, and shifting) coupled with self-monitoring or no self-monitoring. Participants were 90 high school girls. The results showed that the shifting-goal group had the best performances and highest self-efficacy scores, followed by the groups with transformed goals, process goals, and product goals. In addition, the scores for each of the goal groups were higher with self-monitoring compared to no self-monitoring. The authors also reported correlations between self-efficacy and goal setting, self-recording, performance, self-reactions, and intrinsic interest. [3, appendix]

References

Abma, C., Fry, M., Li, Y., & Relyea, G. (2002). Differences in imagery content and imagery ability between high and low confident track and field athletes. *Journal of Applied Sport Psychology, 14,* 67-75.

Ackerman, P.L., Kanfer, R., & Goff, M. (1995). Cognitive and noncognitive determinants and consequences of complex skill acquisition. *Journal of Experimental Psychology: Applied, 1,* 270-303.

Acosta, V.A., & Carpenter, J.L. (1985). Status of women in athletics—changes and causes. *Journal of Physical Education, Recreation and Dance, 56*(6), 35-37.

American Academy of Pediatrics, Committee on Sports Medicine and Fitness and Committee on School Health. (2001). Organized sports for children and preadolescents. *Pediatrics, 107,* 1459-1462.

Ames, C. (1992). Achievement goals, motivational climate, and motivational processes. In G.C. Roberts (Ed.), *Motivation in Sport and Exercise* (pp. 161-176). Champaign, IL: Human Kinetics.

Austin, S., & Miller, L. (1992). An empirical study of the SyberVision golf videotape. *Perceptual and Motor Skills, 74,* 875-881.

Axtell, R. (2000). Why agents: On the varied motivations for agent computing in the social sciences. CSED working paper No. 17. Washington, DC: Brookings Institution.

Axtell, R., & Epstein, J. (1996). *Growing artificial societies: Social science from the bottom up.* Cambridge, MA: MIT Press.

Backman, L., & Molander, B. (1986). Effects of adult age and level of skill on the ability to cope with high-stress conditions in a precision sport. *Psychology and Aging, 4,* 334-336.

Bandura, A. (1977). Self-efficacy: Toward a unifying theory of behavioral change. *Psychological Review, 84,* 191-215.

Bandura, A. (1978). Reflections on self-efficacy. In S. Rachman (Ed.), *Advances in behavior research and therapy,* Vol. 1 (pp. 237 269). Oxford: Pergamon Press.

Bandura, A. (1980). Gauging the relationship between self-efficacy judgment and action. *Cognitive Therapy and Research, 4,* 263-268.

Bandura, A. (1982). Self-efficacy mechanism in human agency. *American Psychologist, 37,* 122-147.

Bandura, A. (1986a). The explanatory and predictive scope of self-efficacy theory. *Journal of Clinical and Social Psychology, 4,* 263-268.

Bandura, A. (1986b). *Social foundations of thought and action: A social cognitive theory.* Englewood Cliffs, NJ: Prentice Hall.

Bandura, A. (1988). Self-efficacy conceptualization of anxiety. *Anxiety Research, 1,* 77-98.

Bandura, A. (1990). Perceived self-efficacy in the exercise of personal agency. *Journal of Applied Sport Psychology, 2,* 128-163.

Bandura, A. (1992). On rectifying the comparative anatomy of perceived control: Comments on "Cognates of Personal Control." *Applied and Preventive Psychology, 1,* 121-126.

Bandura, A. (1995). On rectifying conceptual ecumenism. In J.E. Maddux (Ed.), *Self-efficacy, adaptation, and adjustment: Theory, research, and application* (pp. 347-375). New York: Plenum Press.

Bandura, A. (1997). *Self-efficacy: The exercise of control.* New York: Freeman.

Bandura, A. (2000). Exercise of human agency through collective efficacy. *Current Directions in Psychological Science, 9,* 75-78.

Bandura, A. (2001). Social cognitive theory: An agentic perspective. *Annual Review of Psychology, 52,* 1-26.

Bandura, A. (2006). Guide for creating self-efficacy scales. In F. Pajares & T. Urdan (Eds.), *Self-efficacy beliefs of adolescents* (pp. 307-337). Greenwich, CT: Information Age Publishing.

Bandura, A., Adams, N.E., & Beyer, J. (1977). Cognitive processes mediating behavioral change. *Journal of Personality and Social Psychology, 35,* 125-139.

Bandura, A., & Cervone, D. (1983). Self-evaluative and self-efficacy mechanisms governing the motivational effects of goal systems. *Journal of Personality and Social Psychology, 45,* 1017-1028.

Bandura, A., & Cervone, D. (1986). Differential engagement of self-reactive influences in cognitive motivation. *Organizational Behavior and Human Decision Processes, 38,* 92-113.

Bandura, A., & Locke, E.A. (2003). Negative self-efficacy and goal effects revisited. *Journal of Applied Psychology, 88,* 87-99.

Barber, H. (1998). Examining gender differences in sources and levels of perceived competence in interscholastic coaches. *The Sport Psychologist, 12,* 237-252.

Barling, J., & Abel, M. (1983). Self-efficacy beliefs and tennis performance. *Cognitive Therapy and Research, 7,* 265-272.

Beauchamp, M.R., Bray, S.R., & Albinson, J.G. (2002). Pre-competition imagery, self-efficacy and performance in collegiate golfers. *Journal of Sports Sciences, 20,* 697-705.

Beauchamp, M.R., Bray, S.R., Eys, M.A., & Carron, A.V. (2002). Role ambiguity, role efficacy, and role performance: Multidimensional and mediational relationships within interdependent sport teams. *Group Dynamics: Theory, Research, and Practice, 6,* 229-242.

Beauchamp, M.R., & Whinton, L.C. (2005). Self-efficacy and other-efficacy in dyadic performance: Riding as one in equestrian eventing. *Journal of Sport and Exercise Psychology, 27,* 245-252.

Beilock, S.L., & Carr, T.H. (2001). On the fragility of skilled performance: What governs choking under pressure? *Journal of Experimental Psychology: General, 130,* 701-725.

Beilock, S.L., Carr, T.H., MacMahon, C., & Starkes, J.L. (2002). When paying attention becomes counterproductive: Impact of divided versus skill-focused attention on novice and experienced performance of sensorimotor skills. *Journal of Experimental Psychology: Applied, 8,* 6-16.

Beilock, S.L., & Feltz, D.L. (2006). Selbstwirksamkeit und Expertise [Self-efficacy and expertise]. In N. Hagemann, M. Tietjens, & B. Strauss (Eds.), *Die Psychologie der sportlichen Höchstleistung [The psychology of peak performance in sports]* (pp. 156-174). Göttingen, Germany: Hogrefe.

Beilock, S.L., Jellison, W.A., Rydell, R.J., McConnell, A.R., & Carr, T.H. (2006). On the causal mechanisms of stereotype threat: Can skills that don't rely heavily on working memory still be threatened? *Personality and Social Psychology Bulletin, 32,* 1059-1071.

Beilock, S.L., & McConnell, A.R. (2004). Stereotype threat and sport: Can athletic performance be threatened? *Journal of Sport and Exercise Psychology, 26,* 597-609.

Bernstein, D.A. (1973). Behavioral fear assessment: Anxiety or artifact? In H. Adams & P. Unikel (Eds.), *Issues and trends in behavior therapy.* Springfield, IL: Charles C Thomas.

Biddle, S.J.H. (1985). Personal beliefs and mental preparation in strength and muscular endurance tasks: A review. *Physical Education Review, 8,* 90-103.

Biglan, A. (1987). A behavior-analytic critique of Bandura's self-efficacy theory. *Behavior Analyst, 10,* 1-15.

Bird, A.M., & Brame, J.M. (1978). Self versus team attributions: A test of the "I'm OK, but the team's so-so" phenomenon. *Research Quarterly, 49,* 260-268.

Bond, K.A., Biddle, S.J.H., & Ntoumanis, N. (2001). Self-efficacy and causal attributions in female golfers. *International Journal of Sport Psychology, 31,* 243-256.

Borg, G. (1985). *An introduction to Borg's RPE-scale.* Ithaca, NY: Mouvement.

Borg, G. (1998). *Borg's perceived exertion and pain scales.* Champaign, IL: Human Kinetics.

Borkovec, T.D. (1978). Self-efficacy: Cause or reflection of behaviour change? In S. Rachman (Ed.), *Advances in behavior research and therapy,* Vol. 1 (pp. 231-236). Oxford: Pergamon Press.

Boyce, B.A., & Bingham, S.M. (1997). The effects of self-efficacy and goal-setting on bowling performance. *Journal of Teaching in Physical Education, 16,* 312-323.

Brachlow, M., & Sullivan, P.J. (2006). Coach certification and coaching efficacy. *Canadian Journal of Coaching and Sport Sciences, 1*(1), retrievable at www.coach.ca/eng/sportscience/journal/May2006/content.cfm.

Bray, S.R. (2004). Collective efficacy, group goals, and group performance of a muscular endurance task. *Small Group Research, 35,* 230-238.

Bray, S.R., Brawley, L.R., & Carron, A.V. (2002). Efficacy for interdependent role functions: Evidence from the sport domain. *Small Group Research, 33,* 644-666.

Bray, S.R., Gyurcsik, N.C., Martin Ginis, K.A., & Culos-Reed, S.N. (2004). The Proxy Efficacy Exercise Questionnaire: Development of an instrument to assess female exercisers' proxy efficacy beliefs in structured group exercise classes. *Journal of Sport and Exercise Psychology, 26,* 442-456.

Bray, S.R., & Widmeyer, W.N. (2000). Athletes' perceptions of the home advantage: An investigation of perceived causal factors. *Journal of Sport Behavior, 23,* 1-10.

Brody, E.B., Hatfield, B.D., & Spalding, T.W. (1988). Generalization of self-efficacy to a continuum of stressors upon mastery of a high-risk sport skill. *Journal of Sport and Exercise Psychology, 10,* 32-44.

Brown, E.W. (Ed.). (1992). *Youth soccer: A complete handbook.* Dubuque, IA: Brown & Benchmark.

Brown, L.J., Malouff, M.J., & Schutte, N.S. (2005). The effectiveness of a self-efficacy intervention for helping adolescents cope with sport-competition loss. *Journal of Sport Behavior, 28,* 136-151.

Browne, M.W., & Cudeck, R. (1993). Alternative ways of assessing model fit. In K.A. Bollen & J.S. Long (Eds.), *Testing structural equation models* (pp. 136-162). Beverly Hills, CA: Sage.

Bull, S.J. (1991). Personal and situational influences on adherence to mental skills training. *Journal of Sport and Exercise Psychology, 13,* 121-132.

Burke, K.L. (2006). Using sport psychology to improve basketball performance. In J. Dosil (Ed.), *The sport psychologist's handbook: A guide for sport-specific performance enhancement* (pp. 121-137). London: Wiley.

Burke, S.T., & Jin, P. (1996). Predicting performance from a triathlon event. *Journal of Sport Behavior, 19,* 272-287.

Burton, D. (1989). Winning isn't everything: Examining the impact of performance goals on collegiate swimmers' cognitions and performance. *The Sport Psychologist, 3,* 105-132.

Burton, D., Naylor, S., & Holliday, B. (2001). Goal setting in sport: Investigating the goal effectiveness paradox. In R.N. Singer, H.A. Hausenblas, & C.M. Janelle (Eds.), *Handbook of sport psychology* (2nd ed., pp. 497-528). New York: Wiley.

Callow, N., & Hardy, L. (2001). Types of imagery associated with sport confidence in netball players of varying skill levels. *Journal of Applied Sport Psychology, 13,* 1-17.

Callow, N., Hardy, L., & Hall, C. (2001). The effects of a motivational general-mastery imagery intervention on the sport confidence of high-level badminton players. *Research Quarterly for Exercise and Sport, 72,* 389-400.

Cal South: Excellence in youth soccer. Retrieved December 8, 2005, from www.calsouth.com/coachyouthsoccer_overview.htm.

Campbell, S. (1993). Coaching education around the world. *Sport Science Review, 2,* 62-74.

Campbell, T., & Sullivan, P.J. (2005). The effect of a standardized coaching education program on the efficacy of novice coaches. *Avante, 11,* 56-68.

Caprara, G.V., Barbaranelli, C., Borgogni, L., & Steca, P. (2003). Efficacy beliefs as determinants of teachers' job satisfaction. *Journal of Educational Psychology, 95,* 821-832.

Carnahan, B.J., Shea, J.B., & Davis, G.S. (1990). Motivational cue effects on bench-press performance and self-efficacy. *Journal of Sport Behavior, 13,* 240-254.

Carron, A.V., Brawley, L.R., & Widmeyer, W.N. (1985). The development of an instrument to assess cohesion in sport teams: The Group Environment Questionnaire. *Journal of Sport Psychology, 7,* 244-266.

Carron, A.V., Brawley, L.R., & Widmeyer, W.N. (1990). The impact of group size in an exercise setting. *Journal of Sport and Exercise Psychology, 12,* 376-387.

Carron, A.V., Brawley, L.R., & Widmeyer, W.N. (1997). The measurement of cohesiveness in sport groups. In J.L. Duda (Ed.), *Advancements in sport and exercise psychology measurement.* Morgantown, WV: Fitness Information Technology.

Carron, A.V., Bray, S.R., & Eys, M.A. (2002). Team cohesion and team success in sport. *Journal of Sports Sciences, 20,* 119-126.

Carron, A.V., Hausenblas, H.A., & Eys, M.A. (2005). *Group dynamics in sport* (3rd ed.). Morgantown, WV: Fitness Information Technology.

Cartoni, A.C., Minganti, C., & Zelli, A. (2005). Gender, age, and professional-level differences in the psychological correlates of fear of injury in Italian gymnasts. *Journal of Sport Behavior, 28,* 3-17.

Carver, C.S., & Scheier, M.F. (1981). *Attention and self-regulation: A control theory approach to human behavior.* New York: Springer-Verlag.

Carver, C.S., & Scheier, M.F. (1990b). Origins and functions of positive and negative affect: A control-process view. *Psychological Review, 97,* 19-35.

Cervone, D. (1985). Randomization tests to determine significance levels for microanalytic congruences between self-efficacy and behavior. *Cognitive Therapy and Research, 9,* 357-365.

Chase, M.A. (1995). Children's sources of self-efficacy, accuracy of appraisal and motivation in sport skills and physical activities. Unpublished doctoral dissertation, Michigan State University, East Lansing.

Chase, M.A. (1998). Sources of self-efficacy in physical education and sport. *Journal of Teaching in Physical Education, 18,* 76-89.

Chase, M.A. (2001). Children's self-efficacy, motivational intentions, and attributions in physical education and sport. *Research Quarterly for Exercise and Sport, 72,* 47-54.

Chase, M.A. (2006). Competition plans and performance routines. In R. Bartlett, C. Gratton, & C. Rolf (Eds.), *Encyclopedia of international sports studies* (pp. 290-292). London: Taylor and Francis.

Chase, M.A., Ewing, M.E., Lirgg, C.D., & George, T.R. (1994). The effects of equipment modification on children's self-efficacy and basketball shooting performance. *Research Quarterly for Exercise and Sport, 65,* 159-168.

Chase, M.A., Feltz, D.L., Hayashi, S.W., & Hepler, T.J. (2005). Sources of coaching efficacy: The coaches' perspective. *International Journal of Exercise and Sport Psychology, 1,* 7-25.

Chase, M.A., Feltz, D.L., & Lirgg, C.D. (2003). Sources of collective and individual efficacy of collegiate athletes. *International Journal of Exercise and Sport Psychology, 1,* 180-191.

Chase, M.A., Lirgg, C.D., & Feltz, D.L. (1997). Do coaches' efficacy expectations for their teams predict team performance? *The Sport Psychologist, 11,* 8-23.

Chelladurai, P. (1999). *Human resource management in sport and recreation.* Champaign, IL: Human Kinetics.

Chelladurai, P., & Arnott, M. (1985). Decision styles in coaching: Preferences of basketball players. *Research Quarterly for Exercise and Sport, 56,* 15-24.

Chelladurai, P., & Saleh, S.D. (1980). Dimensions of leader behavior in sports: Development of a leadership scale. *Journal of Sport Psychology, 2,* 34-45.

Chow, G.M., & Feltz, D.L. (2006). *Exploring relationships between collective efficacy, perceptions of success, and team attributions.* Manuscript submitted for publication.

Chow, G.M., & Feltz, D.L. (in press). Exploring new directions in collective efficacy and sport. In M. Beauchamp & M. Eys (Eds.), *Group dynamics advances in sport and exercise psychology: Contemporary themes.* London: Routledge.

Cilz, J., & Short, S.E. (2006). The relationship between self-efficacy, other-efficacy, and relation-inferred self-efficacy with performance in soccer. Unpublished manuscript, University of North Dakota, Grand Forks.

Cleary, T.J., & Zimmerman, B.J. (2001). Self-regulation differences during athletic practice by experts, non-experts and novices. *Journal of Applied Sport Psychology, 13,* 185-206.

Clifton, R.T., & Gill, D.L. (1994). Gender differences in self-confidence on a feminine-typed task. *Journal of Sport and Exercise Psychology, 16,* 150-162.

Coaching: How to become a coach. Retrieved December 8, 2005, from www.ausport.gov.au/coach/ncas.asp.

Coakley, J. (2004). *Sports in society (8th ed.)* Boston:McGraw-Hill

Corbin, C.B., Landers, D.M., Feltz, D.L., & Senior, K. (1983). Sex differences in performance estimates. Female lack of confidence vs. male boastfulness. *Research Quarterly for Exercise and Sport, 54,* 407-410.

Corcoran, J.P., & Feltz, D.L. (1993). Evaluation of chemical health education for high school athletic coaches. *The Sport Psychologist, 1,* 298-308.

Cox, R.H. (2000). Confirmatory factor analysis of the Competitive State Anxiety Inventory-2. Paper presented at the Association for the Advancement of Applied Sport Psychology Conference, Nashville, TN.

Craft, L.L., Magyar, T.M., Becker, B.J., & Feltz, D.L. (2003). The relationship between the Competitive State Anxiety Inventory-2 and sport performance: A meta-analysis. *Journal of Sport and Exercise Psychology, 25,* 44-65.

Cumming, J., Clark, S.E., McCullagh, P., Ste-Marie, D.M., & Hall, C. (2005). The functions of observational learning questionnaire (FOLQ). *Psychology of Sport and Exercise, 6,* 517-537.

Cumming, J., Nordin, S.M., Horton, R., & Reynolds, S. (2006). Examining the direction of imagery and self-talk on dart-throwing performance and self-efficacy. *The Sport Psychologist, 20,* 257-274.

Cunningham, G.B., Sagas, M., & Ashley, F.B. (2003). Coaching self-efficacy, desire to become a head coach, and occupational turnover intent: Gender differences between NCAA coaches of women's teams. *International Journal of Sport Psychology, 34,* 125-137.

Dawson, K.A., Gyurcsik, N.C., Culos-Reed, S.N., & Brawley, L.R. (2001). Perceived control: A construct that bridges theories of motivated behavior. In G.C. Roberts (Ed.), *Advances in motivation in sport and exercise.* Champaign, IL: Human Kinetics.

Denham, C.H., & Michael, J.J. (1981). Teacher sense of efficacy: A definition of the construct and a model for further research. *Educational Research Quarterly, 5,* 39-63.

DeRue, D.S., Hollenbeck, J.R., Ilgen, D.R., & Feltz, D.L. (2005). A theory of efficacy dispersion and trajectory in teams: Beyond agreement and aggregation. Manuscript submitted for publication.

Dils, A.K., & Ziatz, D.H. (2000). The application of teacher education curriculum theory to interscholastic coaching education: Learning outcomes associated with a quality interscholastic athletic program. *Physical Educator,* 88-98.

Dowrick, P.W. (1991). *Practical guide to using video in the behavioral sciences.* New York: Wiley.

Dowrick, P.W., & Dove, C. (1980). The use of modeling to improve the swimming performance of spina bifida children. *Journal of Applied Behavior Analysis, 13,* 51-56.

Driskell, J.E., Copper, C., & Moran, A. (1994). Does mental practice enhance performance? *Journal of Applied Psychology, 79,* 481-492.

Druckman, D., & Bjork, R.A. (Eds.). (1991). *In the mind's eye: Enhancing human performance.* Washington, DC: National Academy Press.

Druckman, D., & Swets, J.A. (Eds.). (1988). *Enhancing human performance: Issues, theories, and techniques.* Washington, DC: National Academy Press.

Duda, J.L., & Nicholls, J.G. (1992). Dimensions of achievement motivation in schoolwork and sport. *Journal of Educational Psychology, 84,* 290-299.

Dunn, J.G., & Holt, N.L. (2004). A qualitative investigation of a personal-disclosure mutual-sharing team building activity. *The Sport Psychologist, 18,* 363-382.

Edmonds, W.A. (2003). The role of collective efficacy in adventure racing teams. Unpublished doctoral dissertation, Florida State University, Tallahassee.

Elston, T.L., & Martin Ginis, K.A. (2004). The effects of self-set versus assigned goals on exercisers' self-efficacy for an unfamiliar task. *Journal of Sport and Exercise Psychology, 26,* 500-504.

Endler, N.S., & Parker, J.D.A. (1990). *Coping inventory for stressful situations (CISS): Manual.* Toronto: Multihealth Systems, Inc.

Ericsson, K.A., & Charness, N. (1994). Expert performance—its structure and acquisition. *American Psychologist, 49,* 725-747.

Ericsson, K.A., Krampe, R.T., & Tesch-Romer, C. (1993). The role of deliberate practice in the acquisition of expert performance. *Psychological Review, 100,* 363-406.

Escarti, A., & Guzman, J.F. (1999). Effects of feedback on self-efficacy, performance, and choice on an athletic task. *Journal of Applied Sport Psychology, 11,* 83-96.

Evans, L., Hardy, L., & Fleming, S. (2000). Intervention strategies with injured athletes: An action research study. *The Sport Psychologist, 14,* 188-206.

Evans, L., Jones, L., & Mullen, R. (2004). An imagery intervention during the competitive season with an elite rugby union player. *The Sport Psychologist, 18,* 252-271.

Everhart, C.B., & Chelladurai, P. (1998). Gender differences in preferences for coaching as an occupation: The role of self-efficacy, valence, and perceived barriers. *Research Quarterly for Exercise and Sport, 69,* 188-200.

Ewing, M., Feltz, D.L., & Brown, E.W. (1992). Working effectively with parents. In E.W. Brown (Ed.), *Youth soccer: A complete handbook* (pp. 31-49). Dubuque, IA: Brown and Benchmark.

Eyal, N., Bar-Eli, M., Tenenbaum, G., & Pie, J.S. (1995). Manipulated outcome expectations and competitive performance in motor tasks with gradually increasing difficulty. *The Sport Psychologist, 9,* 188-200.

Eys, M.A., & Carron, A.V. (2001). Role ambiguity, task cohesion, and task self-efficacy. *Small Group Research, 32,* 356-373.

Eysenck, H.J. (1978). Expectations as causal elements in behavioral change. In S. Rachman (Ed.), *Advances in behavior research and therapy,* Vol. 1 (pp. 171-175). Oxford: Pergamon Press.

Farber, M. (1994, June 22). Seven games to glory. Retrieved December 9, 2005, from http://sportsillustrated.cnn.com/magazine/features/si50/states/new_york/flashback.

Farber, M. (2005). The $90 million ragtag wonders. *Sports Illustrated, 102*(18), 43-45.

Feltz, D. L. (1980). Teaching a high-avoidance motor task to a retarded child through participant modeling. *Education and Training of the Mentally Retarded, 15,* 152-155.

Feltz, D.L. (1982). A path analysis of the causal elements in Bandura's theory of self-efficacy and an anxiety-based model of avoidance behavior. *Journal of Personality and Social Psychology, 42,* 764-781.

Feltz, D.L. (1988a). Gender differences in the causal elements of self-efficacy on a high-avoidance motor task. *Journal of Sport and Exercise Psychology, 10,* 151-166.

Feltz, D.L. (1988b). Self-confidence and sports performance. In K.B. Pandolf (Ed.), *Exercise and sport sciences reviews* (pp. 423-456). New York: Macmillan.

Feltz, D.L. (1992). Understanding motivation in sport: A self-efficacy perspective. In G.C. Roberts (Ed.), *Motivation in sport and exercise* (pp. 107-128). Champaign, IL: Human Kinetics.

Feltz, D.L. (1994). Self-confidence and performance. In D. Druckman & R.A. Bjork (Eds.), *Learning, remembering, believing: Enhancing human performance* (pp. 173-206). Washington, DC: National Academy Press.

Feltz, D.L., & Albrecht, R.R. (1986). The influence of self-efficacy on the approach/avoidance of a high-avoidance motor task. In J.H. Humphrey & L. Vander Velden (Eds.), *Psychology and sociology of sport* (pp. 3-25). New York: AMS Press.

Feltz, D.L., Bandura, A., Albrecht, R.R., & Corcoran, J.P. (1988, June). Perceived team efficacy in ice hockey. Paper presented at the annual meeting of the North American Society for the Psychology of Sport and Physical Activity, Knoxville, TN.

Feltz, D.L., & Brown, E.W. (1984). Perceived competence in soccer skills among young soccer players. *Journal of Sport Psychology, 6,* 385-394.

Feltz, D.L., & Chase, M.A. (1998). The measurement of self-efficacy and confidence in sport. In J. Duda (Ed.), *Advancements in sport and exercise psychology measurement* (pp. 63-78). Morgantown, WV: Fitness Information Technology.

Feltz, D.L., Chase, M.A., Moritz, S.A., & Sullivan, P.J. (1999). A conceptual model of coaching efficacy: Preliminary investigation and instrument development. *Journal of Educational Psychology, 91,* 765-776.

Feltz, D.L., Chow, G., & Hepler, T.J. (2006). Path analysis of self-efficacy and performance: Revisited. *Journal of Sport and Exercise Psychology, 28,* S66.

Feltz, D.L., Hepler, T.J., Roman, N., & Paiement, C.A. (2006). Coaching efficacy of youth sport coaches: Extending validity evidence for the Coaching Efficacy Scale. Unpublished manuscript, Michigan State University, East Lansing.

Feltz, D.L., & Landers, D.M. (1983). The effects of mental practice on motor skill learning and performance: A meta-analysis. *Journal of Sport Psychology, 5,* 25-57.

Feltz, D.L., Landers, D.M., & Raeder, U. (1979). Enhancing self-efficacy in high-avoidance motor tasks: A comparison of modeling techniques. *Journal of Sport Psychology, 1,* 112-122.

Feltz, D.L., & Lirgg, C.D. (1998). Perceived team and player efficacy in hockey. *Journal of Applied Psychology, 83,* 557-564.

Feltz, D.L., & Lirgg, C.D. (2001). Self-efficacy beliefs of athletes, teams, and coaches. In R.N. Singer, H.A. Hausenblas, & C.M. Janelle (Eds.), *Handbook of sport psychology* (2nd ed., pp. 340-361). New York: Wiley.

Feltz, D.L., & Magyar, T.M. (2006). Self-efficacy and youth in sport and physical activity. In F. Pajares & T. Urdan (Eds.), *Self-efficacy beliefs of adolescents* (pp. 161-179). Greenwich, CT: Information Age.

Feltz, D.L., & Mugno, D.A. (1983). A replication of the path analysis of the causal elements in Bandura's theory of self-efficacy and the influence of autonomic perception. *Journal of Sport Psychology, 5,* 263-277.

Feltz, D.L., & Riessinger, C.A. (1990). Effects on in vivo emotive imagery and performance feedback on self-efficacy and muscular endurance. *Journal of Sport and Exercise Psychology, 12,* 132-143.

Fink, J.S. (1995). Female leadership in sport: Dueling debates surrounding existing inequities. *Future Focus, 16*(2), 37-43.

Fitzsimmons, P.A., Landers, D.M., Thomas, J.R., & Van der Mars, H. (1991). Does self-efficacy predict performance in experienced weightlifters? *Research Quarterly for Exercise and Sport, 62,* 424-431.

Fox, K.R. (Ed.) (1997). *The physical self.* Champaign, IL: Human Kinetics.

Fox, K.R., & Corbin, C.B. (1989). The Physical Self-Perception Profile: Development and preliminary validation. *Journal of Sport and Exercise Psychology, 11,* 408-430.

Frank, J.D. (1935). Individual differences in certain aspects of the level of aspiration. *American Journal of Psychology, 47,* 119-128.

Franks, I.M., & Maile, L.J. (1991). The use of video in sport skill acquisition. In P.W. Dowrick (Ed.), *Practical guide to using video in the behavioral sciences* (pp. 231-243). New York: Wiley.

Frey, K.S., & Ruble, D.N. (1990). Strategies for comparative evaluation: Maintaining a sense of competence across the life span. In R.J. Sternberg & J. Kolligian (Eds.), *Competence considered* (pp. 167-189). New Haven: Yale University Press.

Fuller, B., Wood, K., Rapport, T., & Dornbusch, S. (1982). The organizational context of individual efficacy. *Review of Educational Research, 52,* 7-30.

Fung, L. (2003). Coaching efficacy as indicators of coach education program needs. *Athletic Insight, 5.*

Gallmeier, C.P. (1987). Putting on the game face: The staging of emotions in professional hockey. *Sociology of Sport Journal, 4,* 347-362.

Galloway, S. (2003). Motivation theory for elite karate athletes: A psycho-physiological approach. *Physical Training Fitness for Combatives,* 1-17. Retrieved August 20, 2005, from www.ejmas.com/pt/ptart_galloway_0703.html.

Garland, J., Kolodny, R., & Jones, H. (1965) A model for stages o development in social work groups. In S. Bernstein (Ed.), *Exploration in group work* (pp. 17-71). Boston: Milford House.

Garza, D.L., & Feltz, D.L. (1998). Effects of selected mental practice techniques on performance ratings, self-efficacy, and competition confidence of competitive figure skaters. *The Sport Psychologist, 12,* 1-15.

Gayton, W.F., & Nickless, C.J. (1987). An investigation of the validity of the trait and state sport-confidence inventories in predicting marathon performance. *Perceptual and Motor Skills, 65,* 481-482.

Gee, C., & Sullivan, P.J. (2005). The effect of different coaching education content on the efficacy of coaches. Manuscript submitted for publication.

George, T.R. (1994). Self-confidence and baseball performance: A causal examination of self-efficacy theory. *Journal of Sport and Exercise Psychology, 16,* 381-399.

George, T.R., & Feltz, D.L. (1995). Motivation in sport from a collective efficacy perspective. *International Journal of Sport Psychology, 26,* 98-116.

George, T.R., Feltz, D.L., & Chase, M.A. (1992). The effects of model similarity on self-efficacy and muscular endurance: A second look. *Journal of Sport and Exercise Psychology, 14,* 237-248.

Gernigon, C., & Delloye, J.B. (2003). Self-efficacy, causal attribution, and track athletic performance following unexpected success or failure among elite sprinters. *The Sport Psychologist, 17,* 55-76.

Gernigon, C., Fleurance, P., & Reine, B. (2000). Effects of uncontrollability and failure on the development of learned helplessness in perceptual-motor tasks. *Research Quarterly for Exercise and Sport, 71,* 44-54.

Gilbert, N., & Bankes, S. (2000). Platforms and methods for agent-based modeling. *Proceedings of the National Academy of Sciences, 99,* 7197-7198.

Gilbert, W.D., & Trudel, P. (2001). Learning to coach through experience: Reflection in model youth sport coaches. *Journal of Teaching in Physical Education, 21,* 16-34.

Gill, D.L., Ruder, M.K., & Gross, J.B. (1982). Open-ended attributions in team competition. *Journal of Sport Psychology, 4,* 159-169.

Gould, D. (1987). Your role as a youth sports coach. In V. Seefeldt (Ed.), *Handbook for Youth Sport Coaches* (pp. 17-32). Reston, VA: American Alliance for Health, Physical Education, Recreation, and Dance.

Gould, D. (2001). Goal setting for peak performance. In J.M. Williams (Ed.), *Applied sport psychology: Personal growth to peak performance* (pp. 190-205). Toronto: Mayfield.

Gould, D., Giannini, J., Krane, V., & Hodge, K. (1990). Educational needs of elite U.S. national teams, Pan American, and Olympic coaches. *Journal of Teaching in Physical Education, 9,* 332-344.

Gould, D., Greenleaf, C., & Krane, V. (2002). Arousal-anxiety and sport. In T. Horn (Ed.), *Advances in sport psychology* (2nd ed., pp. 207-241). Champaign, IL: Human Kinetics.

Gould, D., Hodge, K., Peterson, K., & Giannini, J. (1989). An exploratory examination of strategies used by elite coaches to enhance self-efficacy in athletes. *Journal of Sport and Exercise Psychology, 11,* 128-140.

Gould, D., & Weiss, M.R. (1981). Effect of model similarity and model self-talk on self-efficacy in muscular endurance. *Journal of Sport Psychology, 3,* 17-29.

Greenlees, I.A., Bradley, A., Holder, T., & Thelwell, R.C. (2005). The impact of opponents' non-verbal behaviour on the first impressions and outcome expectations of table tennis players. *Psychology of Sport and Exercise, 6,* 103-115.

Greenlees, I.A., Buscombe, R., Thelwell, R.C., Holder, T., & Rimmer, M (2005). Perception of opponents in tennis: The impact of opponents' clothing and body language on impression formation and outcome expectations. *Journal of Sport and Exercise Psychology, 27,* 39-52.

Greenlees, I.A., Graydon, J.K., & Maynard, I.A. (1999). The impact of collective efficacy beliefs on effort and persistence in a group task. *Journal of Sports Sciences, 17,* 151-158.

Greenlees, I.A., Graydon, J.K., & Maynard, I.A. (2000). The impact of individual efficacy beliefs on group goal commitment. *Journal of Sports Sciences, 18,* 451-459.

Greenlees, I.A., Nunn, R.L., Graydon, J.K., & Maynard, I.A. (1999). The relationship between collective efficacy and precompetitive affect in rugby players: Testing Bandura's model of collective efficacy. *Perceptual and Motor Skills, 89,* 431-440.

Grieve, F.G., Whelan, J.P., Kottke, R., & Meyers, A.W. (1994). Manipulating adults' achievement goals in a sport task: Effects on cognitive, affective, and behavioral variables. *Journal of Sport Behavior, 17,* 227-245.

Grove, J.R., & Heard, N.P. (1997). Optimism and sport confidence as correlates of slump-related coping among athletes. *The Sport Psychologist, 11,* 400-410.

Gruetter, D., & Davis, T. (1985). Oversized vs. standard racquets: Does it really make a difference? *Research Quarterly for Exercise and Sport, 56,* 31-36.

Gully, S.M., Incalcaterra, K.A., Joshi, A., & Beaubien, J.M. (2002). A meta-analysis of team-efficacy, potency, and performance: Interdependence and level analysis as moderators of observed relationships. *Journal of Applied Psychology, 87,* 819-832.

Guzzo, R.A., Yost, P.R., Campbell, R.J., & Shea, G.P. (1993). Potency in groups: Articulating a construct. *British Journal of Social Psychology, 32,* 87-106.

Haberl, P., & Zaichkowsky, L. (2003). The US womens' Olympic gold medal ice hockey team: Optimal use of sport psychology for developing confidence. In R. Lidor & K.P. Henschen (Eds.), *The psychology of team sports* (pp. 217-231). Morgantown, WV: Fitness Information Technology.

Hackett, G., & Betz, N.E. (1981). A self-efficacy approach to the career development of women. *Journal of Vocational Behavior, 18*, 326-339.

Hackfort, D., & Schwenkmezger, P. (1993). Anxiety. In R.N. Singer, M. Murphey, & L.K. Tennant (Eds.), *Handbook of sport psychology* (2nd ed., pp. 529-549). New York: Macmillan.

Hall, C.R. (2001). Imagery in sport and exercise. In R.N. Singer, H.A. Hausenblas, & C.M. Janelle (Eds.), *Handbook of sport psychology* (2nd ed., pp. 529-549). New York: Wiley.

Hall, E.G., & Erffmeyer, E.S. (1983). The effect of visuomotor behavior rehearsal with videotaped modeling on free throw accuracy of intercollegiate basketball players. *Journal of Sport Psychology, 5*, 343-346.

Hall, C.R., Mack, D., Paivio, A., & Hausenblas, H.A. (1998). Imagery use by athletes: Development of the sport imagery questionnaire. *International Journal of Sport Psychology, 29*, 73-89.

Halliwell, W. (1990). Providing sport psychology consulting services in professional hockey. *The Sport Psychologist, 4*, 369-377.

Haney, C.J., & Long, B.C. (1995). Coping effectiveness: A path analysis of self-efficacy, control, coping, and performance in sport competitions. *Journal of Applied Social Psychology, 25*, 1726-1746.

Hanton, S., & Jones, G. (1997). Antecedents of competitive state anxiety as a function of skill level. *Psychological Reports, 81*, 1139-1147.

Hanton, S., & Jones, G. (1999). The effects of a multimodal intervention program on performers: II. Training the butterflies to fly in formation. *The Sport Psychologist, 13*, 22-41.

Hanton, S., Mellalieu, S.D., & Hall, R. (2004). Self-confidence and anxiety interpretation: A qualitative investigation. *Psychology of Sport and Exercise, 5*, 477-495.

Hardy, J., Gammage, K., & Hall, C. (2001). A descriptive study of athlete self-talk. *The Sport Psychologist, 15*, 306-318.

Hardy, J., Hall, C.R., Gibbs, C., & Greenslade, C. (2005). Self-talk and gross motor skill performance: An experimental approach? *Athletic Insight.* Retrieved September 1, 2005, from www.athleticinsight.com/Vol7Iss2/SelfTalkPerformance.htm.

Hardy, L., Jones, G., & Gould, D. (1996). *Understanding psychological preparation for sport: Theory and practice of elite performers.* Chichester, UK: Wiley.

Hargreaves, A. (1990). *Skills and strategies for coaching soccer.* Champaign, IL: Leisure Press.

Harris Poll #77. (2004, October 13). Professional football leads baseball 2-1 as nation's favorite sport. Accessed October 22, 2004, from http://harrisinteractive.com/harris_poll/index.asp?PID=506.

Harrison, J.M., Blakemore, C.L., Buck, M.M., & Pellett, T.L. (1996). *Instructional strategies for secondary physical education* (4th ed.). St. Louis: Times/Mirror/Mosby.

Hart, B., Hasbrook, C., & Mathes, S. (1986). An examination of the reduction in the number of female interscholastic coaches. *Research Quarterly for Exercise and Sport, 57*, 68-77.

Harter, S. (1978). Effectance motivation reconsidered: Toward a developmental model. *Human Development, 21*, 34-64.

Harter, S. (1981). The development of competence motivation in the master of cognitive and physical skills: Is there still a place for joy? In G.C. Roberts & D.M. Landers (Eds.), *Psychology of motor behavior and sport, 1980* (pp. 3-29). Champaign, IL: Human Kinetics.

Haugen, C., & Short, S.E. (2006). The relationship between coaching efficacy and coaching burnout. Manuscript submitted for publication.

Heggestad, E.D., & Kanfer, R. (2005). The predictive validity of self-efficacy in training performance: Little more than past performance. *Journal of Experimental Psychology: Applied, 11*, 84-97.

Heil, J. (1993). *Psychology of sport injury.* Champaign, IL: Human Kinetics.

Hepler, T.J., & Feltz, D.L. (2006). Self-efficacy and decision-making performance in baseball. Manuscript submitted for publication.

Heuze, J.P., Raimbault, N., & Fontayne, P. (2006). Relationships between cohesion, collective efficacy, and performance in professional basketball teams: Investigating mediating effects. *Journal of Sports Sciences, 24*, 59-68.

Highlen, P.S., & Bennett, B.B. (1983). Elite divers and wrestlers: A comparison between open- and closed-skill athletes. *Journal of Sport Psychology, 5*, 390-409.

Hill, G. (1982). Group versus individual performance: Are N + 1 heads really better than one? *Psychological Bulletin, 91*, 517-539.

Hodge, K., Lonsdale, C., & McKenzie, A. (2006). Thinking rugby: Using sport psychology to improve rugby performance. In J. Dosil (Ed.), *The sport psychologist's handbook: A guide for sport-specific performance enhancement* (pp. 183-209). London: Wiley.

Hodges, L., & Carron, A. (1992). Collective efficacy and group performance. *International Journal of Sport Psychology, 23*, 48-59.

Hodges, N.J., & Starkes, J.L. (1996). Wrestling with the nature of expertise: A sport specific test of Ericsson, Krampe and Tesch-Romer's (1993) theory of deliberate practice. *International Journal of Sport Psychology, 27*, 400-424.

Holloway, J.B., Beuter, A., & Duda, J.L. (1988). Self-efficacy and training for strength in adolescent girls. *Journal of Applied Social Psychology, 18*, 699-719.

Horn, T.S. (1985). Coaches' feedback and changes in children's perceptions of their physical competence. *Journal of Educational Psychology, 77*, 174-186.

Horn, T.S. (2002). Coaching effectiveness in the sports domain. In T.S. Horn (Ed.), *Advances in sport psychology* (pp. 309-354). Champaign, IL: Human Kinetics.

Houseworth, S.D., Davis, M.L., & Dobbs, R.D. (1990). A survey of coaching education program features. *Journal of Education, Recreation, and Dance, May/June*, 26-30.

Hu, L., & Bentler, P.M. (1999). Cutoff criteria for fit indexes in covariance structure analysis: Conventional criteria versus new alternatives. *Structural Equation Modeling, 6*, 1-55.

Hu, L., McAuley, E., & Elavsky, S. (2005). Does the Physical Self-Efficacy Scale assess self-efficacy or self-esteem? *Journal of Sport and Exercise Psychology, 27*, 152-170.

Jackson, P., & Delehanty, H. (1995). *Sacred hoops: Spiritual lessons of a hardwood warrior.* New York: Hyperion.

James, L.R. (1982). Aggregation bias in estimates of perceptual agreement. *Journal of Applied Psychology, 67*, 219-229.

James, L.R., Demaree, R.G., & Wolf, G. (1984). Estimating within-group rater reliability with and without response bias. *Journal of Applied Psychology, 69*, 85-98.

Jones, G., Hanton, S., & Connaughton, D. (2002). What is this thing called mental toughness? An investigation of elite sport performers. *Journal of Applied Sport Psychology, 14*, 205-218.

Jones, G., & Swain, A.B.J. (1992). Intensity and direction dimensions of competitive state anxiety and relationships with competitiveness. *Perceptual and Motor Skills, 74*, 467-472.

Jones, M.V., Mace, R.D., Bray, S.R., MacRae, A.W., & Stockbride, C. (2002). The impact of motivational imagery on the emotional state and self-efficacy levels of novice climbers. *Journal of Sport Behavior, 25*, 57-73.

Joreskog, K., & Sorbom, D. (1996). *LISREL 8.14: Structural equation modeling with the SIMPLIS common language.* Chicago: Scientific Software International.

Jourden, F.J., Bandura, A., & Banfield, J.T. (1991). The impact of conceptions of ability on self regulatory factors and motor skill acquisition. *Journal of Sport and Exercise Psychology, 8*, 213-226.

Kane, T.D., Marks, M.A., Zaccaro, S.J., & Blair, V. (1996). Self-efficacy, personal goals, and wrestlers' self-regulation. *Journal of Sport and Exercise Psychology, 18*, 36-48.

Kanfer, F.H. (1984). Introduction. In R.P. McGlynn, J.E. Maddux, C.D. Stoltenberg, & J.H. Harvey (Eds.), *Social perception in clinical and counseling psychology* (pp. 1-6). Lubbock, TX: Texas Tech Press.

Kavanagh, D.J., & Bower, G.H. (1985). Mood and self-efficacy: Impact of joy and sadness on perceived capabilities. *Cognitive Therapy and Research, 9*, 507-525.

Kavanagh, D., & Hausfeld, S. (1986). Physical performance and self-efficacy under happy and sad moods. *Journal of Sport Psychology, 8*, 112-123.

Kavussanu, M., Crews, D., & Gill, D. (1998). The effects of single versus multiple measures of biofeedback on basketball free throw shooting performance. *International Journal of Sport Psychology, 29*, 132-144.

Kavussanu, M., & McAuley, E. (1995). Exercise and optimism: Are highly active individuals more optimistic? *Journal of Sport and Exercise Psychology, 17*, 246-258.

Kazdin, A.E. (1978). Conceptual and assessment issues raised by self-efficacy theory. In S. Rachman (Ed.), *Advances in behavior research and therapy*, Vol. 1 (pp. 177-185). Oxford: Pergamon Press.

Kent, A., & Sullivan, P.J. (2003). Coaching efficacy as a predictor of university coaches' commitment. *International Sports Journal, 7*, 78-88.

Kent, G. (1987). Self-efficacious control over reported physiological, cognitive and behavioral symptoms of dental anxiety. *Behavior Research and Therapy, 25*, 341-347.

Kent, G., & Gibbons, R. (1987). Self-efficacy and the control of anxious cognitions. *Journal of Behavior Therapy and Experimental Psychiatry, 18*, 33-40.

Kirsch, I. (1982). Efficacy expectations as response predictors: The meaning of efficacy ratings as a function of task characteristics. *Journal of Personality and Social Psychology, 42*, 132-136.

Kirsch, I. (1990). *Changing expectations: A key to effective psychotherapy.* Pacific Grove, CA: Brooks/Cole.

Kirsch, I. (1995). Self-efficacy and outcome expectancy: A concluding commentary. In J.E. Maddux (Ed.), *Self-efficacy, adaptation, and adjustment: Theory, research, and application* (pp. 331-345). New York: Plenum Press.

Kitsantas, A., & Zimmerman, B.J. (1998). Self-regulation of motoric learning: A strategic cycle view. *Journal of Applied Sport Psychology, 10,* 220-239.

Kitsantas, A., & Zimmerman, B.J. (2002). Comparing self-regulatory processes among novice, non-expert, and expert volleyball players: A microanalytic study. *Journal of Applied Sport Psychology, 14,* 91-105.

Knoppers, A. (1987). Gender and the coaching profession. *Quest, 39,* 9-22.

Kozlowski, W.J., & Hattrup, K. (1992). A disagreement about within-group agreement: Disentangling issues of consistency versus consensus. *Journal of Applied Psychology, 77,* 161-167.

Kozub, S.A., & McDonnell, J.F. (2000). Exploring the relationship between cohesion and collective efficacy in rugby teams. *Journal of Sport Behavior, 23,* 120-129.

Krane, V. (1994). The mental readiness form as a measure of competitive state anxiety. *The Sport Psychologist, 8,* 189-202

Kyllo, L.B., & Landers, D.M. (1995). Goal setting in sport and exercise: A research synthesis to resolve the controversy. *Journal of Sport and Exercise Psychology, 17,* 117-137.

LaGuardia, R., & Labbe, E.E. (1993). Self-efficacy and anxiety and their relationship to training and race performance. *Perceptual and Motor Skills, 77,* 27-34.

Landers, D.M., & Landers, D.M. (1973). Teacher versus peer models: Effects of model's presence and performance level on motor behavior. *Journal of Motor Behavior, 5,* 129-139.

Landin, D., & Hebert, E.P. (1999). The influence of self-talk on the performance of skilled female tennis players. *Journal of Applied Sport Psychology, 11,* 263-282.

Lane, A.M. (2002). Relationships between performance toward accomplishment and self efficacy in amateur boxing. *Perceptual and Motor Skills, 94,* 1056.

Lane, A.M., Jones, L., & Stevens, M.J. (2002). Coping with failure: The effects of self-esteem and coping on changes in self-efficacy. *Journal of Sport Behavior, 25,* 331-345.

Langley, D.J., & Knight, S.M. (1999). Continuity in sport participation as an adaptive strategy in the aging process: A lifespan narrative. *Journal of Aging and Physical Activity, 7,* 32-54.

Latané, B., Williams, K., & Harkins, S. (1979). Many hands make light the work: The causes and consequences of social loafing. *Journal of Personality and Social Psychology, 37,* 822-832.

Lee, A.M., Nelson, K., & Nelson, J.K. (1988). Success estimations and performance in children as influenced by age, gender, and task. *Sex Roles, 48,* 719-726.

Lee, C. (1982). Self-efficacy as a predictor of performance in competitive gymnastics. *Journal of Sport Psychology, 4,* 405-409.

Lee, C. (1986). Efficacy expectations, training performance, and competitive performance in women's artistic gymnastics. *Behaviour Change, 3,* 100-104.

Lee, C. (1988). The relationship between goal setting, self-efficacy, and female field hockey team performance. *International Journal of Sport Psychology, 20,* 147-161.

Lee, C., & Bobko, P. (1994). Self-efficacy beliefs: Comparison of five measures. *Journal of Applied Psychology, 79,* 364-369.

Lee, K.S., Malete, L., & Feltz, D.L. (2002). The strength of coaching efficacy between certified and noncertified Singapore coaches. *International Journal of Applied Sport Science, 14,* 55-67.

Lenney, E. (1977). Women's self-confidence in achievement settings. *Psychological Bulletin, 84,* 1-13.

Lent, R.W., Brown, S.D., & Larkin, K.C. (1984). Relation of self-efficacy expectations to academic achievement and persistence. *Journal of Counseling Psychology, 31,* 356-362.

Lent, R.W., Brown, S.D., & Larkin, K.C. (1986). Self-efficacy in the prediction of academic performance and perceived career options. *Journal of Counseling Psychology, 33,* 279-291.

Lent, R.W., & Lopez, F.G. (2002). Cognitive ties that bind: A tripartite view of efficacy beliefs in growth-promoting relationships. *Journal of Social and Clinical Psychology, 21,* 256-286.

Lerner, B.S., & Locke, E.A. (1995). The effects of goal setting, self-efficacy, competition, and personal traits on the performance of an endurance task. *Journal of Sport and Exercise Psychology, 17,* 138-152.

Lewin, K., Dembo, T., Festinger, L., & Sears, P.S. (1944). Level of aspiration. In J.M. Hunt (Ed.), *Personality and the behavior disorders.* New York: Ronald Press.

Lichacz, F.M., & Partington, J.T. (1996). Collective efficacy and true group performance. *International Journal of Sport Psychology, 27,* 146-158.

Likert, R. (1932). A technique for the measurement of attitudes. *Archives of Psychology, 140,* 1-55.

Linacre, J.M. (2002). Optimizing rating scale category effectiveness. *Journal of Applied Measurement, 3,* 85-106.

Lindsley, D.H., Brass, D.J., & Thomas, J.B. (1995). Efficacy-performance spirals: A multilevel perspective. *Academy of Management Review, 20,* 645-678.

Lirgg, C.D. (1991). Gender differences in self-confidence in physical activity: A meta-analysis of recent studies. *Journal of Sport and Exercise Psychology, 8,* 294-310.

Lirgg, C.D., Dibrezzo, R., & Smith, A.N. (1994). Influence of gender of coach on perceptions of basketball and coaching self-efficacy and aspirations of high school female basketball players. *Women in Sport and Physical Activity Journal, 3,* 1-14.

Lirgg, C.D., & Feltz, D.L. (1989). Female self-confidence in sport: Myths, realities, and enhancement strategies. *Journal of Physical Education and Recreation, 60,* 49-54.

Lirgg, C.D., & Feltz, D.L. (1991). Teacher versus peer models revisited: Effects on motor performance and self-efficacy. *Research Quarterly for Exercise and Sport, 62,* 217-224.

Lirgg, C.D., George, T.R., Chase, M.A., & Ferguson, R.H. (1996). Impact of conception of ability and sex-type of task on male and female self-efficacy. *Journal of Sport and Exercise Psychology, 18,* 426-343.

Locke, E.A., Frederick, E., Lee, C., & Bobko, P. (1984). Effect of self-efficacy, goals, and task strategies on task performance. *Journal of Applied Psychology, 69,* 241-251.

Locke, E.A., & Latham, G.P. (1990). *A theory of goal setting and task performance.* Englewood Cliffs, NJ: Prentice Hall.

Locke, E.A., Shaw, K.N., Saari, L.M., & Latham, G.P. (1981). Goal setting and task performance. *Psychological Bulletin, 90,* 125-152.

Lohasz, P.G., & Leith, L.M. (1997). The effect of three mental preparation strategies on the performance of a complex response time task. *International Journal of Sport Psychology, 28,* 25-34.

Lopez, F.G., & Lent, R.W. (1991). Efficacy-based predictors of relationship adjustment and persistence among college students. *Journal of College Student Development, 32,* 223-229.

Lyle, J. (1999). The coaching process: An overview. In N. Cros & J. Lyle (Eds.), *The coaching process* (pp. 3-24). Edinburgh: Butterworth Heineman.

Maccoby, E.E., & Jacklin, C.N. (1974). *The psychology of sex differences.* Stanford, CA: Stanford University Press.

Mack, M.G., & Stephens, D.E. (2000). An empirical test of Taylor and Demick's multidimensional model of momentum in sport. *Journal of Sport Behavior, 23,* 349-363.

MacLean, D., & Sullivan, P.J. (2003). A season long case study of collective efficacy in male inter-collegiate basketball. *Athletic Insight, 5* (3), retrievable at www.athleticinsight.com.

Maddalozzo, G.F., Stuart, M.E., Rose, D.J., & Cardinal, B.J. (1999). Enhancing chip shot performance in golf: Evaluation of modeled and queuing plus modeled instructional. *International Sports Journal, 9,* 66-79.

Maddux, J.E. (1995). Self efficacy theory. An introduction. In J.E. Maddux (Ed.), *Self-efficacy, adaptation, and adjustment: Theory, research, and application* (pp. 3-33). New York: Plenum Press.

Maddux, J.E. (1999). The collective construction of collective efficacy: Comment on Paskevich, Brawley, Dorsch, and Widmeyer. *Group Dynamics: Theory, Research, and Practice, 3,* 223-226.

Maddux, J.E., & Lewis, J. (1995). Self-efficacy and adjustment: Basic principles and issues. In J.E. Maddux (Ed.), *Self-efficacy, adaptation, and adjustment: Theory, research, and application* (pp. 37-68). New York: Plenum Press.

Maddux, J.E., & Meier, L.J. (1995). Self-efficacy and depression. In J.E. Maddux (Ed.), *Self-efficacy, adaptation, and adjustment: Theory, research, and application* (pp. 143-172). New York: Plenum Press.

Magill, R.A. (1998). *Motor learning: Concepts and applications.* Boston: WCB/McGraw-Hill.

Magyar, T.M., & Chase, M.A. (1996). Psychological strategies used by competitive gymnasts to overcome fear of injury. www.usa-gymnastics.org/publications/technique/1996/10/psychological-strategies.html.

Magyar, T.M., & Feltz, D.L. (2003). The influence of dispositional and situational tendencies on adolescent girls' selection of sport confidence sources. *Psychology of Sport and Exercise, 4,* 175-190.

Magyar, T.M., Feltz, D.L., & Simpson, I.P. (2004). Individual and crew level determinants of collective efficacy in rowing. *Journal of Sport and Exercise Psychology, 26,* 136-153.

Malete, L., & Feltz, D.L. (2000). The effect of a coaching education program on coaching efficacy. *The Sport Psychologist, 14,* 410-417.

Mamassis, G., & Doganis, G. (2004). The effects of a mental training program on juniors pre-competitive anxiety, self-confidence, and tennis performance. *Journal of Applied Sport Psychology, 16,* 118-137.

Manzo, L.G., & Silva, J.M. (1994, October). Construction and initial validation of the Carolina Sport Confidence Inventory. Paper presented at the annual meeting of the Association for the Advancement of Applied Sport Psychology, Lake Tahoe, NV.

Manzo, L.G., Silva, J.M., & Mink, R. (2001). The Carolina Sport Confidence Inventory. *Journal of Applied Sport Psychology, 13,* 260-274.

Marback, T.L., Short, S.E., Short, M.W., & Sullivan, P.J. (2005). Coaching confidence: An exploratory investigation of sources and gender differences. *Journal of Sport Behavior, 28*(1), 18-34.

Marsh, H.W. (1994). Sport motivation orientations: Beware of the jingle-jangle fallacies. *Journal of Sport and Exercise Psychology, 16,* 331-345.

Marsh, H.W., Hau, K-T, & Wen, Z. (2004). In search of golden rules: Comment on hypothesis-testing approaches to setting cutoff values for fit indexes and dangers in overgeneralizing Hu and Bentler's (1999) findings. *Structural Equation Modeling, 11,* 320-341.

Marsh, H.W., Richards, G.E., Johnson, S., Roche, L., & Tremayne, P. (1994). Physical self-description questionnaire: Psychometric properties and multitrait-multi-method analysis of relations to existing instruments. *Journal of Sport and Exercise Psychology, 16,* 270-305.

Martens, R. (1987). *Coaches guide to sport psychology.* Champaign, IL: Human Kinetics.

Martens, R. (2005). *Successful coaching* (3rd ed.). Champaign, IL: Human Kinetics.

Martens, R., Burton, D., Vealey, R.S., Bump, L., & Smith, D.E. (1990). Competitive State Anxiety Inventory-2. In R. Martens, R.S. Vealey, & D. Burton, *Competitive anxiety in sport* (pp. 117-213). Champaign, IL: Human Kinetics.

Martens, R., Vealey, R.S., & Burton, D. (1990). *Competitive anxiety in sport.* Champaign, IL: Human Kinetics.

Martin, J.J. (2002). Training and performance self-efficacy, affect, and performance in wheelchair road racers. *The Sport Psychologist, 16,* 384-395.

Martin, J.J., & Gill, D.L. (1991). The relationship among competitive orientation, sport-confidence, self-efficacy, anxiety and performance. *Journal of Sport and Exercise Psychology, 13,* 149-159.

Martin, J.J., & Gill, D.L. (1995). The relationships of competitive orientations and self-efficacy to goal importance, thoughts, and performance in high school distance runners. *Journal of Applied Sport Psychology, 7,* 50-62.

Martin, K.A., & Hall, C.R. (1995). Using mental imagery to enhance intrinsic motivation. *Journal of Sport and Exercise Psychology, 17,* 54-69.

Martin, K.A., Moritz, S.E., & Hall, C.R. (1999). Imagery use in sport: A literature review and applied model. *The Sport Psychologist, 13,* 245-268.

Mascarenhas, D.R., Collins, D., & Mortimer, R. (2005). The accuracy, agreement and coherence of decision making in rugby union officials. *Journal of Sport Behavior, 28,* 253-271.

Maurer, T.J., & Pierce, H.R. (1998). A comparison of Likert scale and traditional measures of self-efficacy. *Journal of Applied Psychology, 83,* 324-329.

McAuley, E. (1985). Modeling and self-efficacy: A test of Bandura's model. *Journal of Sport Psychology, 7,* 283-295.

McAuley, E. (1992a). Self-referent thought in sport and physical activity. In T.S. Horn (Ed.), *Advances in sport psychology* (pp. 101-118). Champaign, IL: Human Kinetics.

McAuley, E. (1992b). Understanding exercise behavior: A self-efficacy perspective. In G.C. Roberts (Ed.), *Motivation in sport and exercise* (pp. 107-127). Champaign, IL: Human Kinetics.

McAuley, E., & Courneya, K.S. (1992). Self-efficacy relationships with affective and exertion responses to exercise. *Journal of Applied Social Psychology, 22,* 312-326.

McAuley, E., & Gill, D. (1983). Reliability and validity of the physical self-efficacy scale in a competitive sport setting. *Journal of Sport Psychology, 5,* 410-418.

McAuley, E., & Mihalko, S.L. (1998). Measuring exercise related self-efficacy. In J.L. Duda (Ed.), *Advances in sport and exercise psychology measurement* (pp. 371-390). Morgantown, WV: Fitness Information Technology.

McCullagh, P. (1987). Model similarity effects on motor performance. *Journal of Sport Psychology, 9,* 249-260.

McCullagh, P., & Weiss, M.R. (2001). Modeling: Considerations for motor skill performance and psychological responses. In R.N. Singer, H.A. Hausenblas, & C.M. Janelle (Eds.), *Handbook of sport psychology* (pp. 205-238). New York: Wiley.

McCullagh, P., & Weiss, M.R. (2002). Observational learning: The forgotten psychological method in sport psychology. In J.L. Van Raalte & B.W. Brewer (Eds.), *Exploring sport and exercise psychology* (pp. 131-149). Washington, DC: American Psychological Association.

McKenzie, A.D., & Howe, B. (1997). The effect of imagery on self-efficacy for a motor skill. *International Journal of Sport Psychology, 28,* 196-210.

McNair, D.M., Lorr, M., & Droppleman, L.F. (1971). *Manual for the profile of mood states.* San Diego: Educational and Industrial Testing Services.

McPherson, S.L. (2000). Expert-novice differences in planning strategies during collegiate singles tennis competition. *Journal of Sport and Exercise Psychology, 22,* 39-62.

Mellalieu, S.D., Hanton, S., & Fletcher, D. (2006). A competitive anxiety review: Recent directions in sport psychology research. In S. Hanton & S.D. Mellalieu (Eds.), *Literature reviews in sport psychology.* Hauppauge, NY: Nova Science.

Mellalieu, S.D., Neil, R., & Hanton, S. (2006). Self-confidence as a mediator of the relationship between competitive anxiety intensity and interpretation. *Research Quarterly for Exercise and Sport, 77,* 263-270.

Mercier, R. (2003). Analysing the impact of the Women in Coaching Apprenticeship Program. *Canadian Journal for Women in Coaching,* 4. Retrieved December 8, 2005, from www.coach.ca/WOMEN/e/journal/oct2003/october2003.pdf.

Messick, S. (1989). Validity. In R.L. Linn (Ed.), *Educational measurement* (3rd ed., pp. 13-103). New York: Macmillan.

Meyer, J.P., & Allen, N.J. (1991). A three-component conceptualization of organizational commitment. *Human Resource Management Review, 1,* 61-89.

Miller, J.T., & McAuley, E. (1987). Effects of a goal-setting training program on basketball free-throw self-efficacy and performance. *The Sport Psychologist, 1,* 103-113.

Miller, M. (1993). Efficacy strength and performance in competitive swimmers of different skill levels. *International Journal of Sport Psychology, 24,* 284-296.

Mills, K.D., Munroe, K.J., & Hall, C.R. (2000). The relationship between imagery and self efficacy in competitive athletics. *Imagination, Cognition, and Personality, 20,* 33-39.

Milne, M., Hall, C., & Forwell, L. (2005). Self-efficacy, imagery use, and adherence to rehabilitation by injured athletes. *Journal of Sport Rehabilitation, 14,* 150-167.

Milner, H.R., & Hoy, A.W. (2003). A case study of an African American teacher's self-efficacy, stereotype threat, and persistence. *Teaching and Teacher Education, 19,* 263-276.

Molstad, S.M. (1993). Coaching qualities, gender and role modeling. *Women in Sport and Physical Activity Journal, 2,* 11-19.

Monsma, E.A., & Feltz, D.L. (2006). Psychological consulting with figure skaters. In J. Dosil (Ed.), *The sport psychologist's handbook: A guide for sport-specific performance enhancement* (pp. 427-454). Chichester, UK: Wiley.

Moran, A.P. (2004). *Sport and exercise psychology: A critical introduction.* New York: Routledge.

Moritz, S.E. (1998). The effect of task type on the relationship between efficacy beliefs and performance. Unpublished doctoral dissertation, Michigan State University, East Lansing.

Moritz, S.E., Feltz, D.L., Fahrbach, K.R., & Mack, D.E. (2000). The relation of self-efficacy measures to sport performance. A meta-analytic review. *Research Quarterly for Exercise and Sport, 71,* 280-294.

Moritz, S.E., Hall, C.R., Martin, K.A., & Vadocz, E. (1996). What are confident athletes imaging? An examination of image content. *The Sport Psychologist, 10,* 171-179.

Moritz, S.E., & Watson, C.B. (1998). Levels of analysis issues in group psychology: Using efficacy as an example of a multilevel model. *Group Dynamics: Theory, Research, and Practice, 2,* 285-298.

Mullen, B., & Cooper, C. (1994). The relation between group cohesiveness and performance: An integration. *Psychological Bulletin, 115,* 210-227.

Munroe, K.J., Giacobbi, P.R., Hall, C.R., & Weinberg, R.S. (2000). The four Ws of imagery use: Where, when, why, and what. *The Sport Psychologist, 14,* 119-137.

Murphy, S.M., Nordin, S.M., & Cumming, J. (2006). Imagery in sport, exercise and dance. In T. Horn (Ed.), *Advances in sport psychology* (3rd ed.). Champaign, IL: Human Kinetics.

Murphy, S.M., & Woolfolk, R.L. (1987). The effect of cognitive interventions on competitive anxiety and performance on a fine motor skill accuracy task. *International Journal of Sport Psychology, 18,* 152-166.

Myers, N.D., & Feltz, D.L. (2007). From self-efficacy to collective efficacy in sport: Transitional issues. In G. Tenenbaum & R.C. Eklund (Eds.), *Handbook of sport psychology* (3rd ed.) (pp. 799-819). New York: Wiley.

Myers, N.D., Feltz, D.L., Maier, K.S., Wolfe, E.W., & Reckase, M.D. (2006). Athletes' evaluations of their head coach's coaching competency. *Research Quarterly for Exercise and Sport, 77,* 111-121.

Myers, N.D., Feltz, D.L., & Short, S.E. (2004). Collective efficacy and team performance: A longitudinal study of collegiate football teams. *Group Dynamics: Theory, Research, and Practice, 8,* 126-138.

Myers, N.D., Feltz, D.L., & Wolfe, E.W. (2006). A confirmatory study of rating scale category effectiveness for the Coaching Efficacy Scale. Manuscript submitted for publication.

Myers, N.D., Paiement, C.A., & Feltz, D.L. (2007). Regressing team performance on collective efficacy: Considerations of temporal proximity and concordance. *Measurement in Physical Education and Exercise Science, 11*, 1-24.

Myers, N.D., Payment, C.A., & Feltz, D.L. (2004). Reciprocal relationships between collective efficacy and team performance in women's ice hockey. *Group Dynamics: Theory, Research, and Practice, 8*, 182-195.

Myers, N.D., Vargas-Tonsing, T.M., & Feltz, D.L. (2005). Coaching efficacy in intercollegiate coaches: Sources, coaching behavior, and team variables. *Psychology of Sport and Exercise, 6*, 129-143.

Myers, N.D., Wolfe, E.W., & Feltz, D.L. (2005). An evaluation of the psychometric properties of the coaching efficacy scale for American coaches. *Measurement in Physical Education and Exercise Science, 9*, 135-160.

National Association for Sport and Physical Education. (1995). *Quality coaches, quality sports: National standards for athletic coaches.* Dubuque, IA: Kendall/Hunt.

NBA at 50: Phil Jackson, The. (2003). Retrieved October 4, 2004, from www.nba.com/history/jackson_50.html.

Neiss, R. (1989). Expectancy in motor behavior: A crucial element of the psychobiological states that affect performance. *Human Performance, 2*, 273-300.

Ness, R.G., & Patton, R.W. (1979). The effect of beliefs on maximum weight-lifting performance. *Cognitive Therapy and Research, 3*, 205-211.

Newton, M., Duda, J.L., & Yin, Z. (2000). Examination of the psychometric properties of the Perceived Motivational Climate in Sport Questionnaire-2 in a sample of female athletes. *Journal of Sports Sciences, 18*, 275-290.

Nicholls, J.G. (1984a). Achievement motivation: Conception of ability, subjective experience, task choice, and performance. *Psychological Review, 91*, 328-346.

Nicholls, J.G. (1984b). Concepts of ability and achievement motivation. In R. Amers & C. Ames (Eds.), *Research on motivation in education*, Vol. 1 (pp. 39-73). New York: Academic Press.

Nicholls, J.G. (1989). *The competitive ethos and democratic education.* Cambridge, MA: Harvard University Press.

Nordin, S.M., & Cumming, J. (2005). More than meets the eye: Investigating imagery type, direction, and outcome. *The Sport Psychologist, 19*, 1-17.

Okwumabua, T.M. (1986). Psychological and physical contributions to marathon performance: An exploratory investigation. *Journal of Sport Behavior, 8*, 163-171.

O'Leary, A. (1985). Self-efficacy and health. *Behavioral Research and Therapy, 23*, 437-451.

Orbach, I., Singer, R.N., & Price, S. (1999). An attribution training program and achievement in sport. *The Sport Psychologist, 13*, 69-82.

Orlick, T. (2000). *In pursuit of excellence* (3rd ed.). Champaign, IL: Human Kinetics.

Paivio, A. (1985). Cognitive and motivational functions of imagery in human performance. *Canadian Journal of Applied Sport Sciences, 10*, 22S-28S.

Pajares, F., Hartley, J., & Valiante, G. (2001). Response format in writing self-efficacy assessment: Greater discrimination increases prediction. *Measurement and Evaluation in Counseling and Development, 33*, 214-221.

Park, J.K. (1992). Construction of the coaching confidence scale. Unpublished doctoral dissertation, Michigan State University, East Lansing.

Parent, J. (2002). *Zen golf: Mastering the mental game.* New York: Doubleday.

Paskevich, D.M., Brawley, L.R., Dorsch, K.D., & Widmeyer, W.N. (1999). Relationship between collective efficacy and team cohesion: Conceptual and measurement issues. *Group Dynamics: Theory, Research, and Practice, 3*, 210-222.

Pastore, D.L. (1991). Male and female coaches of women's athletic teams: Reasons for entering and leaving the profession. *Journal of Sport Management, 5*, 128-143.

Pellett, T.L., Henschel-Pellett, H.A., & Harrison, J.M. (1994). Influence of ball weight on junior high school girls' volleyball performance. *Perceptual and Motor Skills, 78*, 1379-1384.

Pellett, T.L., & Lox, C.L. (1997). Tennis racket length comparisons and their effect on beginning college players' playing success and achievement. *Journal of Teaching in Physical Education, 16*, 490-499.

Pellett, T.L., & Lox, C.L. (1998). Tennis racket head-size comparisons and their effect on beginning college players' achievement and self-efficacy. *Journal of Teaching in Physical Education, 17*, 453-467.

Piltz, W. (1999). Mentor apprenticeship program in lacrosse coaching education. Retrieved December 9, 2005, from www.ausport.gov.au/fulltext/1999/acc/ncd/piltz.htm.

Pintrich, P.R., & Schunk, D.H. (2002). *Motivation in education: Theory, research, and applications* (2nd ed.). Upper Saddle River, NJ: Prentice Hall.

Powers, W.T. (1978). Quantitative analysis of purposive systems: Some spadework at the foundations of scientific psychology. *Psychological Review, 85,* 417-435.

Powers, W.T. (1991). Comment on Bandura's "human agency." *American Psychologist, 46,* 151-153.

Prapavessis, H., & Grove, J.R. (1994). Personality variables as antecedents of precompetitive mood state temporal patterning. *International Journal of Sport Psychology, 22,* 347-365.

Prussia, G.E., & Kinicki, A.J. (1996). A motivational investigation of group effectiveness using social cognitive theory. *Journal of Applied Psychology, 81,* 187-198.

Quinn, A.M., & Fallon, B.J. (2000). Predictors of recovery time. *Journal of Sport Rehabilitation, 9,* 62-76.

Rainey, D.W., Larsen, J.D., & Williard, M.J. (1987). A computer simulation of sport officiating behavior. *Journal of Sport Behavior, 10,* 183-191.

Ram, N., & McCullagh, P. (2003). Self-modeling: Influence on psychological responses and physical performance. *The Sport Psychologist, 17,* 220-241.

Ramey-Gassert, L., Shroyer, M.G., & Staver, J.R. (1996). A qualitative study of factors influencing science teaching self-efficacy of elementary level teachers. *Science Education, 80,* 283-315.

Raudenbush, S.W., & Bryk, A.S. (2002). *Hierarchical linear models: Applications and data analysis methods.* Newbury Park, CA: Sage.

Renfro, B. (2004, October 1). Despite setbacks, volleyball team keeps "family" spirit alive. Retrieved December 9, 2005, from www.thenews.org/media/paper651/news/2004/10/01/Sports/Despite.Setbacks.Volleyball.Team. Keeps.family.Spirit.Alive-738034.shtml.

Reuter, J.M., & Short, S.E. (2005). The relationships among three components of perceived risk of injury, previous injuries, and gender in non-contact/limited contact sport athletes. *Athletic Insight, 7.* Retrieved September 1, 2005, from www.athleticinsight.com/Vol7Iss1/PerceivedRiskofInjuryNoContact.htm.

Richardson, A. (1969). *Mental Imagery.* New York: Springer Publishing Company, Inc.

Rink, J. (1992). *Teaching physical education for learning* (2nd ed.). St. Louis: Times/Mirror/Mosby.

Roberts, G.C. (1992). Motivation in sport and exercise: Conceptual constraints and convergence. In G.C. Roberts (Ed.), *Motivation in sport and exercise* (pp. 3-29). Champaign, IL: Human Kinetics.

Roberts, G.C. (2001). Understanding the dynamics of motivation in physical activity: The influence of achievement goals on motivational processes. In G.C. Roberts (Ed.), *Advances in motivation in sport and exercise* (pp. 1-50). Champaign, IL: Human Kinetics.

Roberts, W., & Vealey, R.S. (1992, October). Attention in sport: Measurement issues, psychological concomitants, and the prediction of performance. Paper presented at the Association for the Advancement of Applied Sport Psychology Conference, Colorado Springs, CO.

Robertson, S. (2005). Career pathways of great coaches: An inside look at success. *Coaches Reports, 12*(1), 7-13.

Rogers, R.W. (1983). Cognitive and physiological processes in fear appeals and attitude change: A revised theory of protection motivation. In J.T. Cacioppo & R.E. Petty (Eds.), *Social psychophysiology* (pp. 153-176). New York: Guilford.

Rotter, J.B. (1966). Generalized expectancies from internal versus external control of reinforcement. *Psychological Monographs, 80*(1, Whole No. 609).

Rousseau, D.M. (1985). Issues of levels in organizational research: Multi-level and cross-level perspectives. *Research in Organizational Behavior, 7,* 1-37.

Rudisill, M.E. (1988). The influence of causal dimension orientations and perceived competence on adult's expectations, persistence, performance and the selection of causal dimensions. *International Journal of Sport Psychology, 19,* 184-198.

Rudisill, M.E. (1989). Influence of perceived competence and causal dimension orientation on expectation, persistence, and performance during perceived failure. *Research Quarterly for Exercise and Sport, 60,* 166-175.

Rudolph, D.L., & Butki, B.D. (1998). Self-efficacy and affective responses to short bouts of exercise. *Journal of Applied Sport Psychology, 10,* 268-280.

Rudolph, D.L., & McAuley, E. (1996). Self-efficacy and perceptions of effort: A reciprocal relationship. *Journal of Sport and Exercise Psychology, 18,* 216-223.

Rushall, B.S. (1988). Covert modeling as a procedure for altering an elite athlete's psychological state. *The Sport Psychologist, 2,* 131-140.

Ryckman, R., Robbins, M., Thornton, B., & Cantrell, P. (1982). Development and validation of a physical self-efficacy scale. *Journal of Personality and Social Psychology, 42,* 891-900.

Ryska, T.A. (2002). Predicting prosocial intentions among young athletes: The mediating role of negative mood and comparative efficacy. *International Sports Journal, 6,* 14-30.

Salmela, J.H. (1996). *Great job coach: Getting the edge from proven winners.* Ottawa, ON: Potentium.

Sanguinetti, C., Lee, A.M., & Nelson, J. (1985). Reliability estimates and age and gender comparisons of expectations of success in sex-typed activities. *Journal of Sport Psychology, 7,* 379-388.

Satern, M.N., Messier, S.P., & Keller-McNulty, S. (1989). The effects of ball size and basket height on the mechanics of a basketball free throw. *Journal of Human Movement Studies, 16,* 123-137.

Scheier, M.F., & Carver, C.S. (1985). Optimism, coping and health: Assessment and implications of generalized outcome expectancies. *Health Psychology, 4,* 219-247.

Schön, D.A. (1983). *The reflective practitioner: How professionals think in action.* New York: Basic Books.

Schultz, R., & Short, S.E. (2006). Who do athletes compare to?: How the standard of comparison affects confidence ratings. *AAASP Conference Proceedings,* 82-83.

Schunk, D.H. (1995a). Self-efficacy and education and instruction. In J.E. Maddux (Ed.), *Self-efficacy, adaptation, and adjustment: Theory, research, and application* (pp. 281-303). New York: Plenum Press.

Schunk, D.H. (1995b). Self-efficacy, motivation, and performance. *Journal of Applied Sport Psychology, 7,* 112-137.

Schunk, D.H., & Hanson, A.R. (1985). Peer models: Influence on children's self-efficacy and achievement. *Journal of Educational Psychology, 81,* 201-209.

Schutz, W.C. (1966). *The interpersonal underworld* (5th ed.). Palo Alto, CA: Science & Behavior Books.

Seefeldt, V. (Ed.). (1987). *Handbook for youth sport coaches.* Reston, VA: American Alliance for Health, Physical Education, Recreation, and Dance.

Seefeldt, V. & Brown, E.W. (Eds.) (1990). *Program for athletic coaches education.* Carmel, IN: Benchmark Press, Inc.

Shaw, J.M., Dzewaltowski, D.A., & McElroy, M. (1992). Self-efficacy and causal attributions as mediators of perceptions of psychological momentum. *Journal of Sport and Exercise Psychology, 14,* 134-147.

Short, S.E. (2006a, October). A comprehensive study of imagery use by coaches. Paper presented at the annual conference of the Association for the Advancement of Applied Sport Psychology, Miami, FL.

Short, S.E. (2006b). The effect of team size, type of sport, time of season and gender on collective efficacy beliefs in sport. Manuscript submitted for publication.

Short, S.E., Apostal, K., Harris, C., Poltavski, D., Young, J., Zostautas, N., Sullivan, P., & Feltz, D.L. (2002). Assessing collective efficacy: A comparison of two approaches. *Journal of Sport and Exercise Psychology, 24,* S115-S116.

Short, S.E., Bruggeman, J.M., Engel, S.G., Marback, T.L., Wang, L.J., Willadsen, A., & Short, M.W. (2002). The effect of imagery function and imagery direction on self-efficacy and performance on a golf-putting task. *The Sport Psychologist, 16,* 48-67.

Short, S.E., Monsma, E.V., & Short, M.W. (2004). Is what you see really what you get? Athlete's perceptions of imagery functions. *The Sport Psychologist, 18,* 341-349.

Short, S.E., Reuter, J., Brandt, J., Short, M.W., & Kontos, A.P. (2004). The relationships among three components of perceived risk of injury, previous injuries, and gender in contact sport athletes. *Athletic Insight, 6.* Retrieved September 1, 2005, from www.athleticinsight.com/Vol6Iss3/PerceivedRiskofInjury.htm.

Short, S.E., Ross-Stewart, L., & Monsma, E. (2006). Onwards with the evolution of imagery research in sport psychology. *Athletic Insight.* Retrieved October 12, 2006, from www.athleticinsight.com/Vol8Iss3/ImageryResearch.htm.

Short, S.E., & Short, M.W. (2004). Coaching efficacy: Coaches' assessments compared to athletes' perceptions. *Perceptual and Motor Skills, 99,* 729-736.

Short, S.E., & Short, M.W. (2005a). Differences between high- and low-confident football players on imagery functions: A consideration of the athletes' perceptions. *Journal of Applied Sport Psychology, 17,* 197-208.

Short, S.E., & Short, M.W. (2005b). Role of the coach in the coach-athlete relationship. *Lancet: Medicine and Sport, 366*(Suppl. 1), S29-30.

Short, S.E., Smiley, M., & Ross-Stewart, L. (2005). The relationships among imagery use and efficacy beliefs in coaches. *The Sport Psychologist, 19,* 380-394.

Short, S.E., Sullivan, P.J., & Feltz, D.L. (2005). Development and preliminary validation of the Collective Efficacy Questionnaire for Sports. *Measurement in Physical Education and Exercise Science, 9,* 181-202.

Short, S.E., Tenute, A., & Feltz, D.L. (2005). Imagery use in sport: Mediational effects for efficacy. *Journal of Sports Sciences, 23,* 951-960.

Short, S.E., & Vadocz, E.A. (2002). Testing the modifiability of the State Sport Confidence Inventory. *Perceptual and Motor Skills, 94,* 1025-1028.

Singleton, D.A., & Feltz, D.L. (1999). The effects of self-modeling on shooting performance and self-efficacy among intercollegiate hockey players. Unpublished manuscript, Michigan State University, East Lansing.

Slobounov, S., Yukelson, D., & O'Brien, R. (1997). Self-efficacy and movement variability of Olympic-level springboard divers. *Journal of Applied Sport Psychology, 9,* 171-190.

Smith, E.V. (2000). Metric development and score reporting in Rasch measurement. *Journal of Applied Measurement, 1,* 303-326.

Smith, R.E., Smoll, F.L., & Curtis, B. (1979). Coach effectiveness training: A cognitive-behavioral approach to enhancing relationship skills in youth sports. *Journal of Sport Psychology, 1,* 59-75.

Smith, R.E., Smoll, F.L., & Hunt, E. (1977). A system for the behavioral assessment of athletic coaches. *Research Quarterly, 48,* 401-407.

Smoll, F.L., & Smith, R.E. (1989). Leadership behaviors in sport: A theoretical model and research paradigm. *Journal of Applied Social Psychology, 19,* 1522-1551.

Smoll, F.L., & Smith, R.E. (2001). Conducting sport psychology training programs for coaches: Cognitive-behavioral principles and techniques. In J.M. Williams (Ed.), *Applied sport psychology (4th ed)* (pp. 378-400). Mountain View, CA: Mayfield.

Smylie, M.A. (1988). The enhancement function of staff development: Organizational and psychological antecedents to teacher change. *American Educational Research Journal, 25,* 1-30.

Solmon, M.A., Lee, A.M., Belcher, D., Harrison, L., & Wells, L. (2003). Beliefs about gender appropriateness, ability, and competence in physical activity. *Journal of Teaching in Physical Education, 22,* 261-279.

Solomon, G.B. (2001). Performance and personality impression cues as predictors of athletic performance: An extension of athlete expectancy theory. *International Journal of Sport Psychology, 32,* 88-100.

Solomon, G.B. (2002). Confidence as a source of expectancy information: A follow-up investigation. *International Sports Journal, 6,* 119-127.

Soohoo, S., Takemoto, K.Y., & McCullagh, P. (2004). A comparison of modeling and imagery on the performance of a motor skill. *Journal of Sport Behavior, 27,* 349-365.

Spink, K.S. (1990a). Collective efficacy in the sport setting. *International Journal of Sport Psychology, 21,* 380-395.

Spink, K.S. (1990b). Group cohesion and collective efficacy of volleyball teams. *Journal of Sport and Exercise Psychology, 12,* 301-311.

Spink, K.S., Nickel, D., Wilson, K., & Odnokon, P. (2005). Using a multilevel approach to examine the relationship between task cohesion and team task satisfaction in elite ice hockey players. *Small Group Research, 36,* 539-554.

Starek, J., & McCullagh, P. (1999). The effect of self-modeling on the performance of beginning swimmers. *The Sport Psychologist, 13,* 269-287.

Steele, C.M. (1997). A threat in the air: How stereotypes shape intellectual identity and performance. *American Psychologist, 52,* 613-629.

Steiner, I.D. (1972). *Group processes and group productivity.* New York: Academic.

Stidwell, H.F. (1994). Application of self-efficacy theory: A treatment approach for sport performance phobias. *Journal of Mental Health Counseling, 16,* 196-204.

Stone, J., Lynch, C.I., Sjomeling, M., & Darley, J.M. (1999). Stereotype threat effects on black and white athletic performance. *Journal of Personality and Social Psychology, 77,* 1213-1227.

Sturm, R., & Short, S.E. (2004). The relationships among self-efficacy, team efficacy, and team performance in baseball. Manuscript in preparation.

Sullivan, P., & Feltz, D.L. (2005). Applying social psychology to sports teams. In F.W. Schneider, J. Gruman, & L. Coutts (Eds.), *Applied social psychology: Understanding and addressing social problems* (pp. 129-149). Thousand Oaks, CA: Sage.

Sullivan, P.J., Gee, C.J., & Feltz, D.L. (2006). Playing experience: The content knowledge source of coaching efficacy beliefs. In A.V. Mitel (Ed.), *Trends in Educational Psychology.* New York: Nova Publishers.

Sullivan, P.J., & Kent, A. (2003). Coaching efficacy as a predictor of leadership style in intercollegiate athletics. *Journal of Applied Sport Psychology, 15,* 1-11.

Sullivan, P.J., Paiement, C., Brachlow, M., & Bagnell, K.(2005). The psychological effect of coaching education. *Journal of Sport and Exercise Psychology, 27*(Suppl), S8.

Smylie, M.A. (1988). The enhancement function of staff development: Organizational and psychological antecedents to teacher change. *American Educational Research Journal, 25,* 1-30.

Swain, A.B.J., & Jones, G. (1993). Intensity and frequency dimensions of competitive state anxiety. *Journal of Sports Sciences, 11,* 533-542

Tabachnick, B.G., & Fidell, L.S. (2001). *Using multivariate statistics.* Boston: Allyn & Bacon.

Taylor, A.H., & May, S. (1996). Threat and coping appraisal as determinants of compliance with sports injury rehabilitation: An application of Protection Motivation Theory. *Journal of Sports Sciences, 14,* 471-482.

Taylor, C.B., Bandura, A., Ewart, C.K., Miller, N.H. & DeBusk, R.F. (1985). Exercise testing to enhance wives' confidence in their husbands' cardiac capabilities soon after clinically uncomplicated acute myocardial infarction. *American Journal of Cardiology, 55,* 635-638.

Taylor, D.M., & Doria, J.R. (1981). Self-serving and group-serving bias in attribution. *Journal of Social Psychology, 113,* 201-211.

Taylor, D.M., Doria, J.R., & Tyler, K.J. (1983). Group performance and cohesiveness: An attribution analysis. *Journal of Social Psychology, 119,* 187-198.

Taylor, J. (1988). Slumpbusting: A systematic analysis of slumps in sports. *The Sport Psychologist, 2,* 39-48.

Taylor, J.A., & Shaw, D.F. (2002). The effects of outcome imagery on golf putting performance. *Journal of Sports Science, 20,* 607-613.

Taylor, J., & Taylor, S. (1997). *Psychological approaches to sports injury rehabilitation.* Gaithersburg, MD: Aspen.

Telch, M.J., Bandura, A., Vinciguerra, P., Agras, A., & Stout, A.L. (1982). Social demand for consistency and congruence between self-efficacy and performance. *Behavior Therapy, 13,* 694-701.

Tenenbaum, G., Levy-Kolker, K.N., Sade, S., Liebermann, D.G., & Lidor, R. (1996). Anticipation and confidence of decisions related to skill performance. *International Journal of Sport Psychology, 27,* 293-307.

Thelwell, R.C., & Greenlees, I.A. (2003). Developing competitive endurance performance using mental skills training. *The Sport Psychologist, 17,* 318-337.

Theodorakis, Y. (1995). Effects of self-efficacy, satisfaction, and personal goals on swimming performance. *The Sport Psychologist, 9,* 245-253.

Theodorakis, Y. (1996). The influence of goals, commitment, self-efficacy and self-satisfaction on motor performance. *Journal of Applied Sport Psychology, 8,* 171-182.

Theodorakis, Y., Beneca, A., Malliou, P., & Goudas, M. (1997). Examining psychological factors during injury. *Journal of Sport Rehabilitation, 6,* 355-363.

Thomas, O., Hanton, S., & Jones, G. (2002). An alternative approach to short-form self-assessment of competitive anxiety: A research note. *International Journal of Sport Psychology, 33,* 325-336.

Treasure, D.C., Monson, J., & Lox, C.L. (1996). Relationship between self-efficacy, wrestling performance, and affect prior to competition. *The Sport Psychologist, 10,* 73-83.

Trungpa, C. (1984). *Shambhala: The sacred path of the warrior.* Boston: Shambhala.

Tuckman, B.W. (1965). Development sequences in small groups. *Psychological Bulletin, 63,* 384-399.

Tuckman, B.W., & Jensen, M.C. (1977). Stages of small group development revisited. *Group and Organizational Studies, 2,* 419-427.

Tuton, K., & Short, S.E. (2004). Sources of coaching efficacy among female women's softball coaches. Unpublished manuscript, University of North Dakota.

United States Census. (2000). Index to the statistical abstract of the United States, 2000 Accessed October 23, 2004, from www.census.gov/prod/www/INDEX00S.HTM#Sports.

Vadocz, E.A., Hall, C.R., & Moritz, S.E. (1997). The relationship between competitive anxiety and imagery use. *Journal of Applied Sport Psychology, 9,* 241-253.

Vancouver, J.B., Thompson, C.M., Tischner, E.C., & Putka, D.J. (2002). Two studies examining the negative effect of self-efficacy on performance. *Journal of Applied Psychology, 87,* 506-516.

Vancouver, J.B., Thompson, C.M., & Williams, A.A. (2001). The changing signs in the relationships between self-efficacy, personal goals, and performance. *Journal of Applied Psychology, 86,* 605-620.

Vargas-Tonsing, T. (2004). An examination of pre-game speeches and their effectiveness in increasing athletes' levels of self-efficacy and emotion. Unpublished doctoral dissertation, Michigan State University, East Lansing.

Vargas-Tonsing, T., & Bartholomew, J.B. (2006). An exploratory study of the effects of pre-game speeches on team-efficacy beliefs. *Journal of Applied Sport Psychology, 36,* 918-933.

Vargas-Tonsing, T.M., Myers, N.D., & Feltz, D.L. (2004). Coaches' and athletes' perceptions of efficacy enhancing techniques. *The Sport Psychologist, 18,* 397-414.

Vargas-Tonsing, T.M., Warners, A.L., & Feltz, D.L. (2003). The predictability of coaching efficacy on team efficacy and player efficacy in volleyball. *Journal of Sport Behavior, 26,* 396-407.

Vealey, R.S. (1986). Conceptualization of sport-confidence and competitive orientation: Preliminary investigation and instrument development. *Journal of Sport Psychology, 8,* 221-246.

Vealey, R.S., & Greenleaf, C.A. (2001). Seeing is believing: Understanding and using imagery in sport. In J.M. Williams (Ed.), *Applied sport psychology: Personal growth to peak performance* (pp. 247-283). Mountain View, CA: Mayfield.

Vealey, R.S., Hayashi, S.W., Garner-Holman, M., & Giacobbi, P. (1998). Sources of sport-confidence: Conceptualization and instrument development. *Journal of Sport and Exercise Psychology, 20,* 54-80.

Vealey, R.S., & Knight, B.J. (2003). Conceptualization and measurement of multidimensional sport-confidence: A social-cognitive approach. Unpublished manuscript, Miami University, Oxford, OH.

Vealey, R.S., & Sinclair, D.A. (1987). The analysis and prediction of stability in sport-confidence. Paper presented at the Association for the Advancement of Applied Sport Psychology, Newport Beach, CA.

Wahl, G. (2005). Yes, hard feelings. *Sports Illustrated, 102*(13), 54-57.

Watkins, B., Garcia, A.W., & Turek, E. (1994). The relation between self-efficacy and sport performance: Evidence from a sample of youth baseball players. *Journal of Applied Sport Psychology, 6,* 21-31.

Watson, C.B., Chemers, M.M., & Preiser, N. (2001). Collective efficacy: A multilevel analysis. *Personality and Social Psychology Bulletin, 27,* 1056-1068.

Watson, D., Clark, L.A., & Tellegen, A. (1988). Development and validation of brief measures of positive and negative affect: The PANAS scales. *Journal of Personality and Social Psychology, 54,* 1063-1070.

Weaver, M.A., & Chelladurai, P. (1999). A mentoring model for management in sport and physical education. *Quest, 51,* 24-38.

Weaver, M.A., & Chelladurai, P. (2002). Mentoring in intercollegiate athletic administration. *Journal of Sport Management, 16,* 96-116.

Wegner, L.D.M. (1989). *White bears and other unwanted thoughts.* New York: Viking Press.

Weinberg, R. (1985). Relationship between self-efficacy and cognitive strategies in enhancing endurance performance. *International Journal of Sport Psychology, 17,* 280-292.

Weinberg, R.S., & Gould, D. (2003). *Foundations of sport and exercise psychology* (3rd ed.). Champaign, IL: Human Kinetics.

Weinberg, R., Gould, D., & Jackson, A. (1979). Expectations and performance: An empirical test of Bandura's self-efficacy theory. *Journal of Sport Psychology, 1,* 320-331.

Weinberg, R.S., Gould, D., Yukelson, D., & Jackson, A. (1981). The effects of pre-existing and manipulated self-efficacy on a competitive muscular endurance task. *Journal of Sport Psychology, 3,* 345-354.

Weinberg, R., Grove, R., & Jackson, A. (1992). Strategies for building self-efficacy in tennis players: A comparative analysis of Australian and American coaches. *The Sport Psychologist, 6,* 3-13.

Weinberg, R.S., & Jackson, A. (1990). Building self-efficacy in tennis players: A coach's perspective. *Journal of Applied Sport Psychology, 2,* 164-174.

Weinberg, R.S., Yukelson, D., & Jackson, A. (1980). Effect of public and private efficacy expectations on competitive performance. *Journal of Sport Psychology, 2,* 340-349.

Weiner, B. (1985). An attributional theory of achievement motivation and emotion. *Psychological Review, 92,* 548-573.

Weiss, M.R., Barber, H., Sisley, B.L., & Ebbeck, V. (1991). Developing competence and confidence in novice female coaches: II. Perceptions of ability and affective experiences following a season-long coaching internship. *Journal of Sport and Exercise Psychology, 13,* 336-363.

Weiss, M.R., & Hayashi, C.T. (1996). The United States. In P. De Knop, L.M. Engstrom, B. Skirstad, & M.R. Weiss (Eds.), *Worldwide trends in youth sport* (pp. 43-57). Champaign, IL: Human Kinetics.

Weiss, M.R., McCullagh, P., Smith, A.L., & Berlant, A.R. (1998). Observational learning and the fearful child: Influence of peer models on swimming skill performance and psychological responses. *Research Quarterly for Exercise and Sport, 69,* 380-394.

Weiss, M.R., Wiese, D.M., & Klint, K.A. (1989). Head over heels with success: The relationship between self-efficacy and performance in competitive youth gymnastics. *Journal of Sport and Exercise Psychology, 11,* 444-451.

Wells, C.M., Collins, D., & Hale, B.D. (1993). The self-efficacy-performance link in maximum strength performance. *Journal of Sports Sciences, 11,* 167-175.

Werthner, P. (2003). Coaches rate WiCAP. *Canadian Journal for Women in Coaching, 4.* Retrieved December 8, 2005, from www.coach.ca/WOMEN/e/journal/oct2003/october2003.pdf.

Wheeler, S.C., & Petty, R.E. (2001). The effects of stereotype activation on behavior: A review of possible mechanisms. *Psychological Bulletin, 127,* 797-826.

White, A., & Hardy, L. (1998). An in-depth analysis of the uses of imagery by high-level slalom canoeists and artistic gymnasts. *The Sport Psychologist, 12,* 387-403.

Widmeyer, A.V., Brawley, L.R., & Carron, A.V. (1990). Group size in sport. *Journal of Sport and Exercise Psychology, 12,* 177-190.

Widmeyer, W.N., Brawley, L.R., & Carron, A.V. (1985). *The measurement of cohesion in sport teams: The group environment questionnaire.* London, ON: Sports Dynamics.

Widmeyer, W.N., & DuCharme, K. (1997). Team building through team goal setting. *Journal of Applied Sport Psychology, 9,* 97-113.

Wiersma, L.D., & Sherman, C.P. (2005). Volunteer youth sport coaches' perspectives of coaching education/ certification and parental codes of conduct. *Research Quarterly for Exercise and Sport, 76,* 324-338.

Wiese-Bjornstal, D.H., Smith, A.N., Shaffer, S.M., & Morrey, M.A. (1998). An integrated model of response to sport injury: Psychological and sociological dynamics. *Journal of Applied Sport Psychology, 10,* 46-69.

Wiggins, M.S. (1998). The relationship between the Competitive State Anxiety Inventory-2 and sport performance: A meta-analysis. *Journal of Applied Sport Psychology, 10,* 201-211.

Wilkes, R.L., & Summers, J.J. (1984). Cognitions, mediating variables, and strength performance. *Journal of Sport Psychology, 6,* 351-359.

Williams, J.M., & Krane, V. (2001). Psychological characteristics of peak performance. In J.M. Williams (Ed.), *Applied sport psychology: Personal growth to peak performance.* Mountain View, CA: Mayfield.

Williams, J.M., & Leffingwell, T.R. (2002). Cognitive strategies in sport and exercise psychology. In J.L. Van Raalte & B.W. Brewer (Eds.), *Exploring sport and exercise psychology* (2nd ed., pp. 75-98). Washington, DC: American Psychological Association.

Williams, S.L. (1995). Self-efficacy and anxiety and phobic disorders. In J.E. Maddux (Ed.), *Self-efficacy, adaptation, and adjustment: Theory, research, and application* (pp. 69-102). New York: Plenum Press.

Wilson, R.C., Sullivan, P.J., Myers, N.D., & Feltz, D.L. (2004). Sources of sport confidence of master athletes. *Journal of Sport and Exercise Psychology, 26,* 369-384.

Winfrey, M.L., & Weeks, D.L. (1993). Effects of self-modeling on self-efficacy and balance beam performance. *Perceptual and Motor Skills, 77,* 907-913.

Wise, J.B., & Trunnell, E.P. (2001). The influence of sources of self-efficacy upon efficacy strength. *Journal of Sport and Exercise Psychology, 23,* 268-280.

Wood, R.E., & Bandura, A. (1989). Impact of conceptions of ability on self-regulatory mechanisms and complex decision-making. *Journal of Personality and Social Psychology, 56,* 407-415.

Woodman, L. (1993). Coaching: A science, an art, an emerging profession. *Sport Science Review, 2* (2), 1-13.

Woodman, T., & Hardy, L. (2003). The relative impact of cognitive anxiety and self-confidence upon sport performance: A meta-analysis. *Journal of Sports Sciences, 21,* 443-457.

Woolfolk, R.L., Murphy, S.M., Gottesfeld, D., & Aitken, D. (1985). Effects of mental rehearsal of task motor activity and mental depiction of task outcome on motor skill performance. *Journal of Sport Psychology, 7,* 191-197.

Woolfolk, R.L., Parrish, M.W., & Murphy, S.M. (1985). The effects of positive and negative imagery on motor skill performance. *Cognitive Therapy and Research, 9,* 335-341.

Wurtele, S.K. (1986). Self-efficacy and athletic performance: A review. *Journal of Social and Clinical Psychology, 4,* 290-301.

Yan Lan, L., & Gill, D.L. (1984). The relationships among self-efficacy, stress responses, and a cognitive feedback manipulation. *Journal of Sport Psychology, 6,* 227-238.

Yukelson, D. (1997). Principles of effective team building interventions in sport: A direct services approach at Penn State University. *Journal of Applied Sport Psychology, 9,* 73-96.

Zaccaro, S.J., Blair, V., Peterson, C., & Zazanis, M. (1995). Collective efficacy. In J.E. Maddux (Ed.), *Self-efficacy, adaptation, and adjustment: Theory, research, and application* (pp. 308-330). New York: Plenum Press.

Zhu, W., & Kang, S.J. (1998). Cross-cultural stability of the optimal categorization of a self-efficacy scale. A Rasch analysis. *Measurement in Physical Education and Exercise Science, 2,* 225-241.

Zhu, W., Updyke, W.F., & Lewandowski, C. (1997). Post-hoc Rasch analysis of optimal categorization of ordered-response scale. *Journal of Outcome Measurement, 1,* 286-304.

Zimmerman, B.J. (1989). A social cognitive view of self-regulated academic learning. *Journal of Educational Psychology, 81,* 329-339.

Zimmerman, B.J. (1996, April). Misconceptions, problems, and dimensions in measuring self-efficacy. Paper presented at the annual meeting of the American Educational Research Association, New York.

Zimmerman, B.J. (2000). Attaining self-regulation: A social-cognitive perspective. In M. Bockaerts, P.R. Pintrich, & M. Zeidner (Eds.), *Handbook of self-regulation* (pp. 13 39). San Diego: Academic Press.

Zimmerman, B.J., & Cleary, T.J. (2006). Adolsecents' development of personal agency: The role of self-efficacy beliefs and self-regulatory skill. In F. Pajares & T. Urdan (Ed.), *Self-efficacy beliefs of adolescents* (pp. 45-69). Greenwich, CT: Information Age.

Zimmerman, B.J., & Kitsantas, A. (1996). Self-regulated learning of a motoric skill: The role of goal setting and self-monitoring. *Journal of Applied Sport Psychology, 8,* 60-75.

Zimmerman, B.J., & Kitsantas, A. (1997). Developmental phases in self-regulation: Shifting from process goals to outcome goals. *Journal of Educational Psychology, 89,* 29-36.

Zinsser, N., Bunker, L., & Williams, J.M. (2006). Cognitive techniques for building confidence and enhancing performance. In J.M. Williams, *Applied sport psychology* (5th ed., pp. 349-381). New York: McGraw-Hill.

Index

Page numbers followed by an *f* or a *t* indicate a figure or a table, respectively.

About the Authors

Philip Sullivan, Deborah Feltz, and Sandra Short

Deborah Feltz, PhD, is professor and chairperson of the department of kinesiology at Michigan State University in East Lansing. She has devoted more than 30 years to researching the relationship between self-efficacy and sport performance.

Dr. Feltz has written more than 70 publications on the topic. Her dissertation focused on self-efficacy and was published in the prestigious *Journal of Personality and Social Psychology* in 1982. She was invited to write the first review of her research on self-confidence and sport performance for *Exercise and Sport Sciences Reviews* in 1988. In 1986, while on sabbatical at Stanford University, she studied with Albert Bandura, who triggered her interest in the concept of team efficacy. She is an American Psychological Association fellow, former president of the American Academy of Kinesiology and Physical Education, and president-elect of the North American Society for the Study of Sport and Physical Activity. She earned her PhD in physical education and sport psychology from Pennsylvania State University. Her major professor was Daniel M. Landers.

Sandra Short, PhD, is professor and chairperson of the Department of Physical Education, Exercise Science, and Wellness at the University of North Dakota in Grand Forks, where she also holds an adjunct appointment in the Psychology department. She is the recipient of several scholarships and awards, including the Franklin Henry Young Scientist Award and a New Faculty Scholar Award. Dr. Short is an associate editor for *The Sport Psychologist,* the founding coeditor for the *Journal of Imagery Research in Sport and Physical Activity*, and a guest reviewer for 15 different journals. She has coauthored more than 25 peer-reviewed articles, mostly focused on efficacy beliefs and imagery. She has been the advisor to more than 25 master's degree students. She earned her PhD in the psychosocial aspects of sport and physical activity from Michigan State University.

Philip Sullivan, PhD, is an associate professor in the department of physical education and kinesiology at Brock University in St. Catharines, Ontario, Canada. He is a research fellow with the Coaching Association of Canada, coeditor of the *International Journal of Coaching Science,* and codirector of the Center for Healthy Development Through Sport and Physical Activity.

Dr. Sullivan has coauthored more than 25 peer-reviewed articles, most of them focusing on coaching and team efficacy. He coauthored with Dr. Feltz a chapter on applying social psychology to sport teams, which appeared in the book *Applied Social Psychology.* He earned a PhD with specialization in sport psychology and degrees in psychology and human kinetics. Dr. Sullivan is a certified rugby coach with 15 years of experience.